D1453385

HUNTING NATURE

HUNTING NATURE

IVAN TURGENEV AND THE ORGANIC WORLD

THOMAS P. HODGE

CORNELL UNIVERSITY PRESS
Ithaca and London

First published 2020 by Cornell University Press

Printed in the United States of America

Library of Congress Cataloging-in-Publication Data
Names: Hodge, Thomas P., author.
Title: Hunting nature : Ivan Turgenev and the organic
    world / Thomas P. Hodge.
Description: Ithaca [New York] : Cornell University Press,
    2020. | Includes bibliographical references and index.
Identifiers: LCCN 2019050822 (print) | LCCN 2019050823
    (ebook) | ISBN 9781501750847 (hardcover) | ISBN
    9781501750854 (ebook) | ISBN 9781501750861 (pdf)
Subjects: LCSH: Turgenev, Ivan Sergeevich, 1818-
    1883—Knowledge—Natural history. | Turgenev,
    Ivan Sergeevich, 1818-1883—Knowledge--Hunting. |
    Turgenev, Ivan Sergeevich, 1818-1883—Criticism and
    interpretation. | Hunting in literature. | Nature in
    literature.
Classification: LCC PG3444.N3 H63 2020 (print) | LCC
    PG3444.N3 (ebook) | DDC 891.72/3—dc23
LC record available at https://lccn.loc.gov/2019050822
LC ebook record available at https://lccn.loc.gov/2019050823

The face of creation takes in everything with a level stare. . . . The excessive busy-ness complained of is rooted in fear; fear: of mortality, and then of the pain of loss and separation. Only in the observation of nature can we recover that view of eternity that consoled our ancestors.

—Thomas McGuane ("Spring," in *The Longest Silence*, 1999)

CONTENTS

ILLUSTRATIONS

ACKNOWLEDGMENTS

This project unfolded over the course of almost two decades. I was inspired and guided time and again by a group of skillful ecocritical analysts of Russian history and literature. Following in the footsteps of pioneers like Robert L. Jackson, Andrew Durkin, and Loren Graham, innovative scholars such as Douglas Weiner, Christopher Ely, Amy Nelson, Jane Costlow, Rachel May, Thomas Newlin, Ian Helfant, Kevin Windle, and Margarita Odesskaia—to name a few—have in recent years been producing excellent studies of Russians' responses to the natural environment. Their work has constantly stimulated and informed my own.

Various institutions have rendered crucial assistance. I particularly wish to thank the Slavic Reference Service, University of Illinois, Urbana-Champagne (especially Jan Adamczyk and Victoria Jacobs); the Ernst Mayr Library, Museum of Comparative Zoology, Harvard University; the Davis Center for Russian and Eurasian Studies, Harvard University; the Russian State Library, Moscow; and the Russian National Library, St. Petersburg (especially Ol'ga Gurbanova). Wellesley College has unfailingly supported my work with a series of generous grants and has frequently sent me to teach at Lake Baikal, where I have been privileged to experience "Russian nature" at its most breathtaking; special thanks to Marianne Moore for being an ideal colleague on those expeditions. The Inter-Library Loan Department of Wellesley College's Clapp Library (especially Susan Goodman, Karen Jensen, and Angie Batson) has tirelessly helped me obtain a large number of elusive sources. Steve Smith at Clapp furnished essential assistance with Turgenev's correspondence. Mary Pat Navins, Jessica Gaudreau, Brittany Bailey, and Kathy Sanger provided expert help with logistics year in, year out.

This book has benefited enormously from the contributions of friends and colleagues. Petra Schiller, Bernhard Geiger, and Anjeana Hans helped me with German sources. From outside the world of Slavic Studies, Sally Cerny, Raymond Starr, Elliott Gorn, Louis Warren, Lawrence Buell, Daniel Herman, Alison Hickey, Nicholas Rodenhouse, Brendon Reay, Joanne Pierce, Susan Ashbrook Harvey, Thomas Hansen, William Cain, Timothy Peltason,

Jonathan Imber, Carolyn Ayers, Joela Jacobs, Laura O'Brien, Sarah Barbrow, Ed Silver, Nick Lyons, Andrew Shennan, and Caroline Johnson Hodge all gave me generous assistance. Within my field, I received help and inspiration from Konstantin Polivanov, Douglas Weiner, Andrew Durkin, Rachel May, Amy Nelson, Adam Weiner, Alla Epsteyn, Sarah Bishop, Nina Tumarkin, and Jennifer Flaherty. Ian Helfant told me what ecocriticism was and guided me over the years with great generosity. Turgenev authority Nicholas Žekulin read a draft of the manuscript and made a host of immensely helpful suggestions. Very special thanks go to Jane Costlow and Thomas Newlin, who not only commented on the manuscript, but offered patient counsel and fine insights over many years; this book is in large measure a response to their wonderful scholarship and has been substantially improved by their scrutiny.

A number of my Wellesley students, several of whom have since become colleagues at other institutions during my work on this project, provided vital assistance: Sarah Stone, Olga Kaplan, Jeenah Jung, Caroline Parsons, Miriam Neirick, Megan Gross, Laura Crisafulli Morais, Valerie Morozov, Elena Mironciuc, Genesis Barrios, Lyubov Kapko, Annie Roth Blumfield, Sarah Smith-Tripp, Zoë Swarzenski, Evan Williams, and Samantha English. Sincere thanks also to Oberlin College's Samuel Morrow. I am also grateful to Viktoriia Kadochnikova, Sofron Osipov, Anastasiia Gryzlova, and especially to Daria Osipova and Margaret Samu, for their help obtaining the images reproduced in this book. To three Wellesley women who acted as perspicacious and energetic research assistants during their undergraduate years, I tender particular thanks: Sarah Bidgood, Adrien Smith, and Cheryl Hojnowski.

At Cornell University Press, I am very grateful to Mahinder Kingra, Karen Laun, Glenn Novak, and two anonymous reviewers who passed along extraordinarily helpful comments.

Finally, and most importantly, I must thank the inhabitants of the nest I call home—Caroline, Peter, and Annie. I can never adequately express my gratitude for the love and patience they have shown to a frequently eremitic husband and father.

A NOTE ON TECHNICAL MATTERS

The authoritative scholarly edition of Turgenev's works is *Polnoe sobranie sochinenii i pisem v tridtsati tomakh* (*Complete Collection of Works and Letters in Thirty Volumes*), second edition, Moscow, Izdatel'stvo Nauka, 1978–present, to which I refer in citations as *Pssp*. The *Sochineniia* (*Works*) appear in volumes 1–12 (1978–86). The *Pis'ma* (*Letters*) appear in a separately numbered set of eighteen volumes, of which only sixteen have been published as of 2020 (1982–). The acronym *Pssp* is followed by *S* for volumes of *Works* (*Sochineniia*) or *P* for volumes of *Letters* (*Pis'ma*). For example, *PsspS4*:182 refers to volume 4 of the *Works*, page 182. The three final *Letters* volumes are divided into two books each; thus, for example, *PsspP15.2*:63 refers to volume 15, book 2, page 63 of the *Letters*.

For Turgenev's letters written after 1878, the last year covered by the portion of *PsspP* (second edition) published thus far, I cite volumes 12.2 (1967), 13.1 (1968) and 13.2 (1968) from the formerly definitive first edition, published a half century ago: *Polnoe sobranie sochinenii i pisem v dvadtsati vos'mi tomakh* (*Complete Collection of Works and Letters in Twenty-Eight Volumes*), Moscow–Leningrad: Izdatel'stvo Akademii Nauk SSSR, 1960–68. When citing from that older edition, I include the publication date to distinguish it from the second edition, for example, *PsspP13.1* (1968). I do the same when citing variants or drafts of Turgenev's non-epistolary writing from the *Works* volumes of the earlier complete edition (1960–68).

For events taking place in Russia, dates before 1918 are given according to the Old Style (Julian calendar). For Turgenev's letters, I provide both the Old Style and New Style (Gregorian calendar) dates. In Turgenev's lifetime, the New Style was twelve days ahead of the Old Style. On the first mention of a literary work, I give, whenever possible, the year written (as opposed to published).

In the main text, I have consistently used the Library of Congress transliteration system (without diacritics), except in certain proper names that have widely accepted spellings in English (e.g., Tolstoy, Dostoevsky, Gogol, Herzen, Asya, Semyon). In the notes, bibliography, and index, all Russian words, including names, are strictly transliterated (without diacritics) according to the Library of Congress system (e.g., Tolstoi, Dostoevskii, Gogol', Gertsen).

Unless otherwise noted, all translations are my own. When I have modified others' translations for the sake of clarity or accuracy, I note this.

Earlier versions of some material in this book have appeared in two articles: "Ivan Turgenev on the Nature of Hunting," in *Words, Music, History: A Festschrift for Caryl Emerson, Stanford Slavic Studies* 29, part 1 (2005): 291–311; and "The 'Hunter in Terror of Hunters': A Cynegetic Reading of Turgenev's *Fathers and Children*," *Slavic and East European Journal* 51, no. 3 (Fall 2007): 453–73.

HUNTING NATURE

Introduction

The Hunting Writer: An Ecocritical Approach

> My knowledge, confirmed by the wisdom of
> the sages, has revealed to me that everything on
> earth—organic and inorganic—is all extraordinarily
> arranged—only my own position is stupid. And those
> fools—the enormous masses of simple people—know
> nothing about how everything organic and inorganic
> is arranged in the world, but they live, and it seems to
> them that their life is very reasonably arranged!
>
> —Tolstoy, *A Confession*

Ivan Sergeevich Turgenev (1818–83) is remembered and honored today, two hundred years after his birth, for a host of reasons, prominent among them that his novels and stories encapsulated nineteenth-century Russian ideologies and social anxieties with extraordinary sophistication, and that he was a pioneer in bringing Russian literature to the writers and readers of Western Europe.[1]

Turgenev is, however, also renowned for his ability to describe the natural world, and we can confidently include him among the most skillful of Russia's nature writers. When he turned away from composing poetry and embraced prose in the mid-1840s, Turgenev's gift for nature description soon attracted notice. The earliest conspicuous praise came from his friend, the critic Vissarion Belinskii, in 1848: "We must not fail to mention Mr. Turgenev's extraordinary talent for painting pictures of Russian nature. He loves nature not as a dilettante, but as an artist, and therefore never attempts to portray it only in its poetic aspects, but takes it just as it presents itself to him. His depictions are always faithful; you always recognize in them our own native Russian nature."[2]

As Tolstoy put it decades later, "There is one thing at which [Turgenev] is such a master that your hands go numb when you touch the subject—nature . . . his depictions of nature! These are true pearls, beyond the reach of any other writer."[3] Typical of Turgenev's reception in the early twentieth century is K. K. Arsen'ev's assessment in 1905: "For [none of our novelists] do descriptions of nature play such a prominent role, and for no one are they distinguished by such variety, such vitality, such impeccable form."[4] In his academic lectures fifty years later, Vladimir Nabokov declared that "Turgenev's best" was "in the way of Russian landscape."[5] Most recently, Daniyal Mueenuddin opined that "no one [describes landscape] better, because he observes nature so closely and because he knows it so well."[6] Turgenev's nature descriptions have been so consistently celebrated by readers, writers, and critics—in Russia and abroad—that presenting anything like an exhaustive survey of the relevant critical commentary here would be impossible. Two entire books devoted exclusively to Turgenev's natural depictions have been published,[7] and numerous articles address the topic.

Artfully observed natural scenes abound in Turgenev's work. Here, as an example from his early prose, is a passage from "Diary of a Superfluous Man" (1850):

> We came out, stopped, and both of us involuntarily squinted: directly opposite us, amid the incandescent mist, a huge, crimson sun was setting. Half the sky had caught fire and glowed; red beams beat down here and there among the fields, throwing a scarlet gleam upon even the shady side of the ravines, and the rays settled like fiery lead along the stream in those places where it wasn't hidden beneath overhanging bushes, as if they were resting against the bosom of the bluff and the grove. We stood drenched in fervid radiance. I am unable to convey all the passionate solemnity of the scene. They say that to a certain blind man the color red resembled the sound of a trumpet; I don't know how just the comparison may be, but there really was something of an invocation in the burning gold of the evening air, in the crimson gleam of the sky and earth.[8]

Another sample, from a later period, in the novel *Smoke* (1867):

> For about three hours Litvinov wandered among the hills [around Baden-Baden]. Sometimes he'd leave the path and jump from rock to rock, occasionally slipping on the smooth moss; sometimes he'd sit down on a fragment of the crag beneath an oak or beech and think pleasant thoughts accompanied by the ceaseless whispering of the tiny brooks overgrown with fern, by the soothing rustle of leaves, by the ringing song of a solitary blackbird. A light, similarly pleasant drowsiness would steal upon him, as if embracing him from behind, and he

would fall asleep . . . But suddenly he'd smile and look around: the gold
and green of the woods and of the forest air would strike his eyes—and
again he'd smile and close them.[9]

Or, finally, a passage written six years before the end of Turgenev's life, from
"The Blackbird I" (1877):

> Like a whitish stain the apparition of the window stood before me;
> all objects in the room became dimly visible: they seemed even more
> immovable and quieter in the smoky half-light of an early summer
> morning. I looked at the clock: it was a quarter to three. And beyond
> the walls of the house that same immovability could be felt . . . And the
> dew, an entire sea of dew!
>
> And in this dew, in the garden, below my very window, a blackbird
> already sang, whistled, trilled—unceasingly, loudly, confidently. The
> modulating sounds penetrated my quiet room, filled it completely,
> filled my ears, and my head, which was irritated by the aridness of
> insomnia, by the bitter taste of unhealthy thoughts.
>
> They breathed eternity, those sounds—breathed all the freshness, all
> the indifference, all the force of eternity. The voice of nature herself
> could be heard in them—that beautiful, unconscious voice that never
> began and will never end.[10]

There is extraordinary descriptive richness in all these passages: chromatic
variety, biological precision, explicit synesthesia, broad sensory engagement,
and several dexterously deployed kinds of metaphor, to name just a few of
the more obvious tropes, and without delving into the role these excerpts
play in the larger works of which they are a part. Just as remarkable is the
writer's sensitivity to the emotional and philosophical reaction of the person
who witnesses these phenomena and their settings. Such multifarious complexity is typical of the care Turgenev lavished on his treatments of "nature,"
a term that merits careful consideration here.

Nature and the Hunting Writer

In Turgenev's era, there were three basic, interconnected Russian terms
for "nature": *natura*, *estestvo*, and *priroda*. The great lexicographer Vladimir
Dal'—who happened to be Turgenev's department head at the Ministry of
Internal Affairs from 1843 to 1845—published definitions of them in the
1860s. According to Dal', *natura*, a direct borrowing from Latin, had as its
fundamental sense "all that is created, especially on our earth; creation; all

that is made, all that is material collectively." That usage is archaic today and was already obsolescent in Turgenev's time; he used *natura* almost exclusively in the sense of "trait, characteristic, attribute, feature; way of life, that which is natural or inborn," such as "[Nezhdanov] was an idealist by nature [*natura*], passionate and chaste."[11]

Estestvo—derived from the Russian word for "is" (*est'*)—meant "all that is; *priroda*, *natura* and its order or laws; essence." The "nature" sense of *estestvo*, as with *natura*, was archaic by Turgenev's time and had already been replaced by the chief sense it still bears in modern Russian: "essence."[12] Turgenev only ever used the adjectival form, *estestvennyi*—which was then, as now, a common word for "natural," as in "the natural sciences" (*estestvennye nauki*)—and compounds of *estestvo*, such as *estestvoispytatel'*, "naturalist" (literally "nature tester").

Priroda, the dominant term today and for Turgenev, refers to the kind of "nature" that we would readily associate in English with a "nature writer." Etymologically, it is a combination of the prefix *pri-*, which indicates an additional characteristic of the root, and the root itself, *rod*, which means family, origin, kin, genus, kind, gender. Dal' defined the chief senses of *priroda* as "*estestvo*, all that is material, the universe, the entire world [*mirozdanie*], all that is visible, subject to the five senses; our world, the earth, with all that is created upon it (as opposed to the Creator); the open air, forests, mountains, etc.; all that is earthly, fleshly, bodily, oppressive, material (as opposed to the spiritual); all natural [*prirodnye*] or *estestvennye* productions on earth, the three kingdoms (or, with man, four), in their primordial form (as opposed to art or the product of human hands)."[13] Turgenev's usage of *priroda* most often coincided with the third and fifth senses ("the open air, forests, mountains, etc." and "the three kingdoms"), and at times contradicted the fourth ("oppressive, material . . . as opposed to the spiritual"), but his explorations of the nonhuman environment ranged into all these shades of meaning. Modern Russian dictionaries give the two primary definitions of *priroda* as "the material environment not created by human activity; the totality of *estestvennye* conditions (landscape, flora, fauna, climate, etc.),"[14] and these two contemporary senses neatly summarize the organic essentials Turgenev encompassed when he used the word.

In his fiction and nonfiction, Turgenev employed *priroda* and its forms frequently—hundreds of times, in fact. A close friend, the poet Iakov Polonskii, described it as one Turgenev's favorite words.[15] It is also a favorite of Russians generally, a term to which considerable affection is attached. *Priroda* is a friendly, flexible word in the modern language. It accepts modifiers more readily than does English "nature": *russkaia priroda*—"Russian nature"; *rodnaia priroda*—"one's native nature"; *dikaia priroda*—"wild nature." It is something that human beings can be "in" if not quite inhabit, and go "to" if not quite reach: Russians routinely speak of spending time *na prirode* ("in nature") and traveling *na prirodu* ("into nature"). *Priroda* is therefore quite a common term, and it covers territory that English speakers often identify with a variety of other nouns and phrases such as "environment," "natural setting," "outdoors," "outside," "natural world," "the country."

When I refer to "nature," "the natural world," or "the organic world" in this book, I generally intend it to coincide with Turgenev's own basic usage of *priroda*. As we will see, however, he persistently ventured well beyond the basics in discussing and depicting "nature," so I will endeavor to make sense of what Turgenev thought *priroda* was, or might be, or should be.

In short, this book is my attempt to document and analyze Ivan Turgenev's relationship to nature (*priroda*) chiefly by scrutinizing his conception and practice of hunting—the most unquenchable passion of his life.

He was not alone. A lifelong craving to pursue and kill animals for sport united Turgenev with an older Russian writer who was his political antithesis: the Slavophile patriarch Sergei Timofeevich Aksakov (1791–1859). General readers remember Aksakov today chiefly for his luminous autobiographical trilogy, completed in the mid-1850s: *A Family Chronicle, Childhood Years of a Bagrov Grandson*, and *Memoirs*. Aksakov, however, preceded the trilogy with large-scale treatises on fishing and hunting that have become Russian classics of the genre, his observations suffused with what Ian Helfant calls a "proto-ecological consciousness."[16] As Thomas Newlin has observed, "Both [Aksakov and Turgenev] seem to have been working at the same time toward a very similar personal philosophy of restraint and equilibrium that had deep and very concrete ecological (as well as existential) implications, and that for each of them found its truest model in nature itself."[17] Aksakov was drawn to the brilliant young liberal largely because he admired Turgenev's epochal *Notes of a Hunter*, a cycle of stories published in book form the same year—1852—as Aksakov's own *Notes of an Orenburg-Province Hunter*, a work that in turn delighted Turgenev and prompted him to write two prominent reviews.

It was in the second of these reviews that Turgenev chose to set forth his own *profession de foi* as a serious observer of nature. This choice of venue—the review of a hunting book—was no accident: Turgenev's perception of the natural world was, throughout his life, inextricably bound to the practice and circumstances of hunting. He declares in the final paragraph of his Aksakov review that "hunting draws us close to nature: only the hunter sees her

at all times of the day and night, in all her beauty, in all her horror."[18] Soon
after reading this, Aksakov's youngest son, Ivan, wrote to Turgenev and confirmed the special status of hunters as observers of nature: "Hunters . . . are
generally more familiar with the natural world, with all its particulars and
details; the hunter knows what to call them, and for him they are not lost in
that vagueness of feeling possessed by a 'lover of nature.'"[19]

An accident of biography—arrest and exile to his country estate in the
spring of 1852—steeped Turgenev in hunting and Aksakovian nature writing just as he began searching for a new literary direction. In the early to
mid-1850s, immediately before the period when he would create his finest
novels—*Rudin, A Gentry Nest, On the Eve, Fathers and Children*—fiction was
for him eclipsed by field sport and especially intense rumination on the
organic world. Thanks to the splendid accounts of rural Russia's humble
beauty in *Notes of a Hunter*, Turgenev was already, on the brink of exile, such
an acknowledged master of natural description that his editor, Ivan Panaev,
could jestingly accuse him of allowing observational zeal to supersede hunting itself:

> [Turgenev] forever roams about in his hunter's garb, endlessly stop-
> ping along the way to look around from side to side or up in the sky.
> You'd think that he, as a hunter, would be tracking the flight of birds
> or, when standing still, would be listening for the rustle of leaves in the
> bushes, afraid of spooking his quarry . . . Now you might expect a shot
> to ring out—but there's nothing of the kind! You can relax . . . this shot
> will never come. My hunter never shoots; his yellow piebald English
> dog Dianka sadly trails behind him with nothing to do, wagging her
> tail and despondently blinking her tired eyes while her master continu-
> ally returns home with an empty game-bag. He's not tracking a bird's
> flight the better to shoot it, but is instead tracking these white-edged,
> golden-gray clouds scattered about the sky just as if they floated in an
> endlessly overflowing river that skirts them with deeply transparent
> channels of unwavering blue; he's listening not for the rustle of leaves
> in the bushes, afraid of spooking his quarry, not for the cry of quail,
> but for the solemn silence of approaching night; he's looking at these
> endless fields sinking into the gloom, at the water's steely gleam that
> shimmers every now and then . . . Nothing in nature escapes his reli-
> able, poetic and inquiring glance, and birds calmly, tenderly, fearlessly
> fly circles around this strange hunter, as if begging to be included in
> his *Notes*.[20]

Banished to his estate a few months after this was printed, Turgenev actually confirmed in his actions the precise opposite of what Panaev's satiric sketch purports: field sport took clear precedence over writing. Initially, at least, he greeted his punishment as a hunting holiday, a respite from literary concerns. Nonetheless, this sketch sets out one of the cardinal dualities of Turgenev's identity: observer versus killer.

Once he had completed eighteen months of rural exile, hunting frequently, Turgenev somehow emerged with a fortified sense of purpose as a writer. From the mid-1850s on, biota and landscape would become even more subtle, integral components of characterization, plot, ideological gesture, and philosophical exploration. Hunting moved by and large from text to subtext, but it continued to play a crucial role by influencing Turgenev to choose natural details with a hunter-naturalist's expertise and to portray human beings not as outside observers but as participants—whether they realize it or not—in nature's vast totality. As in *Notes of a Hunter*, Turgenev's venatically conditioned persona does not stand above the landscape but becomes one with it, as do the forests, fields, dogs, and birds that populate his fiction. In the words of Galina Kurliandskaia, Turgenev "came to recognize the inclusion of the human individual in the general current of life on earth, to recognize the unity of man and nature."[21]

The earliest succinct expression of how Turgenev's hunting molded his aesthetic vision comes from an obituary article on him that appeared in the autumn of 1883. Here, nuanced analysis of the hunting writer's faculties of observation refutes Panaev's jocular characterization of three decades before:

Everywhere Turgenev took notice of artistic images, but it was the forest that provided him his richest material, the forest that he, as a passionate hunter, studied in all its types. Turgenev was not a landscape-writer by profession; during his travels he had seen a great deal of natural beauty, but he sincerely perceived only the natural world of his homeland. . . . He studied it not as an idle passerby, but as a hunter. Every sound in nature must be comprehensible to the hunter; the slightest trembling of a bough, a breath of wind, each momentary shadow, can divulge the presence of game. The hunter must get into the habit of intensifying all his senses—he is obliged to listen, to see, to smell with equal attentiveness. The voice of every bird is known to him; he takes earnest interest in each of them, which, however, does not prevent him from killing them. Turgenev's hunting pictures engender absolute trust: all his senses act simultaneously, and the landscape he depicts ceases to be merely a picture; with him, living reality is in the air. How wonderfully handsome are these sometimes momentary, airy pictures of light![22]

The author, Heinrich Julian Schmidt, was a respected German literary historian and hunting companion of Turgenev's, well qualified to make such an assertion. Five years later, another critic, Arsen'ev, suggested that "in his efforts to study and appraise the natural world of Russia, to attach himself with all his heart to the often 'joyless,' but often also peaceful, soothing scenes of his homeland, Turgenev received a great deal of assistance from the 'noble passion' of hunting."[23]

If we accept this basic view of Turgenev as valid, then hunting is not an irrelevant amusement but a force that lastingly shaped his perceptual and artistic capacities. The hunting self, for Turgenev, was not a separate identity but a fundamental component of the philosophical and literary self. Hunting is much more than a metaphor for his writing, though such comparisons can be illuminating. The hunt supplied Turgenev with a wide assortment of tools that he continually deployed to craft his narratives. Analysis of Turgenev's experience afield thus offers significant insight into his literary methods and their intellectual underpinnings.

The Outdoor Turgenev

The canonical image of Turgenev is an 1872 portrait by Vasilii Perov.[24] Here we have a hoary-bearded sage, seated in a velvet armchair, looking off to the left—lost in thought or ennui—through heavy eyelids. In one hand he holds a closed, leather-bound book perched upright on his lap, in the other his pince-nez. This is the indoor Turgenev. My aim is to explore another Turgenev, the zealous hunter who gazes out at us from Nikolai Dmitriev-Orenburgskii's portrait of the writer from eight years later.[25] In knee boots, with a hunting bowler on his head and powder bag slung at his side, this less familiar figure holds not a book but a double-barreled shotgun, his finger on the triggers, thumb poised over the hammers. This Turgenev, pince-nez in place, eyes ablaze, stands alone at the edge of a thicket, two white birches twisting upward at his back, the faint prospect of an evergreen forest fading behind him in the far distance. This is the Turgenev whose hunting experience informed the nature descriptions that have intrigued scholars and delighted readers since the 1840s. This is Turgenev viewed through the Aksakovian prism.

Figure I.2. N. D. Dmitriev-Orenburgskii, *I. S. Turgenev Hunting* (1880). Courtesy Institute of Russian Literature of the Russian Academy of Sciences (Pushkin House), St. Petersburg.

Figure I.1. V. G. Perov, *I. S. Turgenev* (1872). Courtesy State Russian Museum, St. Petersburg.

Turgenev's lifelong devotion to the hunt instilled and reinforced in him a perceptual habit that became an ideal: venatic equipoise—a balance in humans that emulates what he saw as nature's organic, eternal balance. Jane Costlow refers to Turgenev's political, social, and aesthetic aim as a "contemplative equilibrium" modeled on the balance he saw in nature.[26] It is my contention that this equilibrium was originally and persistently venatic: conceived and achieved through the kind of observation of nature that was, in Turgenev's day, most readily available to hunters.[27]

As I analyze the role of nature in Turgenev's novels, stories, essays, plays, and correspondence, drawing on both famous and less-known works, I adopt an approach both interpretive and documentarian, seeking to ground my observations thoroughly in Russian cultural and linguistic context. Aside from Turgenev, the author most central to my arguments is Aksakov, and one fundamental purpose of this book is to foreground his deeply consequential link with Turgenev.[28] Many other writers and thinkers play an important role, especially Herzen and Fet, but also, among others, Pushkin, Goncharov, Tolstoy, Tiutchev, Nekrasov, Dal', Leopardi, Goethe, Schelling, Shakespeare, Ovid, Flaubert, and Buffon. I frequently draw upon details of Turgenev's biography, relationships, and personal activities—first and foremost hunting—because they shaped many important features of his art and thought.

This project has from the start been informed by ecocritical methods. The definition of ecocriticism is notoriously flexible, but Cheryll Glotfelty's widely cited 1996 discussion of the term frames it in a way that closely resembles my own impulse: "the study of the relationship between literature and the physical environment . . . an earth-centered approach to literary studies. . . [which] takes as its subject the interconnections between nature and culture, specifically the cultural artifacts of language and literature."[29] Ten years later, Camilo Gomides defined ecocriticism in a more activist light that has been well received by many scholars: "The field of enquiry that analyzes and promotes works of art which raise moral questions about human interactions with nature, while also motivating audiences to live within a limit that will be binding over generations."[30]

My first two chapters offer historical, theoretical, and biographical observations that convey the significant textures and terrain of a nineteenth-century Russian hunter-writer's inner life and physical reality. In chapter 1, I describe Turgenev's early grounding in German Romantic nature philosophy and trace the development of his own conception of nature's indifference in relation to Herzen's thought on the subject. I propose and explain the concepts of venatic equipoise, ecotropism, and anthropotropism as tools for analyzing Turgenev as a nature writer. Chapter 2 explores the three most prevalent kinds of sport hunting pursued in nineteenth-century Russia—coursing, hounding, shooting—and suggests that their essential differences pointed to very distinct modes of interacting with nature. Illustrative examples of Turgenev's zealous devotion to shooting are then taken from memoir accounts of his actual hunting praxis.

In chapter 3, I review the rise of Russian hunting literature and survey Turgenev's own venatic writing. The remainder of the chapter is devoted to *Notes of a Hunter*, which, I propose, shares key structural features with hunting manuals. The interplay of ecotropic and anthropotropic modes in this extraordinarily influential cycle of short stories reinforces moral opposition to the arbitrary exercise of power (*proizvol*). Chapter 4 examines Turgenev's personal and literary encounter with Sergei Aksakov, focusing on the philosophical and aesthetic implications of his second review of Aksakov's classic hunting treatise, then turns to Turgenev's story "The Inn" as an unyielding embodiment of the principles set forth in the review. For Turgenev, Aksakov represented an admirable model of unself-conscious, ecotropic nature description that was nonetheless difficult for him to follow. Chapters 5 and 6 trace Turgenev's venatically informed exploitation of natural elements in the fiction he created during the ten years that followed his intimate involvement with Aksakov's work: nature illuminates the aspiration, fear, victimization, and frustrated love that suffuse these texts. The story "Journey to the Forest-Belt" and novels *Rudin* and *A Gentry Nest* are the chief focus of chapter 5, while chapter 6 tackles the major works that brought Turgenev's most fertile period to a close: *On the Eve*, "First Love," and *Fathers and Children*. The hunter's conception of nesting and mating dominates these final two chapters, which investigate zoological, botanical, and celestial motifs as well as Turgenev's deft use of hunting lore, history, language, music, religion, philosophy, classical mythology, and folk culture to enrich his complex narratives.

My conclusion reflects on the treatment of nature and hunting themes in the last two decades of Turgenev's life, when, though his passion for the chase persisted, palpable doubts about its freshness and moral legitimacy appeared with greater force and frequency. In this late period, Turgenev gravitated toward the paranormal in his short stories. His last two novels, *Smoke* and *Virgin Soil*, continue to use nature as a touchstone in ideologically charged settings, though *Virgin Soil* does so with considerably more finesse. In the appendices, I provide translations of four source documents vital to any understanding of Turgenev's nature philosophy: a chronology of his references to nature's indifference, his two reviews of Aksakov's hunting treatise, and his codified precepts for hunters and their dogs. In selecting images for the book, I have attempted to illustrate concrete details of nineteenth-century Russian life, especially the appurtenances and techniques of hunting. Whenever possible, illustrations are contemporaneous with Turgenev and produced by Russian artists.

Turgenev was an expert on the natural world who paid very serious attention to wildlife and landscape. From the outset, therefore, I have sought biological exactitude: I am interested in what Turgenev's field knowledge of actual animals and plants can tell us about the structure of his writing and aesthetics. I have attempted to trace specific nature images in order to answer such modest questions as "Why *this* bird? Why *this* insect? Why *that* tree? And why mention them *here?*" as a preliminary to tackling deeper issues, including the place of humanity in nature, the ethics of using figurative language connected to nature, and the complex role of natural beauty in human consciousness. In this effort I will be as precise as possible in naming the species invoked by Turgenev, which I hope will also go some way toward rectifying a century and a half of English translations that have frequently misidentified and misrepresented his flora and fauna.

My discussion of animals, particularly birds, and the diverse roles they played in Turgenev's literary strategies places much of my commentary within the field of animal studies, one of whose main concerns, as expressed by Jane Costlow and Amy Nelson, is how "animals shape and inform the human experience in real and symbolic ways."[31] In addition, as Michael Lundblad has pointed out, "animal studies can be seen as work that explores representations of animality and related discourses with an emphasis on advocacy for nonhuman animals."[32] Turgenev certainly explores the moral implications of how humans—especially hunters and artists—interact with the natural world, and he clearly favors strictures on how hunters should go about their sport, but it would be difficult to argue that he offers systematic conservationism or animal-rights advocacy in the modern sense, as powerful as his rueful representations of cruelty to animals and of vanishing habitat might be. Instead, he is an environmentalist in the more basic sense that he is intensely aware of the organic world surrounding his characters, and surrounding himself, in a large portion of what he writes. I too will not explicitly act as an environmental advocate here, which means that certain parts of my study may be more accurately seen as aligned with "animality studies," defined by Lundblad as "work that emphasizes the history of animality in relation to human cultural studies, without an explicit call for nonhuman advocacy."[33]

As I suggest in chapter 1, it is particularly illuminating in Turgenev's case to consider the tension between animals presented as such and animals that seem to have a calculated symbolic function. The burgeoning subfield of human-animal studies, however, makes it clear that it is impossible to describe animals "as such," since "understandings of animals only ever emerge within the context of the cultural events or perspectives that draw our attention to them. . . . All forms of representation insert a human filter that effectively creates distance from the very same human-animal relations that we purport to represent, let alone study."[34] Though I agree that it is ultimately impossible for a human being to communicate animal representations uncontaminated by human priorities and preoccupations, I believe that the effort to identify and contrast degrees of such contamination can tell us a great deal about Turgenev's self-conception as a moral participant in the natural world. The same also applies to arguments I will present about natural features beyond the animal kingdom: plants, heavens, landforms.

Costlow and Nelson point out that "Russians have often understood themselves to be more 'natural' than their western European counterparts" and "have tended to point out the *difference* of their natural environment."[35] Though his nature passages frequently intersect with issues of nationality, Turgenev approached the question of Russianness far less chauvinistically than such contemporaries as Tolstoy and Dostoevsky. He largely shared the view expressed by Potugin in the novel *Smoke*: "I both love and hate my Russia, my strange, sweet, horrid, dear homeland."[36] Turgenev's chief concern was with what is universally human, and his Russian characters are primarily *people*, albeit people whose intellectual and psychological habits, whose struggles in the spheres of love and death, have been shaped by political, social, and economic conditions unique to Russia. Many of the peasants he depicts are indeed close to nature, but in general this is because that is the place allotted to them by a system over which they have no control, not because they share a mystical bond with birds, beasts, trees, and soil. Nonetheless, Turgenev extols the formidable outdoor expertise of Russian peasants, and there are extraordinary passages too in which the national consciousness, even patriotism, of Russian noblemen swells when they commune with their country's unpretentiously beautiful natural settings.

Turgenev was an exceedingly sophisticated and subtle thinker. His art resists monolithic interpretations and systematic solutions; it does not accommodate simple keys that unlock cleverly hidden meanings. If at times I seem to propose such solutions and keys, I have misrepresented Turgenev. I do, however, believe that we stand to learn a great deal about his thought and literary technique when we read him in both cultural and environmental context, remaining mindful of how textual detail is wedded to the organic world—the *priroda* that he observed, and ached for, more keenly than perhaps any other Russian writer.

CHAPTER 1

Catching Nature by the Tail

> Systems are prized only by those to whom the whole truth is not given, who want to catch truth by the tail. A system is exactly like the truth's tail, but the truth is like a lizard: it will leave the tail in your hand and the lizard will run away. It knows that it will soon grow another one.
>
> —Turgenev, letter to Tolstoy (1857)

> Gagin was in that particular state of artistic ardor and fury which, like a fit, suddenly seizes dilettantes when they imagine that they have succeeded, as they express it, in "catching nature by the tail."
>
> —Turgenev, "Asya" (1857)

Identifying Turgenev's philosophical outlook in a straightforward, comprehensive way is a daunting task. As many observers have pointed out, he was an eclectic intellectual of towering erudition, deeply read in Western thought, for whom an all-encompassing philosophy is difficult to pin down precisely.[1] The many particular thinkers who influenced him—Pascal, Spinoza, Herder, Goethe, Schelling, Hegel, Feuerbach, Schopenhauer, to name only a few—seem to hold more or less sway depending on the period of writing and the particular sphere of Turgenev's fiction: Hegel in the conflicts of characters and ideas; Pascal and Feuerbach in matters of faith, hope, despair; Schopenhauer in the shape of plots and mood; and so on. None dominates completely or definitively. In Turgenev's representations of and thoughts on the natural world, though these shifted and evolved over the course of his life, Schelling and Goethe seem to have left the deepest imprint.

The Roots of Turgenev's Nature Philosophy

The *Naturphilosophie* of Friedrich Schelling (1775–1854) took shape at the end of the 1790s and exerted a profound influence on Russian thought in the first three decades of the nineteenth century. Imported and promulgated by several professors in Russia's capitals—Danilo Vellanskii at the Imperial

Medical-Surgical Academy in St. Petersburg, Aleksandr Galich (Govorov) at St. Petersburg University, Ivan Davydov and Mikhail Pavlov at Moscow University—Schelling's Romantic theories sought to rescue nature from the Enlightenment view of the nonhuman world as a rationally structured, mechanistic array of animals and plants ruled by the immutable laws of Newtonian physics.[2] Schelling posited nature not as an inert zoological-phytological specimen cabinet validated by human perception, but as a living being, an organism in and of itself, that could perceive and act. With Schelling, nature evolved from beheld to beholder, and humans themselves were part of it, not external spectators. This new status, predicated on a rejection of Descartes's dualistic worldview of mind and body, has been summed up well by Aileen Kelly:

> In Schelling's monistic vision of the universe, matter and mind, spirit and nature, are not distinct kinds of entities, but simply differing degrees of organization and development of an evolving organic whole, a single primal force or absolute, striving upward in a process of self-discovery, whose highest manifestation is achieved in human consciousness. The Cartesian model of the world gave primacy to reason as the tool for apprehending reality; in Schelling's organicist vision, imagination and intuition (as expressed in art and religion) are the primary instruments for penetrating the mysterious underlying unity of the universe. At the summit of being is the artist, whose creativity represents the fusion of consciousness and the unconscious, expressing their foreordained identity.[3]

In the early to mid-1820s, such thinking particularly infected and inspired the so-called Wisdom Lovers (*liubomudry*), led by Prince Vladimir Odoevskii, who knew Schelling personally, and by the poet Dmitrii Venevitinov. Schelling, wrote Isaiah Berlin, "is largely responsible for the characteristically romantic notion that poets or painters may understand the spirit of their age more profoundly and express it in a more vivid and lasting manner than academic historians."[4]

As a student at Moscow University in 1833–34, Turgenev imbibed the lectures of Pavlov, whom he called, in his autobiography, "a follower of Schelling's philosophy who lectured on physics in keeping with that philosophy."[5] During Turgenev's graduate studies at the University of Berlin from 1838 to 1841, Schelling was read and discussed at length with his friends, including Mikhail Bakunin and Nikolai Stankevich. Seven years later, Turgenev wrote that, in 1840, "we [students] would excitedly await Schelling."[6] Turgenev soon came to view Schelling's ideas with a certain ironical distance, commenting in 1847 on the dramatic shift in philosophical fashion and noting that the philosopher had been forgotten in Berlin.[7] Discussing the title character's devotion to German Romantic Idealism in the 1855 story "Iakov Pasynkov," Turgenev wrote that "Romantics, as we know, are almost extinct now," and by the late 1850s, Schelling appears in the novel *On the Eve* (1859) as an abstruse and musty throwback.[8] Shadows of Schelling's perception of nature and the role of the artist are nonetheless detectable for the entirety of Turgenev's career, as, for example, when Lezhnev describes his youthful tree-hugging in *Rudin* (1855), or when the narrator of the prose poem "The Dog" (1878) meditates on the oneness of human and animal: "I understand that in this moment, in both [the dog] and in me, there lives one and the same feeling, that there is no difference between us. We are identical; in each of us burns and shines the same trembling little flame . . . This is not an animal and a man exchanging glances . . . These are two pairs of the same eyes fastened upon one other. And in each of these pairs—in the animal and in the man— one identical life fearfully draws closer to the other."[9] His Schellingian education no doubt played some role in the conspicuous way Turgenev, one of nineteenth-century Russia's more prominent dog-fanciers, explored canine characters and themes.[10]

Turgenev's admiration for Goethe was deep, unequivocal, and lasting.[11] His responses to *Faust*, for example, can be found in a lengthy review article (1844–45), the story entitled "Faust" (1856), and numerous letters.[12] In Berlin, Turgenev conversed at length with Bettina von Arnim, Goethe's former lover, and the German master's work and thought were hotly debated by Russian émigré students at the time. As Peter Thiergen has convincingly shown, Goethe, who was something of a proto-Lamarckian evolutionist, challenged the eighteenth-century notion of nature as a well-ordered paradise, consistently depicting the merciless voracity (in *Werther*, 1774–87) and indifference (in *Die Wahlverwandtschaften* [*Elective Affinities*], 1808–9) of the constantly metamorphosing natural world, and this stance was readily taken up by such writers as Novalis and Heine.[13]

The most important Goethe source for students of Turgenev's nature philosophy is the rhapsodic essay entitled "Nature" ("Die Natur," 1782–83), which proffers concepts that would be repeated and reshaped in many of Turgenev's own depictions of the natural world.[14] In a brief series of paradoxical aphorisms, the essay portrays Nature as an engulfing, maternal, goddess-like figure:

> We are surrounded by her and locked in her clasp: powerless to leave her, and powerless to come closer to her . . . She creates new forms

without end: what exists now, never was before; what was, comes not again; all is new and yet always the old . . . She speaks to us unceasingly and betrays not her secret . . . Individuality seems to be all her aim, and she cares nought for individuals. She is always building and always destroying, and her workshop is not to be approached . . . Nature lives in her children only, and the mother . . . is the sole artist—out of the simplest materials [she creates] the greatest diversity, attaining, with no trace of effort, the finest perfection . . . She has thought, and she ponders unceasingly; not as a man, but as Nature. The meaning of the whole she keeps to herself, and no one can learn it of her . . . She is rough and gentle, loving and terrible, powerless and almighty.[15]

Anticipating Schelling's vitalist views, Goethe suggests that nature has conscious agency. All species of animals and plants are children of the great mother and therefore as similar to one another as siblings, all variations on an *Urtier* and an *Urpflanze*—a single, idealized animal prototype and plant prototype.[16] Thus humans are one with nature and, distinct from Schelling's conception, do not occupy a higher place within it. Instead, nature is indifferent to individuals, including humans, and can be both destructive and constructive—remorselessly so.[17] In the concluding paragraph of "Nature," Goethe's narrator seeks requited affection from nature: "She has placed me in this world; she will also lead me out of it. I trust myself to her. She may do with me as she pleases. *She will not hate her work.*"[18]

From the complex of Goethe's and Schelling's thoughts on the natural world, Turgenev seems to have assimilated a number of ideas that become central figurations in his own nature writing: the natural world is unitary and monistic, and therefore inclusive of humanity. "With Turgenev," as Robert L. Jackson explained, "we are certainly in the presence of an archetypal vision of the epic unity, wholeness, and organic character of nature and the vital life processes."[19] Nature is a living entity, with thoughts and feelings, and yet is pitiless and mute before the totality of organisms that constitute her. She is endlessly fertile, beautiful, attractive, enigmatic, and creative—even artistic.[20]

Of all her traits, however, it was perhaps nature's *indifference* that most haunted Turgenev. For his entire life, Goethe's reassurance that "She will not hate her work" was neutralized by a grim Turgenevian corollary: she is, in equal measure, by no means bound to love her work. Turgenev's writing, not surprisingly in his ideologically contentious age, is saturated with procatalepsis, and this extends to his imaginative conceptualization of nature's intentions. How will she ignore me? What reason will she have to abandon me? he frequently seems to be thinking about nature, just as so many of his hapless male protagonists think about women, when they find themselves on the brink of never attaining, or losing, the joy of mutual affection. Margarita Odesskaia has called nature's indifference "perhaps the principal [motif] over the course of Turgenev's entire creative life."[21]

It is therefore instructive to assemble a comprehensive collection of Turgenev's statements on nature's indifference, as I have done in appendix 1. Surveying Turgenev's own ruminations on nature over nearly five decades, we see distinct patterns emerge, and they bear clear traces of Schelling and Goethe. In Turgenev's statements, both in his fictions and his letters, nature is beautiful, majestic, silent, deaf, calm, maternal, pitiless, devouring, amoral, unstoppable, eternal. Twice, in the closing sentence of two of his most important works—"Diary of a Superfluous Man" ("Dnevnik lishnego cheloveka," 1850) and *Fathers and Children* (*Ottsy i deti*, 1860–61)—he concludes the text by quoting the final stanza of Pushkin's "Whether I wander along noisy streets" (1829), a contemplation of human mortality and the inevitability of being replaced:

И пусть у гробового входа
Младая будет жизнь играть,
И равнодушная природа
Красою вечною сиять.

And may youthful life play
At the crypt's entrance,
And may indifferent nature
Shine with eternal beauty.[22]

As we see in appendix 1, Turgenev even chose to imitate this quatrain in one of his own poems, "The Tit" ("Sinitsa," 1863), and quoted Pushkin's "indifferent nature" in two letters—once in jest, to the poet Afanasii Fet (1860), and once in dead earnest, fatally ill at the end of his life (1882).

If Pushkin ushered the notion of indifferent nature into Russian high culture, it was Aleksandr Herzen who developed it, from the mid- to late 1840s, as a key sociopolitical concept in the Russian context. Herzen wrote the second of his *Letters on the Study of Nature* (1844–46) in August 1844 and published it in the April 1845 issue of *Notes of the Fatherland*. Like Turgenev a student of Goethe, he even appended to Letter II his own complete Russian translation of Goethe's "Nature." In the body of the Letter, Herzen describes nature as "a harmonious whole, an integral organism," whose elements "are characterized by self-sufficient independence from man; they existed before him and they showed no concern for him after he appeared; they are unending, unlimited; they continue to arise and disappear everywhere."[23] Herzen's narrator sounds the same note in the 1846 novel *Who Is to Blame?*: "It has long been remarked by poets that nature is, to a disgusting degree, indifferent to what people do upon her spine."[24]

In 1847–48, Herzen prominently addresses the topic of nature's unconcern for humanity in the essays of *From the Other Shore*, first in "Before the Storm":

> Life and nature disinterestedly pursue their own ends, yielding to man only in so far as he learns to apply nature's own means. . . .
>
> . . . In nature, as in the soul of man, there slumbers an infinite multitude of forces and possibilities; as soon as the conditions arise necessary to awaken them, they will develop and will continue to develop to the nth degree . . . Actually, it makes no difference to nature: it will not diminish; nothing can be detracted from it. Change nature as much as you like, yet everything will remain within it and, after burying the human race, it will most lovingly start anew with its monstrous ferns and lizards half a mile long, but with some improvements, taken from the new environment and from the new conditions.[25]

Later in *From the Other Shore*, the dispassionate essence of nature's balance appears in statistical terms: "Nature is merciless: like a certain well-known shrub it is both mother and stepmother. It does not mind if two-thirds of what it produces goes to feed the one-third, providing the latter develops properly."[26]

Not surprisingly, Herzen the abolitionist is keen to draw a distinction between what he sees as the unnatural human penchant for enforcing subjugation and the natural relationship of predator and prey:

> The wolf devours the lamb because it is hungry and because the lamb is weaker; but the wolf does not demand slavery from the lamb, nor does the lamb submit to him. It protests by bleating and running away. Into the wildly independent and self-sufficient world of the animals man has introduced an element of subservience [*vernopoddannichestvo*], the element of Caliban, and it is owing to this that a Prospero could appear. And here we find the same ruthless economy of nature, conservation of means: should it indulge in some excess at one point, it will curtail itself in another: when it chose to enormously extend the neck and forelegs of the giraffe, it at the same time shortened its hind legs.[27]

Here, nature's balance (*ravnovesie*) is tied to nature's indifference (*ravnodu-shie*), the antithesis of humanity's thirst to domineer—over humans and non-humans alike.[28] As late as 1860, Herzen could write, "The elements, matter, are indifferent. . . . Nature never fights against man; this is a base, religious calumny. She is not intelligent enough to fight: she is indifferent."[29]

Herzen made Turgenev's acquaintance in Moscow in February 1844, and the two became close in Paris, meeting frequently from the spring of 1848 through May of 1849.[30] At this extraordinary juncture—while the revolutions of 1848 were raging throughout Europe, Turgenev was working on stories for *Notes of a Hunter*, and Herzen was composing much of *From the Other Shore*—there can be little doubt that the two men discussed their concepts of nature, which had much in common even before they met. It is difficult to characterize the mutual influence precisely, but Herzen's unflinching tone could well have shaped Turgenev's remarks to Pauline Viardot on the "brutal indifference of nature" in the summer of 1849: "This indifferent, powerful, voracious, selfish, pervasive thing is life; it is nature, it is God. Call it what you like, but do not worship it. Please understand me: when it is beautiful, when it is good (which does not always happen), worship it for its beauty, for its goodness, but do not worship it for its glory or its grandeur!"[31]

It is telling that Turgenev invokes beauty and worship, concepts alien to Herzen's more scientifically inflected formulations. In truth, Turgenev was frequently impelled to depict the natural world as a beautiful, mysterious, feminized, godlike personage. Here again the Schellingian notion of nature as one with the Absolute, perhaps even God, makes itself felt. In "Journey to the Forest-Belt" (1850–57), for example, Turgenev described nature's attitude toward humanity as "the cold gaze of eternal Isis apathetically fixed upon [man]."[32] This tendency to deify found its purest expression toward the end of his life, in the prose poem entitled "Nature," composed in 1879. This short work offers an allegorical dream vision in which a majestic woman, clad in green and lost in thought, personifies the natural world. Echoing the mother-child trope of Goethe's "Nature," the narrator addresses her in Goethean fashion as "our universal mother" and asks her about her plans for human-ity. The goddess-like figure replies anticlimactically that she is contemplat-ing how best to impart more power to the legs of the flea to restore equi-librium (*ravnovesie*) between attack and defense. To the narrator's shocked response—Is not Man the favorite child of Nature?—Nature responds that "all creatures are my children . . . and I look after them equally—and destroy them equally . . . I know neither good nor evil . . . I gave you life—and I will take it away and give it to others, to worms and to people . . . it's all the same to me [*vsë ravno*]."[33] The crucial message, a pithy recapitulation of Goethe's

"Nature," is clear: nature's essential goal is balance (*ravnovesie*), and she can attain this only through perfect indifference (*ravnodushie*).

Turgenev's "Nature" has been persuasively linked by Russian critics to Giacomo Leopardi's "Dialogue between Nature and an Icelander" (from his *Operette Morali*), written in May 1824 and published three years later. In Leopardi's dialogue, a native of Iceland finds himself in an unexplored region of Africa, where he stumbles across a gigantic, beautiful, and terrible woman who declares herself to be Nature. The beleaguered Icelander suggests that nature is the enemy of all living things, including humans, to which the goddess figure replies:

> Did you think by any chance that the world was made for you alone? Now let me tell you that in my works, laws, and operations, except for very few of them, my purpose was not, and is not, the happiness or unhappiness of men. When I harm you in any way and with whatever means, I don't notice it, except very rarely; just as I ordinarily don't know whether I please or help you; nor have I done those things, nor do I perform those actions, as you believe, to please or to help you. Finally, even if I happened to wipe out your entire species, I wouldn't notice it. . . .
>
> . . . Evidently, you have not considered that in this universe life is a perpetual cycle of production and destruction—both functions being so closely bound together that one is continuously working toward the other, thus bringing about the conservation of the world, which, if either one of them were to cease, would likewise dissolve. Therefore, were anything free from suffering, it would be harmful to the world.[34]

Leopardi gives the story a pair of possible endings: two starving lions eat the argumentative Icelander and thereby survive another day, or a sandstorm rises up and buries the Icelander, whose perfectly desiccated body is "later discovered by some travelers and placed in the museum of a European city."[35]

For Turgenev, as for Leopardi, it is a foolish delusion to believe that Nature is humanlike and therefore has compassion and a conscience, since she—despite the ancient tradition of personification—is simultaneously and fundamentally not a *she*, but an *it*, an insensate aggregation of species and phenomena. Hence the envisioning by Turgenev's narrator and Leopardi's Icelander of Nature as a woman is absurd, and yet neither writer could escape the compulsion to personify the Goethean abstractions through dialogues between a humanoid goddess and thwarted worshipper.

Turgenev was able to achieve a Leopardian degree of sardonic irony with regard to nature, but he had a favorite alternative to goddess imagery:

interrelated insect metaphors depicting self-centered predation in the "true field of carnage" (*vrai champ de carnage*) he vividly described in a letter of 1868 to Pauline Viardot.[36] The first of these insect figures appears in an earlier letter to Viardot, from 1849: "That's what [nature] is—she is indifferent; there is a soul in us, and perhaps to some extent around us . . . it is a weak radiance that old night eternally seeks to swallow up. That does not keep wicked nature from being admirably beautiful—and the nightingale can bring us delightful ecstasies while some poor, unfortunate, half-crushed insect dies painfully in the bird's gizzard."[37] Indifferent to the suffering it causes in keeping itself alive, the insectivore goes about its business—even if that business is the creation of beautiful song. In 1859, Turgenev twice used a related image, but this time the predator assumes the form of a parasite, for Shubin's jocose confrontation with Bersenev in *On the Eve*:

I'm struck most of all by the seriousness of ants, beetles and other august insects; they run back and forth with such grave faces, just as if their lives meant something! I'm sorry, but man, the lord of creation, a superior being, looks down at them, and they couldn't care less about him. What's more, maybe some mosquito will land on the lord of creation's nose and use him for food. It's insulting. But on the other hand, how is their life worse than ours? And why shouldn't they put on airs if we allow ourselves to put on airs? Well, philosopher, solve that problem for me! Nothing to say? Eh?[38]

In "Hamlet and Don Quixote," written at about the same time, Turgenev musters a more sharply dramatic example: "Every living thing considers itself the center of creation and considers all else to be things that exist solely in order to benefit this center. Thus the mosquito, having landed on the forehead of Alexander the Great, sucked his blood as its appropriate food, calmly convinced of its right to do so."[39] In his second review of Sergei Aksakov's 1852 hunting treatise, Turgenev had illustrated the same concept with "the fly that freely flits from your nose to a lump of sugar, to a drop of honey in the heart of a flower."[40] The nihilist hero Bazarov muses over an ant dragging away a half-dead fly in *Fathers and Children*: "Pull, brother, pull! Take no notice that she's resisting; make use of the fact that you, as an animal, have the right not to recognize a sense of compassion, unlike us self-destructive human beings!"[41] The self-beneficial predation all around us demonstrates nature's great indifference writ small, as it were—the indifference of individual organisms as they perpetrate violence to satisfy their own physical imperatives.

For Turgenev, insect metaphors can also embody the despair born of contemplating natural indifference. "This sphinx," he wrote to Valentine Delessert in 1864, "that will present itself eternally to us all has looked at me with its great, immobile, empty eyes, all the more terrible in that they do not seek to instill fear. It's cruel not to know the riddle's solution; it's crueler still, perhaps, to admit to oneself that there is no solution, since the riddle itself no longer exists. Flies beating themselves endlessly against a pane of glass—that, I believe, is our most perfect symbol."[42]

On Venatic Equipoise

The thoughtful observer of the natural world, then, faces a problem. Nature is exquisitely beautiful, even attaining to the divine in her ability to elicit wonder and worship from those who behold her. Without meaning to, she compels love, but she does not, cannot, love in return. The famous dictum of Spinoza, so influential in Goethe's life, comes to mind: "He who loves God cannot endeavor that God should love him in return."[43] Kant would put it differently almost a century later, in the wake of the 1755 Lisbon earthquake: "Man must learn to yield to nature, but he wants it to yield to him."[44] What posture should the nature-loving artist, an artist like Turgenev, adopt before the indifferent and all-powerful goddess?

In his seminal 1974 essay, "The Root and the Flower," Robert L. Jackson surveys Turgenev's aesthetic outlook and characterizes it with such terms as *unity, conservative, centripetal, harmony, clarity, serenity, even-handed, indifferent, balance, restraint, equilibrium, tranquility, objectivity, calm, measure, detachment, reconciliation, armistice.*[45] Jackson notes the similarity between these hallmarks of Turgenev's literary equanimity and the essential features Turgenev perceived in the natural world itself, concluding that

> as artist he accepts Nature as a guide. Nature's evenhanded justice may be bad news for [man], but this same Nature provides a model for art and the artist precisely in her restraint, her Olympian tranquility and objectivity. . . .
>
> . . . The artist par excellence for Turgenev . . . finds nature in himself, and with nature's calm and measure apprehends life in its essential relationships, laws, and continuities.[46]

Turgenev's ideal as a hunter-writer was indeed to imitate nature's balance, as Jackson observed, but it was also an equilibrium that rested on far more violence—the crushing and dragging of half-dead insects, the sucking of blood—than Jackson implies. It is "armistice," but the setting is a "field of carnage." The balance Turgenev achieved was a specifically venatic equipoise, marked by the tensions and insights to which hunters had special access. The way in which nature served as a "guide" and a "model" for Turgenev was fundamentally influenced by his experience as a relentless observer, pursuer, and killer of animals. In fact, such experience could well be what prompted Turgenev to embrace nature's even-handed indifference in the first place. Turgenev's love of hunting, which began in early boyhood, and to which he devoted a great deal of mature thought, plunged him into a set of physical activities and observational habits that informed his aesthetics for the rest of his life. By studying the structure of his hunting life and the meaning he sought to give it, we draw closer to an essential source of Turgenev's artistic proclivities, of his persistent literary projects, and of his philosophy.

For Turgenev, hunters were not like other spectators of nature. Though profoundly responsive to natural beauty, he joined Sergei Aksakov in detesting the Romantic vogue for idolizing outdoor scenery, which was a disservice to the art of hunting and a desecration of the quasi-religious reverence for the natural world that field sport instilled in its practitioners:

> Hardly a single person can be found [wrote Aksakov] who is absolutely indifferent to so-called natural beauty, that is, to a lovely natural scene, a picturesque vista, a sunrise or sunset, or a bright moonlit night. This, however, is still not love of nature. This is love of landscape, stage-sets, prismatic refractions of light . . . To [such people], none of [the side of nature seen by sportsmen] qualifies as "natural beauty" . . . Their love for nature is shallow and obvious. They prefer pretty pictures, and even then not for long.[47]

Turgenev, in his early tale "The Duelist" ("Breter," 1846), implied much the same attitude through the drawing-room small talk of Küster, a kindly but shallow Romantic: "'I've found such nice society here . . . and nature! . . .' Küster embarked on a description of nature."[48] Vasilii Vasil'ich, the eponymous "Hamlet of the Shchigry District," tells the narrator in *Notes of a Hunter*, "I suppose I can pass over in silence my first impressions of country life and any allusions to the beauty of nature, the quiet charm of solitude, and so on," to which the relieved hunter-narrator insistently responds, "You can, you can."[49]

Observing nature for enjoyment is not enough. Hunters find themselves outdoors not because they are following an itinerary dictated by superficial notions of beauty. In Aksakov and Turgenev's worldview—if not always in their fictional hunters—the goal is game, not scenery. Sportsmen's long and frequent presence in natural settings is ancillary to the aim of killing birds and beasts, which, as Julian Schmidt asserted, makes hunters open and attentive to whatever natural phenomena they may encounter as they pursue that aim. Moreover, even hunters who have no connection to conventional literary activity still report on what they see and do in the outdoors: hunting stories are told around the campfire, kills are meticulously recorded in bag lists, letters to fellow sportsmen are filled with details of outings. Andrew Durkin sums up the way Aksakov's *Notes of an Orenburg-Province Hunter* projects the hunter as an attentive, integral presence in the organic world: "Hunting survives as a means of direct participation in nature, which is conceived as a complex system of signs that one must learn to interpret and control through *nabliudatel'nost'* [perceptual acuity] and *opyt* [experience]."[50]

It is a commonplace of Turgenev criticism to describe him as a detached observer, and as such he may be seen as mimicking nature's indifference. But while hunters fully immerse themselves in the never-ending interaction of predator and prey that reveals nature's indifference, they are anything but indifferent themselves. "Passionate"—the antithesis of "indifferent"—as an epithet for "hunter" is extraordinarily common in Russian hunting texts, including Turgenev's and Aksakov's.[51] On the other hand, Turgenev is noted for mercilessly dispatching his major characters (Girshel', Küster, Chulkaturin, Mumu, Rudin, Insarov, Bazarov, and so on). Here, when controlling the world of his fiction, Turgenev does seem to cast himself in the role of the indifferent Nature god, exercising complete and arbitrary power over his creations to serve the goal of aesthetic balance: killing them, making them fall in love, moving them from place to place—"letting nature take its course," as the cliché has it.

Tensions such as these, inherent in venatic equipoise, have serious implications for literary technique. As we explore those implications in the chapters ahead, such familiar ecocritical concepts as anthropocentrism and ecocentrism can be helpful, but a more nuanced set of terms is necessary if we are to do justice to Turgenev's specific representations of how human observers interact with the natural world.

Recently, Aaron Moe has developed the powerful term *zoopoetic* to describe poetry that achieves "breakthroughs in meaning" because the poet has shown keen "attentiveness to another species' bodily *poiesis*," resulting in a "co-making" by two separate species.[52] In the case of Turgenev, essentially a prosaist, I propose the term *zootropic*, derived from the Greek nouns *zoion* (animal) and *tropos* (turn). By *zootropic*, I mean a mode of literary perception and representation in which an animal is not manifestly used as a device (symbol, metaphor, emblem, metonym, personification, and so on) to allude to or stand for something in the human world, but is taken on its own terms and described as it is; the author *turns* toward the animal, instead of turning the animal toward humans, and merely observes it as an element of the organic world.[53] The human defers to—instead of demanding deference from—the nonhuman creature. *Zootropic* writing refrains from appropriating the animal or, to extend this idea into the realm of moral philosophy, does not subjugate the animal's will (Russian *volia*) to the writer's will by using it as a tool to create some larger, human-directed meaning. Zootropism rejects "catching nature by the tail."[54] Expanding this terminological framework, we can also speak of *phytotropism* for non-subordinating depictions of plants and trees, *geotropism* for such depictions of the earth and landscape, and *caelotropism* for the heavens. At a general level, we can group all four concepts together as *ecotropism* to signify the movement of the writer's attention outward, toward the environment.[55]

I will employ *anthropotropism* as the opposite of ecotropic modes, that is, to denote the tendency of writers to exploit animals and plants as obvious tropes for, or pointers to, human concepts and concerns.[56] This kind of allusive art can be seen as a form of *proizvol*, the arbitrary assertion of the author's will over the autonomy of another living thing.[57] Anthropotropism is the writer's bending what is nonhuman toward the human species, a rhetorical maneuver that instrumentalizes elements of the natural environment. While it is true that artists who subscribe to anthropocentrism—in which humankind is seen as the center and all else as the periphery—tend to generate anthropotropic art, I do not intend anthropotropism (an aesthetic mode) and anthropocentrism (a worldview) to function as synonyms. Turgenev's overwhelming tendency in writing about nature, and about human beings, is not to describe whole *categories* of beings (all of humanity, say, or all animals) as viewing themselves as a center or core. Instead, he perennially trains his focus on the strivings of *individuals*, a teeming multiplicity of micro-centers: the individual mosquito, the individual nightingale, the individual emperor. Thus, as we will see in chapter 4, the governing contrast for Turgenev is not typically center vs. periphery, but who is subordinated vs. who subordinates.

The tension between ecotropism and anthrotropism animates Turgenev's writing about nature, and examples of these opposing modes in Turgenev's orbit are not difficult to find. As Jane Costlow puts it so well in the context of woodland descriptions, the conflict is between "the forest 'as such' and the one that is rustling with allusions."[58] As was typical for a person of his time and place, Turgenev was steeped in anthropotropic figurations. Modern visitors to the writer's family estate of Spasskoe-Lutovinovo, near Mtsensk, learn that, a decade or so before Turgenev was born, his great uncle, Ivan

Ivanovich Lutovinov, had the property's linden alleys laid out in the shape of a gigantic "XIX," to signify the new nineteenth century. For his entire life, Turgenev thus walked paths that literally inscribed the symbols of human history on the landscape. He grew up with such books as *Buffon for Young People* (1814), a Russian adaptation of the French naturalist's writings, in which he read, "Of all the quadrupeds domesticated by man, the most sublime is the horse. This proud and fiery animal shares with him martial labors and the glory of battle. The horse, being as intrepid as her rider, scorns all hazards."[59] No literate Russian of the early nineteenth century could avoid exceedingly anthropotropic texts, from animal fables (by Krylov, Dmitriev, and others) to the pervasive presence of classical mythology (particularly Ovid's *Metamorphoses*), merely to name the most obvious examples.

Among the books on flora and fauna that sought to portray the natural world as a repository of useful symbols, Nestor Maksimovich Maksimovich-Ambodik's *Emblems and Symbols* (*Emvlemy i simvoly*), published in St. Petersburg in 1788, held particular fascination for Turgenev from boyhood on. In 1840, he wrote to Mikhail Bakunin and Aleksandr Efremov of his experience with this peculiar compendium when he was eight or nine years old:

> To my lot fell *The Book of Emblems*, etc., an imprint of the 1780s, the thickest of volumes . . . I leafed through my enormous book all day and went to bed with an entire world of vague images in my head . . . I myself fell in among the emblems, I myself "signified"—was illuminated by the sun, was plunged into murk, sat in a tree, sat in a pit, sat on the clouds, sat in a bell tower and with all my sitting, lying, running and standing nearly caught a fever. A servant came to wake me, and I was on the point of asking him, "What sort of emblem are you?" Since then I've avoided *The Book of Emblems* like the devil, and even last year, at Spasskoe, took it into my hands with trembling.[60]

The volume is an emblem book of complicated lineage, and the first widely available Russian example of that popular Renaissance and Enlightenment genre, whose function was, in the words of one nineteenth-century Russian commentator, "to synchronize an allegorical drawing with the expression of moral maxims or generally witty and elaborate aphorisms."[61] With "*emvlemy*" (allegorical drawings) on the left-hand page and "*simvoly*" (meanings) presented on the facing page in Russian, Latin, French, German, and English, the 840 images and their textual explanations represent the anthropotropic mode at perhaps its purest, a far cry from the Schellingian-Goethean vision of nature as an autonomous, sentient being.[62] The book thus represents a provocative early influence on Turgenev's view of the natural world: the notion that natural images should mean something specific and profound. Indeed, Turgenev's late conceptualization of natural balance in the form of a goddess ("Nature") may derive in part from Ambodik's description: "Nature [*Natura*] is . . . sometimes [depicted] as a young maiden in simple clothing and a crown of flowers who offers her hand to art."[63]

As we will see in chapter 4, Turgenev nonetheless declared his scorn for the anthropotropic mode: "We love nature in relation to us; we gaze at her as if she is on a pedestal of our own making. It is because of this, by the way, that time and again, in so-called 'natural descriptions,' we find either comparisons with the dynamics of human emotion . . . or the simple and clear transmission of external phenomena is replaced by disquisitions about those phenomena."[64] In crowning Sergei Aksakov Russia's greatest practitioner of what I am calling ecotropic prose, Turgenev denounced Buffon's flagrant anthropotropism: "I dare not deny the great merits of 'the father of natural history,' but I must confess that such glittering rhetorical descriptions as, for example, the description, familiar to us all since childhood, of a horse—'The horse is man's noblest conquest,' etc.—in essence do very little to acquaint us with the animals to which they are dedicated."[65] He goes on to upbraid the poet Benediktov and Victor Hugo for the same tendency, then praises the nature descriptions of Shakespeare and Pushkin by contrast (see appendix 3).

Though he held up ecotropic nature writing as an ideal, in practice Turgenev himself regularly, especially in his novels, made anthropotropic forays to further the aesthetic, social, and political goals of his fiction. In fact, as we will see in his commentary on Aksakov, he admitted this. For a vivid example, consider how Turgenev "catches nature by the tail" in his story "Asya" (1857): the eponymous heroine is described by the narrator as a "chameleon," "wild, nimble and silent as a little animal," possessed of "half-wild charm"; she longs to grow wings and fly away, and hides her head like a "frightened little bird."[66] She is a hybrid of human and animal features, the latter serving as metaphors for her unpredictable personality and yearning for freedom. Most striking of all is the narrator's attempt to map his relationship with Asya onto the myth of Acis and Galatea: "She is put together [*slozhena*] like Raphael's little Galatea in the Farnesina . . . Asya needs a hero, an extraordinary man— or a picturesque shepherd in a mountain gorge."[67] The famous fresco (ca. 1514) in Rome's Villa Farnesina portrays the Nereid Galatea's apotheosis, as she escapes the amorous advances of Polyphemus, who has killed her lover, the shepherd Acis.[68] Half in sea and half in sky, Galatea stands atop her seashell chariot, drawn by two dolphins (one of whom consumes an octopus), surrounded by several figures who unite the human and nonhuman: Triton (half man, half fish) ravishing a sea nymph, a female human-sea-serpent hybrid embracing a centaur, a partially fish-skinned man blowing a horn, a horseman blowing a conch, and winged putti swooping high and low. Especially in the human-animal crossbreeds—literally "put together" (*slozheny*) just as Asya is "put together" (*slozhena*) in the image of Galatea—we are confronted with a swirl of animals and animal traits being put to allegorical human use in an orgy of pictorial anthropotropism. Moreover, every figure is under subjugation of some kind, except two: Triton and Galatea. As we will see in subsequent chapters, Turgenev's intense interest in this kind of human-focused natural imagery surfaces time and again.

By extension, anthropotropic orientation can be built into characters. Consider the following example from Turgenev's most famous work, *Fathers and Children*. The protagonist is a medical student, the young nihilist Evgenii Bazarov. His apparent nemesis, the chief representative of the older generation's Romantic liberalism, is a fastidious and opinionated anglomane—Pavel Petrovich Kirsanov. In chapter 5 of the novel, Bazarov returns from a morning of outdoor specimen gathering:

> "What's that you have?" asked Pavel Petrovich. "Leeches?"
> "No, frogs."
> "Do you eat them or breed them?
> "They're for experiments," said Bazarov indifferently, and went into the house.[69]

The exchange seems trivial, but is in fact an expertly constructed biological illustration of the profound generational difference between these two men. When doctors ventured into the marsh in Pavel Petrovich's time, it was for the gathering of leeches, aquatic annelids that could be applied to patients' bodies to draw their blood for a number of reasons, some, from our modern standpoint, medically ridiculous, some valid; the parasite is tricked by humans into becoming a symbiont. Bazarov's medical worldview is entirely different: he gathers amphibians, a far more complex form of life than leeches, whose anatomy resembles that of people. "I'll split open the frog," Bazarov explains earlier in the same chapter to a curious peasant boy, "and take a look at what's inside, and since you and I are just frogs walking on two legs, I'll know what's going on inside of us too."[70] Bazarov's advanced approach is based on anthropotropic assumptions: the frog is an analogue for human beings, unlike the leech, whose method of nourishment can be harnessed by human beings to improve human health. Bazarov mutilates the frog and destroys its life, sacrificing the animal, because it is, in essence, a useful medical metaphor. The human benefits, and the animal dies in agony on the vivisection table. Bazarov's frog-harvesting provides a subtle but distressing hint at the mercilessness of his revolutionary outlook and at the vast difference between how the two generations believe people can or should interact with the natural environment.

Another passage from much later in the novel further illustrates Turgenev's subtly anthropotropic techniques. Bazarov's erstwhile disciple, the young college graduate Arkadii Kirsanov, falls deeply in love. Excited, terrified, stumbling over his words, he proposes marriage to his beloved Katia Lokteva, and she accepts. At the start of this scene, however, that outcome is in doubt: Arkadii stammers about non sequiturs, while "a chaffinch [*ziablik*] in carefree fashion sang his song above Arkadii in the foliage of a birch tree."[71] Here Turgenev, with the hunter's expert knowledge of birds, gently mocks Arkadii's timeless predicament by allowing a classical avian symbol of bachelorhood to achieve the happy fluency that eludes a nervous young man on the verge of leaving his own bachelorhood behind; it is the only appearance of this particular bird in the entire novel. The chaffinch's Latin name, *Fringilla coelebs*, means "celibate finch." It is "derived from the Latin word for 'without marriage,' and acknowledges the preponderance of male chaffinches that winter in northern parts of their range, while females migrate further to the south."[72]

What seem to be incidental zootropic elements of setting—frogs, chaffinches—actually contain, when taken seriously, a great deal of information that deepens character, plot, moral outlook, and atmosphere in Turgenev's fiction. Such examples are numerous, and exploring them reveals illuminating particulars that perhaps have gone unnoticed, or have had a subliminal effect on readers, or might have been detected by shrewd naturalists—or hunters—drawn to Turgenev's work. Unfortunately, in English editions, such passages are often obscured by translators who fail to emulate in their renderings Turgenev's own Aksakovian precision in naming inhabitants of the organic world.

Perhaps the chief tension of Turgenev's venatic equipoise is the unstable balance between representing the natural world ecotropically and exploiting it anthropotropically, between reporting a natural scene and putting it to conspicuously clever use. Though he professed (to paraphrase Archibald MacLeish) that nature should not *mean*, but *be*, he was frequently torn between two poles.[73] At one stood Aksakov, ecotropism, the gun, and the outdoors; at the other—Ambodik, anthropotropism, the book, and the indoor world. To frame the two descriptive modes in terms of Turgenev's most famous dichotomy, ecotropism is in many ways Quixote-esque (simple, direct, certain), while anthropotropism is Hamlet-esque (complex, solipsistic, unsure).[74] "In the art of Turgenev," Jackson observes, "understanding emerges more often through the objective representation of phenomena and not through the author's demonstratively burrowing into their significance."[75] His hunter's eye equipped him to engage the entire spectrum spanning these poles with supreme skill, and, as I hope will become evident in the chapters ahead, it is often the complex interplay of the two opposing methods that imbues Turgenev's nature descriptions with such vividness and power. If, as he emphatically declared in his second Aksakov review, the ecotropic mode was superior, we might wonder whether Turgenev at times felt a sense of guilt as he habitually yoked his observations of nature to human problems and strivings, perhaps even to the extent that he believed himself to *deserve* nature's indifference as a form of punishment for anthropotropic transgression.

As we will see, Turgenev's distress before nature seems to stem from a painful irony: his expert ability to convey the essence of the natural world is a byproduct of pursuing the goal of becoming a better killer of wild creatures, an aim that dramatically diverges from imitation of "indifferent" nature. The snuffing out of life is what brings sport hunters into field and forest; their careful observation of flora and fauna is ultimately motivated by the desire to dominate and destroy, however reverently, affectionately, or scrupulously such a desire is carried out. If nature is in balance, as Turgenev clearly believed, hunters deliberately tip that balance toward the human at the expense of the nonhuman, especially when they hunt for sport. Turgenev could not reassure himself, as a peasant might, that he was forced to hunt, for sustenance. As a wealthy sportsman of noble birth, he hunted out of inner desire (*okhota*) and not because he was externally compelled to do so, which makes his taking the lives of birds and beasts an act of *proizvol*. In his earliest play, *Indiscretion* (1843), he captured the hunter's excitement at arbitrarily controlling the lives of wild creatures:

> Have you never been on a bird hunt? Never set snares? Never spread nets? . . . Ah! So you have! Don't you agree that it's pleasant to lie in wait, wait for a long time? Now the little birds, beautiful and merry, gradually begin to alight together; at first they're skittish and shy; then they start to peck at your feed; finally, they settle down and whistle a bit, and so nicely, so carefree! . . . You stretch out your hand and pull the cord: bang! The net falls and all the birds are yours; it only remains to crush their little heads—what pleasant satisfaction![76]

We must of course differentiate here between Don Pablo's netting and Turgenev's real-life shooting. Moreover, Turgenev was no sadist: especially later in life, he expressed deep misgivings about the suffering hunters inflicted on animals. And yet, despite their clear differences, Don Pablo's and Turgenev's urges to hunt stem from the same fundamental impulse to control the life of another being.

One potential source of reassurance for the hunting writer is the ancient notion, emphasized by Schelling and Goethe, that the hunter is also the prey, because it assumes that humans too are animals, that humans do not stand apart from nature. Just as hunters passionately plunge into the landscape, they are subject to nature's merciless equanimity, part of the organic world, not superior to it. But the redemptive power of recognizing that hunter and hunted are one and the same is blunted by the horror of one's own inevitable weakness and mortality, one's insignificance in the grand ecosystem, illustrated by Turgenev's prose poem "Partridges" ("Kuropatki," 1882). This is the dilemma of the nineteenth-century thinker and artist caught between the reassurances of religious faith, on the one hand, and the pitiless contingency that follows from Feuerbach and Darwin, on the other. All the same, in spite of his atheism, Turgenev could never fully embrace a godless or unsupernaturally scientific view of nature, which explains his personifying her as a goddess, or turning to pagan visions (as in "Nymphs" ["Nimfy"], 1878), or invoking the Christian notion of eternal life (the conclusion of *Fathers and Children*), or—late in his career—creating tales about supernatural subjects, which can be seen in part as responses to the frustration arising from nature's insuperability.

For Turgenev, whose own worldview was mutable, hunting offered a pragmatic, unchanging, rule-based undertaking—a code of conduct, an anchor in his life. At the same time, hunting set before him the metaphorical vision of a suspended balance scale, with fulcrum, beam, and two pans, the contents of which varied greatly: human vs. nonhuman, passion vs. dispassion, allegory vs. observation, prescription vs. description, persuading vs. recording, literature vs. natural history, and so on. And with Turgenev, "The doubtful Beam long nods from side to side," as Alexander Pope put it.[77] The question of who, if anyone, holds the scale, was likewise an artistically productive torment to Turgenev. His ideal hunter-writer nonetheless lovingly observes nature's balance and can even fitfully attain her indifference. Such venatic equipoise is fleeting, precarious, and hard to come by. Through careful attention to his portrayal of the natural world in a broad spectrum of works, we may comprehend how Turgenev arrived at his conception of this delicate balance, exploited it in his portrayals of the nonhuman world, and despaired at some of its implications.

CHAPTER 2

The Gun before the Lyre

Turgenev Afield

> Esau was a skillful hunter, a man of the field, while Jacob was a quiet man, living in tents. . . . "Look, my brother Esau is a hairy man, and I am a man of smooth skin."
>
> —Genesis 25:27, 27:11 (NRSV)

> [Turgenev] had always been a passionate sportsman; to wander in the woods or the steppes, with his dog and gun, was the pleasure of his heart. . . . It would have been impossible to imagine a better representation of a Nimrod of the north.
>
> —Henry James, 1888

In a letter to Sofia Andreevna Tolstaia, Tolstoy's wife, novelist Ivan Goncharov wrote, "Turgenev is a troubadour (perhaps the first) who wanders the villages and fields with a gun and a lyre and sings of the natural world of the countryside."[1] Thanks to Turgenev's talent for distilling ideological debates and the vicissitudes of love, traditional interpretations of his work have naturally tended to emphasize the lyre and downplay the gun. Or, to invoke the dichotomy of Jacob and Esau, critics have favored Turgenev the smooth and artful tent-dweller over Turgenev the hirsute hunter. The urbane, impossibly accomplished, multilingual habitué of salons across Europe, the erudite companion of Pauline Viardot, the honorary doctor of civil law at Oxford—these are perhaps the regnant images of Turgenev today. Yet, to use the Puritan Thomas Brooks's phrase, Turgenev was in some ways "a Jacob without, and an Esau within."[2] The tension between the intellectual and the hunter in Turgenev's life and writing was a remarkably complex and generative one. It fed his lifelong craving to immerse himself in the natural world, and it nourished his skill in charting the two great massifs of nineteenth-century Russian social life—the nobles and the peasants—with a sharp and knowing contrast worthy of Jacob and Esau.

Turgenev flaunted his penchant for hunting, in Europe as well as Russia, and enjoyed the seeming contradiction between the civilized and the primal in his personality, as if he were living out the shopworn stereotype of Russians as hybrids of Mongol barbarity and European progress, or playing, in V. S. Pritchett's phrase, adapted from Edmond de Goncourt, "the gentle barbarian."[3] It would, however, be entirely wrong to see Turgenev's hunting as a mere pose: all the evidence clearly points to the sincerity of his love for field sport, from childhood on.

Like Aksakov, Turgenev relished taking the field, with a shotgun and a well-trained pointer or setter, in pursuit of upland game birds, primarily black grouse, woodcock, snipe, partridge, and quail.[4] He approached field sport with a rich man's devotion to connoisseurship: relieved by affluence of the need to obtain food with his gun, he scrupulously adhered to the latest European standards of gentlemanly hunting. In nineteenth-century Europe, these rules emphasized the *means* of making a kill, and were designed to render the killing difficult; in subsistence hunting, the norms made killing as easy as possible and emphasized the *end* of the activity: putting meat on the table.[5]

Few scholars have seriously dealt with what it meant to be a hunter for a man of Turgenev's time, class, nationality, and intellectual pedigree.[6] By doing so, however, we can begin to explain what a Russian nobleman hunter of the mid-nineteenth century was and how such a person was conditioned to observe and interact with the natural world. Turgenev's pivotal role in the evolution of hunting in Russia helps explain his particular ability to perceive and transmit the organic world. In other words, if we ignore the gun, we will remain partially deaf to the lyre.

The etymology and application of the basic Russian term for hunting (*okhota*) diverge from most West European linguistic practice. In French, *chasse* emphasizes pursuit, as do the English term *chase*, Italian *caccia*, and Spanish *caza*, all of which stress the seeking of game, though they ultimately derive from Latin *capere* (to capture, to take, to seize). English *hunt*, too, descends from terms meaning "to take," "to capture." Russian *okhota*, however, is based on the same lexical root (-*khot*-) from which we have "to want" (*khotet'*)—not to mention "lust" (*pokhot'*)—and it denotes desire, keenness to do something. *Okhota* can be applied to numerous everyday activities or hobbies that have nothing to do with the capture or killing of animals.[7]

The Russian conception of hunting, therefore, inheres in the personality and proclivity of the hunter rather than in a particular physical activity. Etymologically, at least, *okhota* is a feeling, not a practice. Oleg Egorov, the foremost modern scholar of Russian hunting, expands—in modestly nationalistic and religious ways—on this crucial distinction:

> The fact that in Russian the bagging of wild beasts and birds is denoted by the word *okhota*—which in its primordial sense means joy, merriment, satisfaction, desire—tells us a great deal. . . . *Okhota* reflected with utmost precision the internal world of the Russian hunter [*okhotnik*], his conception of God's world surrounding him, of himself within this world, and the significance for him of the killing of wild beasts and birds. Not trophies, and not their quality, still more not their quantity; not ritual, not sporting behavior, and still more not the competitiveness of the activity; not the idle titillation of one's nerves during a dangerous hunt, still more not the testing of one's character by the overcoming of certain farfetched obstacles, and not the search for some kind of analogue for a healthy way of life in the bosom of nature. *Okhota* for the Russian is not labor, not entertainment, not competition, but a condition of the soul, one might even say a way of life, when everything in one's life is subordinated to and aligned with a passion. It is a profound, unconscious sensation of the beauty, reason, and harmony of God's world, a delight and joy stemming from complicity in it and merging with it. For the Russian hunter the fact itself of bagging game is not as important as how it was bagged, in what setting and under what circumstances. It is precisely a case of the process being more important than the result.[8]

In Russian, *okhota* did not develop its modern sense of "hunting" until almost 1600, and the usage of *okhotnik* to mean "hunter" actually predated by over a century the usage of *okhota* to mean "hunting."[9] "The first and fundamental meaning of the word *okhotnik* in Old Russian," Egorov points out, "is a person who voluntarily undertakes something or occupies himself with something according to his own wishes or will. Moreover, quite frequently *okhotnik* or *okhochie liudi* [wanting-people] was used for persons who volunteered to participate in some sort of dangerous undertaking."[10]

In spite of the distinctive linguistic and cultural heritage of hunting in Russia, Russian sport hunters in the nineteenth century—as they did in many spheres of cultural life—generally used the techniques of English, French, and German enthusiasts and adhered to the same distinctions among various forms of European hunting by the end of the eighteenth century: hawking, netting, coursing, hounding, and shooting.[11] By the nineteenth century, members of the Russian nobility mostly limited themselves to these last three activities, all of which depended on the participation of well-trained dogs and rested upon a generally recognized code of what constituted "sporting" behavior. The two principal forms of hunting widely embraced by the gentry and later the middle class were based on two very different tactics: coursing (and closely related hounding), on the one hand, and shooting, on the other. It is essential to grasp the distinctions between these two practices—one of which Turgenev rejected, the other he eagerly accepted and promoted—if we hope to gain insight into his view of the natural environment, a view rooted in his identity as *okhotnik*.

Coursing and Hounding

Because it did not depend on the use of firearms, coursing is by far the older form of the hunt, dating back at least to ancient Egypt, where gazelles were chased by ancestors of the modern greyhound. In Russia, such hunting had developed by the early nineteenth century into two carefully distinguished types: *psovaia okhota*, and *gon'ba*.[12]

The oldest and probably best-known style of Russian hunting, *psovaia okhota*—traditional coursing—consisted of releasing a group of swift and silent hounds that relied on their keen eyesight (gazehounds, sight hounds) to pursue game (*dich'*) while hunters (*okhotniki*) on horseback attempted to catch up. In the meantime, the hounds surrounded the game animal, pinned it to the ground, or—less desirably—killed it. If this last eventuality was avoided, hunters could arrive on the scene and capture the prey or kill it with clubs, spears, arrows, or, in later periods, firearms. The most famous of all Russian breeds, the borzoi (*borzaia sobaka*—"swift dog"), was a large gaze-hound bred expressly to course wolves, though in practice borzois were most often employed to chase down hares, a far more common game animal.[13] *Gon'ba*, or hounding, on the other hand, relied on a pack of slow-moving, noisily baying scent hounds (*gonchie sobaki*; also *vyzhletsy/vyzhlitsy*) that used their keen sense of smell to track the game. Hunters carrying weapons followed on foot and shot the quarry—foxes, wolves, hares—once the hounds had cornered it and held it at bay. Russian breeds existed, such as the sideburn hound (*russkaia brudastaia gonchaia sobaka*), but by the 1800s various Western hounds—beagles, foxhounds, harriers, the Gascon Saintongeois, and so on—were most popular.

Coursing with gazehounds (*psovaia okhota*) is known to have been practiced in Kievan Rus' at least as far back as the eleventh century, but reached its heyday as an aristocratic pastime in the late 1700s, after Tsar Peter III released Russian nobles from government service in 1762.[14] Lavish, highly ritualized, and noisy, this was a rich man's sport that depended on large numbers of specially trained peasant assistants and vast tracts of open land. Aleksei Kamernitskii (1926–2009), distinguished chemist and modern authority on the history of Russian hunting, writes that in the decades before 1800, large coursing parties flourished among the gentry, with some forays employing hounds numbering in the thousands.[15] Typically, the hunting landowner would keep a large kennel (*psarnia*), and his borzois were tended by skilled peasants—houndsmen (*psari*)—who wore elaborate livery on hunt days. Before the hunt, the dogs were normally led two on a single leash (*svora*). The senior houndsman was called the "rider-up" (*doezzhachii*); the hounds-man in charge of the entire hunt, the "catchman" (*lovchii*). These men in general could also be called huntsmen (*egeria*, from German *Jäger*, "hunter"). Large game (*krasnye zveri*), such as wolves and foxes, was pursued with spe-cialized cries from the hunters and houndsmen—"O-go-go!" (*porskan'e*) or "U-liu-liu!" (*uliuliukan'e*)—while hares were chased down with shouts of "O-to-to-to!" or "Atu!" (*atukan'e*), from the French "à tout."[16] Large-scale hunts were frequently conducted as a battue (*oblava*), in which numerous peasants were employed as beaters (*zagonshchiki*) to scare up game animals from their isolated brushy or woodland cover (*ostrov*), at which point they would be pursued by any borzois that caught sight of them. The hunters themselves—normally men, but occasionally also women—would either ride horseback in pursuit of the borzois or take up station at a specified location (*nomer*)—determined by drawing lots—and wait for the hounds and game to come within riding range. These mounted nobles could number in the dozens or even hundreds. They carried special riding whips (*arapniki*, *nagaiki*) with stout handles that could be used, when necessary, to club to death the captured game animal.

Hounding boasted a similarly complex set of roles, techniques, and hier-archies. Scent hounds were led in pairs on a single leash (*smychok*), and their handlers were called "whippers-in" (*vyzhliatniki*), as distinct from the *bor-ziatniki* and *borzovshchiki* who worked with gazehounds. Writing in 1897, Leonid Sabaneev linked the distinction between hounding and coursing to the interaction of terrain with canine breeds:

> The difference between the scent-hound and the borzoi is that the lat-ter is much swifter than the former and for the most part much nimbler than the animal it pursues; the borzoi captures, while the scent-hound catches up and brings to bay. The speed of its gallop prevents the bor-zoi from giving voice, and therefore it captures silently; that same speed cannot fully manifest itself in overgrown or rugged country, and therefore the borzoi is a dog of steppes and plains. The scent-hound's

FIGURE 2.1. Russian coursing. A. D. Kivshenko, *Muzzled Wolf* (1891). Courtesy V. P. Sukachev Irkutsk Oblast' Art Museum, Irkutsk.

arena, however, is forests and mountains. The borzoi captures only what it sees and has very keen eyesight and a poor sense of smell; the scent-hound rarely sees the animal it pursues, and therefore its vision is little developed, but, on the other hand, it possesses a remarkably fine nose which enables it to track quickly.[17]

It was also possible to combine hounding and coursing, with the scent hounds and beaters flushing game until the borzois caught sight of it and chased it down. Such a combined hunt (*komplektnaia psovaia okhota*), as can be imagined, required especially large, complicated contingents of handlers and hounds.

Despite their differences, however, coursing and hounding shared fundamental features. Both relied primarily on dogs to chase, corner, and capture the quarry. Both relied secondarily on teams of peasants to train and handle the dogs. Both were noisy, either from the constant baying of the scent hounds or the shouting and horn blowing of the houndsmen and hunters. Both were methods of pursuing predominantly inedible mammals—and never birds— that were considered dangerous or detrimental to humans. Both required large, intricately organized groups of people and therefore tended to have the character of festivals. Both were temporally concentrated, normally lasting a single morning or day, by focusing on a single specimen of game and concluding when that one specimen (and perhaps its young) was killed or caught. Neither actually required the use of firearms—these were essentially tests of horsemanship, not marksmanship. Neither demanded that hunters

FIGURE 2.2.   Russian hounding. A. D. Kivshenko, *Hounding* (1894). By permission of M. P. Kroshitskii Sevastopol' Art Museum, Sevastopol'.

have intimate knowledge of the natural world, since the houndsmen did the spotting—often days in advance—and the dogs did the tracking.

These characteristics of coursing and hounding can readily be recognized in nineteenth-century Russian literature. Coursing is portrayed with particular vividness in the opening lines of Pushkin's *Count Nulin* (*Graf Nulin*, 1825):

Пора, пора! рога трубят;
Псари в охотничьих уборах
Чем свет уж на конях сидят,
Борзые прыгают на сворах.[18]

It's time, it's time! Horns are blaring;
The houndsmen are in their hunting attire
In whose radiance they sit upon their mounts;
Borzoi pairs jump in their leashes.

In this instance, Pushkin portrays the noisy, boisterous moments before a hunting party sets out after wolves. In his poem "Before the Hunt" ("Pered okhotoi," 1846), Turgenev himself described a similar scene, as did Fet in "Coursing" ("Psovaia okhota," 1857), which contains a clear echo of Pushkin's lines:

В поля! В поля! Там с зелени бугров
Охотников внимательные взоры

Натешатся на острова лесов
И пестрые лесные косогоры.[19]

To the fields! To the fields! From the green of knolls
The hunters' careful gazes
Disport themselves on forest-islands
And dappled woodland slopes.

In *Coursing* (*Psovaia okhota*, 1846), Nekrasov responded to the excitement and tension of Turgenev's "Before the Hunt" with a vividly detailed, satirical vision of the sport, emphasizing its violence and the enormous peasant labor it required. The larger context of Nekrasov's poem suggests that the lowly houndsmen are indifferent to natural beauty because they are being forced to do a job whose sole purpose is to provide pleasure to their master:

А за долиной, слегка беловатой,
Лес, освещённый зарёй полосатой . . .

Но равнодушно встречают псари
Яркую ленту огнистой зари,

И пробуждённой природы картиной,
Не насладился из них ни единый.[20]

And beyond the slightly whitish valley,
The forest was illuminated by a brindled dawn. . .

But the houndsmen greet with indifference
The bright ribbon of fiery daybreak,

And not one of them took pleasure in
This picture of wakened nature.[21]

The narrator's uncle in Leskov's Christmas story "The Beast" ("Zver'," 1883) is an Orel landowner devoted to coursing. Most famous, however, are surely Lev Tolstoy's wolf-hunt scenes in *War and Peace*, which function as a virtual encyclopedia of coursing and clearly illustrate its chaotic and (metaphorically) martial character.[22]

Shooting

For the bagging of birds, and sometimes hares, a hunting method utterly distinct from coursing and hounding was developed: *ruzheinaia okhota*, literally "gun hunting." Originally known in Russian as *egerskaia okhota*—"the peasant-huntsmen's style of hunting"—this sport is normally referred to in

English as shooting or fowling. *Ruzheinaia okhota*, which originated in six-teenth-century Europe, depends on the expert use of a smooth-bore firearm designed to propel a large number of small pellets—essentially a shotgun. Before firing, hunters must be relatively close to their prey—Turgenev in 1876 considered one hundred paces a maximum—and therefore quiet stalking is essential.[23] The most desirable game (*krasnaia dich'*)—analogous to the *krasnye zveri* in coursing—consisted of black grouse, woodcock, partridge, common snipe, great snipe, and jack snipe.[24] Unlike the earthbound mammals targeted by coursers and hounders, birds were particularly elusive thanks to their ability to escape by taking flight.

As an aid in this stealthy pursuit, quiet dogs trained to listen for, detect, and retrieve the game—field dogs, also known as gun dogs (*legavye / podru-zheinye / polevye sobaki*)—are indispensable.[25] When such dogs discovered hidden quarry, they would stop and take up a set (*stoika*)—hence the French term *chiens d'arrêt* (stopping-dogs)—which clearly communicated the location of the intended victim. In his *Notes of an Orenburg-Province Hunter*, Sergei Aksakov vividly described the gun dog's behavior in taking up a set: "Only dedicated sportsmen can appreciate all the charm of the scene when a dog, pausing frequently, finally goes right up to a sitting woodcock, raises its paw and stands trembling as in a fever, its eager eyes spellbound and seeming to turn green, fixed to the spot where the bird is sitting. It stands as if graven in stone, rooted to the spot, as sportsmen say."[26] In English parlance, as Turgenev explained it to his Russian readers in 1852, short-haired dogs who set by stretching forward and raising their heads toward the game were called pointers; long-haired dogs who set by sitting or lying down were called setters.[27]

Shooting encouraged a close relationship between a highly skilled hunter and an exceptionally intelligent dog that had to understand numerous complex verbal commands under often rugged and trying circumstances. In the late eighteenth century, Russians employed German imperatives with their dogs; the fashion for French arose in the first third of the nineteenth century.[28] The basic commands in Turgenev's day were *À terre!* (down), *Pille!* (seize), *Apporte!* (fetch), *Donne!* (give), *Tout beau!* (don't touch), *Derrière!* (heel), *Cherche!* (seek), *Tourne!* (turn). Aksakov held that the field dog and the hunter constituted a self-contained whole, bound together by deep mutual affection:

> Every hunter understands the need for a gun dog: this is the life and soul of shooting . . . a hunter with a field-piece but lacking a dog is something deficient, incomplete . . . a dog's searching can be so

expressive and clear that it's exactly as though she is speaking with the hunter . . . A good dog has an unselfish and natural passion for seeking out game and she will devote herself to it selflessly; she will love her master warmly too and unless she is forced to she will part with the hunter neither day nor night.[29]

French hunting authority Elzéar Blaze summed up the symbiotic human-canine relationship by frequently citing a hunting proverb: "A good dog makes a good hunter, and a good hunter makes a good dog."[30]

Originally, shooting was—as reflected in the term *egerskaia okhota*—a technique employed by serf huntsmen in their spare time or to provide game for the master's table. Egorov credits the original establishment of shooting in Russia to the Empress Anna Ioannovna's fondness for it during her reign from 1730 to 1740.[31] Kamernitskii emphasizes that this form of sport gained popularity in Russia much more recently than had coursing and hounding: "Russian shooting underwent a rapid upsurge following the Napoleonic wars, especially after 1812, when Russian officers, who had passed through Europe and become widely familiar with all facets of life there, brought their interest in shooting home to their estates."[32] Improvements in gun technology in the early 1800s—percussion caps replacing flintlocks, breechloaders replacing muzzle loaders, and so on—also contributed to the rapid spread of shooting by making guns more convenient to load, clean, and carry.

For guidance in delineating the status of shooting versus coursing and hounding in Turgenev's day, we may once again turn to Sabaneev:

Originally shooting had a purely commercial character, that is, it was the exclusive property of peasants, house-serfs, the petty bourgeois, and, perhaps, of minor clerks. Not without reason was it said then: falconry is the sport of tsars; coursing—of noblemen; shooting—of huntsmen or houndsmen. Indeed, before the start of Catherine the Great's reign, birds were hunted chiefly with falcons and hawks; beasts—with borzois, guardian dogs, and scent-hounds. Even later, when falconry had almost disappeared, noblemen nonetheless long considered, almost up the 1840s, the title of huntsman [*eger'*] degrading and for hunting feathered game would send out houndsmen or special hunters who were obliged to put game on the landowner's table.[33]

Egorov offers a vivid modern characterization:

The point was that in falconry, hounding and coursing, the main emphasis of the hunt falls specifically upon the birds or the hounds. On them depends not only the success of the hunt, but also all its

FIGURE 2.3.   Russian shooting. I. M. Prianishnikov, *At the Roding* (1881). By permission of Tver' Oblast' Picture Gallery, Tver'.

beauty. And it is they who capture the wild beasts and birds, not the human, who merely "amuses himself" with their work. . . . In shooting [*egerskaia okhota*], the human was transformed from semi-passive spectator into active participant, into the chief figure in the hunt, having pushed the hunting-birds and hounds into the background.[34]

Shooting could thus be a small-scale activity undertaken by a solitary person. It required only four elements: hunter, gun, dog, and bird. It was a quiet and secretive undertaking, at least until shots were fired. It fostered an intimate relationship between hunter and dog. It was predominantly directed at killing birds, which served as food—either for the hunter or the household. It was done slowly, on foot, and favored the hunter who was attentive to natural surroundings as well as to the dog's behavior. It focused on a wide variety of avian quarry, such as grouse, partridge, quail, snipe, woodcock, various waterfowl and wading birds, but also hares. It could be practiced at length, for days or even weeks on end, which fostered long hunting trips with overnight stays in or near wilderness areas. It frequently involved the services of a single peasant guide (*eger'*), with whom the hunter spent a great deal of time alone during the search for game. It encouraged marksmanship as well as expertise with rapidly advancing firearm technology and other hunting paraphernalia. Wolf hunters could argue that they were protecting human lives and livestock by coursing,[35] but shooting did not explicitly seek to exert a protective effect. Its practitioners were, in the end, obtaining viands, not exterminating enemies or pests.[36] Shooting enabled hunters to immerse themselves in the natural world, to merge with the landscape—a state clearly depicted by Ivan Shishkin in 1867 (figure 2.4). In literary terms, coursing was epic; shooting was lyrical. The progressive sociopolitical connotations of this new form of hunting play a prominent role in Turgenev's *Notes of a Hunter*, as we will see in chapter 3.

FIGURE 2.4. I. I. Shishkin, *Landscape with Hunter. Valaam Island* (1867). By permission of State Russian Museum, St. Petersburg.

Shooting, which could be undertaken far more often in a single season than coursing and hounding, encouraged daily and yearly bag lists that detailed the wider range of species and number of specimens killed. This demanded expertise on fauna and a naturalist's focus, and the practice implied that in the struggle with nature, score could be kept—a ledger of conquest could be compiled. The exact species *matters* in this kind of hunting: there was a hierarchy of prestige among the various kinds of often closely related birds, so knowing exactly what they were was essential. This hierarchy was modified according to the personal taste of the hunter. For example, Count Aleksei Tolstoy preferred to stalk capercaillie, while Turgenev favored black grouse.[37] In his shooting treatise, Aksakov provided detailed descriptions of forty-five species of birds and one mammal (the hare). Through 1868, Turgenev mentions pursuing twenty-two different species (seventeen birds, five mammals)—a staggering difference from the three species targeted by coursing and hounding. It is therefore not surprising that some of Russia's most prominent naturalists (*estestvoispytateli*), such as Karl Rul'e, came to the fore—and willingly collaborated with sportsmen—precisely during the widespread rise of Russian shooting in the mid-1800s.[38]

As shooting grew in popularity throughout the nineteenth century, it naturally appeared with greater and greater frequency in contemporaneous Russian literature. Pushkin offers an early reference, in "The Squire's Daughter" ("Baryshnia-krest'ianka," 1830) from his *Tales of Belkin* (*Povesti Belkina*): "And so, she [Liza] was walking, lost in thought, along the road canopied from both sides by tall trees, when suddenly a fine gun dog began to bark at her. Liza was frightened and cried out. At the same time, a voice rang out, 'Tout beau, Sbogar, ici,' and a young hunter appeared from behind the shrubbery. 'Don't be scared, my dear,' he said to Liza, 'my dog doesn't bite.'"[39] Some four decades later, Tolstoy provides a fine example of Russian marshland shooting, in Levin's hunting scenes from *Anna Karenina*.[40] Aksakov's *Notes of an Orenburg-Province Hunter* was devoted entirely to shooting, the cumbersome title explicitly declaring that these are the notes of a *ruzheinyi okhotnik*. It was Turgenev, however, who wrote the most celebrated fictional depictions of shooting, particularly in *Notes of a Hunter*, and whose experience of hunting would help mold him into a student of nature without rival among his Russian literary peers.

Turgenev's Hunting Experience and Proclivities

In general, nineteenth-century Russian hunters, like their West European counterparts, preferred either shooting or coursing and tended not to engage in both; Lev Tolstoy was an exception. Aleksei Khomiakov was an enthusiastic breeder of borzois and an expert in coursing, while Aleksei Tolstoy, Nikolai Nekrasov, Iakov Polonskii, and Afanasii Fet by and large devoted themselves to shooting.

Turgenev far surpassed all these writers in the depth of his devotion to field sport in general and shooting in particular. His maternal grandfather, Petr Ivanovich Lutovinov, and great uncle, Ivan Ivanovich Lutovinov, were keen coursers and hounders who frequently organized grand hunts at the family estates, including Spasskoe-Lutovinovo, where Turgenev grew up.[41] Both of his parents hunted regularly, and by all accounts as a boy Turgenev spent a great deal of time outdoors at Spasskoe. Our best evidence suggests that he was fascinated by the birds in his mother's aviary, and was catching songbirds by the age of seven.[42] After numerous bird-watching trips led by huntsmen on the estate, Turgenev at age ten began to shoot sitting birds and gradually learned to kill birds on the wing.[43] He seems to have begun hunting seriously in the late summer of 1835, at the age of sixteen. In addition to the peasants on the estate, his chief hunting instructors at that time were his uncle Nikolai Turgenev, Aleksandr Bers (brother of Lev Tolstoy's future father-in-law), and Aleksandr Kupferschmidt, a musician who lived at Spasskoe in his youth and in later years went on to lead the Moscow Hunting Society (Moskovskoe obshchestvo okhoty).[44]

Of all Turgenev's hunting mentors, however, Afanasii Timofeevich Alifanov (1802–72) was no doubt the most influential. It was by chance that Turgenev met Alifanov, a serf owned by his neighbor I. Cheremisinov, in 1837, when Turgenev was not yet nineteen.[45] That summer he hunted a great deal in the Mtsensk District with Alifanov, and the young nobleman formed a close attachment to the peasant outdoorsman, who was a locally famous master of many forms of hunting and fishing, but prized shooting above all. Turgenev's mother, Varvara Petrovna, later purchased Alifanov, and he and his family were freed by Turgenev after her death in 1850.[46] Afanasii moved his family—wife, son, five daughters—to a village about two miles from Spasskoe, and lived there the rest of his life.[47] Elisei Kolbasin, a close friend of Turgenev who knew Alifanov personally, offers this portrait: "As if it were now, I can remember this tall, well-built peasant in a sort of short, knee-length, homespun caftan, belted with a rope and reporting in a monotone to Turgenev on broods of corncrake, great-snipe, and so forth. Turgenev would listen to him attentively, never interrupting his smooth speech, and then take money out of his purse, saying, 'Now make arrangements for me, Afanasii, as usual' . . . [Alifanov was] a great expert in all forms of sport, from bear to dace."[48] Though he was an incorrigible alcoholic who occasionally drank up his master's provisions, Afanasii—"Athanase" in letters to the Viardots—served as Turgenev's indefatigable guide and chief huntsman at Spasskoe, breeding and training Turgenev's beloved gun dogs and caring for them during the writer's frequent and lengthy trips abroad. Until Alifanov's death in 1872, he and Turgenev were inseparable shooting partners, and contemporaries averred that when the pair took the field it was difficult to tell who was the peasant and who the nobleman, an observation perhaps due in part to Turgenev's practice of constantly buying Alifanov new hunting gear.[49] Other hunters who visited Turgenev and made forays at and around Spasskoe—Fet and Nekrasov among them—came to know Afanasii well. Turgenev immortalized Alifanov by transparently using him as the prototype for Ermolai, the narrator's hunting guide, in six of the *Notes of a Hunter* stories, most notably "Ermolai and the Miller's Wife" ("Ermolai i mel'nichikha," 1847), second in the cycle. Turgenev's sketch "On Nightingales" ("O solov'iakh," 1853) is actually a verbatim transcription of Afanasii's own words, preserving all the colorful oddities of the peasant's speech.[50]

From the late 1830s on, Turgenev seems to have limited himself almost exclusively to shooting. When his friends urged him, as a young man, to take up hounding, Turgenev reportedly answered, alluding to the din of the baying dogs, "The music's there, but not enough poetry."[51] His mother bought him scent hounds and borzois as a welcome-home surprise when he returned from abroad in 1841, and one doubtful anecdote describes Turgenev's grief at the death of a borzoi, but in his voluminous correspondence, we find nothing but references—countless references—to shooting, and no mention of his engagement in coursing or hounding.[52]

Hunting became one of the most important aspects of Turgenev's existence, even an obsession. He called himself "a true hunter—a hunter body and soul."[53] In his brief autobiographical "Memorial" (1852–53), in which the thirty-five-year-old writer tersely noted the most significant events of his life—first love, loss of virginity, first publications, grave illnesses, meeting Pauline Viardot, birth of his illegitimate daughter, the 1848 Revolution, and so on—he lists with startling prominence his hunting trips (five), and mentions by name his hunting companions (four) as well as hunting dogs (four). In a published questionnaire he filled out for a French journal in 1869, Turgenev, when asked his favorite activity, responded, "Hunting!"[54] His letters—to the Viardots, the Aksakovs, Nekrasov, Fet, and many others—are rife with passionate, detailed references to hunting. In the late autumn of 1852, to cite one example, Turgenev wrote to Sergei Aksakov that he had killed that season 304 animals: 69 woodcock, 66 common snipe, 39 great snipe, 33 black grouse, 31 willow grouse, 25 quail, 16 hares, 11 corncrake, 8 moorhens, 4 ducks, one jack snipe, and one black-tailed godwit.[55] Hunting with Louis Viardot was one of the earliest and sturdiest bases for the long-standing friendship between the two men. In fact, the earliest extant letter from Turgenev to either of the Viardots is a note to Louis in late 1843 or early 1844 in which Turgenev offers to help the visiting Frenchman arrange a hunt in the countryside southeast of St. Petersburg for roe deer and moose.[56] "They introduced [Turgenev] to me," Pauline Viardot allegedly said, "with the words, 'This is a young Russian landowner, magnificent hunter, and bad poet.' "[57] For his own part, Turgenev hunted not only in Russia, but all over Europe, including France, Germany, and Great Britain. Analysis of published Turgenev chronologies suggests that the writer spent an average of one to two months per year hunting, for the entirety of his adult life.

Turgenev Afield in Memoirs and Letters

Since the realia of nineteenth-century sport directly shaped Turgenev's sense of venatic equipoise, it is crucial to grasp the form of his day-to-day hunting praxis. Despite his titanic devotion to field sport, memoirs that offer specifics on Turgenev the hunter are relatively scarce. Among these, three sources stand out for their richness and reliability: notes by Dmitrii Kolbasin as well as by Afanasii Fet, and the set of reminiscences compiled by Ivan Rynda in the last years of the nineteenth century.[58] Many of the material details from these accounts can also be found in Turgenev's fiction; though it is conceivable that the memoirists might have included such information as a way of retroactively validating certain particulars of Turgenev's published works, it is impossible to determine the extent to which they might have done so.

Turgenev's close friend Dmitrii Iakovlevich Kolbasin (1827–90) published his short hunting memoir in 1892, nearly a decade after Turgenev's death.[59] Kolbasin's account is particularly useful for a number of reasons. Unlike the reminiscences of Turgenev's other contemporaries, it focuses solely on hunting. Kolbasin was a novice at the time, which makes his commentary simple and comprehensive, and Turgenev's role as hunting tutor affords us many glimpses of his attitude toward field sport. The memoir focuses on July 1852, the first summer of Turgenev's exile at Spasskoe, when he abandoned literary work in order to hunt full time. Finally, though Kolbasin was an admiring friend of Turgenev, his notes were published posthumously and deal as frankly with the writer's personal foibles as they do with his virtues.

The typical equipment of the mid-nineteenth-century Russian *ruzheinyi okhotnik* consisted, according to Kolbasin, of a fowling piece (in this case, an old Lepage for Kolbasin), hat, bag with powder and shot, an old caftan, and water-resistant knee boots. Karl Briullov's 1836 portrait of nineteen-year-old Count A. K. Tolstoy (figure 2.5), freshly graduated from Moscow University, presents a refined view of this outfit, dating from the period when shooting was gaining tremendous popularity among the Russian gentry.

For an even closer look at the hunter's accoutrements, we may turn to Ivan Kramskoi's populist depiction, painted thirty-five years later (figure 2.6).

FIGURE 2.5.   K. P. Briullov, *Portrait of Count A. K. Tolstoy in His Youth* (1836). By permission of State Russian Museum, St. Petersburg.

Figure 2.6. I. I. Kramskoi, *At the Roding* (1871). Courtesy National Art Museum of the Republic of Belarus, Minsk.

Here is a shabbier sportsman who embodies the eventual spread of shooting beyond the upper classes, an earthy figure crouching at the edge of a murky woodland, hat tossed on the ground beside him, his body entwined by an abundance of hunting gear.[60]

In Turgenev's case, as we have seen, from the late 1830s through the 1860s the role of *eger'* was played by Afanasii Alifanov. For the hunting forays with Kolbasin in 1852, Afanasii assisted Turgenev, while a peasant by the name of Aleksandr served Kolbasin. The two gentlemen traveled to the hunting ground in a tarantass, together with their valet, Ivan; the huntsmen rode in a separate cart, harnessed to a troika, which also carried a driver, provisions, and a primitive refrigerator consisting of a large, double-walled tin box with ice between the walls, for preserving the game they hoped to shoot.[61] In one outing, the men stay in a peasant's house; in another, they spend the night at an inn (*postoialyi dvor*) on a main road in the countryside; for another, they put up in a woodland hunting hut located on land belonging to one of Turgenev's uncles.

For the first foray, into marshland near the Raspberry Water spring (Malinovaia voda), three dogs are taken along: Turgenev's favorite, Diana; her untried daughter, Bouboule (Bobul'ka); and Afanasii's Shamil'. For the other outings, in pursuit of forest-dwelling black grouse, only Diana and Shamil' are present. The first day, Kolbasin sees a curlew that stops running and trembles in place, and he lets his dog pounce on the bird and try to retrieve it. Turgenev immediately admonishes his inexperienced friend: "Listen, Kolbasin, you mustn't do that. Shooting a sitting bird or sleeping animal is considered murder and only proper for commercial hunters, not sportsmen." Bouboule then hears Kolbasin's shot and tries to run away, straining at her leash in fear. Turgenev loses his temper, complaining bitterly, "Hopeless dog! This is what it means to be raised by women: it's the cowardice of an indoor dog—take her and shoot her! . . . Drag her—let her choke." On the way home, however, as the sun sets, Turgenev brings down a black grouse, and Bouboule retrieves the bird successfully, so it is officially decided that the young dog will not be shot.[62] Kolbasin chides Turgenev about his cruel treatment of Bouboule, and the writer ridicules himself for his uncharacteristic outburst. The next morning, Turgenev announces that the hunters will have to return home to Spasskoe because he's having an attack of illness; he worries about what he'll tell the women when they ask him what's wrong.[63] The exact nature of his physical maladies is difficult to pinpoint—in a letter to Aksakov from this period, Turgenev describes suffering from "gastritis or a chronic stomach disorder, often accompanied by fever and insomnia."[64]

Two weeks later, Kolbasin and Turgenev are after woodland fowl again. The first morning, they depart to hunt young black grouse in forest glades, ordering their horses to be taken back to the inn for the day and to be returned to the edge of the woods at dusk. Diana points effectively, and all members of the party, except neophyte Kolbasin, kill grouse. When the birds are scattered by the sound of gunshots, Afanasii expertly lures them back by imitating their calls. The grouse arrive and answer, the dogs are released, the birds fly up and are shot; the huntsmen gut the birds and stuff them with green pine needles to keep them from spoiling before evening. Turgenev, troubled that Kolbasin has brought nothing for himself to eat, tells him, "I don't eat all day and only quench my thirst with red wine mixed half and half with water. We'll eat by candlelight." Kolbasin finally bags a black grouse and demands that he, not Aleksandr, carry it—a departure from normal practice. The party returns at dusk to the horses and count the bag: thirty birds. They hunt in this fashion for three days at this place, and Kolbasin's technique improves. He notes that Turgenev is tireless, always cheerful, refrains from grumbling, and constantly gathers information by conferring with other hunters and their guides on the best locations.[65]

They now drive to the forest hut of Turgenev's uncle for their final hunt. The valet, Ivan, prepares some paté, which is quickly swarmed by cockroaches. Turgenev advises the worried Kolbasin not to trouble about the roaches: "Leave them . . . you can't do anything about it; at least once in their lives they can regale themselves with a delicious dish! And besides, this will distract them from the other provisions." That evening, Turgenev suffers from great pain in his shoulder, almost to the point of delirium, then settles down. Kolbasin summons a young doctor who comes the next morning and prescribes various powders. An expert on his own maladies, Turgenev quibbles with the prescriptions. "Subsequently," writes Kolbasin, "I became truly convinced that this athletically built man was subject to many bouts of illness, which made him a hypochondriac and unsure of himself. But when he was healthy, I never in my life met such a clever, fascinating, and warmhearted person." As Kolbasin was leaving Spasskoe, Turgenev gave him the Lepage gun as well as a hunting dog from his kennels. Kolbasin proudly declares that the summer of 1852 made him a hunter for the rest of his life.[66]

Rynda's sources in "Features of I. S. Turgenev's Hunting Life" (1903) emphasize the writer's serious approach to hunting, his tirelessness in the field, and his habit of rising long before his comrades.[67] He was an excellent marksman, particularly after he struck his quarry with the first shot, though an early miss could throw off his aim for the rest of the day. A courteous companion, Turgenev offered to draw lots for left, right, and center positions when he and another hunting party arrived at the same grounds simultaneously. In his youth, he walked great distances to the best locations, though he sometimes drove in a racing sulky. As he grew older, Turgenev added creature comforts to his outings: guests were invited, carriages with drivers were employed, wine was added to the icebox, and a cook would cater the meals. Game was generally not eaten in the field, as Turgenev preferred it to age before it reached the table. He loved his dogs—Napoleon I, Napoleon II, Tolly, Napl' (Naples), Diana, Bouboule (Bubul', Bubul'ka), Zima (Winter), Osen' (Autumn), Nochka (Little Night), Don-dan, Flambeau, Pégase—and pampered them constantly. Diana, whom he brought to Russia from France in 1850, was a particular favorite: he gave her a velvet sofa to lie on in her old age, and when she finally died, in 1858, Turgenev buried her at Spasskoe beneath an oak tree he himself had planted on the grounds (and which flourishes into the twenty-first century). He wrote to his daughter of the dog's passing: "My poor Diana died day before yesterday—and yesterday morning we buried her. I cried at this event—and I'm not ashamed to admit it, for this was a friend who has left me—and they are so rare, whether on two legs or four."[68] His favorite guns were a custom-made Tula field-piece as well as weapons crafted by such famous European smiths as Lepage, Mortimer, Blanchard, and Lebeda.

The memoirs of Afanasii Fet—for many years one of Turgenev's intimate acquaintances and most valued hunting partners, not to mention one of Russia's foremost poets—offer insightful details of their hunting trips during the summer and fall of 1858, precisely the span of Turgenev's work on *A Gentry Nest (Dvorianskoe gnezdo)*.[69] Near-contemporaries, Fet and Turgenev had met in late May 1853. They soon became close friends and collaborators, with Turgenev editing Fet's poetry throughout the 1850s, even acting as best man at Fet's wedding in 1857, before the two fell out over politics in the 1860s. Fet published his reminiscences of Turgenev eight years after the latter's death.

In the most detailed firsthand account we have of Turgenev's hunting customs, Fet describes an eight-day grousing trip he made with Turgenev to Shchigrovka, in the Forest-Belt (Poles'e), Zhidra District, Kaluga Province, thirty-three miles from Spasskoe. This was the same region that had inspired one of Turgenev's most important pieces of nature writing, "Journey to the Forest-Belt" ("Poezdka v Poles'e," 1853–57), a fictionalization of hunts undertaken there five years before.

The two writers set out on 30 June 1858—the day after St. Peter's Day, the start of the legal shooting season and a celebrated occasion among Russian hunters in the nineteenth century.[70] Two troikas are dispatched: one, a day before Turgenev and Fet depart, containing "the renowned Afanasii

[Alifanov]," a kitchen boy, and another hunter; the other, a covered tarantass, carrying the writers. Fet had never visited this part of Russia, and he puts himself completely in the hands of his companion. When the hunters spend the first night at a wayside inn (*postoialyi dvor*), Fet tells us, Turgenev is greatly distressed when his Bouboule—now a seasoned gun dog—is not allowed to stay in her master's room: "Bubul'ka always slept in Turgenev's bedroom, on a little mattress, protected from flies and cold by a flannel blanket. And when by some chance the blanket would fall off, she would go and unceremoniously poke Turgenev with her paw. 'Just see what a spoiled dog you are,' he would say, rising and covering her up again."[71] The innkeeper's officious wife insists that a cur (*pës*) must not be allowed to stay with guests. With great difficulty Turgenev finally convinces her that Bouboule is, among all dogs, an exception, and cannot be considered a cur: "A cur barks and is slovenly, but she never does this." The next evening is spent at the Apukhtin estate, where the young poet Aleksei Apukhtin, who had recently disseminated a stinging parody of Fet, is chagrined to meet the target of his wit. When the hunters depart next morning, Fet comments on the "rather sizable leather-covered chest" that crowds his feet in the tarantass: "Without this little chest, which contained a home apothecary, Turgenev never left his house, seeing it as a talisman against cholera." When a servant spills food on the precious chest, Turgenev berates him in his "piercing falsetto."

The noblemen finally rendezvous with Alifanov at the hunting ground near Shchigrovka, and the peasant is skeptical about prospects for a good bag of black grouse: "Stern Afanasii . . . viewed shooting as a matter that was far from trifling." The next day, at 5:00 a.m., the hunters rise and move to a burned area (*gar'*) in the enormous forest, Fet with his dog Napier (Nepir) and a serf guide, Turgenev with Bouboule and Alifanov. Fet worries that Napier, with whom he has not hunted in two years, will misbehave and irritate Turgenev, but the poet manages to bring down the first grouse, to his companion's consternation. Unlike Turgenev, Fet lacks prepared cartridges of gunpowder and therefore takes longer to reload than does Turgenev, who calls Fet's shells "devilish." They generally hunt morning and evening, returning home for lunch by 1:00, resting during the hottest part of the afternoon, then setting out again at 5:00 p.m. Fet remembers outshooting Turgenev, whom he nonetheless acknowledges as "a much better shot," by killing twelve black grouse in the morning, then four in the evening. At day's end, the birds are dressed, cooked, and preserved in vinegar. The game is invariably carried by their guides.

The two friends pass the week hunting daily, often resting in bivouacs during the hot July afternoons, though sometimes they do so in their carriages, with curtains drawn to keep out the flies.[72] On the trail of grouse, they often part company to hunt separately, with their respective *egeria*, then find each other for lunch and light meals: "We took from our game bags bread, salt, fried chicken and fresh cucumbers and, tossing off a silver glass of sherry as a preliminary, set about having a snack in the pouring rain . . . 'Good heavens!' exclaimed Turgenev. 'What would our ladies say if they could see us now!'" The outdoor repasts were memorable:

> I can't refrain from recalling with pleasure our lunches and rests after a wearying hike. With what delight we sat down at the table and treated ourselves to rich chicken soup, so beloved by Turgenev, who considered it inferior only to haslet soup. Young black grouse with their flesh still white may justly be called a delicacy, and afterward Turgenev could not help laughing as he watched how zealously I consumed whole plate-fuls of large, ripe wild strawberries. He said that my mouth yawned open as I did this "like a baby jackdaw's."

Fet affirms that the hunters slept well after evening shooting but that it was difficult to get up before dawn and wash themselves in the ice-cold well-water brought to them by servants: "Turgenev, seeing my indecisive splashing accompanied by pained gaggling, maintained that he could discern on my nose the un-washed-off remains of yesterday's flies." After their successful outing in the Forest-Belt concludes, Fet and Turgenev hunt two more times that same season, in the neighborhood of Spasskoe, for common snipe and partridge, in September and October, but during the October trip, Turgenev catches cold and is bedridden for an entire week.[73] The following summer, while Turgenev is abroad, Fet returns to Shchigrovka to pursue black grouse in the Forest-Belt, guided by Alifanov himself, but with considerably less success.[74] Evidence from later sources, such as Ludwig Pietsch's 1883 memoir of Turgenev's hunting at Baden-Baden in the 1860s, confirms the same basic patterns and habits we see in the foregoing accounts.[75]

If these descriptions of Turgenev afield furnish significant external details, his letters offer suggestive evidence of his internal state while hunting. The letters to Fet from abroad reveal a vibrant, avid devotion to shooting, as Turgenev's imagination is set ablaze by his memories of hunting in the Forest-Belt. His experience of field sport seems to gain vividness when he is recalling it from afar and recording it in written form. Almost exactly a year after the first 1858 outing with Fet, Turgenev writes to him from Vichy:

> I often think about Russia, about my Russian friends, about you, about our trips last year—about the arguments we had . . . What about

hunting?—This letter will probably find you after your return from Shchigrovka, where you probably drove with Afanasii. Let me know, for God's sake: how was the hunting? Were there many black grouse? How did the dogs perform—especially Vesna [Spring], Nochka's daughter? Does she give reason to hope? All of this interests me in the extreme. You wouldn't believe how much I'd like to be with you now: everything earthly passes away,[76] all is dust and vanity, except hunting:

> [In German] As blows the pillar of smoke,
>   Each earthly life shrinks,
> Only the—snipe, hare, black grouse, partridge, hazel grouse,
>   And other fowl, the hare, duck,
>   Common snipe, great snipe and woodcock—
>   remain constant.[77]

A month later, Turgenev writes again (from Bellefontaine), this time invoking the pleasurable shooting that Lev Tolstoy's elder brother, Nikolai, had enjoyed the summer before, and disparaging Nikolai's fondness for coursing: "I await the description of your hunting in Shchigrovka. Nikolai Tolstoy managed to like it. I was drooling at the thought that I could be there with both of you. . . . What's to be done! During woodcock season he'll ride out after his hares and foxes. . . . There's a pity! I would like to watch him in conversation with the 'Frenchman' Afanasii [Alifanov]. What dog have you been hunting with?"[78] Even two years after their original visit to the Forest-Belt, Turgenev marks St. Peter's Day, 1860, with another avid letter to Fet, this time from Germany:

> Today is St. Peter's Day, my dearest Afanasii Afanas'evich—St. Peter's Day, and I'm not out hunting! I picture to myself you, [Fet's brother-in-law, Ivan Petrovich] Borisov, Afanasii [Alifanov], Snob, Vesna, and Don-dan hunting in the Forest-Belt . . . A black grouse rises from the bushes—bang! Red-brow starts tumbling to the ground . . . or bolts off toward the forest that's turning blue in the distance, beats his wings hard, as both shooter and dog watch from behind . . . Will he fall? Will he go mad? . . . No, the son of a bitch is moving farther and farther away—he's made it to the woods—good-bye! And I sit here in Soden, taking the waters and just sighing! Today, though, I walked around the local fields and tested a dog: she turned out to have a sluggish search-and-take [pil'-avans]. They wanted to bring another one tomorrow; they say she's much better. We'll see . . . but in my heart I know that I'll never replace Dianka or Bubul'ka.[79]

Less than three weeks later, Turgenev dispatches from Courtavenel one of his most remarkable hunting letters. Fet has complained of depression, and his friend responds with sympathy and the prospect of grouse hunting:

> Youth has passed, but old age has not yet set in—that's why you need a kick in the pants. I myself am living through that difficult, twilight period, a period of impulses made that much stronger by the fact that nothing justifies them—a period of repose without rest, of hopes resembling regrets, and of regrets resembling hopes. We'll be patient a bit longer, we'll be patient, my dearest Afanasii Afanas'evich, and we'll at last arrive at the quiet haven of old age, and then will appear the possibility of old age's pursuits and even the pleasures of old age, about which Marcus Tullius Cicero speaks so eloquently in his treatise "De senectute." A few more gray hairs in the beard, another tooth or two falls out, a little rheumatism in the lower back or legs—and everything will be just fine! But meanwhile, to keep the time from dragging, let's go shoot these:

> Speaking of black grouse, I was hoping to receive from you a description of your first hunts [of 1860] in the Forest-Belt—and you're only just getting ready! That's bad. I'm sure that by now you've made amends and had your fill of hunting. Here in France, God knows when the hunting season will arrive! We've got real winter here, your teeth chatter, weekly rains—abysmal! No one can say when the harvest will start or end. What about the hunting, though! Endless partridge and hare! As to the timing of my return home, I can't yet say anything definite. In a few days the matter will be decided—whether I'll have to spend the winter in Paris, or if I'll return to Spasskoe in time for the woodcock.[80]

In his earlier letter, Turgenev had joked with Fet that "all is dust and vanity, except hunting," but now the vagaries of middle age are more real, and Turgenev's earnest response about regrets and hopes resonated to such a degree that he transplanted precisely the same phrases into chapter 7 of *Fathers and Children* to describe Pavel Petrovich's desolate life after his loss of Nellie, the enigmatic Princess R.[81] Moreover, something prompted Turgenev, an inveterate doodler, to draw a sketch of the black grouse—instantly recognizable as such—to accompany his words of commiseration, as if the verbal invocation alone were inadequate to balm Fet's melancholy.

The memoirs and letters illustrate how Turgenev saw life's fragility juxtaposed with the exhilaration of hunting. That fragility could manifest itself in emotional weakness as well as physical illness, but in either case, he consistently perceived shooting, even tales of shooting, as a tonic: "I'm very sorry to hear that both rheumatism and melancholy are tormenting you," he wrote to Lev Vaksel' in 1853. "I know of no remedies for rheumatism—but to dispel your melancholy, I'll tell you a bit about my hunting this year."[82] The tension between human frailty and hunting was also evident in the many examples of Turgenev's having to curtail, postpone, or cancel his outings because of ill health. While out hunting with Nekrasov in the fall of 1854, Turgenev almost put his eye out with a tree branch and had to stay home for two days.[83] As Turgenev, by then in his mid-fifties, put it to Gustave Flaubert in 1873, "My unrestrained passion for hunting is the only passion I have left . . . [but] I don't know if my gout will permit me such tricks."[84] The outdoor world was a place of matchless beauty and excitement, but accessible only when the hunter was strong enough to enter it and bear up under its physical demands. Turgenev was a delicate Esau.

And yet, in the memoirs of Turgenev's actual hunting practice, and in his own numerous letters on hunting, the allure of nature as such is not something that occupies the foreground—his companions do not describe a man who sat idly meditating on natural beauty during the hunt. A reliable observer quoted Turgenev late in 1880:

I can't admire nature when I'm hunting—that's all nonsense: you admire her when you lie down or sit down to rest after the hunt. Hunting is a passion, and I, except for some partridge that sits under a bush, don't and can't see anything else. Whoever goes to hunting grounds with a gun and admires nature is not a hunter. I'm an old man now; about five years ago, when I saw a bird sitting near me (though if it were in a cage, I was indifferent), and I knew that my dog would track it down and take up a set, my heart beat 180 times a minute. Passion is a slippery business. Ask yourself why you enjoy something, and a minute later you'll no longer enjoy it.[85]

This closely resembles the serious, intensely focused mentality of the peasant hunter—of Turgenev's tutor, Afanasii Alifanov, for whom shooting, in Fet's direct observation of him, was "a matter that was far from trifling." Another witness captured this quality well when he described Turgenev on a foray for woodcock: "After this we set out to hunt, in different corners of the forest, of course. But in the woods I nevertheless happened to meet up with Turgenev. He stood in one of the little glades, beneath a birch, with his gun cocked, having fixed his gaze upon the scarlet sunset, and, saying nothing, only waved his hand at me, so that I wouldn't bother him."[86] This description is provided by an anonymous hunter from Mtsensk who chanced to meet Turgenev in the forest in the 1850s but who only later realized who he was— the famous writer and describer of the Russian landscape. Instead of the Romantic fixating the sublimity of the setting sun, Turgenev, this observer found, was the diligent marksman who knows that careful attention must be paid to the evening sky at dusk during roding season, when woodcock appear overhead on their noisy courtship flights. He merely waves the intruder away and scans the twilight sky for his quarry.

The practical aspects of Turgenev's interaction with the natural world while hunting will by now be clear: zeal for the chase, seriousness, indefatigability, expertise in the norms of hunting, careful planning, desire to introduce his friends to outdoor sport, extreme affection for his dogs, separation from the world of women, willingness to spend weeks at a time in the field, splendid equipment, attentive service from peasant assistants and huntsmen, bountiful meals, physical frailty, and morbid fear of disease.[87] This last concern was a constant feature of Turgenev's life, both outdoors and in, and it contrasts tormentingly with his unflagging desire to be in the woods and fields pursuing game. Nonetheless, for Turgenev, shooting was clearly an active, practical endeavor that required vigor, nerve, and skill. It yielded concrete, quantifiable results, as we see in his many bag lists, and demanded organization and practical acumen. Its complexities were also codifiable in reference works such as hunting manuals and treatises, which entered their Russian heyday at this time.

These pragmatic and palpable aspects of hunting are crucial to our understanding of the impotent "superfluous men" and strong but thwarted women who abundantly populate Turgenev's stories and novels. Hunting gives Russian nobles the satisfaction of tangible achievement that constantly eludes them in the fictional worlds Turgenev fashioned. He extracted from the hunter's natural métier glimpses of the fulfillment and permanence that were nearly always just beyond the grasp of his characters, and the freedom and accomplishment possible in the field throw into vivid relief the endless frustration and failure explored in his literary works. Finally, a successful hunt always results in the death of another being: the hunter's best day is always the worst day for his individual prey animal. This strange form of equipoise—the joy of one depending on the destruction of another—is fundamental to field sport and became one of Turgenev's most distressing themes.

CHAPTER 3

"A Different Kind of Game"

Notes of a Hunter

> Let us suppose that you were not born a hunter, but that you nonetheless love nature. It stands to reason that you can't but envy us hunters.
>
> —Turgenev, "Forest and Steppe," 1848

> [In *Notes of a Hunter*,] Turgenev had his own special hatred; he wasn't picking up crumbs from Gogol's table. He was hunting a different kind of game: the landowner, his wife, his entourage, his steward, and village elder.
>
> —Herzen, 1857

The rise of hunting literature—fiction and nonfiction—helped usher Turgenev and Aksakov into prominence, and these two writers created by far the most celebrated examples in Russia: *Notes of a Hunter* (published 1847–52) and *Notes of an Orenburg-Province Hunter* (published 1852).[1] To appreciate the concepts and conflicts of natural elements with which Turgenev experimented in *Notes of a Hunter*, we must explore the context in which the famous cycle was conceived, written, and received. In my analysis of the structure and ecological thematics of the work, I will frequently touch on the oppression of the Russian peasantry under Tsar Nicholas I. The notion that *Notes of a Hunter* was a weapon in the abolitionist movement (a cause célèbre for Turgenev's generation), that it may have influenced Alexander II to emancipate the serfs in 1861, and so on, is an old one, showcased in Russian school curricula to this day. An assemblage as bountiful and skillfully written as *Notes of a Hunter*, however, is a great many other things as well, and there is a wealth of critical commentary that goes far beyond the traditional interpretation of the cycle as a social tract that illuminated the plight of Russia's underclass. Nonetheless, by focusing on features of ecocritical importance, we can, I believe, recover some of the freshness of the cycle's sociopolitical signals. That result is a welcome byproduct of taking *Notes of a Hunter* seriously as a laboratory of venatic equipoise, a proving ground in which Turgenev tested the limits of Aksakovian nature writing and ultimately moved beyond it into a complex interleaving of ecotropic and anthropotropic modes.

Hunting Literature in Nineteenth-Century Russia

The Russian literary vogue for hunting was part of a general European trend. Depictions of hunting were by no means unheard of in early nineteenth-century Russian writing, as we have seen, but by the 1840s the Russian literary scene—like French and English writing—was inundated by sporting literature in which the hunt became the central setting or thematic concern rather than an incidental element of atmosphere.[2] As the popularity of hunting surged among European landowners in the 1820s and 1830s, vivid written descriptions of their adventures in forest and field were soon to follow, first in England, then in France.[3] Hunting sketches, as Margarita Odesskaia has demonstrated, began to turn up in Russian periodicals during the 1840s.[4] Created by such writers as Nestor Kukol'nik, Nikolai Nekrasov, and Aleksei Khomiakov, the first specimens of Russian hunting literature in the early 1840s seemed to betoken a bright future for the genre.[5] Polish-born Napoleon Reutt founded the popular monthly *Journal of Horse Breeding and Hunting* (*Zhurnal konnozavodstva i okhoty*) in 1842, and soon published the first serious Russian monograph on hunting dogs, his two-volume *Coursing* (*Psovaia okhota*), in 1846. That same year Sergei Aksakov completed the first edition of his *Notes on Fishing*, and in October 1847 a Russian translation of Louis Viardot's memoirs of his Russian hunting trips—organized in part by Turgenev four years earlier—appeared in *Forest Journal* (*Lesnoi zhurnal*).[6] A keen hunter and close friend of Turgenev, Nekrasov, as editor of Russia's most influential midcentury literary journal, the *Contemporary* (*Sovremennik*), boosted the publication potential and prestige for hunting works in the late 1840s and 1850s.

Turgenev, whose literary skill and profound devotion to shooting put him in the perfect position to produce venatically oriented writing of superior quality, found himself at the center of the trend. In 1846 he created his nine-poem cycle *The Countryside* (*Derevnia*), which contains two fine hunting lyrics—"Before the Hunt" ("Pered okhotoi") and "Summer Hunting" ("Na okhote—letom")—and by November of that year had completed "Khor' and Kalinych." Both the poem cycle and the story appeared in the January 1847 issue of Nekrasov's *Contemporary*. This was the first issue edited by Nekrasov, who the following month published in his newly acquired journal a poem entitled "Coursing" ("Psovaia okhota"), his own satiric reply to Turgenev's "Before the Hunt"; Nekrasov took both his title and epigraph from Reutt's 1846 treatise.

This issue of the *Contemporary* was a turning point for Turgenev. *The Countryside* was the last poetry he would publish in his lifetime, while "Khor' and Kalinych" became the first sketch in the famous collection of tales eventually known as *Notes of a Hunter*, based on the subtitle ("From the notes of a hunter") given to "Khor' and Kalinych" by Nekrasov's coeditor, Ivan Panaev, when the story first appeared that January.[7]

Alongside the hunting works of established writers, the production of far less literary, far more pragmatic, hunting manuals, such as Reutt's, and hunting articles, thrived at this time. In fact, Odesskaia has persuasively argued it was these periodical pieces that came first and stimulated the more refined literary products remembered today: "The parochial exclusivity of specialized hunting journals and almanacs was disrupted [in the 1840s–50s], and articles on dog breeds and horses, and on varieties of firearms, began to be diluted by small lyrical sketches of landscapes, and by ethnographic notes connected not only with descriptions of landscapes suitable for hunting, but also with sketches of characters." She contends, however, that after a fleeting golden age, under Aksakov and Turgenev, Russian sporting literature of high literary merit was overtaken by the work of epigones: "Born on the periphery, in the 'backyard' of literature, this genre by the middle of the nineteenth century moved to the center, to the proscenium of literary life, but then, seized by second-rate hunter-writers—who in their compositions 'conserved' or 'preserved the freshness' of the images, compositional structure, and style of their works of 'high' literature—it slipped down and once again retreated to the periphery."[8] Turgenev's enthusiastic involvement with the world of manuals, less well known than his relationships with established members of the literary scene who wrote hunting works, reflects his meticulous, technically sophisticated fascination with the outdoors and helps explain his intense interest in Aksakov's limpid and thorough *Notes*, which we will examine in chapter 4. A brief overview of Turgenev's relations with two manual writers may suffice to demonstrate his proximity to those for whom technical connoisseurship in hunting was of paramount importance.

Writer and publisher Nil Andreevich Osnovskii (1819–71) met Turgenev sometime before 1855 and published the first, four-volume collection of Turgenev's works, in 1860–61; he performed the same service for Dostoevsky in 1860. Osnovskii's claim to fame in hunting literature is *Remarks of a Muscovite Hunter on Shooting with a Gun Dog*, which came out in 1856 and quickly earned a second edition the following year.[9] Clearly modeled on Aksakov's 1852 treatise, *Remarks* was, according to S. I. Romanov, "well known to many Russian hunters and in its time had good success."[10]

To improve their ability to pursue and kill, hunters like Osnovskii acquired and shared, via manuals, detailed information on the appearance, habits, and habitats of their quarry. For this reason, troves of valuable biological field notes were to be found in mid-nineteenth-century hunting treatises. Karl Frantsevich Rul'e (Rouillier, 1814–58), a brilliant professor of zoology at Moscow University, whom Thomas Newlin has called "perhaps the leading Russian biologist of the era,"[11] was attracted to the best sporting books of the 1850s, including Osnovskii's manual, for which Rul'e acted as ornithological consultant. For the last edition of *Notes of an Orenburg-Province Hunter* to be published in his lifetime (the third edition, 1857), Aksakov too turned to Rul'e, who furnished the volume with annotations and illustrations, just as he did for the definitive third edition of *Notes on Fishing* the same year.

The most important of the midcentury manual writers was Lev Nikolaevich Vaksel' (1811–85). Son of one of the first Russian importers of English-bred setters, Vaksel' had befriended Turgenev by 1852.[12] In late May that year, just after his imprisonment, Turgenev sent Vaksel' an inscribed copy of Aksakov's *Notes of an Orenburg-Province Hunter* and inquired about English firearms.[13] Turgenev tried to have Vaksel' come to Spasskoe for some shooting in the summer and fall of 1852, and by early 1853, in a letter to Louis Viardot, could refer to him as "one of my best friends": "He's an excellent hunter—a perfect 'gentleman' in the best sense of the word. I am certain you will like him; his appearance wins him favor and unless I am much mistaken, Madame Viardot will want to have a sketch of his energetic and handsome head in her album."[14] Turgenev's six extant letters to Vaksel', dating from 1852 to 1854, are filled with evidence of their affection and mutual admiration with respect to hunting, dog breeding, dog training, and the treatment of canine illnesses. Vaksel', who lived in Petersburg, served as outfitter to the exiled Turgenev, sending him well-bred puppies, excellent shotguns, and other gear.

In 1856, Vaksel' published what would become the most popular of the practical Russian hunting manuals of the nineteenth century, *Beginner's Pocket Guide to Hunting with Gun and Gun Dog*, which went through five editions before 1900, four in its author's lifetime.[15] In his preface, Vaksel' marked the sub-literary status of his own work and extolled the writers he saw as his exemplars: "I do not consider myself knowledgeable enough to go into detail on the very essence of this kind of hunting [i.e., shooting], and after the poetic narrative of S. A[ksako]v's *Orenburg Hunter* and I. Turgenev's *Notes*, I cannot hope to add anything new to the description of the delights of this pastime."[16] According to Romanov, the quality of Vaksel''s straightforward, down-to-earth prose was one of the book's signal advantages: "It's impossible not to feel great regret that amid the mass of our splendid practical experts on hunting, only two writers have turned up: Aksakov and Vaksel'."[17]

Afanasii Fet published an anonymous review of Vaksel's manual in 1856.[18] "It would not be appropriate here," he writes, "to contend that shooting is more refined and elegant, that it demands the effort of all a man's physical and moral abilities; much quarry will be bagged by someone with access to good coursing, but only a genuine and completely developed wildfowler will be able to kill a great deal of game."[19] Fet sees Vaksel' as both an instructor and friend in this superior form of hunting and asserts that the manual emanates "poetic truth," reinvigorating the reader's memories of adventures afield.[20] It is a belief among hunters, Fet contends, that a person's mind is fully revealed when that person is made to study an animal, which makes his encomium to Aksakov—a gemlike review of Aksakov's *Notes* embedded within the review of Vaksel's *Pocket Guide*—an especially significant endorsement of the zootropic mode:

> Anyone wishing to become acquainted with [birds] can read Mr. A[ksako]v's *Notes of an Orenburg-Province Hunter*; in them he will find peerless description of all our existing bird species. Mr. A[ksako]v has so artfully presented their portraits, so faithfully described the habits of different kinds of game, even demonstrating how some of them fly, that, when reading his book, you not only see the bird, but hear its flight; it seems as though you could take a shot. One hunter has assured me in absolute seriousness that his gun dog comes to attention and takes up a set over his copy of *Notes of an Orenburg Hunter*.[21]

Fet sees Vaksel's work as "imbued with precisely the same artistic truth" as Aksakov's *Notes* and concludes the review on a humorous note: "Young hunters, having learned the rules set down in Mr. Vaksel's *Pocket Guide*, will not be shot by anybody, themselves will not shoot their companions, and will train their gun dogs in marvelous fashion."[22] Fet's review documents the competition between shooting and coursing, and jibes with Aksakov's avowed emphasis—so common in Fet's own nature poetry too—on writing that revives the author's and reader's recollections of actual, lived experience in the organic world. As Aksakov himself put it in the very first words he ever published on outdoor sport, "I wrote these notes . . . to reinvigorate my memories."[23] While Fet's anonymous, lighthearted review of Vaksel's manual offers reasonably substantial commentary, Turgenev's own response to Aksakov's *Notes of an Orenburg-Province Hunter* is of an entirely different order. As we will see in chapter 4, it contains Turgenev's most direct and profound observations about the natural world.

Turgenev's Venatic Writing

Turgenev, who retained his zeal for sport to the end of his life, did produce a few nonfiction works in the 1870s and 1880s that are, in the spirit of Aksakov, explicitly devoted to hunting and strikingly consistent with his own early writing about field sport. He had been conspicuously unable to produce practical essays for Aksakov's hunting miscellany two decades earlier, but now, with the apex of his fiction behind him, he found his resistance to undertaking such efforts subsiding. The first of these works is "Pégase," written in Paris in December 1871 as a tribute to Turgenev's eponymous hunting dog, a beloved German shepherd–English setter cross who had performed some truly extraordinary exploits in the field.[24]

Though Turgenev never wrote a hunting manual after the fashion of Vaksel', his devotion to sporting praxis found direct expression in a short, often overlooked work called "The Hunter's Fifty Flaws and Fifty Flaws of a Gun Dog" (1876), which he published in *Hunting Journal* (*Zhurnal okhoty*) seven years before his death (see appendix 4 for a complete translation).[25] Though entirely couched in terse, negative terms, "Fifty Flaws" is a hunting manual in miniature, a repository of the ideals and codes of shooting that Turgenev had cherished his entire life and in various ways subsumed into his fiction. It is thus is a crucial source document.

The negative structure of "Fifty Flaws" is also typical of Turgenev's approach to his stories and novels, in which he naturally gravitated toward accounts of deficiency and misfortune; positive heroes and happy outcomes, à la Chernyshevskii, were alien to his artistic vision. The negative rhetorical stance of "Fifty Flaws" is likewise in keeping with Turgenev's perception of hunting as the exercise of restraint over misguided impulses, reflective of the balance he perceived as essential in the workings of the natural world. The occasional glimmers of humor, especially in human flaw no. 50 ("Does not permit his companions to boast or even to tell a fib or two in his presence . . . an inhumane trait!"), are overwhelmed by the earnest view of sport that Turgenev imbibed from Afanasii Alifanov: hunting is a serious business. The decision to include equal numbers of flaws for both hunter and dog echoes Turgenev's practice, inherited from Goethe and Schelling, to place animals and people on the same existential plane, and reminds us of his belief, consonant with that of both Aksakov and Blaze, that "a good dog makes a good hunter, and a good hunter makes a good dog."[26] This technique foregrounds the human-canine partnership on which shooting depends. The prevalence of binary oppositions in his work, reinforced by Turgenev's early immersion in Hegelian thinking, is reprised here not only in the human/dog dichotomy of "Fifty Flaws," but also in the author's professed intention for how the miniature manual itself is to be read: "If it should occur to someone to ask me why I have not enumerated the hunter's and dog's virtues, then I will answer that these virtues are implied by the flaws themselves: one need only take their opposite."

The virtues we can infer from the list clearly reflect Turgenev's actual hunting practice as we observed it in chapter 2: early rising (human flaw no. 1), quietness (human flaw no. 39), stamina (human flaws nos. 2, 47), use of the proper clothing and gear (human flaws nos. 6, 7, 43, 44), and attentiveness to the dog's needs (human flaws nos. 10–16). Some of the censure seems self-directed: "Is impatient, easily irritated, becomes annoyed with himself, loses his composure and inevitably begins to shoot poorly" (human flaw no. 3), or "Eats and drinks too much during a hunt" (human flaw no. 45). Some are uncomfortably reminiscent of the episodes with gun-shy Bouboule (canine flaw no. 35) or the hesitant dog at Bad Soden in 1860 (canine flaws nos. 2, 6).

The most significant of all Turgenev's reproofs, however, is also one of the longest—human flaw no. 9: "Is unobservant, fails to pay attention to the habits of his quarry, to the local conditions and to the time—or he wants to prove himself more stiff-necked than everything around him: the quarry, the dog, the weather, and nature herself." This comment encapsulates the very essence of shooting as expressed in Aksakov's *Orenburg-Province Hunter* and Turgenev's review of it: keen observation of one's prey and one's dog, and careful study of the natural world itself. The ecotropic virtues implied by flaw no. 9, in fact, sum up *all* the virtues suggested by the other human flaws in Turgenev's inventory. Human flaw no. 9, the cardinal flaw, is an inherent feature of hounding and coursing that helped drive Russian hunters away from these traditional forms in the mid-1800s and led to the rapid rise of shooting. "Fifty Flaws" thus serves as an indictment of the epic hunting styles that Turgenev rejected and as a codified glorification of the norms of shooting. The sporting ideals enshrined in "Fifty Flaws" can easily be applied to the hallmarks of Turgenev's literary style as well: watchfulness, attentiveness to detail, mindfulness of the era, flexibility, and willingness to subjugate characters and plots to the unpredictable course of indifferent nature. The value Turgenev placed on not "proving himself more stiff-necked than everything around him" is reflected, moreover, in his notorious willingness to suspend moral judgment, to reject dogmas and streamlined systems.

Turgenev returned to sporting subjects in the series of "poems in prose," which he classified as *Senilia* and composed from 1878 to 1882, especially "The Sparrow" ("Vorobei," 1878) and "Partridges" ("Kuropatki"). The plots of "The Sparrow" and another late story not included in *Senilia*, "The

Quail" ("Perepelka," 1882), revolve around the instinct of parent birds to decoy predators away from their young, a form of behavior frequently noted by Aksakov, especially among shorebirds and waders.[27] In "The Sparrow" (April 1878), the narrator returns from a hunting sally with his dog Trésor and witnesses an adult sparrow boldly defend a fallen fledgling. The prose poem "Partridges" was completed in June 1882, when Turgenev was already tortured by the spinal cancer that would take his life fourteen months later. Late at night, lying awake in agony, the narrator asks why he must suffer and refuses to accept that he deserves his torment. He then envisions a large family of young partridges, happily hidden in the underbrush. Suddenly, a dog flushes them, they fly up in unison, a shot is heard, and one of them falls, its wing broken. The victim hides in a thicket of wormwood.[28] As the dog searches, the wounded bird asks, "Why, out of those twenty, must I die? How do I deserve this more than my sisters? It's not fair!" The narrator concludes the sketch by applying the example of the dying partridge to his own life and issuing himself a desolate imperative: "Just lie there, ailing creature, until death finds you."[29] The last hunting story he completed before his death was "The Quail," in which the narrator, as a child, grieves over a mother quail who is killed by his father's gun dog when she flies out to distract the hunters from her concealed young. Turgenev was intrigued all his life by this kind of courageous parental self-sacrifice, claiming that he first witnessed it at ten years of age and writing to Pauline Viardot in 1849 of a similar feat performed by a partridge in France that summer.[30]

Notes of a Hunter and the Structure of Field Notes

Notes of a Hunter appeared at the zenith of Russian hunting literature's brief rise near midcentury, but Turgenev does something far more ambitious than his contemporaries by adding formidable stylistic sophistication and infusing his hunting tales with abundant demonstrations of the human craving to subjugate: we are confronted time and again by characters' desire to subject another's will (volia) to the arbitrary dictates of their own will—to engage in proizvol. Or, as Thomas Hoisington put it in his study of the cycle, "The world as a whole can be divided into two general groups: the persecutors and those persecuted."[31] In biological terms, the stories offer field notes on the behavior of predators and prey—the painful interactions of human beings who occupy different trophic levels. Nature scenes serve as stark contrasts to the sickeningly common victimization of one person by another, reminding readers constantly, yet unobtrusively, of how egregious such behavior is in the organic world of which humans are an integral, if discordant, part. This technique is at times couched in ecotropic terms, respecting the autonomy of animals and the way natural phenomena are indifferent to their human observers. At other times, Turgenev engages in anthropotropic appropriation of flora and fauna to serve as human figures or emblems. Structurally, *Notes of a Hunter* in some ways resembles a hunter's field guide offering observations in which Turgenev first tested the limits of venatic equipoise and explored the paradoxes of what Dale Peterson has called "the cultural ecology of rural Russia."[32]

As we survey the original context of *Notes of a Hunter*, the abolitionist impulse and its ties to Turgenev's love of hunting are difficult to ignore. In 1852, Vaksel', who also happened to be a talented illustrator, drew a caricature of senator Mikhail Musin-Pushkin, director of the St. Petersburg Education District, overseeing the burning of Turgenev's *Notes of a Hunter* (figure 3.1). Musin-Pushkin, thought to be "the chief instigator of Turgenev's imprisonment," has confiscated Turgenev's gun and manuscripts, and gestures toward a hilltop prison fortress as Turgenev, in full hunting garb, but with ankles fettered, looks impassively on.[33] Behind Turgenev's back, a policeman quietly withdraws something—is it manuscript pages or a dead bird?—from the writer's game bag. Vaksel' sketches Turgenev as a hunter who has been rudely interrupted in the field, as if by game wardens enforcing regulations.

FIGURE 3.1.   L. N. Vaksel', *Director of the St. Petersburg Education District M. N. Musin-Pushkin Burns the Manuscript of I. S. Turgenev's "Notes of a Hunter"* (1852). By permission of V. I. Dal' State Museum of the History of Russian Literature, Moscow.

Herzen, too, who in 1850 called *Notes of a Hunter* a "masterpiece,"[34] perceived the cycle as Turgenev's hunting down of serfdom: "Aristocratic Russia retreated to a supporting role, and its voice began to grow weak; maybe, like Nicholas, it was embarrassed by the events of 1848. In order to remain popular in literature, it had to abandon urban life, take up a hunting rifle and slaughter, on the ground and on the wing, the wildfowl of serfdom."[35] For Herzen, this metaphorical hunt succeeded in illuminating the recesses of a monstrous institution:

> Never had the inner life of the landowner's house been exposed to such universal mockery, never had it elicited such revulsion and hatred. Moreover it must be noted that Turgenev never lays it on thick, never uses drastic expressions; on the contrary, he tells his stories in a perfectly unruffled manner, using only an elegant style, which greatly strengthens the impression made by this poetically written act of accusation against serfdom. [His artistic mastery,] having withstood double censorship, forces us to shudder with rage at the sight of the heavy, inhuman suffering that has exhausted one generation after another, without hope, not only with an outraged soul, but with a mutilated body.[36]

Turgenev could well have been emboldened in his *Notes of a Hunter* tales by Herzen's own novel, *Who Is to Blame?*—serialized 1845–46, then published as a book in 1847—which Aileen Kelly calls "the most outspoken critique of serfdom to appear in print in the 1840s."[37]

Looking back in 1867, twenty years after he began the cycle, Turgenev himself likewise envisioned *Notes* as the literary embodiment of a struggle against serfdom:

> That mode of life, that kind of environment and, particularly, the social stratum, if one may put it that way, to which I belonged—the landowning and serf-owning stratum of society—did not represent anything that could hold me back. On the contrary, almost everything I saw around me aroused in me a feeling of embarrassment and indignation and, finally, disgust . . . I could not breathe the same air as those who stood for the things I hated so much; I could not remain at their side . . . I had to put a certain distance between myself and my enemy so as to be able to attack him more effectively from the distance that separated us. In my eyes this enemy had a clearly defined form and bore a well-known name: this enemy was—serfdom. Under this name I gathered and concentrated everything against which I had made up my mind to

fight to the very end, which I had sworn never to be reconciled to. . . .
That was my Hannibal oath.[38]

These comments point to the same kind of moral revulsion that Herzen
believes Notes of a Hunter to elicit from its readers. In Turgenev's own telling,
the celebrated cycle resembles not a hunting foray, but a military struggle
between asymmetrical forces: one writer against the embodiment of a vast,
corrupt social system. A journal entry for 2 May 1872 by Edmond de Goncourt records Turgenev's claim that Notes of a Hunter influenced Alexander
II in his decision to abolish serfdom: "If I [Turgenev] set any store by such
things, all I would want to be carved on my tombstone would be a tribute to
what my book had done for the emancipation of the serfs. Tsar Alexander
once sent word to me that my book had been one of the main factors governing his decision."[39] While these assertions display a considerable degree
of retrospective self-valorization, Schapiro is nonetheless right to note that
"of the effectiveness of the stories as a weapon against serfdom there can be
no doubt."[40]

In undertaking this putative battle, Turgenev could have chosen a more
conventional narrator for his cycle of stories, perhaps by adopting something
like the wry pose of Herzen's omniscient observer in the freshly minted Who
Is to Blame? Such a move would have transformed Notes into something more
like a satiric tract, which Herzen's novel at times becomes. Turgenev could
also have concealed himself to a greater extent, by downplaying references to
hunting and retreating behind the multiple narrative frames he had adopted
for three of the stories that preceded Notes of a Hunter: "Andrei Kolosov"
(1844), "Three Portraits" ("Tri portreta," 1845), and "The Jew" ("Zhid,"
1846). It is true that outdoor sport receives mention in two of those early
works: Nikolai Alekseevich, the chief narrator of "Andrei Kolosov," alludes
to his hunting hobby, and the material of "Three Portraits" is conveyed by
the landowner Luchinov as he entertains five "genuine hunters" who have
gathered at his manor house after an autumn day spent coursing foxes and
hares.[41] In "The Duelist" ("Breter," 1846), probably the last story Turgenev
wrote before composing "Khor' and Kalinych," Küster's second speaks of
shooting his opponent, Luchkov, "like a partridge" in their final duel,[42] but
no other clear hunting references are to be found in that text, and in none of
these earlier tales does hunting perform anything like the central function it
has in Notes of a Hunter.

By building his narrator in part out of autobiographical material, however, Turgenev gives the action in Notes of a Hunter intimate proximity with
his lived experience, which lends the cycle a lyrical immediacy and regionalist

(*kraevedcheskii*) authority reinforced by the realia of hunting. Our narrator, who is finally identified as one "Petr Petrovich," hails from the village and estate of Kostomarovo, a short six miles northwest of Turgenev's own Spass-koe-Lutovinovo, just over the border of Tula Province.[43] Making the cycle's mediator a local wildfowler was shrewd in a number of other ways. It enabled Turgenev to write naturally from the vast personal experience he had, by his late twenties, already amassed in the field, and it anchored the action in the countryside, organically embedded in the Russian provincial landscape. The wayfaring hunter could, in quasi-picaresque fashion, stumble upon scores of Russian men, women, and children from all social strata as they went about their lives, and deaths, in a wide variety of social arrangements. As the narrator himself declares in the first sentence of "Lebedian'," "One of the chief advantages of hunting, my dear readers, is that it forces you to move about ceaselessly from place to place, which is very pleasant for an idle man"; or, in "The Singers," "where don't we hunters turn up!"[44] Moreover, the quiet watchfulness required specifically by shooting intensifies our sense that very little escapes this itinerant narrator's attention.

Perhaps more importantly, shooting—unlike coursing and hounding—was in the process of acquiring politically liberal overtones in Turgenev's day. As Henrietta Mondry has asserted, "borzois and hounds were hated by the peasants through their implication with their powerful masters. Borzois in particular were implicated in Russian literary narratives related to the high value placed on landlords' hounds compared to that of serfs and serf-children" in the early nineteenth century.[45] The retrograde character of hounding and coursing is subtly broached a number of times in the cycle. The narrator's shooting was thus both an innocent hobby and a subversion of traditional social modes, including modes of oppression.

And yet, this hunter-narrator is not a transparently autobiographical figure. Turgenev cannily omits the aspects of his own hunting habits, which we observed in chapter 2, that would have undercut his narrator's moral authority as an observer of social injustice. Gone are the lavish bivouac feasts, ill temper, and sickliness. In place of Turgenev's customary team of multiple servants, he includes a single peasant guide, Ermolai, a change that boosts the narrator's status as a reliable observer of the serfs' lot. Though huntsmen (*egeria*) were essential in coursing and hounding, the contact they had with their masters during those pursuits was quite limited. In shooting, on the other hand, the nobleman hunter was accompanied on foot for days on end by a peasant who was, generally, better at what they were doing than was the nobleman himself. Our narrator is careful to point out Ermolai's peerless mastery of outdoor sport at the start of "Ermolai and the Miller's Wife," yet is unsparing in his inclusion of Ermolai's many personal flaws. Petr Petrovich thus emerges as an observer who, on the one hand, acknowledges the superiority of a peasant in an undertaking to which he, a nobleman, is passionately devoted, but who, on the other hand, does not idealize him. Similarly, the narrator, as Newlin has argued, is something of a bumbler, at times "oddly vacuous," and not nearly as focused and skillful a hunter as Turgenev seems to have been in real life.[46] Our Kostomarovo landowner, in other words, is unsparing in his observations of social arrangements, recognizing authority and quality when they are earned, not when they are bestowed by birth. The biographical evidence suggests that Turgenev viewed Afanasii Alifanov in much the same way: as a man whose vices and social station did not prevent him from becoming a hunting master on par with Aksakov or Elzéar Blaze.

Given the nature of its narrator and the timing of its emergence, contemporaneous readers might naturally have perceived Notes of a Hunter in an Aksakovian light, that is, as something like entries in a sportsman-naturalist's field guide or handbook. Aksakov's Notes on Fishing had first appeared in February 1847, about a month after Turgenev published "Khor' and Kalinych," the opening story of the cycle; and Aksakov's hunting Notes were published in March 1852, some five months before Turgenev's collection was available to the public as a single volume. Both Aksakov's sporting treatises and Turgenev's cycle share the designation Notes (zapiski), and while Turgenev himself did not devise the title Notes of a Hunter, he did choose to retain it.[47] Certain passages in both works are strongly reminiscent of one another, as, for example, Turgenev's evocative second-person description of the sights, sounds, and scents of shooting woodcock on their springtime roding flights in "Ermolai and the Miller's Wife" and Aksakov's lyrical account, written about two years later, of precisely the same form of hunting, in the woodcock chapter of Notes of an Orenburg-Province Hunter.[48] Aksakov scholar Valentina Borisova has recently suggested that "in the dialogic context of Turgenev's and Aksakov's life and work, Notes of a Hunter and Notes of an Orenburg-Province Hunter constitute a distinctive diptych, thematically, ideologically, and stylistically homogeneous in many respects."[49]

The vividly described people and places in Turgenev's Notes prompted Mikhail Gershenzon, in the early twentieth century, to see the work as a zoological garden: "Notes of a Hunter is like a wonderful zoo: what fascinating beasts, each of a different kind, but all are special, amusing, original, personal. Khor', Kalinych, Sofron the steward, the Lone Wolf, Chertopkhanov, Radilov, and how many, many more! . . . It's good that Turgenev did not give them to us in plots, like beasts in cages, but portrayed them on the loose. And in their midst, as in large zoos, meadows grow, treetops rustle in their groves, streams flow."[50] If the zoo metaphor seems reductive, perhaps the zoo's literary embodiment, a bestiary, is more apt, or, to ground our discussion more firmly in Turgenev's milieu, the bestiary's mid-nineteenth-century Russian equivalent: the sporting treatise, a reference volume with key details on a variety of fauna (and some flora). To view Turgenev's collection of stories as something of a field guide to various human subspecies inhabiting rural Russia in his day is not as farfetched as it may seem, and, I suggest, heightens our appreciation of the work's rhetorical effectiveness in probing its "powerful emancipationist pathos"[51] and in setting forth some of the most striking lyrical responses to the natural environment in all of Russian literature. I am not suggesting that *Notes of a Hunter* is about hunting per se, but I do see it as constructed of the natural materials and techniques of hunting. In the discussion that follows, I hope to show that even as he employed the template of a hunter's field notes and borrowed the cultural resonance of hunting manuals, Turgenev constantly transcended and flouted that model in ways that added fresh layers of complexity to his conception of the organic world.

Thanks to the Soviet scholar Mikhail Kleman, we know that Turgenev took great pains over the titling and ordering of the cycle's constituent tales when it came time to group them together for publication in a single volume.[52] The titles of the twenty-two stories originally contained in Turgenev's *Notes of a Hunter* can be divided into people and settings: thirteen of the former and eight of the latter.[53] Only one of Turgenev's titles—"Kas'ian from Krasivaia Mech'"—unites both personal name and setting, as befits the deep connection between Kas'ian and the natural environment he defends. The Aksakov-Turgenev connection is strengthened when we recall that Aksakov's two fishing and hunting volumes, if we exclude their dozen or so introductory chapters on outfitting, comprise chapters whose titles likewise name the relevant species of bird or fish ("Redshank," "Woodcock," "Trout," "Carp," etc.), and that in the hunting notes these chapters are accompanied by detailed discussions of habitats, which are also furnished with their own titles: "Marsh," "Waterways," "Steppe," and "Forest."

"The Russian people are masters at devising nicknames," our narrator declares in "Singers," suggesting that careful scrutiny of Turgenev's own technique for naming characters is not misplaced.[54] A few of Turgenev's person titles are occupations or types, or both ("The Steward," "The Lone Wolf," "Farmer Ovsianikov," "Two Landowners"), but most are proper names. The cycle's inaugural tale, "Khor' and Kalinych," significantly, begins with an animal nickname: Polecat (*khor'*). Kalinych, whose forename we never learn, means "son of Kalina," a colloquial variant of Kallinik, from Greek *kallos* (beautiful) and *nike* (victory).[55] In botanical contexts, however, *kalina* denotes plants of the genus *Viburnum*, usually *Viburnum opulus*, whose delicious berries are the subject of Ivan Larionov's famous song in the folk style, "Kalinka" (1860). Thus Khor' and Kalinych, the two titular characters, have names directly and indirectly connected with fauna and flora, symbolically embracing the entirety of the living environment. In fact, of the ninety or so surnames and nicknames for human characters mentioned in *Notes of a Hunter*, over 20 percent are derived from animals, plants, or natural features.[56]

Two decades after Turgenev's *Notes* appeared, Ivan Goncharov emphasized the linkage of character, setting, and social justice in the work: "Turgenev, having created in *Notes of a Hunter* a series of living miniatures of life under serfdom, would of course not have given to literature these exquisite, gentle tales, full of classical simplicity and real, genuine truth about minor gentry and peasants, and these inimitable landscapes of Russian nature, if he had not from childhood been suffused by love of the native soil of his fields and woods and had not preserved in his soul an image of the sufferings of the folk who populated them!"[57] To Goncharov, Turgenev's love of the natural environment dovetails with his sympathy for the enserfed peasants, as though one were impossible without the other. Goncharov's assessment encapsulates the two chief structural elements of the cycle: depiction of Russian social types, and depiction of Russian landscape.

The order of tales in *Notes of a Hunter* tells us something about how Turgenev might have conceptualized his project's balance between people and place. The first five stories to be written bore person titles, with "L'gov" (the name of a village) being the first to interrupt that sequence in the spring of 1847. Thereafter, as he wrote story after story, Turgenev alternated quite regularly between setting titles and person titles, until February 1851, when he completed the entire cycle in "Kas'ian from Krasivaia Mech'," with its hybrid title. To be sure, even the setting-titled stories are largely devoted to the people the narrator encounters in those places: the two old serfs in "Raspberry Water," the horse dealers in "Lebedian'," the young drovers in "Bezhin Meadow," and so on. Yet Kleman's work suggests that Turgenev wished to give persons and settings more equal weight, and therefore chose to insert a setting-titled tale ("Raspberry Water") after "Ermolai and the Miller's Wife" to break up the initial string of person titles. In the final program for the book edition, "Kas'ian," the last tale to be written, is now placed about one-third of the way through the cycle, while "Forest and Steppe," as was the case in all of Turgenev's program drafts, is held in reserve as the final story. One wonders if Aksakov was inspired in part by Turgenev's valedictory tale to use "Forest" and "Steppe" as chapter titles in *Notes of an Orenburg-Province Hunter*.

The focus of *Notes of a Hunter* on character calls to mind Henry James's famous comment about Turgenev's "dossier" technique:

> The germ of a story, with him, was never an affair of plot—that was the last thing he thought of: it was the representation of certain persons. The first form in which a tale appeared to him was as the figure of an individual, or a combination of individuals, whom he wished to see in action. . . . To this end he wrote a sort of biography of each of his characters. . . . He had their *dossier*, as the French say. . . . If one reads Turgenev's stories with the knowledge that they were composed—or rather that they came into being—in this way, one can trace the process in every line.[58]

Turgenev's lifelong tendency to include the name, background, and habits of characters, at or near their first appearance in the text, closely resembles Aksakov's method of providing those same details for the fish and birds he meticulously describes in his sporting treatises. The opening of "Khor' and Kalinych," with its discussion of the habitats and field marks of the peasants of Orel and Kaluga Provinces, serves as a prime example, especially when we recall that the analogous paragraphs that open the very next tale ("Ermolai and the Miller's Wife") are devoted to actual birds (woodcock) and their mating habits.

The sensation that *Notes of a Hunter* is structured like a field guide is heightened by the particularity of Turgenev's identification of nonhuman species in the cycle, a feature Gershenzon and Hoisington have noted.[59] For example, in the space of two sentences in the second paragraph of "Ermolai and the Miller's Wife," the narrator mentions chaffinches, robins, buntings, redstarts, woodpeckers, chiffchaffs, orioles, and nightingales. One effect of such meticulousness is to convince readers that they are in the hands of an expert, a storyteller who resembles a writer of reference works. And if one senses that Turgenev is an authority on the animal world, one might also be more inclined to perceive him as an authority on human beings. The twenty-six footnotes he provides for the cycle reinforce that impression: they have the commanding air of labels in a zoo or technical explanations in a hunting treatise. These notes on *Notes* bristle with expertise on geographic terminology (nine notes), animal terminology (six), technological terminology (five), and miscellaneous local vernacular (six).

When we compare *Notes of a Hunter* to the only actual—if extraordinarily compact—hunting treatise Turgenev ever wrote, "Fifty Flaws," we find a remarkable number of specific connections: the way tired dogs "shine your spurs" in "Raspberry Water" (canine flaw no. 29); the careless hunter who shoots off Vladimir's chin and forefinger in "L'gov" (flaw no. 31); Penochkin's inability to rise early in "The Steward" (flaw no. 1); Chertopkhanov's permitting his borzoi pups to feed on a horse carcass (canine flaw no. 16) and his poor attempts to train his poodle in "Chertopkhanov and Nedopiuskin" (flaws nos. 11 and 14). It is not unreasonable to conjecture that Turgenev, while drafting "Fifty Flaws" in 1876, had mined *Notes of a Hunter* for material. He had, after all, recently returned to the original story ideas for *Notes* in the 1870s in order to develop and add three new tales to the cycle: "The End of Chertopkhanov" ("Konets Chertopkhanova," 1871–72), "The Living Relic" ("Zhivye moshchi," 1873–74), and "It's Clattering!" ("Stuchit!," 1874).

Like the reminiscences that pepper Aksakov's hunting and fishing treatises, *Notes of a Hunter* contains numerous descriptions of forays in the field. With the notable exception of "Forest and Steppe," these are frequently brief mentions of the narrator's own journeys to and from shooting grounds, usually at the start of a tale as a way to frame the narrative: grousing in "Bezhin Meadow" and "Chertopkhanov and Nedopiuskin," snipe-shooting in "Lebedian'," duck-hunting in "L'gov," woodcock-shooting in "Ermolai and the Miller's Wife" and "My Neighbor Radilov," and so on. These unfolding, first-hand accounts are supplemented by passages in which the characters themselves describe or enact hunts in ways that sharply differentiate shooting (our narrator's passion) from coursing and hounding.

In "Raspberry Water," the elderly peasant fisherman, nicknamed Fog (Tuman), admires the narrator's gun dog and asks him if he also "rides to hounds," a clear reference to coursing. Surprisingly, though perhaps merely to make conversation, the wildfowler replies that he has "a couple pair" (*svory dve*) of hounds, implicating himself in an elaborate and elitist form of field sport. This makes the old man smile and recall the extravagant hunts undertaken by his deceased master, Count Petr Il'ich ***: silk leashes, red caftans with gold braid, a head houndsman (*lovchii*), numerous assistant houndsmen (*psari*), noble guests. Fog fondly remembers the way Petr Il'ich was helped into the saddle by his serfs, and "respect was observed" in his opulent bygone hunts. The dead Count had been a kind man, because, Fog says, after "he'd beat you, you see, he'd soon forget all about it." This nostalgic reminiscence of rigid social hierarchy ends abruptly—and ironically—when Fog loses a fish, quietly reminding readers that he and his friend Stepushka angle not for sport, but to fill their empty bellies.[60]

The association of cruelty with hounding is intensified in "Farmer Ovsianikov," whose titular *odnodvorets* (a peasant akin to US sharecroppers), Luka Petrovich Ovsianikov, tells how, years before, his father had been given a severe beating by the narrator's own grandfather for having the temerity to protest the theft of his land. The henchman sent to drag Petr Ovsianikov to his unwarranted punishment is a man called Baush, the landowner's *lovchii* (head houndsman in coursing). Luka Petrovich later conveys the grandeur of a hunt organized by Aleksei Grigor'evich Orlov-Chesmenskii (1737–1837/8), a general and grandee during Catherine II's reign: "And then, when I was in Moscow, he started up a hunt [*sadka*] the likes of which no one had ever seen in Russia: he invited all the hunters in the realm to attend, and he set the date three months in advance. So they came. Dogs and huntsmen [*egeria*] were brought—it was like a whole army, and what an army! First they feasted, as is proper, and then they set out for the city gate. Countless people came running to watch. And what do you think? Your grandfather's dog outran them all."[61] The particular form of competitive hunt described here, a *sadka*, was devoted to the pursuit of previously captured, "planted" (*sazhenyi*) hares, foxes, and wolves which were then released with no real chance of escape. After Luka Petrovich recounts Baush's great skill with hounds, the narrator asks Luka whether he too loves to hunt, which elicits a telling reply: "I *would* love it, that's for sure, but not now. My time's passed. Though in my younger years . . . you know, it's awkward, because of my rank. The likes of us shouldn't strive to become noblemen."[62] Turgenev thus employs hounding as a marker of the constraints that kept peasants as trapped in their social stratum as the prey animals planted in Count Orlov's hunting spectacles. Farmer Ovsianikov is nonetheless an unashamed critic of oppression: "[Young gentry] handle the peasant like a doll: they'll twist him a bit, twist him a bit more, break him, and throw him away."[63] His forthright denunciation of serfdom clearly embarrasses the narrator, who, we are told, either looks away or doesn't know what to say.[64] By frankly depicting the cruel behavior of the narrator's own family, and showing the narrator's own shame, the tale serves as Turgenev's self-implication in a wicked institution, but also offers a modicum of hope: the narrator's grandfather was a hounder, but at least his grandson is now a fowler, and one who feels remorse at social wrongs.

A few other characters, such as Petr Petrovich Karataev, hunt primarily with scent hounds and borzois, but the most clearly satirized of these are the landowners Chertopkhanov and Nedopiuskin, painfully degraded versions of the splendid coursers from a bygone era—of hunters like Orlov-Chesmenskii and Petr Il'ich ***. Chertopkhanov is a ridiculous horn-blowing hare-hounder who ostentatiously forgives the narrator, after the latter accidentally trespasses while shooting grouse: "I'm a nobleman myself and glad to be of service to a fellow nobleman."[65] This pose of elitist camaraderie introduces a scene that displays all the flaws of coursing, especially when it is practiced incompetently, as it is by Chertopkhanov and Nedopiuskin: the riders are badly out of breath, give no clear commands to their ill-bred hounds, and whip their horses mercilessly. Ermolai, a bystander, is forced to kill the hare himself, with a single expert shot, after it outmaneuvers its bumbling pursuers. What follows is the most gruesome depiction of hunting carnage in the cycle: "Chertopkhanov flew down from his horse like a tumbler-pigeon, grabbed his dagger, ran up to the dogs with his legs spread wide, tore the mutilated hare away from them with furious oaths, and, distorting his whole face, plunged his dagger up to the hilt into the hare's throat, and started cackling with laughter . . . He cut off the hare's paws, tied the carcass to his game-straps, and scattered the paws to the dogs."[66]

The narrator points out that Chertopkhanov and Nedopiuskin are coursing out of season, thereby trampling a valuable oat crop, and their sorry peasant *eger'* Fomka is nowhere to be found, his horse having fallen under him in another part of the wood; a few days later, we learn, its body is devoured by bloodstained borzoi pups.

At Chertopkhanov's dilapidated house, its windows resembling the eyes of "aged sluts," the master orders two hounds to be brought to impress the narrator, who inwardly disapproves: "I, out of politeness, made a show of admiring these stupid animals (borzois are all extraordinarily stupid)."[67] The narrator, a practitioner of shooting, pointedly distances himself here from gazehounds, the very foundation of coursing. His ignorant, snobbish hosts lack all hunting expertise and are shown to laugh uncontrollably at the violent disruption they bring about in the organic world. Unlike Ermolai, a shooting *eger'*, Fomka, their putative *lovchii*, is a poor horseman and absentee guide. In the smug and disheveled universe of Chertopkhanov and Nedopiuskin, there is no venatic equipoise—only stupidity, chaos, clumsiness, cruelty. Their loathsome treatment of the natural world is clearly inferior to the narrator's far quieter, more intelligent, egalitarian interaction with his surroundings.

A Landscape of *Proizvol*

Nearly all the scenes of peasant suffering in *Notes of a Hunter* have at their foundation the exercise of *proizvol* by the gentry. The wrongs inflicted on the serfs—the ways in which they are treated like dolls, to use Ovsianikov's expression—are wide-ranging in severity and scope. The most pervasive injustice is the sudden and senseless uprooting of peasant workers: Kas'ian has been arbitrarily moved from his native Krasivaia Mech'; Knot (Suchok) is peremptorily converted from a coachman into his master's fisherman ("L'gov"); Arina is wrenched from her village, transferred to St. Petersburg, then banished back to the country as punishment for becoming pregnant, after which her lover is sent off to the army ("Ermolai and the Miller's Wife"); Losniakova sends away Tat'iana ("The Office"); Matrena's spiteful mistress refuses to sell her to her nobleman lover, then bribes the police to fetch her home when she runs away with him ("Petr Petrovich Karataev"). The text is likewise rife with physical violence perpetrated against the peasants by their masters, with the stories ordered in such a way that the mistreatment generally becomes more savage as the reader moves through the cycle, increasing in intensity from the casually mentioned beating in "Raspberry Water" to the Lone Wolf's manhandling of a wood poacher and Stegunov's beating of Vasia the butler for no clear reason ("Two Landowners").

Perhaps most distressing is the rampant *samodurstvo*, or petty tyranny, in "The Steward," which somehow entitles the mincing landowner Penochkin to treat his serfs—in his words—"like children": the house serf punished for not warming wine, the cook whose stomach is crushed in a carriage accident, the forester whose beard is pulled out at the roots, and the peasant Antip who is "eaten" by the steward Sofron Iakovlevich for complaining of harsh treatment, including having his wife beaten and two sons sent off to conscription.[68] Particularly nauseating to the narrator is Penochkin's pretense of being a delicate and civilized man. The immorality of his gallified charade is only reinforced by Penochkin's distaste for hunting: "It's always off into the field. Oh, these hunters try my patience!"[69] Lounging on a Persian divan in his baggy silk trousers, black velvet jacket, blue-tasseled fez, and backless yellow Chinese slippers, he perhaps vaguely resembles his namesake, the *penochka*—a small, dainty, very common leaf warbler known in English as the chiffchaff (*Phylloscopus collybita*). Yet the innocuous songbird exterior cannot conceal the malignant soul of a sadistic coward whose orders are gleefully carried out by Sofron Iakovlevich—the instrument of his master's *proizvol*. "The Steward" is the only story in the entire cycle supplied with a formal dateline: "Salzbrunn, in Silesia, July 1847." Turgenev added this in the 1880 edition of *Notes*, as if to separate himself temporally and spatially from the matter-of-fact depravity exposed in the story.[70]

As we have seen, during precisely the period of Turgenev's most intensive work on *Notes of a Hunter*, Herzen wrote, "The wolf devours the lamb because it is hungry and because the lamb is weaker; but the wolf does not demand slavery from the lamb, nor does the lamb submit to him."[71] Turgenev's cycle portrays a human world in which *proizvol* is perpetually rampaging—a form of moral violence absent in the organic world that surrounds his stories. Nature's indifference means that predation in the wild will take place unchecked, but it proceeds not from cruelty. It is, instead, a product of the most benign kind of selfishness: the universal will to survive and reproduce. In nature, this self-serving imperative results in beauty and health; in human society, self-interest has mutated into *proizvol*, which spawns only ugliness and misery. Peter Thiergen draws a crucial conclusion about the positive effect of nature's indifference as perceived by Turgenev:

> Since its indifference is equally valid for the entirety of what exists, it is a builder of justice and reconciliation. . . . Nature appears as a *coincidentia oppositorum* [coincidence of opposites], which certainly imposes difference by indifference, but which also guarantees an equidistance by distance, as well as eternity and beauty. Nature, detached from history, is, in its indifference, at the same time a guarantor of endurance and of a higher justice, beyond any act which would be the fruit of some divine choice.[72]

To nature, *vsë ravno*—a common Russian idiom that can be translated as both "it's all the same" and "everything is equal." Turgenev was deeply saddened by this first sense, but took solace in the second. His nonhuman natural world is a place where neither favoritism nor cruelty exists, and all its denizens, in seeking their own advantage, at least find themselves on equal footing. Such a conclusion confirms Liudmila Skokova's assertion that Turgenev shared the conviction of Rousseau that "nature" created all human beings equal.[73]

In *Notes of a Hunter*, Turgenev explicitly calls nature "indifferent" only once, as a way of naming the source of Nedopiuskin's diffidence and delicacy: "Indifferent—and perhaps mocking—nature endows people with various capacities and inclinations, without at all taking into account their place in society and means."[74] Aside from this single instance, instead of *telling* us in *Notes of a Hunter* that nature is indifferent, as he often did in other writings (see appendix 1), Turgenev *shows* us, frequently through instances of death's inexorability and randomness. In a forerunner to the series of entomological images of natural indifference we examined in chapter 1, Radilov recalls with horror how a fly nonchalantly crawled over the exposed eyeball of his dead wife.[75] Similarly, in the long description, in "Hamlet of the Shchigry District," of Vasilii Vasil'ich's wife's springtime funeral after her death in childbirth, a swallow twitters inside the church after flying in through open windows, heedless of the solemn ritual of human death being enacted below.[76] *Vsë ravno*: everything, and everyone, is equally a prey to mortality.

In the story called "Death," Turgenev conveys nature's indifference by stressing the inevitability of succession: the specimen may die, but the species will not, thereby ensuring that the whole will outlast the part. Six decedents are presented: three peasants, one *raznochinets*, one landowner, and one forest. All the characters except for Avenir Sorokoumov and the peasant burn victim are keen to make arrangements for those who will survive them. The narrator's nostalgic vision of the Chaplygino Forest boasts one of his most extensive zootropic and phytotropic catalogues: almost thirty specific examples of flora and fauna appear in a mere three sentences. To describe the old, frost-killed oak and ash trees' replacement by a "young grove" of intermediate species, the narrator quotes Pushkin's elegy to bygone stars of the Russian stage in chapter 1 of *Eugene Onegin*, then quotes Kol'tsov's "The Forest" ("Les," 1837), which is itself a meditation on Pushkin's death.[77] Pushkin's "Whether I wander along noisy streets" echoes repeatedly: in Turgenev's footnote on the cruel winter of 1840, which rues the onslaught of birches and aspens that replace the hardwood forest; in the five-year-old girl who cowers in the burn victim's hut; and in Sorokoumov's reassurance to the narrator that "it's all the same [*vsë ravno*] where one dies":

Гляжу ль на дуб уединенный,
Я мыслю: патриарх лесов
Переживёт мой век забвенный,
Как пережил он век отцов.

Младенца ль милого ласкаю,
Уже я думаю; прости!
Тебе я место уступаю:
Мне время тлеть, тебе цвести.

[. . .]

И хоть бесчувственному телу
Равно повсюду истлевать,
Но ближе к милому пределу
Мне всё б хотелось почивать.

If I gaze upon a solitary oak,
I ponder: the forests' patriarch
Will survive my forgotten age,
As he survived the age of my forefathers.

If I caress a sweet infant,
I already think: farewell!
To you I relinquish my place;
It's time for me to rot, for you to blossom.

[. . .]

Though to the insensate body
All places are alike for decay,
Nonetheless nearer to my dear region
Would I prefer to slumber.[78]

When the narrator reminisces with Sorokoumov about Hegel, now long out of fashion, he uses Pushkin's famous phrase about "days long since gone by" from *Ruslan and Liudmila*.[79] The literary excellence of Pushkin's and Kol'tsov's meditations on death is a world away from the sycophantic French verses devoted in "Death" to the Krasnogor'e hospital and its lovely natural setting, but especially antithetical to the fatuous comment of Jean Kobyliatnikoff—"Et moi aussi j'aime la nature!"—which offers exactly the kind of shallow nature-worship detested by Aksakov and Turgenev. In "Death," the inevitability of disappearing and being replaced—in literature, in philosophy, in work, in family, in the forest—makes one wonder if Turgenev had read Adolphe Dureau de la Malle's pioneering 1825 work on forest succession: "Memoir on alternation or on the problem of alternative succession in the reproduction of plant species living in a community, and whether it is a general law of nature."[80] If there is any "general law" followed by those who perish in the story, it is that "Russians die in astonishing fashion," as the narrator explicitly reminds us three separate times.[81] When the peasant Maksim expires after being struck by a falling ash tree, the narrator generalizes: "[The Russian peasant's] state before the end can be called neither indifference nor dullness; he dies as if observing a ritual, coldly and simply."[82] In other words, these unassuming deaths mirror nature's own detachment, offering a paragon of equipoise for the hunter-narrator to imitate. Such characters are synchronized with nature in a way that mindless Monsieur Kobyliatnikoff—unlike our narrator—could never understand.

These and numerous similar examples culminate in "The Tryst," which functions in part as an allegory of nature's indifference toward her admirers. A pretty, pregnant serf girl, Akulina, is deeply devoted to her lover, a vain house serf, Viktor Aleksandrych, who is in the midst of abandoning her. On a rainy September day, the narrator, concealed by chance under a birch tree twenty paces away, witnesses Akulina's earnest appeals for Viktor's affection, and his unshakable rejections. Her sorrowful gaze is full of "tender devotion, reverent humility, and love," while Viktor responds with "affectedly contemptuous indifference."[83] The scene unfolds like a gender-switched rendition, transposed into the serfs' lowly social stratum, of Turgenev's "Nature" prose poem of three decades later. Akulina, like Turgenev himself, is portrayed as an expert on the outdoors, at least in the sphere of floral and herbal lore, as she fondly explains to Viktor the uses of the four species of flowers she has gathered: tansy (*Tanacetum vulgare*), beggartick (*Bidens tripartita*), forget-me-nots (*Mysotis scorpioides*), and wood violet (*Viola odorata*, called *matkina-dushka*, or "dam's darling," in Orel Province).[84] She presents him with a special posy of blue cornflowers (*Centaurea cyanus*), but the metaphorical offering laid at the altar of this uninterested god is greeted with a yawn: "Akulina was so beautiful at that moment: her entire soul was trustingly, passionately laid open before him, caressingly stretched out to him, and he—he dropped the cornflowers onto the grass."[85] The narrator, clearly feeling deep sympathy for her, emerges from his hiding place and attempts to console Akulina after Viktor leaves her sobbing, but she runs away. In the end, the hunter cannot refrain from mapping Viktor's chilly rejection of Akulina onto the natural environment and sensing the fickle indifference of a personified nature: "I grew sad. Through the cheerless yet fresh smile of fading nature, it seemed, the dismal fear of impending winter was creeping through." The tale concludes with a brief, unusually personal response: "I returned home, but the image of poor Akulina long remained in my mind, and her cornflowers, long since withered, I've kept with me to this day."[86] With his abrupt shift from contemplating Akulina's rejection to contemplating nature and the nearness of winter, the narrator has become Akulina, and the natural world is his Viktor. Nature and a callous house serf ostensibly have little in common, but the agony they induce when they express their indifference to those who love them is identical. The ache of unrequited love is one of the most persistent Turgenevian themes, and it could be argued that the many examples of it in his fiction descend from the author's perception of nature's apathy toward his own infatuation with her beauty and majesty.

In "The Tryst," as with all the stories in this cycle, Turgenev introduces a great deal of anthropotropic representation. His characters are prone to it: Akulina sees her cornflowers not merely as cornflowers but as symbols of love. Vasilii Vasil'ich in "Hamlet of the Shchigry District" compares his wife to a dying Eurasian siskin (*Spinus spinus*); the poacher calls the Lone Wolf a "bloodsucker" and a "beast."[87] Khvalynskii in "Two Landowners" sees the peasants as breeding animals. The narrator, especially, is inclined to anthropotropic characterizations: weather as a harbinger of sadness, abundant comparisons of people to birds, cleverly zoological and phytological character names, even the subtle ways in which the *Notes of a Hunter* collection itself resembles a hunter-naturalist's field notes, to name only a few examples.

We must, however, recall that "The Tryst," like the cycle's other tales, contains another, very different, mode of transmitting nature, in which the environment is described, not exploited prima facie. It is true that the opening paragraph's extended depiction of the autumnal birch forest begins with a cluster of personifications: the blue of the sky looks like "a beautiful eye," "everything in the grove's interior seemed to smile," and the sounds of the leaves in the trees are likened to human trembling, talking, murmuring, and gabbing (*trepet, govor, lepetan'e, boltovnia*).[88] But there follow over three hundred words of nearly pure phytotropic, caelotropic, and zootropic description, in which Turgenev's narrator simply but richly records the species, ages, colors, shapes, sounds, and textures that reach his senses while he traverses and observes the wood:

> The slender trunks of the not-too-densely-growing birches abruptly took on the delicate gleam of white silk, the small leaves lying on the ground suddenly grew multicolored and began to blaze with a deep-red gold, while the lovely stems of tall, curling ferns, already painted with their autumn tint, like the color of overripe grapes, shone through, endlessly entangling and crisscrossing before one's eyes; then suddenly everything would again turn slightly blue: bright colors momentarily dimmed, all the birches stood out white, without luster, as white as new-fallen snow that has yet to be touched by a chilly, playful ray of the winter sun; and furtively, craftily, the faintest drizzle has begun to sprinkle and whisper through the wood. The foliage on the birches was still almost entirely green, though it had perceptibly paled; only in a few places did one tree stand alone, very young, all red or all gold, and one had to notice how it brightly blazed in the sun when its beams abruptly forced their way, sliding and glistening, through the dense network of slender boughs freshly washed by the sparkling rain. Not a single bird was to be heard: they had all taken shelter and gone silent; only now and then would the tit's derisive voice ring out like a little steel bell. Before I stopped in this small birch wood, my dog and I had walked through a grove of tall aspen. I confess that I do not particularly like this tree—the aspen—with its pale-violet trunk and gray-green metallic foliage that it sends up as high as possible and scatters, like a trembling fan, into the air; I don't like the eternal quaking of its round, untidy leaves, awkwardly attached to long pedicels. It's handsome only on certain summer evenings when, rising up over the low bushes, it opposes the ruddy rays of the setting sun and shines and trembles, from root to crown bathed in the same yellowish crimson—or when,

on a clear, windy day, the whole tree noisily streams and murmurs against the dark-blue sky, and every one of its leaves is caught up in the endeavor, as though it wants to break away, fly off, and dash into the distance. But in general I dislike this tree, so, without stopping to rest in the aspen grove, I made for the birch wood, nestled myself beneath a small tree whose branches started close to the ground and could thereby shield me from the rain, and, having admired my surroundings, went to sleep—that serene and gentle sleep known only to hunters.[89]

There are similes in this remarkable passage, but they are generally linked to other natural objects, not human beings. The straightforward, detailed imagery does not preclude frank expression of the narrator's personal taste. The result—thanks also to the way this section contrasts with anthropotropic elements we have observed elsewhere in the tale—is distinctly Aksakovian.

To drive home the corrupting enormity of serfdom in *Notes of a Hunter*, Turgenev deploys his keen eye for nature description with a deftness unseen in his earlier work. Portraying the peasants' arbitrary victimization is perhaps the cycle's unifying anthropotropic macrocosm, and this macrocosm is served, paradoxically, by a series of ecotropic microcosms in which human cruelty is set against natural beauty. The result is to expose the criminality of *proizvol* by showing how the human arrogation of power over other people, and over nature, confounds the beautifully indifferent processes of the organic world. It is a refined strategy that produces harsh juxtapositions. In "The Tryst," a serene ecotropic opening functions as the prelude to Viktor's discordant exercise of *proizvol* over Akulina, just as the ecotropic passages that follow her destitution at story's end serve to bookend the emotional cruelty our narrator has witnessed. Such juxtapositions, in which nature's indifference becomes an instrument of justice, continually remind us that the wolf does not demand slavery from the lamb—that the human addiction to dominion is conspicuously wrong. Turgenev experimented with variations on this basic technique, with fascinating results, in many other *Notes of a Hunter* stories.

Near the conclusion of "Raspberry Water," for example, Fog tells the story of his bygone master's wickedness and womanizing among the lower classes. After a brief pause, the narrator asks, "So it seems your master was severe, then?" Fog, with a perplexingly embittered nostalgia, admits that such things are no longer done, now that Count Petr Il'ich is gone. In a moment, another peasant, Vlas, will appear, and make clear that Fog is either mistaken or dissembling—that masters are still cruel. In fact, Vlas's master is the well-fed absentee landlord Count Valerian Petrovich, son of Petr Il'ich. Valerian has heartlessly rebuffed Vlas's request to have the terms of his quit-rent adjusted owing to the death of Vlas's son, a Moscow cabby who had been sending money home to his parents. Vlas and his wife are now destitute. He sits down by the river, sings a plaintive song, and "Raspberry Water" ends. Between Fog's reminiscence and Vlas's woeful tale, however, Turgenev inserts the following passage:

> We sat in the shade, but in the shade it was stifling. It was as though the heavy, sultry air had come to a standstill. One's burning face wistfully sought the breeze, but there wasn't any breeze. And so the sun beat down from the blue, somewhat darkened sky; directly in front of us, on the opposite bank, an oat-field, in places overgrown with wormwood, shone yellow, and not a single stalk so much as stirred. A little down-stream, a peasant horse stood in the river up to its knees and lazily swished its wet tail; occasionally a fish would surface beneath an over-hanging bush, release some bubbles, and quietly dive to the bottom, leaving behind a faint ripple. Grasshoppers chirred in the reddened grass; quail called as though unwillingly; hawks smoothly soared above the fields and often hovered in place, quickly beating their wings and fanning their tails. We sat motionless, oppressed by the heat.[90]

This is one of the longest natural interludes in the early part of the cycle, and it exemplifies Turgenev's ecotropic mode: the observations are comprehensive, vivid, and devoid of obvious human figurations. The narrator's gaze moves from low to high, from the bottom of the food chain (grasshoppers, fish), to the top (hawks hovering in search of prey). Readers might be tempted to see those raptors as metaphors for the merciless landowners described before and after this passage, but such an assumption ignores the excessiveness of the oppression perpetrated by the older and younger counts, who, unlike hawks, exploit their victims far beyond what they need. Their desire to intimidate transforms predation into depredation.

In "Ermolai and the Miller's Wife," when Arina concludes her shocking account of the reprisals carried out against her by her owners, Turgenev immediately follows up with an ecotropic passage that serves as the conclusion to the entire story: "A flock of wild ducks sped over our heads with a whistle, and we heard them land on the river not far from us. It was already quite dark and starting to get cold; in the grove a nightingale was loudly jugging. We burrowed into the hay and fell asleep."[91] The plainly depicted sights, sounds, and sensations produced by the nonhuman world at day's end retrospectively point up the unnatural vindictiveness of Arina's masters, who, in a transparently anthropotropic touch, bear the speaking surname Zverkov ("Beastie"). These human beasts remind us of another constant in Turgenev's cycle: besides the contrast achieved through oppositions of human cruelty and natural beauty, we gradually but surely become aware that *proizvol* is as integral a part of the moral landscape—the tainted noo-sphere—as the animals and plants are of the natural landscape.

"Kas'ian from Krasivaia Mech'," the last of the original *Notes of a Hunter* stories to be written, is one of Turgenev's most sophisticated commentaries on a hunter's place in the natural order, and it features a character unlike any other in his oeuvre. The peasant Kas'ian is not where he belongs, hence the need to specify where he is "from" in the story's title: his original home is a village in what was then Tula Province (modern-day Lipetsk Oblast'), just upstream from where the picturesque Krasivaia Mech' River (modern Russian "Krasivaia Mecha"), or "Beautiful Mech'," flows into the Don, about ten miles south of Lebedian'. This means he is about 150 miles from his homeland when we meet him in the village of Iudiny vyselki (modern Iudiny dvory, "Judas's Farms"), a dozen miles southwest of Orel, more than twice as far away as the "hundred versts or so" reckoned by Kas'ian himself.[92] In addi-tion to being geographically displaced, he is physically separated from his fellow peasants by his short stature; the narrator describes him as a "dwarf" (*karlik*), whose nickname is Flea (*blokha*).[93] Finally, Kas'ian is spiritually set apart because he is viewed by the other peasants as a *iurodivets*, or holy fool, and his behavior suggests that he is a religious dissenter.[94] In spite of, or per-haps because of, these multiple forms of displacement, Kas'ian carries with him an unshakable sense of the intrinsic value and sacred significance of the natural world, which he sees as his abode. Just as Ovsianikov spoke insubor-dinate truths to the narrator about the oppression of human beings, Kas'ian, following the long tradition of Russian holy fools who challenge the moral-ity of their social superiors, boldly defends the flora and fauna surrounding him. He is an implacable foe of anthropocentric violence.

That violence permeates the story, underscored, in the early pages, by frequent oppositions of *derevo* (tree) to *drevesina* (deadwood). Near the out-set, our narrator and his driver, Erofei, encounter a funeral, twice called "a bad omen": the wooden coffin (mentioned five times) encloses the body of a local carpenter, a man who earned his keep by shaping dead trees to shelter human beings. Suddenly, the wooden axle of the narrator's cart breaks, con-firming the omen. With Kas'ian's reluctant help, the travelers visit a nearby forestry operation to obtain a new axle, which will be fashioned from the trunk of a dead young oak tree: "In the distance, closer to the grove, axes faintly clattered, and from time to time, solemnly and quietly, as if bowing and spreading its arms wide, a curly-topped tree would fall."[95] When the narrator first meets Kas'ian, the peasant is, not unlike one of the felled trees, sprawled on the ground, asleep, intimately embracing the earth, almost part of the soil. Once awoken, he rebukes the narrator without hesitation for hunting birds and beasts and "spilling their innocent blood."[96] Kas'ian's commitment to what we would now call animal rights (not to mention plant rights) is deep and pugnacious. True to his namesake—St. Cassian, the martyred schoolmaster of Imola, killed by his own students—Kas'ian will later enter into impassioned, pedantic dialogue with the narrator in an attempt to teach him about the immorality of harming the natural world.

One of the most striking passages of nature description in *Notes of a Hunter* occurs at the midpoint of "Kas'ian from Krasivaia Mech'," just after the narrator has shot and killed a corncrake in Kas'ian's presence, earning the peasant's profound opprobrium ("A sin! Oh, that's a sin!").[97] Taking refuge from the afternoon heat in a nearby grove, our narrator lies down, supine, and gazes aloft at the towering trees, while Kas'ian, significantly, seats himself on a felled birch (more *drevesina*), and, unlike the narrator, refuses to look up. The hunter now offers a lengthy second-person description of how staring upward at trees and sky is uncannily like looking down into a transparent body of water. The inverted perspective is impressively ingenious: branches have the appearance of roots, clouds become magical submerged islands, and so on. Turgenev concludes the passage with the blissful emotional effect on the person who witnesses such a scene, but that happy reverie is harshly shattered by Kas'ian ("Master! Hey, Master!"), who jerks the narrator's consciousness back to the sin of killing birds, setting off a page-long debate on hunting ethics.[98] In his analysis of this sequence, Thomas Newlin has observed that "there is an oddly vacuous—indeed, at times almost idiotic—quality to the narrator's state of mind," and that the basic imagery was recycled from an 1848 letter to Pauline Viardot.[99] What seemed to be the narrator's cleverly affectionate description of natural beauty and its beneficial effect on the observer is exposed by the context as a smug, self-serving exploitation of the environment that is morally equivalent to killing trees and birds: landscape as narcotic, its beauty a palliative. Here is anthropotropism of a subtle kind: celebratory depiction of the natural world that exists to titillate and reassure a human observer who ignores the natural destruction all around him, including the destruction he himself perpetuates. The narrator's hypocrisy becomes glaring, as we now reconsider, and condemn, his earlier eagerness to use the killing of trees as an opportunity to kill black grouse, because they are often found near newly cleared woodlands. "Kas'ian" is ultimately Turgenev's own complex self-imprecation at the end of his work on the *Notes of a Hunter* cycle: self-indictment for excessive bravura in his nature descriptions and for his own hunting zeal, which for most of his life remained resistant to the moral arguments against the practice of killing for sport. His cognizance of those arguments is obvious once we discern the many purposes of Kas'ian—healer, herbalist, caster of protective spells, theologian, and holy fool.

Turgenev completed "Bezhin Meadow" just before "Kas'ian" and placed the two tales one before the other in the book edition of the cycle, the same order in which they had first appeared in the *Contemporary*. An extended ecotropic account of a July day opens the story, in which the narrator, hunting alone, becomes lost as evening sets in. The smell of wormwood (*Artemisia absinthium*) suffuses the air, hinting that the disoriented hunter will experience on this night something like an absinthian vision of supernatural figures, a vision that only dies away at story's end, near dawn, when "the air was no longer so strongly scented."[100] His English setter, Dianka, though she is named, like artemisia itself, after the goddess of the hunt, can offer no guidance. As in "Kas'ian," the narrator is taught lessons by the peasants, in this case not about ethics and homespun cosmology, but about the uneasy relationship between human consciousness and inexplicable natural phenomena. The schoolmasters here are boys guarding cattle overnight, and the lessons are about "village superstitions" (*sel'skie pover'ia*): water spirits (*rusalki*), forest spirits (*leshie*), house spirits (*domovye*), Trishka (a bogeyman based on the Antichrist), unclean places, and omens. Like Turgenev, Sergei Aksakov was also deeply interested in the origins of such beliefs, which he subjected to his own rational analysis.[101] Turgenev, however, unlike Aksakov, employs a fictional character—skeptical and ungainly Pavlusha—to debunk the anthropotropic process of supernatural myth making. The boy exposes the way people distort and exploit natural occurrences to foretell human destinies, to make sense of misfortune, and to assert some measure of control in a world where they have next to none. He rationally explains, for example, the sudden, brief arrival of a white dove at the campfire circle, and unmasks a putative visitation by Trishka as nothing more than Vavila, the village cooper, walking down the street with an empty keg on top of his head. Pavlusha's exposure of their foolish credulity elicits laughter from the others, and Turgenev chooses precisely that moment to interject one of the finest caelotropic passages in the entire cycle:

> All the boys started laughing and fell silent for a moment, as often happens with people conversing in the outdoors. I looked around: the night stood solemn and regal; the damp freshness of late evening had

been replaced by the dry warmth of midnight, which still had a long while to lie like a soft canopy over the sleeping fields; there was still a long time before the first murmuring, before the first stirrings and rustlings of morning, before the first dewdrops of dawn. There was no moon in the sky: at that time it was rising late. Countless golden stars, it seemed, were constantly and quietly streaming, twinkling in eager rivalry, in the direction of the Milky Way, and, indeed, as you gazed at them, it was as though you yourself could dimly sense the headlong, ceaseless motion of the earth.[102]

This lyrical interlude suggests that level-headed Pavlusha's exposure of the truth is something profound, akin to those moments when we are able to grasp the larger truth of our environment, as when we seem to feel the rotation of our planet. From the narrator's point of view, Pavlusha's honesty and intelligence make him the most endearing of the five boys in the tale, so it comes as a shock when Turgenev's narrator suddenly announces his death in the terse final paragraph: "Unfortunately, I must add that in that same year Pavel passed away. He did not drown [as another boy, Iliusha, had superstitiously predicted], but was killed in a fall from a horse. It's a shame—he was a fine boy!"[103] To Turgenev, no one, not even an admirable rationalist who enlightens others about their fraught relationship with the natural environment, is exempt from the law of indifference that governs that environment. To the peasant boys, it must have seemed as though Pavlusha was punished for having scoffed at the time-honored folk wisdom to which they all subscribe: namely, that misery and mortality must make sense.[104]

Perhaps the most complex admixture of ecotropic and anthropotropic modes is to be found in "The Singers." The hilltop tavern known as the Haven (Pritynnyi), where a peasant singing contest takes place, is located in the village of Kolotovka, named not for the kitchen implement that is the word's ostensible meaning (a branched mixing stick), but apparently because the village is *cleft* (from the verb *kolot'*) by a "horrible ravine which, yawning like an abyss, winds, dug-up and eroded, right down the middle of the street."[105] The opening paragraph dwells on this cleavage in the earth, a split that retrospectively comes to embody the contradiction between the peasants' exquisite vocal artistry and the violent squalor of their material circumstances. At story's end, deeply moved by the singers he has heard, the narrator walks away from the tavern, down along the ravine, and hears the loud voice of a boy, singing out his brother's name—"Antropka!"—at least thirty times, calling him home to be flogged by their father. We are left to wonder whether perhaps the fine singing voices of the local men were developed by such calls to violence in their youth; we face the abyss between breathtaking music and degrading cruelty.[106]

In the early pages of "The Singers," rooks, crows, and sparrows are described as behaving like people as the narrator passes them by outside the Haven, and soon the people inside the tavern will be outsinging the birds. One of the most intriguing of Turgenev's footnotes is placed before the contest begins, when Wild Gent (Dikii-Barin) contemptuously tells Dunce (Obaldui), "Come on, no 'chirring'!" Turgenev glosses the passage: "Hawks 'chirr' [*tsirkaiut*] when they are frightened of something."[107] In a single stroke, the author implies that the peasant singers are like hawks—powerful, aggressive—yet capable of fear, and underscores his own authoritative mastery of the local scene he observes. In the tale's climax, Iashka the Turk sings best of all:

> I confess that I had rarely heard such a voice . . . A truthful, burning, Russian soul resounded and breathed within it and simply seized you by the heart, seized you by the Russian heart-strings . . . I recall once seeing, in the evening, at the ebbing of the tide, on the flat sandy shore of a sea that was sternly and sorrowfully roaring in the distance, a large white gull: it stood motionless, offering its breast to the scarlet radiance of the sunset, and every now and then it slowly spread its long wings toward the familiar sea, toward the low, crimson sun: I remembered that gull as I listened to Iakov . . . He sang, and from every sound of his voice wafted something familiar and boundlessly broad, as if our familiar steppe were opening up before you, stretching away into the endless distance.[108]

Here again the narrator resorts to an avian image, zootropic in itself, but linked to a larger celebration of Russian national character, anthropotropic in its import. That celebration, however, is bittersweet: the gull may bathe in warm crimson light, but the noisy sea in the distance is both pained, like Antropka, and threatening, like Antropka's father. The effect is to illuminate social contradictions through opposing modes of natural description.

"Forest and Steppe," the shortest of the twenty-two stories, jettisons the agonized juxtapositions and social critiques of the other tales to offer an ecstatic tour of the Russian landscape, finally revealing the kind of fervor we observed in Turgenev's hunting correspondence in chapter 2. The narrator's joy seems to blur the boundaries between literary modes. Skokova goes so far as to call the story "a poetic hymn to nature," while Borisova asserts that "Aksakov's 'Forest' and 'Steppe' and Turgenev's 'Forest and Steppe' are exceptional works of lyrical prose which to a considerable degree gravitate toward verse," and she convincingly demonstrates how a key sentence in Turgenev's third paragraph readily scans as iambic dimeter.[109] By melding poetry and prose, such passages echo the amiably inclusive way the story brings together and extols biomes, species, seasons, and times of day. The overall tone is one of sheer childlike delight in the organic world. Perhaps because there are no other major characters in the story aside from the narrator, no other consciousnesses to account for, "Forest and Steppe" fully melds ecotropic observation with emotional response to environmental beauty. Second-person narration, too, bestows the agency of perception directly upon the reader; it is the functional antithesis of the distancing dateline appended to "The Steward."

This lyrical ecotropism brings the story as close to a purely Aksakovian manner as Turgenev ever came. The most striking example here may be the passage on hunting woodcock in late autumn. After a few richly detailed sentences describing the sun, sky, light, color, scent, and the texture of the ground, Turgenev is unrestrained in conveying the psychological effect of the natural environment's glorious abundance:

> You breathe easy, but a strange sense of apprehension comes upon your soul. You walk along the forest edge, you watch the dog, and at the same time beloved images, beloved persons, dead and living, come to mind, impressions long since dormant suddenly awake; your imagination hovers and flies, like a bird, and everything moves and stands still before your eyes so distinctly. Your heart at times suddenly starts to quiver and beat, passionately plunging ahead, and at times irretrievably sinks into reminiscence. The whole of life unrolls as easily and quickly as a scroll; a man controls his entire past, all his feelings, powers, all his soul. And nothing around him can hinder him—there is neither sun, nor wind, nor sound.[110]

In "Forest and Steppe," there is also no Kas'ian to remind the narrator of his hypocrisy, no Ovsianikov to shame him for his disgraceful complicity. The narrator, as it were, sees only the beautiful sunlit gull of which he was reminded by Iashka's singing, unstained by the violence that darkens the conclusion of "The Singers." The narrator is free, in full possession of *volia* and undistracted by any *proizvol* around him.[111]

These lines convey the same basic sentiment as Aksakov's verse epigraph to *Notes on Fishing*, published the previous year: "I venture into nature's world, / The world of serenity and freedom [*volia*]."[112] Yet Aksakov's description, in the preface to that work, of the emotional cleansing that takes place when the sportsman is enveloped by the natural world, brings out a crucial distinction between Aksakov's and Turgenev's visions: "imaginary passions will subside, imaginary storms abate, prideful daydreams disperse, and impossible hopes fly away. *Nature will assert her eternal rights*, and you will hear her voice, hitherto drowned out by vanity, travail, laughter, shouting, and all the vulgarity of human speech" (my italics).[113] When Aksakov experiences the freedom bestowed by outdoor sport, nature herself takes center stage and makes her voice heard over the anthropogenic din. In Turgenev's meditation, however, the hunter's own vivid memories of other *people*, "dead and living," along with a sense of control over one's life, dominate. "Forest and Steppe," despite its celebratory tone, is therefore a more ambivalent story than it may seem at first blush: it presents a great deal of pure nature description, and yet it makes clear that Turgenev, unlike Aksakov, is incapable of stepping back entirely, of ignoring the way his own preoccupation with humanity tints what he experiences outdoors in the nonhuman world. Though readers who reach the conclusion of *Notes of a Hunter* might want to see "Forest and Steppe" as an expression of delight that offsets or even erases the explorations of misery found in the twenty-one tales that precede it, Turgenev denies them complete reassurance.

CHAPTER 4

Thinking Oneself into Nature

The Aksakov Reviews and Their Aftermath

> The tender emotion and delight that we experience
> from the contemplation of nature is our recollection
> of that time when we were animals, trees, flowers,
> earth. Or rather: this is consciousness of the unity in
> everything, unity hidden from us by time.
>
> —Lev Tolstoy, 1906

Just as Turgenev was being lionized in Russia
for the periodical publication of his *Notes of a Hunter* stories, and as that
cycle was being prepared for publication in book form, he was arrested and
detained for a month. While incarcerated in St. Petersburg from April to
May 1852, he wrote the story "Mumu," a short masterpiece of pathos that
is perhaps his most searing treatment of gentry *proizvol*. Turgenev was then
immediately sentenced to over a year and half of exile on his home estate,
deep in the Russian provinces. Already a seasoned part-time resident of Western Europe, he used this as an opportunity to plunge into the countryside
of his boyhood, hunting constantly and immersing himself in provincial culture, even as he agonized over his future path as a writer. During this period,
Turgenev's literary output was meager: he started and abandoned his first,
abortive novel project, *Two Generations*, and wrote only two short stories. But
as much as weather permitted during the months of seclusion, he was out
shooting, while indoors he was devouring Aksakov's just-published hunting
treatise and meditating on the review he had promised to write, which he
worked on fitfully from early June to mid-October 1852. Turgenev's review
is a crucial statement of his own *Naturphilosophie* and one of the most wide-
ranging philosophical documents in nineteenth-century Russian nature
writing. It is the climactic and cardinal statement in a substantial dialogue

between the two writers, but the review would have been impossible without *Notes of a Hunter* to prepare the ground.

For Turgenev, 1852 marked the start of a nearly two-year period of personal upheaval and creative reflection that distilled his thoughts about the organic world and transformed his literary representation of it for the rest of his career. At the center of all this was his collaborative involvement with Aksakov, who was entering a phase of astonishing productivity during the last ten years of his life.

Turgenev's Encounter with Aksakov

Turgenev had known Konstantin Aksakov since 1841 but did not meet his father, Sergei, until the end of 1850: "A few days ago," wrote Sergei, "I made the acquaintance of Turgenev and liked him very much; perhaps his [political] convictions are false or, at least, run counter to my own, but he is by nature kind, simple and superstitiously open to impressions of the dark, enigmatic world of the human soul."[1] In January 1851, twenty months before his *Notes of a Hunter* stories were published as a single volume, Turgenev visited Sergei Aksakov in Moscow and listened with pleasure to a reading of the older man's still-unfinished manuscript of *Orenburg-Province Hunter*, much to the delight of Aksakov, who immediately wrote to his son Ivan: "When Turgenev's *Notes of a Hunter* appeared, I thought of how nice it would be to read him my own *Notes*! My impossible dream has come true: they read him several excerpts, and these were fully appreciated by him. He wanted to listen to more, and tomorrow evening Konstantin will read him several further excerpts. I was very happy with the first audition."[2]

A year later, after Turgenev had continued to show great curiosity about Aksakov's project, Sergei wrote, "Your interest in my *Hunter's Notes* and approving words are dearer to me than all others, and it's no wonder: you bring together expertise on both the literary and hunting aspects."[3] To reciprocate, Turgenev read uncensored excerpts from *Notes of a Hunter* to Aksakov.[4] In February 1852, three weeks before he learned of Gogol's death, Turgenev expressed his deep admiration for Aksakov's hunting book and welcomed its imminent appearance in print: "Your *Notes* will be valuable not only to hunters; they will afford genuine pleasure to any person in possession of a nose for poetry; and I therefore stand ready to answer for both their literary and material success. Writing a review of them would simply be a holiday for me."[5] Aksakov's treatise finally appeared in March 1852, the same month that the book version of Turgenev's own *Notes of Hunter* was cleared for publication.

Exactly one week before Turgenev's arrest, his first review of Aksakov's *Notes* appeared, in the April 1852 issue of the *Contemporary*.[6] This notice consists of a one-paragraph introduction to the Aksakov work, then eight long excerpts from it (each prefaced with a single sentence), capped off by a short conclusion: "It is impossible to read this book without a kind of joyful, bright and complete feeling similar to those feelings that nature herself awakens in us; we know of no higher praise than this."[7] Though brief, this review, written in haste, offers hints at what was to come in Turgenev's second response to the book.

On 5 March 1852, Turgenev's own *Notes of a Hunter* received censor's approval. Aksakov's old friend Gogol had died in Moscow on 21 February, and Turgenev heard the news in Petersburg three days later. His lament over Gogol's passing—brief and modest in form but life-changing in its effect— appeared in the *Moscow Gazette* (*Moskovskie vedomosti*) on 13 March; Sergei Aksakov published a short obituary on Gogol, "A Letter to Gogol's Friends," on the same page of the newspaper.[8] By 16 April, Turgenev had been imprisoned in St. Petersburg for publishing the Gogol death notice in Moscow after having skirted the ban being enforced in the capital, clearly a trumped-up charge, while Aksakov, writing in Moscow, received no official censure for his obituary. Turgenev habitually put a brave face on the peripeteia of 1852, writing from jail to the Viardots about his excitement at the prospect of exploiting his impending exile as a chance for frequent hunting.[9] Exactly one month later, he was banished to his home estate of Spasskoe-Lutovinovo. In early June, he wrote to the Aksakovs, "I see nothing terrible about my fate, especially now, in the country . . . Just between us, I can tell you that I'm glad that I was in prison for a month; there I was able to look at the Russian from a side that was, until then, little known to me."[10] In more distant retrospect, at the end of the 1860s, Turgenev could write that "it all turned out for the best; my time under arrest, and then in the country, was of undoubted benefit to me. It acquainted me with certain sides of Russian life that would probably have escaped my attention in the normal course of things."[11] With the exception of one (probable) clandestine trip to Moscow in the spring of 1853 to visit Pauline Viardot, he would remain at Spasskoe and environs for the next eighteen months, until December 1853.[12]

While in exile, Turgenev utterly immersed himself in the world of hunting. Inhabitants of the local village relate that he began hunting with his favorite dog, Diana, as soon as he arrived, and spent most of the summer in the field instead of at his writing desk.[13] From Spasskoe, Turgenev corresponded constantly at this time with Aksakov, who deeply sympathized with his plight. In early August 1852 the book version of Turgenev's *Notes of a Hunter* was published. He had promised at the beginning of June "to get to work on an article" devoted to Aksakov's "much-read and much-loved book" right away, but the task was not so easily completed and occupied Turgenev's thoughts the entire summer and autumn.[14] Aksakov had been exceedingly grateful for the first, brief review, and eagerly anticipated the forthcoming "critical remarks of a literary man and hunter," which he hoped to use as he made revisions for a second edition.[15] Finally, on 17 October, Turgenev informed Aksakov that the piece was done, though its final version would not reach Nekrasov until December. With certain key passages removed by the censor, the review appeared in the January 1853 issue of the *Contemporary*.[16]

Notes of an Orenburg-Province Hunter was met with what Semyon Mashinskii calls "rare unanimity" of acclaim; the book was widely reviewed, and those notices were universally positive.[17] Turgenev's appraisal, however, is by far the most important: no other had been developed in such close collaboration with Aksakov himself, no other was as long, and no other delved as deeply into the historical and philosophical implications of hunting.

Leonid Maikov, who in 1894 edited the publication of the Aksakovs' letters to Turgenev, suggests that the first review, written in St. Petersburg before Turgenev's exile, was an outline for the second review, written at Spasskoe: "This notice served as a program that he employed in the country to write his large article about the same book."[18] To judge from that first review, there can be little doubt that Turgenev saw it as a placeholder, an initial outburst of delight that would suffice until he could gather his thoughts in earnest: "We will allow ourselves the pleasure, in an upcoming issue of the *Contemporary*," Turgenev wrote, "to speak in detail about this work that was written with so much love and such knowledge of the subject; and we will speak about that love 'on location,' since we will be in the country, in the natural world of which this love serves as such a faithful and poetic reflection, and we ourselves will be indulging in sport."[19] This is typical of Turgenev's view that nature writing is best undertaken by those who spend a great deal of time in the outdoors and thereby reaffirm their experience of humanity's status as part of nature: "Anyone who simply loves nature in all her variety, in all her beauty and strength; anyone who cherishes a display of universal life—in the midst of which man himself stands as a living link, higher, but tightly bound to the other links—will not be able to tear himself away from Mr. A[ksako]v's work."[20]

Turgenev casts his second, far longer review as a letter, perhaps in imitation of virtually the only kind of writing he accomplished during the first half-year of his exile.[21] Unlike the first review, which was written anonymously, the second is signed "I. T." and addressed to "N. A." (for N. A. Nekrasov). The epistle-review opens with an epigraph Aksakov himself had chosen five years earlier for his first sporting treatise, *Notes on Fishing*, which signals Turgenev's affectionate familiarity with Aksakov's work but also subtly indicates the ambition of the review: if it displays the same epigraph that opened a famous 163-page treatise, the review itself perhaps makes a claim to similar comprehensiveness and depth. This impression is intensified by the paucity of quotations from Aksakov's *Notes of an Orenburg-Province Hunter*: while seven-eighths of the first review consisted of long block-quotations from Aksakov, in the second review Turgenev quotes him only twice, and very briefly. More of Pushkin, and even more of Shakespeare, is quoted than of Aksakov.

It soon becomes clear that in this second review Turgenev has, to a considerable extent, crafted a self-reflective monograph in miniature. We are made to witness *Turgenev's* deep knowledge of hunting manuals, dogs, firearm technology, and other accoutrements; *Turgenev's* expertise on the history of hunting in Western culture from the ancient Hebrews to the present; *Turgenev's* philosophy of nature; *Turgenev's* views on the proper aesthetic depiction of nature. Three times he needs to remind himself, and the reader, that he has strayed too far and must return to Aksakov's *Notes*, his ostensible subject. It is no wonder that an anonymous reviewer of the same treatise expressed puzzlement at Turgenev's second review: "This is all marvelous! But how did it end up in a review of a book about hunting? We live in a strange time! You open an article on hunting—and you find wonderful aesthetic propositions; you glance into an article on poetry—and there is no mention of anything to do with aesthetics."[22] Running counter to what can at times seem Turgenev's showy emphasis on his own connoisseurship, however, there is a refreshing vein of self-criticism that he exposes by contrasting Aksakov with other writers, including himself.

Turgenev consistently praises Aksakov for the simplicity and directness of his largely ecotropic approach:

How much freshness, grace, observation, understanding and love of nature it contains! . . . [Aksakov] looks upon nature (both animate and inanimate) not from some exclusive point of view, but as one should look at her: clearly, simply, and with complete sympathy; he does not complicate things unnecessarily, use cunning or add extraneous motives and goals; he observes intelligently, conscientiously and keenly; he only wants to learn, to see . . . This is authentic Russian speech: genial and direct, supple and adroit. There is nothing pretentious and nothing superfluous, nothing strained and nothing sluggish. . . . [I admire] the amiably intelligent, clear and manly tone of the entire book.[23]

It is difficult not to presume here that Turgenev was tacitly contrasting Aksakov's *Notes* with his own *Notes of a Hunter*, which, thanks to its implicitly abolitionist critique of Russian landowners, could easily be seen—and was, by the authorities—as having "extraneous motives and goals."

Turgenev goes on to compare Aksakov's way of describing nature with two faulty descriptive modes he finds in other writers. The first kind of error is characterized, as we observed in chapter 1, by the labored, anthropocentric tropes of figures like Buffon ("the horse is man's noblest conquest"), the poet Vladimir Benediktov (who writes of mountains that are "sprouts of dust into the heavens," a crag that "laughs," and lightning that resembles a "phosphorescent snake"), and Victor Hugo (who commits similar sins in the poems of *Les orientales*).[24]

Later in the review, Turgenev also derides a second kind of bad nature writing practiced by artists much closer to his heart:

> There can sometimes be subtly developed, nervous, irritably poetic personalities who possess some particular outlook on nature, a particular sense of her beauty; they take note of many nuances, many often barely perceptible particulars, and occasionally they succeed in expressing them extremely felicitously, neatly, and gracefully, though the larger outlines of the picture either escape them or they lack sufficient strength to grasp and hold on to them. One could say that they mostly have access to the scent of nature, and their words are fragrant.[25]

A page later, Turgenev refers to these writers as "semi-feminine poetic personalities" and names them as Tiutchev and Fet, poets he admired immensely.[26] The style of Turgenev's own Aksakov review, with its flights of historiographical and philosophical sophistication, places Turgenev himself in the very category of "semi-feminine" nature writers he chides. His letter to Ivan Aksakov written at the time strongly suggests that this was indeed an intentional self-indictment: "My article about your father's book is appearing in the January issue of the *Contemporary* . . . There are a few thoughts there about how nature can be described, and I show no mercy to myself."[27] Thus the subtle yet vivid natural descriptions we explored in *Notes of a Hunter*—the "often barely perceptible particulars" expressed "extremely felicitously, neatly, and gracefully"—seem to have disappointed their creator, at least when he compared them to the products of Aksakov's less anthropotropic approach.

Turgenev's disapproval of the first type of bad nature writing is directed at authors who possess a particular, preconceived notion of nature that they depict through speciously ingenious means, not unlike the way Turgenev himself describes the narrator's skyward gaze in "Kas'ian from Krasivaia Mech'," as we observed in chapter 3. In the Aksakov review, this literary flaw suddenly prompts a remarkable elaboration on the essence of nature itself:

> An outlook of that sort [the sort belonging to Buffon, Benediktov, Hugo] is utterly discordant with the true meaning of nature, with her basic tenor. Without question, in her entirety she constitutes one great, well-proportioned whole—every point within her is united with every other point—but at the same time her aspiration is that precisely each point, each separate unit within her, exist exclusively for itself, consider itself the center of the universe, turn to its own advantage everything around it, negate the independence of those surroundings and take possession of them as its own property. To the mosquito who sucks your blood, you are food, and he makes use of you just as calmly and without shame as the spider into whose net he has toppled does him, just as a root that digs in the dark makes use of the earth's moisture. Direct your attention for a few moments to the fly that freely flits from your nose to a lump of sugar, to a drop of nectar in the heart of a flower—and you will understand what I mean; you will understand that she is resolutely on her own just as much as you are on your own. How, from this disunity and fragmentation by means of which everything seems to live only for itself, how that selfsame universal, endless harmony, in which, conversely, all that lives lives for another and only in another attains its reconciliation or its resolution, and all lives merge into a single, universal life—this is one of those "open" secrets that we all see and do not see.[28]

This is probably the single most important statement Turgenev ever made about the organic world, and it serves as a touchstone for his nature writing, as we will see in the chapters ahead. The paradoxical mutuality of natural solipsism (self-absorption) and natural extroversion (other-absorption) was, however, to have little direct effect at the time, because the lines quoted above were entirely excised by the censor before publication.[29]

We must pause here to acknowledge how Herzen's then-recent writings echo in this key passage. In late 1845, while praising Karl Rul'e, Herzen had disparaged mystically anthropotropic nature writing: "Our imagination is so corrupted and imbued with metaphysics that we have lost the power to convey the events of the physical world directly and simply without introducing . . . false ideas, mistaking metaphors for the real thing, separating in words what is united in reality."[30] In the second of his *Letters on the Study of Nature*, which we touched on in chapter 1, Herzen writes,

> Man did not recognize the autonomy of particular phenomena. Everywhere man played the role of master, considering it within his right *to take possession of all that surrounded him and subject it to his will*. He regarded inanimate objects as slaves, as organs outside his body, belonging to him. We can impose our will [*volia*] only on something which has no will of its own or whose will we refuse to recognize; once we assign our aim to someone else that means either that we regard his aim as unimportant or else regard ourselves as his aim.[31]

Herzen's phraseology here in 1844 is strikingly similar to Turgenev's in the Aksakov review ("negate the independence of those surroundings and take possession of them as its own property"), but there is a crucial difference: while Turgenev seeks to describe the self-centered impetus governing all life, Herzen trains his gaze only on *Homo sapiens* and the *human* yen for exploiting resources of all kinds, clearly gesturing toward the institution of slavery; the subtext is serfdom.[32] Turgenev, intrigued by what he sees as a universal tendency in nature, perceives self-beneficial domination as an ecosystem-wide phenomenon, not limited to humans: it is a tendency that animates and balances the natural world. The structure and vocabulary of his meditation in the Aksakov review could well have come from Herzen, who was, after all, a fellow admirer of Goethe's "Nature." It seems plausible, even likely, that Turgenev reread Herzen's essay on Rul'e and *Letters on the Study of Nature* in preparation for the Aksakov review. Turgenev, however, is more interested than Herzen in that painful, indistinct zone—not unlike Darwin's "entangled bank"—where the infinite expressions of microcosmic *volia* collide, collude, and ultimately produce the macrocosmic harmony and beauty linking all species that constitute the organic world.[33]

Turgenev's basic conception of nature's paradox—the achievement of harmony through disharmony—offers fresh perspective on nature's indifference, and he would restate the paradox, this time in the human context, half a decade later in "Hamlet and Don Quixote":

> We must acknowledge an elemental law of all human life: this life, in sum, is nothing more than the eternal reconciliation and eternal opposition of two ceaselessly separating and ceaselessly converging cores . . . Hamlets constitute the expression of the elemental centripetal force of nature, according to which every living thing considers

itself the center of creation and considers all else to be things that exist solely in order to benefit this center. (Thus the mosquito, having landed on the forehead of Alexander the Great, sucked his blood as its appropriate food, calmly convinced of its right to do so.) . . . Without this centripetal force (the force of egoism), nature itself could not exist, just as it could not exist without another, centrifugal force, according to which everything that exists does so to benefit something else. (This force, this principle of devotion and sacrifice . . . is represented by Don Quixote.) These two forces—of inertia and of motion, of conservation and of progress—constitute the fundamental forces of all that exists. They explain the growth of flowers to us, and they even enable us to comprehend the development of the most powerful nations.[34]

In these comments, the harmony-disharmony dialectic migrates from biology into literature, physics, psychology, and political history, ultimately taking on the character of something like a unified field theory for Turgenev. The disharmonious, egoistic, Hamletesque, centripetal force is in constant tension with the harmonious, altruistic, Quixotic, centrifugal force, and all organisms—from world-historical figures to plants and parasitic insects—are equally at the mercy of both.

To explain where we might find evidence of altruism (Quixote's "devotion and sacrifice") in this bleak world of parasites, predators, and prey, Turgenev falls back on German thought. In the second Aksakov review, immediately after his harmony-from-disharmony discourse, he adds a selection, in his own translation, of paradoxes quoted from the Goethean essay "Nature":

Nature places abysses between all beings, and they all strive to devour one another. She disunites all in order to unite all. . . .

Her crown is love. Only through love can one draw near to her. . . .

It seems that she only troubles herself in order to create individuals— and individuals mean nothing to her. She ceaselessly builds and ceaselessly destroys.[35]

Turgenev has shifted the order in which these aphorisms actually appear in the original German text so that the reader first encounters selfishness and disunity, then love, then an expression of heartless destruction. In a world dominated by the indifferent, self-serving competition of natural forces, Turgenev's unexpected advice, which he now dispenses in his own words directly on the heels of Goethe's perplexing contradictions, is that one must *love*: "If it is only 'through love' that one can draw near to nature, then this love must be unselfish, like any authentic feeling: love nature not by virtue of what she means in relation to you, a person, but because she, in and of herself, is sweet and dear to you—and you will understand her."[36] We can conclude that, in Turgenev's estimation, Buffon, Hugo, and Benediktov must not truly love nature, because their descriptions are full of authorial egoism, of anthropotropic edifices that seek to subjugate the natural world in an act of aesthetic *proizvol*. A Schellingian residue is still perceptible in Turgenev's attitude: nature has agency, is a subject, and deserves to exercise her agency freely, even deserves to be loved.

In elaborating on his view that "all that lives lives for another and only in another attains its reconciliation or its resolution," Turgenev has omitted the obvious implication about reproduction—that organisms seek one another out in order to mate—and instead of discussing how nature's denizens "love" one another, he immediately moves to the question of how people ought to love nature. This is typical of all his writing about the natural world: titanic affection for its beauty constantly underlies his depiction of the nonhuman environment. As Galina Kurliandskaia points out, "For Turgenev, the true meaning of nature is revealed only to loving, unselfish attention to her objective substance."[37] Who, then, is a true lover of nature? An obvious specific answer is Aksakov, who sees her and depicts her as she is; Turgenev had plainly stated in the first review that Aksakov's notes were written "with love," and that the topic of the second review would be a discussion of that love.[38] Turgenev, too, has, earlier in the second review, declared, "I passionately love nature, especially in her living manifestations."[39] The common element that enables them both to love nature, at least as Turgenev has argued she should be loved, is trumpeted in the first sentence of the review, when the author calls himself "a true hunter—a hunter body and soul."[40] Hunting is the answer, the key category, the activity that allows its practitioners to see nature clearly, to enter into a truly loving relationship with her.

Hunters supply the altruism, simply by loving nature. It is another paradox, of course, that they express this love by deliberately killing living things, but, as Aksakov put it, "we [hunters] have our own logic: the more respect you have for a bird, the harder you try to shoot it."[41] Hunters reenact the never-ending struggle that is the essence of the natural world. As we noted in chapter 1, Turgenev's conception of that essence was initially shaped by his exposure to German Idealism, but now, by 1852, he has moved beyond the *Naturphilosophie* embraced by Russian intellectuals of his generation: in the second *Orenburg Hunter* review, he celebrates Aksakov's meticulous descriptions of birds as a rejection of "those sometimes poetic and profound, but nearly always murky and indeterminate hypotheses, with which Schelling used to turn heads at the beginning of the present century."[42] Turgenev expresses delight that Aksakov's nature writing should be of great interest to naturalists (*estestvoispytateli*) rather than philosophers; he even speculates that the recently deceased John James Audubon "would have been deeply moved" by *Notes of an Orenburg-Province Hunter*.[43]

Turgenev makes clear in the second review that human beings do not stand separate from nature but are fully joined to it in a spirit of kinship. This union explains the instinctive human affection for nature that is simultaneously filial and parental: "Man cannot fail to be fascinated by nature; he is connected to her by a thousand unbreakable threads: he is her son; the sympathy that is awakened in one's soul by lower creatures—so similar to man in their outward appearance, inner structure, organs of sensation and feeling—is somewhat reminiscent of that lively interest each of us takes in the development of an infant."[44] Yet the hunter, as shown by the descriptive excellence of Aksakov's *Notes*, enjoys a privileged status as nature observer. In his hunting treatise, Aksakov emphasizes quietness, careful observation, protracted contact with the world outdoors—all salient features of precisely the form of hunting that he and Turgenev embraced and did so much to promote. We must keep in mind that Aksakov's book is exclusively about shooting. His commentary is unsparing of the other forms of hunting practiced in Russia: "All forms of sport are good!" Aksakov declares. "Each has its own ardent devotees who prefer it to other kinds of hunting, but one must acknowledge shooting as superior to all of them . . . I do not dispute the pleasures of [hounding], but we all have our likes and dislikes: I do not enjoy hunting that involves co-operation with others who may not be hunters at all, and I must admit that I am not fond of hounds or borzois so I do not like hunting with [them]."[45]

Turgenev's correspondence makes it abundantly clear that he relished the elite strictures and specialized gear that gentry hunters embraced as they entered the landscape. Early in the second review of Aksakov's treatise, too, he revels in the latest shooting technology, mentioning gunsmiths—Manton, Mortimer, Purdey, Morgenroth, Lepage, Starbus, Becker—and learnedly discussing percussion caps, breechloaders, powder flasks, shotguns, muzzle-loader wads, bandoliers, cartridges, and so forth; his discussion of gun dogs likewise shows off a dazzling store of knowledge.[46] He is also, as we discussed in chapter 2, an expert on hunting manuals, carefully pointing out that Aksakov has not written one of these: "For our part, we will only add that *Notes of an Orenburg-Province Hunter* is not a book like Elzéar Blaze's *Chasseur au chien d'arrêt*, which is considered the classic work on French hunting. Mr. A[ksako]v's *Notes* is not a hunting book in the strict sense; it cannot serve as a complete manual for the beginning hunter, though valuable remarks and pieces of advice are to be found on nearly every page. The author himself perceives this."[47] Aksakov has sought to create a timeless document rather than a practical guide tied to the ceaselessly changing technology of firearms and vogues for certain breeds of dog.

Elzéar Blaze's remarkable book is, as Turgenev asserts, not like Aksakov's. Published in 1836, *Chasseur au chien d'arrêt* was a standard hunting manual in France through the 1840s. Blaze (1786–1848), five years Aksakov's senior, fought in the Napoleonic campaigns, and his treatise is rife with jocular, at times grotesque, war stories that link hunting to military struggle.[48] By contrast, no mention of war is ever made in *Notes of an Orenburg-Province Hunter*. Unlike Aksakov, Blaze offers a meticulous history of hunting, from classical antiquity to the present; he quotes Pythagoras, Rousseau, Bernardin de Saint-Pierre, and many others; he provides entire chapters on weaponry and clothing, as well as four separate chapters on the training and treatment of hunting dogs. Blaze's tone throughout the work is bluff, lighthearted, aphoristic. He does include descriptions of species, but these are far fewer and less detailed than Aksakov's.[49] In the same letter in which Turgenev informed Aksakov that he had finished the review, he told the older hunter that he regretted that Aksakov's treatise had not included as much discussion of dogs as Blaze's volume. At the same time Turgenev seemed to feel that the essential Frenchness of Blaze's *Chasseur* produced a distinct focus, making it "an exemplary book for *French* hunting, which I also know from experience."[50] The differences between Aksakov's *Notes* and Blaze's work reveal two things: that Turgenev, in his Aksakov review, was himself susceptible to the same show of connoisseurship and savoir faire displayed by Blaze, and that Aksakov's *Notes*—in Turgenev's eyes—was more akin to natural history than to a manual.

Erudition was a passion in Turgenev's personal life as well as a trope he frequently employed in his fiction. Strikingly detailed familiarity with history, and particularity in nomenclature, mark the opening pages of the Aksakov review and serve the same rhetorical function they did in *Notes of a Hunter*—to establish Turgenev's status as an expert, disposing the reader to assume that such a learned author is to be trusted in the more speculative matters that follow, such as the harmony-from-disharmony thesis. While Turgenev supplies *connoisseurship* in abundance, Aksakov's writing displays *knowledge*. This difference runs the risk of souring readers on Turgenev, but it soon becomes clear that he genuinely admires Aksakov's knowledge—based on decades of astute, conscientious observation of the natural world—and Turgenev has taken it upon himself to supply the erudition that shows why such knowledge is important, how it is linked to history, philosophy, and science. Aksakov, who frequently expressed hope that his hunting and fishing notes would be of use to science, shied away from philosophical exposition. In fact, as we have seen, Turgenev explicitly praises Aksakov for not freighting nature with intellectual and aesthetic significance: "he only wants to learn, to see. And before such scrutiny, nature opens up and allows him to 'peep in' at her."[51] As Newlin has pointed out, Aksakov's *Orenburg Hunter* furnished a "counterexample" to the metaphysical verbiage in natural descriptions that Herzen had decried in the early 1840s.[52] Aksakov was devoted to scrupulous accuracy in calling physical things by their correct names, a pragmatic tendency that indicates his distaste for metaphysics. "Turgenev was delighted by Aksakov's ability to name each little plant, each living thing," Ella Voitolovskaia, an Aksakov specialist, observes. "Knowledge of nature and unsurpassed familiarity with the scope of Russian peasant language constituted in Turgenev's eyes the basic feature that distinguished Aksakov from 'our entire brotherhood of writers.' . . . Turgenev showed that only knowledge of nature can liberate the writer from commonplaces and stock phrases."[53] These Aksakovian virtues are the foundation of Turgenev's own ecotropically oriented accounts.

The more learned Turgenev appears in the review, the more admirable Aksakov's knowledgeable simplicity seems by contrast. Turgenev tackles the big questions, establishing, like Blaze, the roots of hunting in antiquity, underscoring that what was a sport in his era was an activity essential for human survival in the ancient world: "I could adduce striking proof of the fact that hunting occupies far from the last place in human life and the history of humanity . . . I will remark only that hunting must justly be considered one of man's most important undertakings."[54] Turgenev's erudite survey of hunting lore extends from Nimrod in the Book of Genesis to *The Odyssey* to Henry IV of France to Prime Minister Earl Grey in the early nineteenth century.[55] In a move that must have pleased the Slavophile patriarch, Turgenev gives an overview of Russian hunting history that is no less comprehensive: "From time immemorial, Russians, too, have loved to hunt. This is confirmed by our folksongs, our tales, and all our legends."[56] He covers Grand Prince Vladimir Monomakh, Tsar Aleksei Mikhailovich, and the instinctive urge to hunt he has observed in Russian peasants, accompanying his discussion of Russia with a regretful footnote: "Fairness demands mention that, unfortunately, the quantity of our game is quickly diminishing," owing to habitat loss and the slaughter of breeding birds.[57] This comment resonates with the proto-environmentalist laments that frequently appear in *Notes of an Orenburg-Province Hunter*.[58]

Turgenev's sophisticated commentary in the final pages of the review readily veers into literature, not only adducing negative examples, as noted above—from Benediktov, Hugo, Fet, Tiutchev, and Turgenev himself—but offering up paragons of nature description he believes to be equaled by Aksakov's own work.

Turgenev reminds readers of Pushkin's and Gogol's excellent landscapes, but the first specific exemplar he actually quotes is "the celebrated passage in *King Lear* [IV: 6] where Edgar describes for blind Gloucester the steep sea-cliff that supposedly falls away precipitously at his very feet."[59] The passage—quoted in its entirety—appeals to Turgenev because Shakespeare "wishes neither to say something out of the ordinary nor to find in the picture that appears before his eyes particular, as-yet-unnoticed details; with the true instinct of genius he keeps to the single chief sensation."[60] Ostensibly an example of how a nature description avoids "cunning" or "extraneous motives and goals," of all the straightforward literary landscapes that Turgenev, who was extremely well read in Shakespeare and the Western classics, had at his fingertips, this passage may seem a shocking choice. Indeed, it would be hard to find a nature description in Shakespeare that is more packed with "extraneous motives and goals." This picture is a fake, an imagined vista, concocted by Edgar to dupe his father, the recently blinded Earl of Gloucester, into thinking that he has found an ideal place to commit suicide by leaping from a seaside cliff. Edgar apparently hopes that the short plunge forward, onto the ground at his feet, will convince Gloucester that he has miraculously survived a deadly fall and thereby cure him of his desire for self-destruction. Moreover, beyond its convoluted context within the play, this passage depends on a cascade of figurative language: distant crows and choughs that look like beetles; a man who seems as small as his own head; fishermen who "appear like mice"; a ship that looks as small as her own flag; her flag as small as a tiny buoy. The description is a bravura display of improvised metaphorical detail and nobly motivated falsehood. The complexity of the passage on so many levels might have led readers to wonder if Turgenev could possibly have been serious in naming it as a specimen of straightforward, Aksakovian nature description. And yet, Shakespeare's vision of a precipitous cliff is utterly effective in conveying the distortion that great height imparts to the appearance of familiar objects. Perhaps the success of that "single chief sensation" overrides the complexity of the passage's composition and function. Even more likely is that Turgenev admired the description precisely because nature's majesty is untouched by the tortuous human strivings that surround it.

Pushkin's "The Cloud" ("Tucha," 1835) is now quoted in full as another fulfillment of Turgenev's summary dictum on natural description: "When you describe nature's phenomena the point is not to say everything that may enter your head: say what should enter each person's head, but in such a way that your depiction is as forceful as what you depict, and neither you nor we listeners will have anything more to wish for."[61] Turgenev offers no particular methods for achieving this, but Pushkin's caelotropic poem provides hints of what he might have had in mind. The narrator apostrophizes a cloud, the last remnant of a passing storm. His second-person narration implies that the cloud, as a listening addressee, is animate, but an explicit personifying metaphor is absent. Instead, Pushkin's narrator now makes a series of observations of what the cloud *does*: it speeds, casts a shadow, saddens the day, covers the sky, releases thunder, waters the earth. While these verbs imply agency, once again the narrator stops short of personification. In the final quatrain (of three), the narrator commands the cloud to hide, declaring that it will now be replaced by the wind. The ultimate impression is that nature interacts with human beings by performing familiar acts that people recognize and even hope to control ("Enough—go hide!"), and that nature's elements are part of what human observers see as a natural succession: from storm, to solitary cloud, to wind, and so on. Though the cloud is never humanized, other elements are: "exultant day" is "sadden[ed]," and the wind "caress[es]" the leaves of the trees. As with the Shakespeare passage, Turgenev seems to approve of tropes, but they must, like Pushkin's anthropomorphism here, be subtle and directly descriptive. Rather than indulging "everything that may enter his head," Pushkin deftly avoids the miscues of Buffon, Hugo, and Benediktov.

Repercussions of the Reviews: The Aksakovs, "The Inn"

Turgenev's second review of Aksakov's *Notes* was well received.[62] Lev Vaksel', true to form, seized on the technical comments it contained and peppered Turgenev with half a dozen questions and objections connected to guns, dogs, and ammunition, which Turgenev, true to form, addressed with methodical insouciance.[63]

Before it was completed, Sergei Aksakov had graciously complimented Turgenev on the prospect of the second review: "Never did I think that my modest labor, which provided me so much pleasure in my study, at the time of the work itself, would provide so many comforting notices among whose number I without doubt value yours highest of all."[64] Ivan Aksakov, who was himself a noteworthy poet, welcomed the review, borrowing some of Turgenev's figures, including the aroma of nature and Benediktov's glib descriptions:

All that you write in your article, in the first issue of the *Contemporary*, about methods of describing nature, is entirely just, expressed with exceptional precision and success, and is utterly after my own heart . . . What knowledge of a life lived close to nature, what a close bond with nature is necessary for that high simplicity of description about which you speak! For the most part, we fall short (and here I naturally speak of myself) when it comes to exactitude of expression; we find more accessible the scent, the aroma, of nature, with some kind of indefinite musicality of feeling . . . Nevertheless, I find that you ought to have enlarged upon that modern mode of nature-description which—not to connect this description with my own personality—is similar to a daguerreotype and makes an unpleasant impression . . . It's irritating somehow that nature is placed into our hands so cheaply, that nature-description whose fidelity we can't help but acknowledge demands from the writer neither service to nature, nor an especially ardent love for her . . . These writers of course fail to capture the spirit of life: the point is not to describe minutiae, not to be faithful in every detail. All this is so; but you ought to have reproached these gentlemen too; they have multiplied a great deal. Now they won't start saying "sprouts of dust into the heavens," but they'll describe to you a dust-speck in offensive detail, with repugnant fidelity.[65]

Ivan Aksakov grasps the hunter's special, practical relationship to the natural world but lashes out at nature writers who stray too far into the dry, scientific prose of naturalists. Turgenev's response to these comments has unfortunately not come down to us.

The moment of truth was Sergei Aksakov's own reaction to the published review. If Turgenev had intended his artful commentary on Aksakov's artless *Notes* to be a happy literary symbiosis between observer and explainer, between knowledge and connoisseurship, this was largely lost on Aksakov, who was perplexed by the review. After a first paragraph that gratefully acknowledges the praise Turgenev had lavished on his book, Aksakov gets down to business:

I esteem you so much, dearest Ivan Sergeevich, that I cannot speak to you other than with complete frankness. I am not afraid of appearing in your eyes to be an annoyingly vain, demanding and ungrateful man. And so, more to the point. If you were to ask me whether your article completely satisfied all *my* expectations (mark that: *my own personal* expectations), then I would tell you that I expected and desired something different. To wit: your letter to the publisher of the *Contemporary* is not a critique of my book, but a marvelous article on the occasion of my book. On the other hand, I very much understand that, if your article had stuck to the form of a critique, it might perhaps have come out less interesting and a bit dry; the most important thing is that the time for that manner of analysis has passed, and I entirely agree that such an approach would decidedly lose you the majority of your readers. I nonetheless expected less praise, but on the other hand expected impartial judgment and fair criticisms; I had hoped for a more serious tone, especially regarding language and style. Finally, in speaking of Pushkin and Shakespeare, in citing examples from them (without ulterior motives, it stands to reason), you crushed my small *persona* with their enormous personalities! At least that is what I sensed when I listened to your article; perhaps such a thought will not enter the head of a single other person . . . I'm truly embarrassed to write these lines! Not embarrassed that they will be unpleasant to you; here's what I think: in our friendship, sincerity is indispensable.[66]

Remarkable here is that Aksakov's reaction to Turgenev's review entirely confirms the mode of observation Turgenev has explained as typifying Aksakov. That is, with his disappointed comment that this is a "marvelous article" inspired by the book rather than a critique of the book, Aksakov rightly recognizes that Turgenev, to use Turgenev's own term, is indeed a "semi-feminine" writer whose goal is not merely to observe, but to embellish, speculate, philosophize—to "complicate things unnecessarily." Turgenev has failed to offer observations on Aksakov's treatise that emulate the directness and purity of Aksakov's own observations of nature. Particularly disappointing is Turgenev's lack of attention to Aksakov's linguistic labor, his tireless pursuit of terminological exactitude. Aksakov's review of Turgenev's review of Aksakov's book forcefully confirms the legitimacy of what Turgenev had asserted about Aksakov's book in the first place: that the two writers, though united by sincere mutual admiration and love of hunting, were fundamentally different artists.

By the mid-1850s, nonfiction sporting literature had been abandoned by first-rank authors and on the whole reverted to the pragmatic form promulgated by the writers of manuals.[67] Yet whatever the fate of sporting literature in nineteenth-century Russia, Turgenev and Aksakov together played a vital role in facilitating the rise to primacy of Russian shooting, as S. I. Romanov explains:

Written when coursing with hounds was at the height of its popularity, [Aksakov's *Notes of an Orenburg-Province Hunter* and Turgenev's *Notes of a Hunter*] exerted a wonderful, refreshing influence on the excessively sprawling hound-hunters and thanks to the artistic enthusiasm of the descriptions in these works, confirmed most effectively that the pleasure of hunting by no means consists solely of noisy forays by almost entire districts into the hunting grounds, but rather is to be had in *shooting*—forgotten, pushed aside and almost crushed by the glitter of coursing with hounds—which offers irreplaceable, shining moments and beauty. Without these books, and the books of Mr. Osnovskii and Mr. Vaksel', our society, infatuated with the opulence of coursing raids, would scarcely have taken up shooting so quickly and unobtrusively at that grave juncture for hound-hunters when

> The great chain was broken, / Was broken and leapt apart: / At one end the master, / At the other the peasant!
>
> [Порвалась цепь великая, / Порвалась-расскочилася: / Одним концом по барину, / Другим по мужику!][68]

and when, after the abolition of serfdom, landowners were at once deprived of the means to support their hunting retinue and huge packs of hounds.[69]

Writing at the same time, Sabaneev echoes Romanov's polemical assertion, and is just as explicit about the political implications of shooting: "Times changed, and so did customs: at present [in the late 1870s], shooting stands higher in public esteem than does coursing, probably because it carries a democratic character."[70] Shooting, therefore, held for Turgenev's readers a political, philosophical, and artistic meaning. Paradoxically, he was best able to enunciate that meaning in dialogue with Sergei Aksakov, a writer whose hunting treatise consciously rejected the political, the philosophical, and the overtly artistic.

It is significant that during the first year and a half of Turgenev's exile he finished only one work of fiction, a fifty-page story entitled "The Inn" ("Postoialyi dvor").[71] Named for the form of lodging he often sought on his hunting forays during those years, the tale was conceived during the height of Turgenev's work on the second Aksakov review: he began writing it two days after the letter to Konstantin Aksakov quoted above, and the day after he wrote to Sergei telling him he had completed the review. The story was finished in less than a month.[72] There can be no doubt that both "The Inn" and the *Orenburg Hunter* review simultaneously occupied Turgenev's thoughts, but critics have never seriously explored how the two works might be connected. Voitolovskaia suggested in 1958 that with "The Inn" Turgenev "wanted to put into practice those aesthetic principles which had been expressed by him in the article on *Notes of an Orenburg-Province Hunter*," but she left it at that.[73] In fact, "The Inn," usually considered a minor tale, has been given relatively scant attention by scholars.[74] In light of the explorations that Turgenev had just undertaken, however, the story can be seen as illustrating his central thesis in the review: that nature somehow builds unity out of each separate organism's relentless pursuit of its own interest.

In "The Inn," an industrious serf, Akim, asks his owner, Madame Kuntse, for permission to build and run a hostel to serve the many travelers who pass by her estate. She agrees, and the enterprise thrives for ten years, but Akim fatefully falls in love with Avdot'ia, a servant girl thirty-six years his junior, who reluctantly marries him. After several years have passed, Avdot'ia, childless and an indifferent wife, has reached her mid-twenties, when she falls passionately in love with twenty-year-old Naum, a workman lodger. After a time, she secretly gives Akim's life savings to Naum, who convinces Kuntse to sell him the inn, which Naum buys with Akim's stolen money. Naum immediately evicts the dumbfounded Akim and then without warning expels the equally distraught Avdot'ia, his own lover. Despondent, Akim gets drunk and is caught by Naum trying to burn down the inn. Naum releases Akim after extracting a promise that he will make no further attempts at revenge. In the end, Avdot'ia is taken back as a lowly servant in Kuntse's household; Akim becomes a pious pilgrim who wanders Russia; and Naum takes his place as the new innkeeper, prospering for years, before he eventually sells the inn and retires in comfort.

In his accustomed fashion, Turgenev sent the manuscript to friends for comment, but first and foremost to the Aksakovs, who loved the tale. Ivan and Konstantin tried to give the story an obviously Slavophile slant, while Sergei, now playing the role of reviewer for Turgenev, offered deeper insight, writing that the story featured "Russian people, the Russian drama of life, drama that is outwardly unattractive—but which makes the soul tremble— that is depicted by Russian talent."[75] In another letter a few days later, Aksakov highly commended the liveliness and realism of both the major and minor characters.[76] Turgenev responded that this praise "simply filled me with pride. 'It stands to reason,' I thought, 'that I did not go astray, if Sergei Timofeevich so correctly understood all that I had intended.'"[77] Aksakov could not refrain from offering specific corrections to Turgenev's language in the first paragraph of the story[78] (typical of his pragmatic approach), but it is possible that his delight with the text also stems from the concrete examples of the abstract concepts Turgenev had discussed in his review of Aksakov's *Notes*. If we see the setting of "The Inn" as an ecosystem, with its characters as animals pursuing their interests, then the tale begins to resemble an episode of natural history—a study in ecological resilience, but with a human and decidedly Turgenevian final twist: the triumphant male predator rejects his mate and never, as far as we know, goes on to reproduce. Naum's animalistic victory is also a sterile one—a biological dead end.

"The Inn" depicts a system that maintains its balance, first with Naum thriving at the apex, and then, in flashback, with Akim at the apex. Turgenev unfurls the plot in a startlingly even-handed way, but the reader soon recognizes Naum as a predator who simply uses Akim as prey, and causes temporary havoc, before a new equilibrium is achieved, now with a new dominant predator prospering. Naum's self-serving behavior seems unconscionable only if we apply the standards of conventional human morality. "The Inn" is an illustration, limiting itself to the human world, of what Turgenev claimed about the natural world: that each organism will "exist exclusively for itself, consider itself the center of the universe, turn to its own advantage everything around it, negate the independence of those surroundings and take possession of them as its own property."[79] This perfectly describes Naum's ruthless appropriation of Akim's wife, money, and territory.

Though rational calculations and careful machinations permeate the tale, they are always presented against a backdrop of natural elements that cannot be premeditated, and it is these elements that furnish the story's dramatic infrastructure: the physical attractiveness or unattractiveness of the characters, their lust, or their addiction to alcohol. Akim's one weakness, we are told, is "the female sex," and this mating instinct inexorably leads to his ruin despite Akim's basic decency.[80] Naum gains the upper hand because he happens to command natural superiority: he outsmarts, out-handsomes, out-sings, and out-woos Akim, patiently, over the course of years. In short, Akim is weak, Naum is strong, and Naum does not hesitate to destroy Akim to attain his aims, both sexual and financial.

As Robert Jackson puts it, "This is a very shocking story."[81] "The Inn" is full of blunt, brutal details and sudden reversals that at first resemble the commonplaces of melodrama but that resonate deeply because they can be seen as the natural actions and conflicts of animals competing for advantage before new equilibrium is reached. The predator Naum is shown to flourish most of all, because of—not in spite of—his shameless actions; the natural triumph of the sinner neutralizes any melodramatic overtones. By the end of the tale, vice is not punished, virtue is not rewarded. If *Notes of a Hunter* was a gallery of provincial behavior in which oppression was exposed and at least implicitly condemned, "The Inn" depicts oppressive behavior that remains uncensured. Nature's impartiality becomes a model for the author's moral impartiality—the withholding of judgment, even in the face of shockingly "evil deeds," finally labeled as such only in the story's last paragraph.[82] The narrator's disinterested depiction of beastly behavior serves as a forerunner of Chekhov's much later approach in such works as "Sleepy" ("Spat' khochet-sia," 1888), "Peasants" ("Muzhiki," 1897), and "In the Ravine" ("V ovrage," 1900). Or, viewed retrospectively, in the ten years since the publication of *Dead Souls*, Naum's plot has evolved from Chichikov's comically clumsy economic swindle to showcase *natural* competition: remorseless, bold, skillful.

Turgenev deftly employs hunting references to intensify the animalistic atmosphere of "The Inn." One of them clearly confirms Newlin's connection of *okhota* to sexual desire.[83] Early on, middle-aged Akim knows that he is no ideal match for Avdot'ia but takes a hunter's pride in having won her: "His love for his good-looking wife did not diminish; he was proud of her, especially when he would compare her—not with the other village women or with his former wife, to whom he'd been married off at sixteen—but with the other house-serfs: 'Look, as they say, what kind of birdie we've bagged!' Her slightest caress afforded him great satisfaction."[84] The term for "bagged" here—*zapolevali*—is pure hunter's jargon. In spite of Akim's prosperity and good character, he is doomed by the superiority of his younger, fitter rival, which Turgenev conveys through another hunting metaphor: "The affairs of Akim and his wife went very well—they lived in harmony and were reputed to be an exemplary couple. But like the squirrel who grooms his nose at the very moment when a shot is aimed at him, a man has no premonition of his misfortune, and things give way beneath him, like ice."[85] Later, when Akim asks the sexton Efrem for more vodka, suggesting a second binge, Turgenev describes the dipsomaniac Efrem's excitement through a hounding figure: "He felt within him at this moment a certain shudder; the same kind of sensation is felt by a hunter when his scent-hound suddenly yaps at the edge of a forest from which he thought all the game had already run off."[86]

Perhaps because Turgenev has created his own human ecosystem in "The Inn," he seems to feel little need for descriptions of the nonhuman environment. Only his account of Avdot'ia's assignation with Naum is an exception, if a modest one:

> Avdot'ia had gone out to meet Naum, who waited for her in the unbroken shadow that fell upon the road from the motionless field of tall hemp. Dew moistened every stem from top to bottom; the scent, stupefyingly strong, suffused everything. The moon had just come up, big

and crimson in the blackish and murky mist. Still at a distance, Naum heard Avdot'ia's rapid footsteps and headed in her direction. She came up to him, all pale from running; the moon shone in her face.[87]

As in the depiction—so prized by Turgenev—of the sea-cliff in *King Lear*, the simple beauty of the natural scene contrasts agonizingly with the schemes of the characters: this is the moment when Advdot'ia ruins Akim by passing his money to Naum. In other passages, more animal metaphors are sprinkled in, heightening the sense that we are observing wildlife: when Naum apprehends would-be arsonist Akim, the two are likened to cat and mouse; Akim is compared to a wolf, however, as he contemplates burning down the inn; and Akim's uncle calls Naum a wolf.[88]

The most important of all such metaphors, though, is given to us right away, in the second paragraph of the story: "[Naum's] absences never lasted long; like a kite, to which, especially in the expression of his eyes, he bore a strong resemblance, he would return to his nest. He knew how to keep that nest in order."[89] This choice of animal identity for Naum succeeds in a number of ways that confirm Turgenev's consummate skill with the lore of the organic world—knowledge worthy of Aksakov. The narrator's reference is to the *korshun*, or black kite (*Milvus migrans*), which is widespread and common in Russia: "Found in a variety of habitats . . . often found near settlements and cities . . . one of the most common and frequently seen raptors . . . nests lined with rags, wool, scraps of paper, and other rubbish . . . searches out prey by soaring at a great altitude for a long time."[90]

Here we readily detect echoes of Naum's adaptability, commonness, thievery, and patience in planning his seizure of the inn. The kite's habit of swooping on small prey, rubbish, and carrion has earned it the British slang name of "shite-hawk."[91] In his dictionary entry on the bird, Vladimir Dal' emphasizes the kite's attacks on defenseless domesticated fowl: "most eagerly [*okhotnee*] of all, it captures young chickens in barnyards."[92] Maksimovich-Ambodik's *Emblems and Symbols* portrays the kite as a frightful counterpoise to the nature goddess's nurturing side: "*Nature* is portrayed in the form of Pan, which means All; or in the form of a woman having many breasts full of milk, with a kite sitting on her arm."[93] Aksakov mentions kites five times in *Notes of an Orenburg-Province Hunter*, three times as attackers of chicks, and twice in passages adjacent to excerpts Turgenev had quoted in his first review of the book.[94]

Turgenev himself inserts kites into his other works as well: in *Smoke* ("Along with the darkness, unbearable misery descended upon [Litvinov] like a kite"), in "An Unfortunate Girl" ("It wasn't fear I felt, or despair, but some kind of senseless surprise. It must be that a captured bird dies that way in the

MILVUS MIGRANS, *Bodd.*

FIGURE 4.1. The black kite (*Milvus migrans*). John Gould, *The Birds of Great Britain*, vol. 1 (London: Taylor and Francis, 1873).

talons of a kite"), and in *Spring Torrents*.[95] In all three of those instances, the bird is put to use as a metaphor, as it is in "Mumu," the only Turgenev work in which a kite appears before "The Inn": "Then Stepan, seizing a suitable moment, suddenly threw himself upon her [Mumu], like a kite onto a chick, pressed her breast to the ground, gathered her up in his arms, and without so much as putting on his cap, ran with her out of the yard, got onto the first carriage that presented itself and set off at a gallop for Hunter's Row."[96] The kite image in "Mumu" is used to underscore the shocking abduction of deaf-mute Gerasim's beloved dog, perpetrated by a peasant, Stepan, who is "a sturdy fellow serving as a footman"—not unlike hale young Naum.[97] Readers otherwise unfamiliar with the kite's nefarious reputation as an attacker of the defenseless might well have remembered its associations from "Mumu," the last story Turgenev had published before "The Inn."

In "An End" ("Une fin," 1883), Turgenev's final work of fiction, the kite plays an overwhelmingly sinister role, suggesting that the dire associations of this avian metaphor had changed little for Turgenev after three decades. Dictated to Pauline Viardot about a fortnight before his death, "An End" harks back to the thematic concerns of *Notes of a Hunter* and "The Inn": a violent, debased landowner, Platon Sergeevich Talagaev, terrorizes his rural neighborhood before he is finally murdered, his mangled body left to freeze in the middle of the road. "Talagaev," we are told, "belonged to an ancient noble family from Tula Province, once very rich, but who, thanks to a few generations of petty tyrants [*samadours*], had fallen into poverty."[98] He first appears outside an inn—*auberge* in Turgenev's original French, but translated as *postoialyi dvor* in both the authoritative modern Russian translation and Dmitrii Grigorovich's 1886 Russian version.[99] Turgenev initially titled the story "Un milan" ("A Kite"), and Talagaev is called "notre oiseau de proie" (our bird of prey) when he first appears in the tale, just outside the inn.[100] Though a far less intelligent and devious person than Naum, Talagaev is a careless hunter, a swindler, a bully, and a sexual predator who apparently abducts and nearly rapes a fifteen-year-old girl. Talagaev unites all the kite's despicable features with the destructive wantonness of gentry *proizvol*, though in the end, unlike the cruel masters in *Notes of a Hunter*, and unlike Naum, he is destroyed by the very people he oppressed. Near the conclusion of "The Inn," Akim looks back on how his rival bested him: "I tried to set fire to the place, but he caught me—Naum did; he is too sharp!"[101] The adjective here, *lovkii*—often rendered in English as agile, deft, nimble, or as crafty, cunning—derives from *lov*, another word for hunting or catching; *lovets*, from the same root, means "hunter." It would be hard to devise a more fitting totem for Naum, or for Talagaev, than the kite. These men are human raptors without remorse.

Unlike Naum, however, Talagaev, a monster created long after the meditations of the Aksakov review, is punished for his rapacity, a relict specimen
of what Turgenev calls, in the tale's opening sentence, a "race of tyrants"
that is "extinct or nearly so in Russia."[102] Such judgment of and retribution
for the destructive effects of natural solipsism point to a heightening of Turgenev's moralistic mood at the end of his life, a mood entirely missing from
"The Inn." If love, which Turgenev had identified in the Aksakov review
("all that lives lives for another"; "[nature's] crown is love")[103] as nature's
paradoxical concomitant to self-interest, is absent in "The Inn," it appears
in his late works through the self-sacrificing behavior of brave parent birds,
as we observed in chapter 3. Though he had expressed fascination with this
phenomenon as early as 1849, in a letter to Pauline Viardot, Turgenev was
drawn to literary explorations of parental heroism starting at the end of the
1870s, with "The Sparrow" and "The Quail."[104] In "The Sparrow," a power
"stronger than his will" had impelled the adult bird from the safety of its high
branch to aid its fallen nestling, and Trésor, the hunting dog, respected that
power and kept away: "Love, I thought, is stronger than death and the fear
of death. Only by it, only through love, is life preserved and advanced."[105]

That Turgenev would immediately—the next day—undertake in "The
Inn" a bleak fictional incarnation of the nature philosophy he had just adum-
brated in the *Orenburg Hunter* review seems to validate Aksakov's assessment that Turgenev was "superstitiously open to impressions of the dark,
enigmatic world of the human soul."[106] Unlike Aksakov, Turgenev was by
temperament unable to divorce observation of the natural world from artistic embodiment of human conflict. He was incapable of leaving his theory
of nature unillustrated by fiction. Aksakov was the inverse: he had initially
gravitated toward ecotropic accounts of the natural world, and then gradually worked his way into fiction during the mid-1850s, but even so, this was
autobiographical fiction, a form Turgenev never fully embraced except in
"First Love" ("Pervaia liubov'," 1860). Turgenev produces human characters
who behave like animals; with Aksakov, the animals behave like humans.

Turgenev's encounter with Aksakov made clear that the two writers
admired and understood one another. It also made clear that they could not,
in the end, emulate one another. The long review of *Orenburg Hunter* made
two basic statements: here is what nature is, and here is how one should
write about it. Turgenev declared that the writer, to achieve venatic equipoise, must undertake the difficult task of "thinking oneself [*vdumat'sia*]
into the phenomena of nature" rather than stay indoors and fall back on
sublime images and clever rhetoric. "Try to understand and express what
takes place within even something as simple as a bird that falls silent just

before the rain," he observes, "and you will see that this is not easy."[107] Aksakov excelled at such tasks because his inclination was to see himself as outside of nature, which allowed him "to peep in" (as Turgenev aptly put it), to
observe his way, rather than think his way, "into the phenomena of nature."
Lacking Turgenev's philosophical vision of "universal life in the midst of
which man himself stands as a living link, higher, but tightly bound to the
other links,"[108] Aksakov emerges as a brilliant documentarian, content to
record, lovingly and honestly, from the outside. Aksakov never did, and never
would, write something like "The Inn," or an allegory like Turgenev's prose
poem "Nature"—such things require a penchant for metaphorical equiva-
lences that ran counter to his creative core. Turgenev, on the other hand, saw
human beings and animals blend and merge along a natural continuum; and
he always pined for an audience with the goddess, was always keenly aware
that he was engulfed in her realm, habitually felt the "thousand unbreakable
threads" that bound him tightly to her.[109]

Involvement with Aksakov in the early 1850s helped illuminate Turgenev's
way forward into large-scale forms. He abandoned the intensive distillation
of Russian rural types and hunting settings, gradually coming to submerge
the thematic complex of hunting literature into his stories and novels. He
likewise shifted from conceiving venatic equipoise solely as a problem of
authorial technique to projecting its dilemmas with greater frequency onto
his fictional characters themselves, to portray their own struggles for natural
balance. From now on, his tendency was to allow *okhota* to permeate his
fiction, but predominantly as implicit subtext rather than explicit setting.
After his Aksakov period, Turgenev continues to think himself into nature,
but, more intensively than ever, thinks nature into his fiction, as a subtle, far-
reaching, multifariously symbolic element shaped by the lore and experience
that he felt hunters possessed in greater abundance than all other observers
of the organic world.

CHAPTER 5

Nature and Nidification

"Journey to the Forest-Belt," Rudin, A Gentry Nest

> There is a great difference between hoping
> and having.
>
> —"The Gun Dog and the Pochard," in *The Book
> of Emblems* (1788)

> Even the sparrow finds a home,
> and the swallow a nest for herself,
> where she may lay her young.
>
> —Psalm 84:3 (NRSV)

While in exile at Spasskoe-Lutovinovo, Turgenev endured a creative drought, and the summer and fall of 1852 were a time of intense self-interrogation. The publication of *Notes of a Hunter* left him restless and seeking new directions. Prevented from further hunting by the early onset of foul weather that autumn, Turgenev put down his gun and returned to literary and critical work, completing the Aksakov review but not the ill-fated novel *Two Generations*: his friends were displeased with the few portions he finished, and he ultimately destroyed the manuscript.[1] Very little of it was drafted when he wrote of his crisis to Konstantin Aksakov in October 1852: "'Why did I publish [*Notes of a Hunter*]?' you ask; in order to escape from it, from that *old way*. Now this burden is cast from my shoulders . . . But whether I have the strength to go forward, as you put it, I don't know. Simplicity, serenity, clarity of line, scrupulousness in my work, that scrupulousness that comes with certainty—all these are, for now, ideals that flicker before me. This is why, by the way, I have not yet completed my novel [*Two Generations*]."[2]

Less than a fortnight later, on his own birthday, Turgenev elaborated, in a letter to his close friend Pavel Annenkov:

I have to walk a different road—I have to find it—and part forever with the old way. I've tried enough to draw the concentrated essences—*triples extraits*—from people's characters in order to pour them into little glass bottles—as if to say, "Take a sniff, dear readers—uncork it and take a sniff—doesn't that smell like a Russian type?" Enough—enough! But here's the question: am I capable of something big, something serene? Will simple, clear lines be given to me . . . This I don't know, and I won't know until I try—but believe me—you'll hear something new from me—or you won't hear anything at all. To that end I'm glad of my winter confinement—I'll have time to pluck up my courage—but most important—in solitude a man stands far away from everything—but especially from literature!—journalistic or otherwise; and something can emerge from me only after the destruction of the *littérateur* within me—but I'm 34 years old—and it's hard to be reborn at that age. Well—we'll see.[3]

Over the three years that followed this aesthetic distress call, Turgenev did indeed find a way to craft larger-scale works with "clarity of line" and in which the "triple extracts" of Russian character types—the metaphorical zoo specimens that delighted Gershenzon[4]—would be moderated and integrated into four extraordinarily successful novels: *Rudin* (1855), *A Gentry Nest* (1858), *On the Eve* (1859), and *Fathers and Children* (1861). To achieve the "serenity" he sought, however, Turgenev had to refashion his literary treatment of the natural world, which soon reshaped his creative encounter with Sergei Aksakov.

After the publication of *Notes of an Orenburg-Province Hunter*, Aksakov enthusiastically sought to enlist Turgenev in further joint ventures. In early March of 1853, Aksakov outlined his plan to edit a hunting journal that would publish nonfiction pieces on various forms of field sport. He invited Turgenev, along with Aleksei Khomiakov and Iurii Samarin, among others, to contribute. At first, Turgenev eagerly accepted: "Your 'Hunter's Miscellany' is a brilliant idea and, I hope, a lucrative one as well. It goes without saying that I am your collaborator and my pen and my name are at your service."[5] It was that same spring, in late May, that Turgenev made the acquaintance of Fet, who would become a cherished hunting companion in both Russia and France over the next decade, as we have seen.

In the end, Aksakov's hunting journal failed to receive publication permission from the censorship, and the other authors, apart from Turgenev, reneged on their promises to contribute. Turgenev himself had long delayed sending his contribution to an increasingly exasperated Aksakov, and what he finally did submit was not, strictly speaking, his own work. Instead, he wrote down, verbatim, Afanasii Alifanov's colorful accounts of capturing nightingales to be sold as cage birds, a profitable pursuit at which the peasant huntsman was particularly adept. His hopes for a sporting periodical now dashed, Aksakov converted the project into a book, a one-volume miscellany, published in 1855, that contained his recent essays on sport as well as only a single work that was not his own: the Turgenev transcription of Alifanov's nightingale narrative. If perhaps not a "triple extract," it is the most unadulterated specimen of peasant discourse Turgenev ever published. Aksakov gave the book a title whose inelegance reflected its troubled publication history but paid tribute to the one collaborator who had not deserted the undertaking: *A Sportsman's Stories and Memoirs on Various Kinds of Sport, with the Appended Article "On Nightingales" by I. S. Turgenev*.[6] The failure of Sergei Aksakov's journalistic enterprise marked the end of serious standalone hunting writing by major Russian authors in the nineteenth century.

What the *Koromyslo* Conveys

Turgenev had originally promised to contribute a second article to Aksakov's hunting miscellany, in addition to "On Nightingales." It was to be an account of how peasants pursued bears that invaded their oat fields in the vicinity of Russia's so-called Forest-Belt (Poles'e).[7] A few months later, however, in July 1853, Turgenev went grouse hunting for two weeks along the River Desna in the Forest-Belt, with a peasant guide named Egor, and the experience radically changed his plan for the story. Unable to adapt his more ambitious conception to the needs of the miscellany, he eventually published it separately, in the October 1857 issue of *Library for Reading*.[8] This final version of the story, which had far outgrown its beginnings as a hunting article, was "A Journey to the Forest-Belt" ("Poezdka v Poles'e"), which offers striking evidence of Turgenev's new method for subsuming natural elements into his fiction.

"Journey to the Forest-Belt," one of Turgenev's most powerful explorations of the human interaction with the natural environment, was a transitional work that looked back at the last-written *Notes of a Hunter* stories and forward to his post-Aksakovian techniques. A bleak response to, in some ways a rejection of, the ecstatic communion with nature experienced by the hunter-narrator in "Forest and Steppe," "Journey" seems to have been conceived in the context of "The Singers."[9] When hunter, manual writer, and publisher Nil Osnovskii brought out the first volume of Turgenev's collected works in 1860, he retroactively inserted "Journey" into *Notes of a Hunter*, immediately preceding "Forest and Steppe." Nonetheless, just as it could not find a home in Aksakov's hunting miscellany, the story somehow did not seem to fit *Notes of a Hunter*, and Turgenev never again allowed it to be included in reprintings of the cycle.[10]

The tale is divided into two chapters: "First Day" and "Second Day." Many concrete details of the kind that fill the hunting memoirs we surveyed in chapter 2 make an appearance. A nameless narrator sets out to hunt capercaillie and hazel grouse in the primeval Forest-Belt near the Reseta River with the peasant guide Egor, a taciturn teetotaler who is "the best hunter in the district" but who is also beset by ill fortune: a sickly wife, dead children, poverty.[11] Oppressed by the enormous, ancient woodland, the narrator plunges into a terrifying meditation on nature's indifference, his own insignificance, and the ephemerality of life. Suddenly, he is rescued from his despondency by Egor, who offers the neurasthenic nobleman the simplest of all refreshments: "Here's water for you . . . drink it in good health [literally, 'with God']."[12] Emotionally refreshed, the narrator falls asleep in a hut, which concludes the First Day. During the Second Day, the hunter-narrator pursues his quarry in a large burned area (gar'), where he runs across the peasant Efrem, a transgressive trickster figure. As sunset approaches, the narrator lies down to rest outside the pine forest, and his gloomy mood of the previous day is relieved. The story, and the Second Day, end with the narrator's admiration for Egor's equanimity, as he observes the peasant's uncomplaining contemplation of his ill fortune. In a March 1857 letter to Annenkov, Turgenev discussed adding a Third Day, a few fragments of which have survived, but this plan was never realized.[13]

In "Journey" we are treated to Turgenev's usual particularity with species—such as the calls of the hoopoe, spotted nutcracker, and Eurasian roller we hear early in the story—but the most remarkable of the tale's ostensibly zootropic moments is a celebrated passage, probably written in 1856 or 1857, in which the narrator, reposing at the end of the Second Day, describes a dragonfly:

I raised my head and saw, on the very end of a slender branch, one of those large flies with an emerald head, long body, and four transparent wings, which the coquettish French call "damsels," while our unsophisticated folk have nicknamed them koromysla. For a long time, more than an hour, I did not take my eyes off her. Baked through by the sun, she did not move, but only turned her head occasionally from side to side and stirred her upraised wings . . . that was all. As I looked at her, it suddenly seemed to me that I understood the life of nature, understood her undeniable and manifest—though, for many, secret—meaning. Quiet and slow animation, deliberateness, restraint of sensations and forces, equilibrium of health in each separate being—this is her very foundation, her immutable law; this is what she stands upon and is supported by. All that diverges from this level—whether upward or downward—is discarded by her as worthless. Many insects die as soon as they know the joys of love, which upset the equilibrium of life; a sick beast hides in a thicket and expires there alone: it's as though he senses that he has already lost his right to see the sun, shared by all, and to breathe the free air. He has lost the right to live. And a person—either through his own fault or the fault of others—who has come to grief in this world must at least know how to be silent.[14]

Here, our narrator sees in nature the balance and quietude for which Turgenev had thirsted in his letter to Annenkov of five years earlier, at the outset of his painful metamorphosis from story writer to novelist. Venatic equipoise now moves in the direction of aesthetic balance, as Robert Louis Jackson asserted: "Nature provides a model for art and the artist precisely in her restraint, her Olympian tranquility and objectivity."[15] For Thomas Newlin, the scene constitutes a special form of environmental contemplation, a "visual extroversion, a sort of two-way osmosis in which [the narrator] is both 'absorbed and absorbing'—and not introversion or romantic *self*-absorption—that leads to a moment of true *in-sight*, to a noetic epiphany that is at once intellectual, spiritual, and bodily."[16] For Jane Costlow, "the contemplative delicacy of this moment is indisputable; it feels as though we have come to a calm, safe harbor after the turbulence of the story's opening and the narrator's second plunge into morose solipsism at the end of the first day . . . What is at stake are the ways in which readers or characters analogize between an aesthetic response . . . and ethics: *Does* nature set humans a rule for life?"[17]

The Soviet editors of Turgenev's complete works recognized long ago that the encounter with the emerald-headed insect recapitulates central themes of the second Aksakov review.[18] Indeed, Turgenev's thinking here is not new, but we have entered a phase in which his *method* of pointing to nature, the emblems he uses to represent the organic world, attain a higher level of ingenuity. More intensively than ever before, Turgenev pours his thoughts, and paradoxical meanings, into carefully selected natural images, ecotropic on their face, such as the appearance of this dragonfly, but which are supported by a complex anthropotropic semantics.

In the case of the *koromyslo* in "Journey," this semantic apparatus, deeply dependent on Russian terminology and cultural practices, is unintelligible in English translation. In Turgenev's time, as it does today, *koromyslo* (plural *koromysla*) had three basic meanings.[19] Turgenev obviously intends the word's entomological sense: dragonflies of the genus *Aeshnidae*, known to the British as hawkers and in the United States as darners. More precisely, the insect Turgenev refers to here must be the female *Aeshna viridis*, or green hawker, which Russians call *koromyslo zelenoe*, the only aeshnid that completely fits the physical description in the story (figure 5.1).

Green hawkers are widespread throughout Eastern Europe and Cis-Ural Russia, including the Forest-Belt region.[20] In its original sense, however, *koromyslo* is the name for the long, usually curved, wooden yoke used for centuries by Russian peasant women to carry two pails of water from the well (or river, or pond) into the house (figure 5.2).[21]

Along with such implements as the scythe, sickle, pail, rake, and harrow, this tool was one of the mainstays of Russian peasant material culture and is a common find in Russian archaeological sites dating back as far as the eleventh century.[22] The ancient device is the source of the insect name: "In Russian, the name *koromyslo* is customarily linked to the way females of this genus bend the abdomen in the shape of a shoulder pole when males approach, if the females are not ready to mate."[23] The third basic meaning of *koromyslo* is the balance beam of a traditional beam scale; the Russian

FIGURE 5.1. *Aeshna viridis*, female. Photograph © Sabine Flechtmann.

FIGURE 5.2.   G. V. Soroka, *View of Lake Moldino (Spasskoe Estate, Tambov Province)* (1840s). By permission of Tver' Oblast' Picture Gallery, Tver'.

name for such a scale is *koromyslovye vesy*. The metaphorical implications of this particular species and its name are striking, especially when we consider that Turgenev could simply have used a vague phrase, such as "green drag-onfly" (*zelenaia strekoza*), or selected one of the many other dragonfly species with suggestively colorful Russian names—grannies (*babki*), grandpas (*dedki*), pretty girls (*krasotki*), rivermen (*rechniki*), arrows (*strelki*), watchmen (*dozorshchiki*), to name only a few.[24]

The *koromyslo*, in its primary sense, was the time-honored means for bringing water, the most precious natural resource, from the exterior—from the natural world the narrator of "Journey to the Forest-Belt" sees as indiffer-ent—to the human-built interior, as in the hut where the narrator wishes to seek shelter from "the cold, indifferent gaze of eternal Isis" described at the start of the tale.[25] Egor, as the bringer of what Costlow calls "living water,"[26] literally performs the redemptive act for which the *koromyslo* dragonfly stands as an emblem. The shoulder pole, with its hooked end, was also employed to lower a pail into the well for the purpose of drawing up water, an act closely paralleled by the narrator's reaction to Egor's bringing him water: "It was as though I had fallen into a dark, unexplored pit where all had grown quiet and the only sound was the soft and ceaseless groan of some eternal sorrow . . . I stopped dead, unable to resist, and suddenly a friendly call reached me, someone's mighty hand drew me out into the light of day [literally 'God's light'] at one stroke."[27] Here, Egor's compassionate hand takes the place of the *koromyslo*'s hook. The insect thus embodies the narrator's acceptance of regeneration, and balance, into the interior of his consciousness. Similarly, at the end of the Second Day, spiritual revitalization comes to the narrator, but this time the blessed revelation occurs while he is alone, observing the natural world in a state of serenity, with a dragonfly playing Egor's role of the day before.

The association of the balance beam with this species neatly echoes the equilibrium our narrator perceives in the way the green hawker is perched at the end of a slender branch, and, more importantly, in the way the shape of its abdomen embodies the balance of nature as a whole. Turgenev's habitual identification of nature as feminine in his writings is accommodated here by the fact that only female green hawkers have the emerald head, and by the association of the Russian shoulder pole almost exclusively with women, normally young women, a tradition that has given rise to such proverbs as, "A woman's wit is like a woman's *koromyslo*: curved, notched, and goes both ways."[28] This may help explain Turgenev's otherwise odd invocation of the French word for damselfly in the passage—he spoke French like a native, and surely he could tell a damselfly from a darner. It is possible that he flouted his usual biological exactitude in order to place side by side the image of a maiden (Russian *devitsa*, French *demoiselle*) and the folkish image of the shoulder yoke (*koromyslo*), that is, to unite the yoke itself with the maiden (*devitsa*) who traditionally carries it. Or perhaps Turgenev simply sought to redouble the earthiness of the Russian colloquialism (*koromyslo*) by juxtaposing it with the "coquettishness" of the personification conveyed by the French usage.

The verdant, feminine incarnation of nature here readily brings to mind the prose poem "Nature," of a quarter-century later: with its dream vision of a green-clad nature goddess who is obsessed with the "balance" (*ravnovesie*) between attack and defense, the central figure resembles a divine, if humanoid, embodiment of the Forest-Belt dragonfly, which, significantly, pays no attention to the human being who studies it so intently. Turgenev's Leopardian nature goddess of 1879, joined with the balance beam (*koromyslo*) in "Journey," conjures up an image of the titaness Themis, personification of justice, holding the scale in her hand. In "Nature," however, the goddess explicitly scoffs at the narrator when he desperately questions her about "justice" (*spravedlivost'*): "What is justice? I gave you life, and I will take it away and give it to others."[29] For Turgenev, nature embodies devotion to an elemental justice that is far more profound and pervasive than petty human preoccupations with fairness. Describing the insect's color as "emerald" (*izumrudnyi*), an adjective that Turgenev used (infrequently) in other works, usually to refer to the color of fresh grass or forest moss, links the peaceful close of the story with its fearsome opening, since the emerald is tradition-ally associated with Isis, "who wore an emerald (or at least some sort of green stone) in her headband, and all who looked upon it were guaranteed a safe trip through the land."[30] The hawker's color near the story's end thus hints at the accomplishment of a safe journey in the Forest-Belt, an emerald talisman against the "cold and indifferent gaze of Isis."

Another of Turgenev's *Poems in Prose* explicitly invokes the *koromyslo* dragonfly, but to depict nature as an aggressive force that intrudes upon the human environment, dealing death and dismay—the antithesis of safe pas-sage. "The Insect" ("Nasekomoe"), written in 1878, a year before "Nature," presents another dream vision, or, in this instance, a nightmare: "The insect resembled a fly or a wasp. Its body was dirty-brown; its flat, rigid wings were of the same color; it had splayed, shaggy claws and a large, angular head, as *koromysla* do; both head and claws were bright red, just as if they were bloody."[31] This creature flies into a roomful of people, who shrink back in disgust, even "terror." A young man approaches the intruder unafraid: "Sud-denly the insect seemed to fix its gaze upon him, flew up, landed on his head, and stung his forehead above the eyes . . . The young man gasped faintly—and fell dead."[32] Here, Turgenev stuns the reader with a menacing, blood-red counterweight to the quiescent green dragonfly in "Journey." The two images are in balance. Together, they illustrate the primordial, merciless "justice" of natural equilibrium.

The lethal blood-red insect retroactively clarifies an essential bond between the narrator and green hawker in "Journey": both are hunters in repose. Unlike the stealthy parasites Turgenev frequently invoked to illus-trate nature's indifference (see appendix 1), the dragonfly is one of the most conspicuous and rapacious of predatory insects. With their "huge eyes that provide an almost spherical view of the world. . . [dragonflies] shoot off in pursuit, scooping up victims with their hairy legs in less than half a second. Dragonflies succeed in catching their prey about 95% of the time."[33] They are among the speediest of all flying insects: one *Aeshna* species was clocked at nearly sixteen miles per hour.[34] In Britain, the ability of aeshnids to hunt on the wing is what earned them the name "hawker," a fourteenth-century usage derived explicitly from the human form of hunting known today as falconry. It is no surprise that Turgenev's avid hunter would fix his attention on this particular insect, which, like him, is a killer at rest. They share the deep need of all predators to gather strength between attacks. The narrator suddenly comprehends, through contemplation of his insect counterpart in this tranquil moment, nature's "quiet and slow animation, deliberateness, restraint of sensations and forces, equilibrium of health in each separate being."[35]

A hunter meditates on a dragonfly. The dramatic moment seems simple, worthy of the "unsophisticated folk" who gave this species its homey nickname. The narrator's description is precise, detailed—seemingly ecotropic. The encounter with the *koromyslo*, however, is alarmingly allusive: Isis, nature, green hawker, balance beam, and hunter are all bound tightly together, their meanings blending and reinforcing one another. "Journey to the Forest-Belt" signals a generic and stylistic transition, as Turgenev comes to favor anthropotropic meanings embedded in putatively ecotropic observations. In the first four novels—the most highly regarded among his works in that genre—this new approach comes to dominate. If we seriously consider literary details of flora and fauna in their venatic context, the subtle but profound implications of Turgenev's descriptive choices can open up long-familiar works to new interpretations. Early critics, such as Schmidt and Arsen'ev, rightly sensed the reliance of Turgenev's depictions of nature on what Richard Freeborn called "the hunter's eye."[36]

Rudin

The first of Turgenev's finished novels, *Rudin* was written entirely at Spasskoe-Lutovinovo, in the space of seven weeks during the summer of 1855, while "Journey to the Forest-Belt" was still evolving.[37] In fact, the first four novels were all written, or at least completed, at Spasskoe. Like the three novels that followed it, *Rudin* is set firmly in the Russian countryside, on rural estates that mirror Turgenev's physical surroundings during the process of composition, and call to mind the settings in *Notes of a Hunter*. Turgenev employs subtle hunting motifs and focuses on arboreal and avian images to advance one of the novel's cardinal themes: how intellect and ideology—the protagonist's supposed strengths—can enfeeble as much as they inspire.

In *Rudin*, the only hunting that takes place is figurative, along the lines of Tennyson's 1847 quip, "Man is the hunter; woman is his game."[38] Near the outset, Konstantin Pandalevskii, a devious minor character, happens upon a young and pretty peasant girl on the roadside, and, with lecherous intent, orders her to pick him some cornflowers—the beautiful emblems of unrequited love, and indifferent nature, in "The Tryst." He is interrupted in this amorous pursuit by his antagonist, Basistov, who appears unexpectedly. "My passion is to enjoy nature," claims Pandalevskii. "We saw how you were enjoying nature," mumbles Basistov in disgust.[39] Dar'ia Mikhailovna Lasunskaia, the pretentious landowner at whose estate most of the action takes place, also professes to be a lover of nature, which gives her new visitor, Dmitrii Nikolaevich Rudin, a chance to demonstrate his powers of observation:

> "Now I understand," began Rudin in a slow voice, "I understand why you come to the country every summer. You need the rest; rural quiet, after life in the capital, refreshes and fortifies you. I am certain that you must deeply sympathize with the beauty of nature."
>
> Dar'ia Mikhailovna looked askance at Rudin.
>
> "Nature . . . yes . . . yes, of course . . . I love it terribly, but you know, Dmitrii Nikolaich, in the country, too, one can't manage without people."[40]

Rudin too will eventually be exposed as a shallow, showy lover of nature, but early in the novel he benefits greatly by contrast with such insincere characters as Pandalevskii and Dar'ia Mikhailovna. Two other inferior characters who precede him in the story bolster his impressiveness when he finally arrives on the scene.

First, Rudin is contrasted with a certain junior chamberlain, of German extraction and baronial rank, author of a recent article on political economy, and reportedly eloquent on the subject of Beethoven. This young man, however, never appears, having been called away to St. Petersburg; in his stead he sends Rudin, an old friend, who kindly brings along a recent article by the baron. This is the happenstance through which Rudin inserts himself into the Lasunskii household and sets in motion the events of the novel. The junior chamberlain's name, mentioned repeatedly in chapters 2 and 3, is Muffel, clearly a hunter's joke: German *Muffel* is an old-fashioned hunting term for the muzzle of a gun, as well as a colloquialism for "grouch." Thus the absent baron is the ill-tempered muzzle that fires Rudin into his new environment, and the novel's feckless hero, perhaps without meaning to, finds a target—young Natal'ia Lasunskaia—with bullet-like speed. The surname Rudin, we should recall, derives from *ruda*, meaning "ore," underscoring the question of whether Dmitrii Nikolaevich will remain in his inert state or be refined into something useful.

Rudin's intellectual primacy is also established by a second character, Afrikan Semenovich Pigasov, a bitter misogynist and failed graduate student, who, Turgenev claimed, was the first personage to occur to him and thereby catalyzed the rest of the novel.[41] Pigasov's idea of evoking the true "voice of nature" (*golos prirody*) is to swat a young lady on the hip from behind with an aspen stake and listen to her yowl of pain;[42] his stream of bilious witticisms pervades the Lasunskii home in the pages preceding Rudin's entrance. To test the new arrival's mettle, Pigasov unwisely chooses to debate him. Calmly, with superior mental dexterity, Rudin humiliates Afrikan Semenovich. Here again, Turgenev is playing with names. *Pigasov* is likely derived from the rarely used Russian forename *Pigasii*, itself derived from *Pegas*, Russian for Pegasus, the winged horse of classical myth—perhaps an ironic jab at Pigasov's decidedly earthbound intellect.[43] An important echo of the surname, however, can be heard in *pigalitsa*, the northern lapwing (*Vanellus vanellus*), a smallish bird well known to hunters for its comically showy crest, shrill call, and habit of feigning a broken wing to draw predators away from its nest. Aksakov's chapter on the lapwing provides details that mesh well with Pigasov's ostentatious volubility. The bird is also known in English as *peewit*, an echoic term derived from its cry; according to Aksakov, Russian peasants interpreted this call as "Ch'i vy? Ch'i vy?"—"Whose are you? Whose are you?"[44] Such interrogation is reminiscent of Pigasov's pert questioning of the newly arrived hero's identity in *Rudin*. Its brashness, however, does not endear the lapwing to hunters, who, Aksakov tells us, call it "The wheel that made the carriage lame, the lowest form of marshland game."[45] According to Aksakov, lapwings also boldly defend their nests by flying at the hunter and dog, but are rarely killed, because hunters simply ignore them. Here again we see an instructive reflection of Pigasov's quixotic sallies and Rudin's initial reluctance to argue. His opponent is thus an irritating hybrid of classical majesty and modern nullity—game normally ignored but then effortlessly dispatched by the wayfaring intellectual.

Rudin's masterstroke during his debut in the novel is, characteristically for him, not something he does, but something he says: a speech at the close of chapter 3 that rises above the usual badinage and captures the imagination of the entire household. This performance of what Turgenev's narrator calls "the music of eloquence"[46]—so superior to the nattering of his lapwing opponent, Pigasov—reaches its climax when Rudin asserts what purports to be the eternal significance of humanity's ephemeral existence, by retelling a "Scandinavian legend":

A king sits with his warriors around the fire in a long, dark hall on a winter's night. Suddenly a small bird flies in through the open doors at one end and flies out through the other doors. The king remarks that this bird is like man in the world: it came in out of the darkness and departed into the darkness, experiencing the warmth and light only briefly. . . "Sire," objects the eldest warrior, "even in the dark the bird will not be lost and will find its nest . . ." Just so: our life is brief and insignificant, but all that is great is accomplished through people. Consciousness of being the instrument of those higher powers should supplant for man all other joys: in death itself will he find his life, his nest.[47]

The effect of this tale on its hearers is dazzling: "Vous êtes un poète," whispers Dar'ia Mikhailovna; Pigasov leaves the house, bested once and for all ("I'll go join the idiots"); Basistov, the children's tutor, stays up all night, writing to a friend in Moscow about Rudin's prowess. Most importantly, young Natal'ia—Dar'ia's daughter and the novel's heroine—is deeply moved, unable to sleep a wink. The chapter's final sentence: "With her head propped on her arm, she gazed fixedly into the darkness; her veins were throbbing feverishly and her bosom often heaved with a deep sigh."[48] The basic framework of the simple plot—a potential romance between Natal'ia and Rudin—is now in place.

Dar'ia Mikhailovna's splendid estate is adorned by "many old linden alleys, golden-dark and fragrant, with emerald gleams at their ends, and many arbors [*besedki*] of acacia and lilac,"[49] an image that reinvigorates the German Romantic cliché of the linden as the tree of love with the richly symbolic color of the dragonfly in "Journey to the Forest-Belt," subtly suggesting an environment where love might be pursued successfully. It is, but not in the Rudin-Natal'ia pairing. Later in the novel, Rudin's old acquaintance, Lezhnev, speaks of how, as a university student in Moscow, under the spell of German philosophy, he habitually hugged a young linden tree in the evening: "It seemed I was embracing the entirety of nature, and my heart would broaden out and grow faint, as if all of nature were actually pouring into it."[50] In the end, it is Lezhnev, not Rudin, who defies the heritage of his name—*lezhnem lezhat'* means to "be a layabout"—and proposes to the widow Aleksandra Pavlovna Lipina, whose surname means "linden" (from Russian *lipa*). In acting decisively on his feelings of love, Lezhnev escapes the paralyzing Romantic intellectualism of his youth and graduates from loving the linden tree to loving the "linden" woman, a tangible, forceful action of the kind that continually eludes Rudin. Lipina's enthusiastic acceptance of Lezhnev serves as a stark contrast to Rudin's abortive attempt to join his life with Natal'ia's.

Turgenev freights Rudin's attachment to Natal'ia with a great deal of cleverly emblematic arboreal imagery, none of which bodes well for their future together. "The self-loving person withers like a lonely, fruitless tree,"[51] declares Rudin, in the bosom of Dar'ia Mikhailovna's country salon, just before Pandalevskii performs Schubert's "Erlkönig" at the piano.

Rudin said nothing and went to the open window. A fragrant mist lay over the garden like a soft shroud; the nearby trees breathed a drowsy freshness. Stars quietly glimmered. The summer night surrendered to bliss and offered bliss. Rudin looked at the darkened garden—and turned around.

"This music and this night," he began to say, "have reminded me of my time as a student in Germany: our gatherings, our serenades . . ."[52]

In Goethe's song text (1782), the desperate father reassures his dying son that the Elf King's promises of bliss are merely the wind sighing "through the dry leaves," and that the Elf King's daughters are shimmering gray willow trees.[53] Rudin's Romantic nostalgia, like the phantom images of nature in Goethe's poem, ultimately offers nothing of substance, no practical form of rescue, to the young woman who strains to analyze his every word.

Natal'ia, entranced with his eloquence over a span of two months, pays careful attention when Rudin invites her to consider an apple tree out the window: "It has broken down," he says, "under the weight and abundance of its own fruit. A true emblem of greatness." The tree is an obvious, self-congratulatory metaphor for Rudin himself, burdened with the unplucked fruit of intellectual superiority and social relevance. Natal'ia's response is to offer herself as an orchard crutch: "It broke down because it didn't have any support," she answers.[54] Rudin continues his parabolic dialogue with Natal'ia by comparing the way new love supplants old love to the way an oak's young foliage breaks through and forces the old leaves to detach and fall. Natal'ia, a woman of action and sincerity, is baffled by the simile and queries him about its meaning the next day. "I was talking about myself, about my past—and about you," he replies, alluding vaguely to a "new feeling" she has awakened in him.[55] Rudin's overdone arboreal figurations and wistful Romantic yearnings create an atmosphere of anthropotropism and egocentrism antithetical to the earnestness of Natal'ia, who, in semiotic terms, cares about the signified, while Rudin is infatuated with the signifier.[56]

Rudin's eventual confession of love occurs in a *besedka*, one of Dar'ia Mikhailovna's arbors. These are outdoor spaces composed of living plants, but shaped and forced by human hands into a decorative semblance of human shelter.[57] The natural tranquility of the earlier Schubert scene returns, but is overshadowed by ominous personification:

At half past nine, Rudin was already in the arbor. Little stars had only just begun to show through the distant and pale depth of the sky; the west was still scarlet—there the horizon too seemed clearer and purer; the half-circle of the moon shone gold through the black mesh of a weeping willow. Other trees either stood like morose giants, with a thousand gleaming points of light that resembled eyes, or they merged into gloomy, solid masses. Not a single leaf stirred; the upper branches of the lilacs and acacias seemed to be listening to something and stretched themselves in the warm air. The house nearby was dark; its long windows were illuminated from without by spots that loomed a reddish color. The evening was gentle and quiet, but there was, it seemed, a restrained, passionate sigh in this silence.[58]

According to Vladimir Dal''s dictionary, *besedka* was also nineteenth-century hunter's jargon for a duck blind or grouse blind, where the hunter could lie in wait as unsuspecting birds arrived, deceived by the camouflage.[59] And indeed, on this night, Rudin musters a hunter's fortitude in finally telling Natal'ia that he loves her. The declaration, however, is observed not only by eavesdropping trees—giants who bode as ill as the Elf King in Goethe's ballad—but also by a human eavesdropper: Pandalevskii, who informs Dar'ia Mikhailovna of Rudin's confession. After this assignation, Rudin is left alone in the moonlight, incredulously and momentarily happy—a hunter who has captured a worthy young woman's heart.

The portentous natural details of the declaration scene reach their culmination less than two days later in an ingeniously designed outdoor setting. Natal'ia herself, desperate to speak to Rudin about her mother's opposition to their match, chooses the meeting place: "Avdiukha's Pond, beyond the oak wood."[60] The site of the old millpond, now breached and dry, was abandoned thirty years before and has been reclaimed by the organic world: the dam is in ruins, overrun with burdock and blackened nettle, the miller's house is gone, and "two enormous pines" where it once stood are the only reminders of human habitation. Rumor has it that a third pine fell during a storm and killed a girl, possibly Avdiukha herself.

> The entire area of the old pond was considered unclean; empty and bare, but remote and somber, even on a sunny day it appeared still gloomier and more remote because of its proximity to a decrepit oak wood, long dead and withered [*zasokhshii*]. Here and there, the gray hulks of huge trees loomed out [*vysilis'*] like mournful apparitions over the low, bushy undergrowth. It was eerie to look upon them: they resembled wicked old men who had gathered to plot something evil. A narrow, barely discernible little road crept along, off to one side. No one passed by Avdiukha's Pond without a special reason.[61]

Unlike his measured, phytotropic approach to describing the burned woodland in "Journey to the Forest-Belt," Turgenev has chosen to personify the dead trees here much as he did the Chaplygino Forest in "Death," from *Notes of a Hunter*: "The lethal, snowless winter of 1840 did not spare my old friends, the oaks and ash-trees; withered [*zasokhshie*], denuded, in places covered with a consumptive-looking green, they loomed out [*vysilis'*] sadly over the young grove which had 'succeeded, but not replaced, them.'"[62] As in "Death," a tree has fallen and killed a human being, but the setting in *Rudin* offers no evidence of renewal, no opportunity for an encomium to Russian stoicism in the face of calamity. Instead, at Avdiukha's Pond, we see oaks that will never have new leaves force out the old. This landscape expresses only loss, gloom, and foreboding, all of which intensify the cowardice of Rudin's decision there to "submit to fate" as he reveals himself to Natal'ia as a "craven man" when faced with her mother's disapproval.[63] "When I told you I loved you, I knew what the word meant," says Natal'ia, who, in parting with Rudin, reaffirms her devotion to the preeminence of meaning— to sincerity.[64] Rudin's hollowness and wasted potential find an effective metaphor in the abandoned dam, and his failure is all the more painful when we recall Aksakov's lengthy and ecstatic description of millponds in *Notes on Fishing* as loci of freedom, serenity, beauty, bountiful catches, and bustling productivity.[65]

In his verbose farewell letter to Natal'ia, Rudin extends the arboreal metaphor he had begun with the apple tree remark: "Nature has given me much . . . All my riches will go for naught; I will never see the fruit of my seed."[66] And yet, in spite of all the tree imagery, Rudin, at a deeper figurative level, is more akin to a tree-dwelling bird who has flown into and out of the Lasunskii household as quickly as the "little bird" of his "Scandinavian legend" passes through the legendary king's feasting hall. Scholars have long understood that Rudin's enigmatic tale is not actually Scandinavian, but an altered excerpt from chapter 13 of Bede's eighth-century *Ecclesiastical History of the English People*. N. L. Brodskii convincingly argues that the "legend" was taken by Turgenev from Sergei Solov'ev's *History of Russia from the Earliest Times* (1854); Solov'ev, in his turn, had obtained the story from Augustin Thierry's *History of the Conquest of England by the Normans* (1825).[67] Both Solov'ev and Thierry quite faithfully reproduce Bede's original version, which I quote here in English translation:

> Another of the king's chief men . . . added, "This is how the present life of man on earth, King, appears to me in comparison with that time which is unknown to us. You are sitting feasting with your ealdormen and thegns in winter time; the fire is burning on the hearth in the middle of the hall and all inside is warm, while outside the wintry storms of rain and snow are raging; and a sparrow flies swiftly through the hall. It

enters in at one door and quickly flies out though the other. For the few moments it is inside, the storm and wintry tempest cannot touch it, but after the briefest moment of calm, it flits from your sight, out of the wintry storm and into it again. So this life of man appears but for a moment; what follows or indeed what went before, we know not at all."[68]

Rudin's version follows Bede's original—as well as Solov'ev's and Thierry's adaptation—relatively closely, but Turgenev manufactures a telling natural detail not present in any of these prototypes: the nest. Rudin has the wise old warrior stress that the "little bird" will not lose her way, but find her *nest*, and that death furnishes the final nesting place for human beings.

Rudin's own birdlike character is amply confirmed elsewhere in the text by Lezhnev, the person who has known him longest. He describes Rudin in his youth as having "fledged," as an intrusive "swallow over a pond," and angrily threatens to "shoot him like a partridge."[69] In the epilogue, set in a provincial hotel several years after the Lasunskii debacle, Rudin seems to destroy his avian identity when he confesses to Lezhnev, "How many times have I flown out like a falcon—and returned crawling, like a snail with a crushed shell!"[70] At novel's end, Lezhnev—who finally achieves an agreeable balance between Rudin's Hamletism and the Quixotism of Natal'ia's successful suitor, Sergei Volyntsev—humanely and hospitably revives the bird metaphor when he offers Rudin friendly sanctuary: "Remember: whatever happens to you, you always have a place, a *nest*, where you can find shelter. That's my home . . . do you hear, old man? Philosophy also has its veterans: they need to have a refuge too."[71]

A Gentry Nest

Turgenev's insertion, through Rudin, of nest images into Bede's tale, and the final mention of nest as refuge, reinforce Rudin's superfluity in a typically Turgenevian way: nidification, of which Rudin is incapable, is one of the author's most persistent themes. Mikhail Alekseev called Turgenev's obsession with nests a "fixed formula" in his letters,[72] and the same can be said of the stories, plays, and novels. Regardless of the language he was using, the nest—*gnezdo* or *gnezdyshko* in Russian, *nid* in French, *Nest* in German—appears with such extraordinary frequency that Russian critics have in recent years profitably analyzed Turgenev's work in terms of "nest vs. nestlessness" and "nest vs. abyss."[73]

First appearing in his poetry as early as 1844, nests are mentioned in nearly thirty of his works, including all the novels except *Smoke*, and virtually always as a metaphor for human habitation rather than in the literal sense. The earliest use of "nest" in his extant correspondence occurs in a letter to Pauline Viardot in August 1850, after which it becomes a commonplace, cropping up dozens of times, frequently as a synonym for home, apartment, estate, or manor house, often for Spasskoe itself, especially from the late 1850s on, then Baden-Baden in the 1860s, then Bougival in the late 1870s. Turgenev customarily uses the word in the first paragraph of his letters, discussing his own whereabouts and the whereabouts of his correspondent, regularly embedded in the expression "to weave one's nest" or "build one's nest" (svit'/ustroit' sebe gnezdo), or "on the edge of another's nest" (na kraiushke chuzhogo gnezda).[74]

Hunters are never entirely at home in the natural world: in the most immediate sense, they are there to kill, to erase something from the environment. This is especially true of the gentleman hunter, who is not seeking sustenance. The feeling of being submerged in nature while always being, at least in some measure, an alien, may help account for Turgenev's sense of strangerhood and lack of a "nest" in all his work. It also helps explain his admiration for peasant hunters, who, like animals, kill in order to keep themselves alive.

Some of the connotations Turgenev attached to the concept of nesting emerge most clearly in connection with members of the Tolstoy family. From Paris in 1856, he wrote to Lev Tolstoy's sister, Mariia, "You see, it was painful for me to grow old without having known complete happiness, without having woven myself a tranquil nest."[75] In 1864, Vasilii Botkin wrote to Turgenev of Lev Tolstoy's improved character ("Marriage has greatly changed him for the better; he's become calmer and his angularities are almost gone; you sense that he has found a nest and settled down"), to which Turgenev replied, "Speaking of nests, I was delighted with what you wrote about Tolstoy: I take a lively interest in this remarkable man, even though I can't bear to be in the same room with him."[76] Haunted to the end by his own inability to find a spouse and succeed at traditional family life, Turgenev wrote a despondent poem-in-prose called "Nestless" ("Bez gnezda") in January 1878:

Where shall I go? What can I undertake? I'm like a solitary bird without a nest . . . Her feathers ruffled up, she sits on a bare, dry branch. To stay is sickening . . . but whither to fly?

And there she spreads her wings—and hurls herself into the distance headlong and straight, like a dove frightened by a hawk. Won't some green, sheltered nook open up before her? Will it be impossible for her to weave even a temporary nest somewhere? . . .

The poor bird is weary . . . Her wingbeats grow weak; her flight dips. She wishes she could soar heavenward . . . but it's impossible to weave a nest in that endless emptiness! . . .

At last she folds her wings . . . With outstretched body she has fallen into the sea.

A wave has swallowed her up . . . and it rolls on, senselessly roaring as before.

Where shall I go? And isn't it time for me to fall into the sea?[77]

The impossibility of finding a nest in the heavens, perhaps a gesture toward the futility he perceived in seeking religious solace or notions of an afterlife, leads the narrator of "Nestless"—with his own contemplation of a fatal plunge into the indifferent sea—to echo Rudin's embellishment of the "Scandinavian legend": "in death itself will man find his nest."

As a hunter, Turgenev understood well that the nest's primary purpose was to shelter helpless offspring, not adults, as he stressed in another letter to Tolstaia: "To have one's nest—to live for the children—what can be better on this earth!"[78] In his hunting treatise, Aksakov provides numerous examples of how adult game birds—especially the females—boldly and self-sacrificially defend their young at the nest: redshank (*travnik*), marsh sandpiper (*porucheinik*), lapwing (*pigalitsa*), duck (*utka*), curlew (*kronshnep*), plover (*krechetka*), quail (*perepel*), and black grouse (*teterev*).[79] Aksakov ashamedly confesses that, in his youth, he took advantage of parent birds when he slaughtered common snipe (*bekas*) at their nest sites, also a customary practice at the nesting colonies of black-tailed godwit (*veretennik*) that resulted "in a marsh that hours before teemed with noisy bird life and rang with their bright calls being turned into a still and lifeless place."[80] Turgenev himself, at the conclusion of his semiautobiographical children's story "The Quail," expresses compunction at exploiting the parental instincts of his quarry at the nest.[81] Such examples confirm the hunter's clear perception that, in the natural world, perpetuation of the family supersedes survival of the individual. Like Aksakov a regular firsthand witness to such behavior, Turgenev believed it to offer a moral example, which he chose to honor, in such late works as "The Sparrow" and "The Quail."

Nonetheless, "nest" infrequently appears in Turgenev's work as a place for raising children. Instead, it is most often synonymous with a refuge or home for adults, typically adults of noble birth. It was in *Notes of a Hunter* that he first used the phrase "gentry nest" (*dvorianskoe gnezdo*), for the story "My Neighbor Radilov," in early 1847: "Our forefathers, in choosing a place to live, invariably set aside about five acres of good land for an orchard with linden alleys. After fifty years or so, seventy at the most, these estates, 'gentry nests,' gradually disappeared from the face of the earth, the houses decayed or were sold for salvage, the stone service-buildings turned into heaps of rubble, the apple trees died out or went for firewood, and the walls and wattle fences were destroyed."[82] The association of these "nests" of noble families with abandonment and emptiness actually begins in two poems written three years earlier ("the long-empty and abandoned nest") and is continued in *Notes of a Hunter*, after "My Neighbor Radilov," in "Raspberry Water" ("the masters moved to another nest; the estate fell into neglect") and "Chertopkhanov and Nedopiuskin" ("[Chertopkhanov's father] . . . finally sold the last ancestral nest").[83]

These elegiac undertones are inseparable from the title of Turgenev's second novel, *A Gentry Nest* (*Dvorianskoe gnezdo*, 1858), in which abandoned country estates play a conspicuous role. Mar'ia Dmitrievna Kalitina, mother of the nineteen-year-old heroine, Liza, had to quit her ancestral village of Pokrovskoe to live with her husband in the town of O——: "Mar'ia Dmitrievna often missed her pretty Pokrovskoe with its merry stream, broad fields and green groves."[84] After he is betrayed by his wife, Varvara Pavlovna, the hero, Fedor Ivanovich Lavretskii, refuses to live at Lavriki ("Little Laurels"), his family's main estate, choosing instead to inhabit empty and disused Vasil'evskoe. Lavretskii, like so many of Turgenev's heroes and heroines— among them Chulkaturin in *Diary of a Superfluous Man*, Elena Stakhova in *On the Eve*, Evgenii Bazarov in *Fathers and Children*, Dmitrii Sanin in *Spring Torrents*, Litvinov in *Smoke*—is destined to experience what Bede calls "the briefest moment of calm" before returning to nestlessness. When, in the early days of their marriage, Varvara Pavlovna craftily expels Lavretskii's aunt Glafira Petrovna from Lavriki, Glafira prophetically declares, "I know who's driving me out of here, out of my own family nest. Just mark my words, nephew: nowhere will you be able to weave your own nest; you will wander forever."[85]

Instead of serving as a paragon of maternal defense of her offspring, the sensualist Varvara, not unlike Naum in "The Inn," enacts nature's merciless displacement of the old by the young. An expert builder and abandoner of nests, she begins at Lavriki by surrounding herself with splendid creature comforts, then repeats the process in St. Petersburg, then France: "In Paris, Varvara Pavlovna bloomed like a rose and wove a little nest [*gnezdyshko*] for herself there just as quickly and deftly as she had in Petersburg."[86] In avian fashion, she exhibits a regular migration pattern: Lavriki to St. Petersburg to Paris early in the novel, then Paris to St. Petersburg and back to Lavriki by the end. After returning to Lavretskii's nest, Varvara performs a Rossini duet with Panshin, which disgusts Liza's great-aunt, Marfa Timofeevna: "And all in Italian, 'chi-chi' and 'cha-cha,' like real magpies."[87] Marfa, whom Costlow calls "the voice of truth" in *A Gentry Nest*,[88] enunciates here a deeply significant simile for Varvara. Reflecting the magpie's beautiful black, white, and iridescent plumage, Varvara, when she returns to beg Lavretskii's forgiveness of her adultery, is "in a black silk dress with flounces [*volany* < Fr. *volant*, flying]," carefully coiffed, perfumed, and made up: "her entire figure, from her shiny hair to the tip of her barely displayed shoe, was so elegant."[89]

Russian culture boasts a rich trove of magpie lore. In his classic collection of Russian sayings, Dal', for example, lists nearly fifty on the magpie (*soroka*), largely devoted to its showiness, noisiness, cunning, selfishness, and thievery, including "No magpie soils its own nest," and "The magpie herself will tell where she wove her nest."[90] Writing in the mid-1840s, Dal' discusses folk beliefs regarding the traditional enmity between the magpie, who is often viewed as a witch in disguise, and the house spirit (*domovoi*), and suggests that the magpie is considered an ill-omened bird because it is "semi-predatory, greedy for carrion, intolerably flashy, and prophetic."[91] Marfa Timofeevna, aligned with the Slavophile axis in the novel, carries with her this folk wisdom and intuitively senses the magpie in Varvara. On the other hand, Mar'ia Dmitrievna, "the voice of hypocrisy,"[92] infatuated with Westernism, is taken in by Varvara's Parisian finery and expertly executed Western music, just as she is by Panshin: "'Quite as in the best Paris salon,' thought Mar'ia Dmitrievna, listening to their duplicitous and fidgety speeches."[93]

Varvara and Panshin's Rossini duet, "Serenata," eleventh of the composer's twelve *Soirées musicales* (1830–35), was scored for soprano and tenor. It is a setting of Carlo Pepoli's "Mira la bianca luna" (See the pale moon), in which two lovers watch the moon become obscured by clouds and seize the opportunity for a secret nocturnal tryst in the woods, an echo of the audaciously ungrateful way Varvara and Panshin insult Mar'ia and flirt, barely hiding their faces behind the music book. Taken together with Marfa's magpie reference, the duet invokes Rossini's *La gazza ladra* (*The Thieving Magpie*, 1817), in which an honest young woman, Ninetta, is nearly hanged for theft thanks to a magpie who steals valuable cutlery from the household where she works. Turgenev knew this opera well, expressing his admiration for it in a letter to one of the nineteenth century's most celebrated Ninettas, Pauline Viardot herself, just after she had finished her Italian seasons in St. Petersburg, and discussing *La gazza ladra* in an anonymous article published, like "Khor' and Kalinych," in the first issue of the *Contemporary* in 1847.[94] Russians, like West Europeans, subscribed to the now-discredited belief that magpies habitually steal shiny objects: "The magpie loves a find (i.e. she's a thief)," as Dal' recorded it.[95] Varvara Pavlovna, with her yen for expensive accoutrements to feather her nest, on one level, and, on another, with her ominous reappearance and theft of Lavretskii's happiness, behaves like a thieving magpie.[96] The link between Ninetta and Liza is also worth considering: unlike in Rossini's opera, in which Ninetta is saved from the scaffold when the magpie returns and is unmasked as a thief, the return of Varvara Pavlovna, in which she cunningly conceals her base motives, results only in Liza's misery and permanent break with Lavretskii. *A Gentry Nest* is Russian tragedy, not *opera semiseria*.

Varvara, however, is more than a magpie. Her selfish acquisitiveness has consequences so dire that they move her, on Turgenev's metaphorical plane, from "semi-predatory" to predatory, as we see in Lavretskii's torment when he discovers her adultery: "Then suddenly it seemed that everything happening to him was a dream, and not even a dream, but, yes, some kind of absurdity; that it simply called for shaking oneself off and looking around . . . He did look around and, like a hawk clawing a captured bird, misery was cutting deeper and deeper into his heart. To cap it all off, Lavretskii was hoping to become a father in a few months . . . The past, the future, and his entire life were poisoned."[97] To fall prey to another person's ruthless indulgence of self-interest is to witness firsthand—to participate in—the painful paradox of natural solipsism and love Turgenev had enunciated in his second Aksakov review; it is to be crushed in the raptor's talons without hope of escape.

We find a ready parallel a dozen years later in the agony caused by the ruthless seductress Mar'ia Nikolaevna Polozova in *Spring Torrents* (*Veshnie vody*, 1870–71) as she draws naïve, good-hearted Dmitrii Sanin into infidelity and slavish devotion:

> The gray, predatory eyes, those dimples on the cheeks, those snake-like tresses—could it really be that all of this had attached itself to him, and that he lacked the strength or ability to shake it all off or toss it aside? . . . What a face! It was entirely exposed: exposed, greedy, bright, wild; lips and nostrils, also exposed, which breathed greedily; she gazed straight ahead of herself, as if this soul desired to possess all that it perceived—earth, sky, sun, and the very air . . . She slowly ran her fingers through his obedient hair, drew herself up, with triumph curling her lips—and her eyes, wide and bright, almost white, expressed only the pitiless vacancy and satiety of victory. Such are the eyes of a hawk who claws a captured bird.[98]

Varvara Pavlovna and Mar'ia Nikolaevna embody the same kite-like behavior displayed by Talagaev in "An End" and Naum in "The Inn." When he mercilessly exploits and destroys his rival's wife, Naum calmly informs her of what amounts to the predator's creed: "Please don't be alarmed, Avdot'ia Aref'evna . . . I'll tell you this one thing: people look out for their own interests [*svoia rubashka k telu blizhe*]; but then, that's why the pike's in the sea, Avdot'ia Aref'evna: to keep the crucian carp alert."[99] In an act of authorial empathy akin to his technique in such late works as "The Partridges," Turgenev powerfully employs aerial and aquatic predators to convey the sensation of being utterly dominated by someone who will show no mercy. With a hunter's expertise, he portrays in human interactions both the predator's pleasure and the desperation of its prey. In *Spring Torrents*, Turgenev describes that pleasure in terms that take us back to the gentry *proizvol* he documented in *Notes of a Hunter*: "Mar'ia Nikolaevna looked upon [Sanin] and grinned that grin already familiar to him as an enserfed man—the grin of the proprietor, of the sovereign."[100] Turgenev's narrator gives a similar account of Litvinov, the hapless hero of *Smoke*, once his love for Irina Ratmirova is rekindled: "Since the day before, here, in this room, Irina had reigned [*tsarstvovala*]; everything spoke of her—the very air, it seemed, preserved the secret traces of her visit . . . Litvinov again felt himself to be her slave."[101] And at the end of *A Gentry Nest*, the same fate awaits Panshin: "Varvara Pavlovna had enslaved [*porabotila*] him, literally enslaved him: no other word can possibly express her limitless, irrevocable, unreciprocated power over him."[102]

Varvara, Panshin, and Mar'ia Dmitrievna—the predator and her accessories—are the chief representatives of Westernism in the novel, while Liza, Lavretskii, and Marfa Timofeevna—the prey—generally exemplify the patriotic, nature-loving values of the Slavophiles. Turgenev later expressed consternation at having validated an ideology that ran counter to his personal Westernist convictions,[103] but the moral superiority of the Lavretskii bloc, perhaps in part derived from Turgenev's respect for the Aksakov family, shines out through representations of the natural world in *A Gentry Nest*, often through musical associations.

Panshin's art song, composed to his own words ("The moon sails high above the earth"), is a labored expression of lovelorn longing in which the moon represents his unfeeling beloved, while the sea represents his soul, responding to lunar forces that compel the tides.[104] These words near the beginning of the novel seem directly connected to the moon imagery in the nauseous Rossini duet Panshin will sing with Varvara Pavlovna near the end of the novel. In chapter 22, a few days after Panshin's performance of "The moon sails high," Lavretskii and the German composer Lemm discuss creating their own song. Lemm, now thinking deeply about his own hopeless love for Liza, proposes lyrics along the lines of "O, you pure stars! . . . You gaze upon the righteous and the guilty alike . . . but only the innocent at heart love you . . . And you too know who loves, who is capable of loving, because you alone, pure stars, can give consolation."[105] The simplicity of Lemm's halting lyrics, and their ties to the fidelity and subtler light of the stars rather than Panshin's inconstant moon, mingle in Lavretskii's mind with the natural music of the night when he arrives home before sunrise:

> He returned to his study and sat down before the window. In the garden a nightingale sang his final, pre-dawn song. Lavretskii recalled that at the Kalitins' a nightingale had been singing in the garden; he also recalled the quiet movement of Liza's eyes when, at the bird's first sounds, they had turned toward the dark window. He started thinking about her, and his heart grew calm within him. "Pure girl," he said in an undertone, "—pure stars," he added with a smile, and peacefully lay down to sleep.[106]

A few days later, when Liza performs Lemm's setting of the star text, however, his music is a failure, no match for the power of the evocative and consoling nightingale in Lavretskii's, or the Kalitins', garden. Lavretskii and Liza are now liberated to speak sincerely about their feelings and questions of deep spiritual import, all against the wholesome backdrop of a family fishing trip for crucian carp and stone loach on a summer day—an idyll worthy of Aksakov himself.

Emotionally cleansed by his honest interaction with Liza and the natural environment, in chapter 27 Lavretskii is granted another moment of tranquil contact with nature as he rides home:

> The charm of the summer night took hold of him. The surroundings seemed suddenly so strange and at the same time so long familiar, sweetly familiar. Nearby and far away—he could see far into the distance, though his eyes could not make out much of what he saw—everything lay in repose; young, blossoming life proclaimed itself in this same repose. . . . There was something mystically pleasing in the clop-clop of [his horse's] hooves, something merry and wondrous in the ringing cry of the quail. The stars were disappearing in a kind of luminous mist. The moon, not yet full, shone with a hard luster; its light poured forth in a light-blue stream along the sky and fell as a patch of smoky gold on the delicate little clouds passing close by. The freshness of the air produced a gentle moisture on his eyes, tenderly embraced all his limbs, and freely streamed into his breast.[107]

This is an extension of the earlier moment (chapter 20) in which the narrator describes the "peaceful torpor" that Lavretskii, newly arrived in the country, experiences as he immerses himself in his rural environment as though he were "at the bottom of a river."[108] Newlin sees that justly celebrated river-bottom passage as part of a larger and newly emergent environmental consciousness in Russia, while Costlow aptly describes it as "a symbolic return to the womb of nature, Lavretsky's spiritual rebirth in the motherland."[109] If chapter 20 serves as a metaphorical baptism, then chapter 27, with the liquefied evening air flowing into Lavretskii's body, is a metaphorical communion, a merging of Lavretskii with the natural environment and the congregation of his fellow Russians, including, especially, devout Liza Kalitina.

Beyond the connections it establishes between certain individuals, communion with nature in *A Gentry Nest* aligns characters with what emerges as the morally superior Slavophile element. We must not forget how Lavretskii's sacramental bottom-of-the-river reverie concludes: "strangely, never before had he experienced such a profound and powerful feeling for his homeland [*chuvstvo rodiny*]."[110] Thus when Panshin pompously asserts his Westernizing critique of Russian society in chapter 33, nature's denizens unite with Lavretskii to confute these insults to the homeland:

> Panshin walked about the room and spoke eloquently, but with secret exasperation: it seemed that he was rebuking not an entire generation, but a few personal acquaintances. In the Kalitins' garden, in a large lilac bush, lived a nightingale; his first evening calls resounded during the intervals in [Panshin's] eloquent speech. The first stars came out in the rosy sky above the motionless tops of the linden trees. Lavretskii stood up and started disagreeing with Panshin; a debate began . . . Lavretskii did not become angry, did not raise his voice . . . and he calmly crushed Panshin on every point.[111]

Here, heavens, flora, and (musical) fauna join forces to defend love between true hearts and love of country. In *A Gentry Nest*, communion with nature bestows the blessing of patriotic certainty.

And yet, like the soothing refuge of patriotism itself, the scene is too good to be true, too reassuring to last. While its ostensibly beautiful natural components—lilac, nightingale, stars, lindens, and rose-colored sky—are far less troubling than the imagery connected to Western-oriented Varvara Pavlovna, they nonetheless have ominous connotations. The traditional Persian symbolism of the uncomprehending nightingale and deaf rose, made famous in Russia by Pushkin and Kol'tsov in the 1820s and 1830s, hints that love will be frustrated.[112] The sickly scent of the fast-fading lilac, the unbridgeable distance to the stars, and the Romantic platitude of the linden tree as a lovers' haven are similarly unsettling.[113] These figures have occurred often enough in the text that by now they begin to resemble metaphors whose fixed meanings are perhaps too facile to carry authentic meaning or too brittle to escape shattering. Other totemic images in the novel—Gedeonovskii as a stork, Lemm as an owl, Petr Andreevich Lavretskii as a hawk, Malan'ia Sergeevna as an uprooted sapling, Lavretskii as a steppe marmot (*baibak*), Zakudalo-Skubyrnikov as "le gros taureau de l'Ukraïne," to name a few—are so conspicuous and opportune that they begin to resemble entries in some inscrutable emblem book.[114]

It is perhaps no accident, then, that Turgenev prominently inserts Nestor Maksimovich-Ambodik's *Emblems and Symbols*, which we briefly explored in chapter 1, into *A Gentry Nest*. Chapter 11 of the novel relates how Fedor Lavretskii steeped himself (as did young Turgenev) in allegorical images from Ambodik's compendium, starting at around eight years of age: "Fedia would scrutinize these drawings; they were all familiar to him, down to the smallest details; some, always the same ones, made him fall into deep thought and awakened his imagination; he had no other entertainment . . . He used to sit in a nook with his *Emblems*—and sit, and sit."[115] Upon returning to his estate and settling at Vasil'evskoe as a disillusioned adult, "Lavretskii found several old calendars, dream-interpretation books, and the mysterious work of Mr. Ambodik; the long-forgotten but familiar *Emblems and Symbols* awakened in him many recollections."[116]

The idyllic natural elements associated with Lavretskii and the Slavophile cause can appear distressingly conventional or false when viewed through Ambodik: "The Nightingale and Her Nestlings," emblem no. 302, teaches us that "Our parents are our best masters" (in English), or, in Russian, "Parental teaching is best" and "Fathers are children's best teachers"—all notions called into question by the lengthy, often painful dossier passages on Lavretskii's family background.[117] Liza, associated with the stars, has both her piety and unattainability confirmed in "The Star, Ship, and Compass" (emblem no. 129): "unmovable to an unmovable godhead." The laurel tree (*lavr*), etymon for the family name *Lavretskii*, supplies similarly ominous mottoes. "Laurel" (emblem no. 169) seems to mock Lavretskii's inability to punish Varvara Pavlovna: "I will hurt him that hurts me." Another "Laurel" emblem (no. 805) prophesies his stagnation ("Always the same"), as does the interpretation of emblem no. 328, "Little Laurel Tree" ("Lavrovoe drevtso"): "I change only when dying."[118] The onomastic prominence of the laurel, associated in classical antiquity with fame and victory, is intensely ironic, a mockery of the hero's profound frustration in *A Gentry Nest*. His true motto—the motto of a great many Turgenev protagonists—is better summed up by Lavretskii himself: "I saw close by, and almost held in my hands, the possibility of life-long happiness—but it suddenly vanished. So it is in the lottery, too: turn the wheel a bit more and the beggar, perhaps, would become a rich man."[119]

Lavretskii's early exposure to and adult fascination with Ambodik's styl-ized distortions of nature stand in stark contrast to his participatory percep-tion of the natural world from "the bottom of the river" and to his com-munion with nature on a blissful summer night. These authentic natural encounters have a direct counterpart in the all-encompassing aesthetic rap-ture that Lemm's piano masterpiece offers to Lavretskii on the evening he and Liza acknowledge their mutual love:

> Suddenly it seemed to him [Lavretskii] that some sort of marvelous, triumphant sounds were flooding the air above his head. He stopped: the sounds started to thunder even more magnificently; they flowed in a strong and songful stream—and in them, it seemed, his happiness spoke and sang . . . the sweet, passionate melody seized one's heart from the very first note. It all shined, all pined for inspiration, happi-ness, beauty; it grew and melted; it touched all that is dear, secret and sacred on this earth; it breathed unending sorrow and went off to die in the heavens. Lavretskii drew himself up and stood, frozen and pale with ecstasy. These sounds seemed to sink into his soul, which had only just been stirred by the happiness of love, and the sounds themselves glowed with love.[120]

Turgenev's vision is far more expansive than mere Slavophile communion with nature and tradition: great art, even when embodied in a decidedly Western form, created by a Western artist like Lemm, clarifies and amplifies Lavretskii's awareness of his rapturous emotional state. East and West, Rus-sian and German, Lavretskii and Lemm, are united at the deepest level, if only fleetingly, before Liza is put out of reach. In A Gentry Nest, these moments of "affective awareness" (to use Richard Gustafson's phrase),[121] when a person is steeped in nature, art, or requited love, are perhaps the best these characters' lives can offer, because they are endlessly menaced by predators who enact the processes of indifferent nature. In her wisdom, Marfa Timofeevna knows this, and tells Lavretskii, near the end of the novel: "Oh, my dear man, it's hard for you, I know, but no one has an easy time of it. I used to envy flies: there, I thought, was somebody who had it good in this world. But one time, at night, I heard a fly whimpering in the clutches of a spider. 'No,' I thought, 'they live under threat too. What's to be done, Fedia.'"[122]

Nature's role as an instructor for characters and readers who seek to achieve balance and find true shelter—metaphorically or otherwise—dominated Turgenev's attention in his major works of the mid- to late 1850s. Human relationships, coaxed and frustrated by the same natural forces and images that characterize an organic world of serenity, somehow fail to attain that serenity in his post-Aksakov period. Over the next few years, as he entered a phase in which he would create his most powerful fictions, Turgenev scaled back the use of explicit hunting images but continued to explore debates about the role of nature, never losing sight of the ideals of the *koromyslo*, the nest, and requited love. Yet even as he attenuated the hunting motifs in his work, Turgenev, now distanced from the master of Russian ecotropism, found a new purchase on Aksakov's fundamental observations and exploited them with subtle ingenuity for the works that culminated in *Fathers and Children*.

CHAPTER 6

Life at the Lek

On the Eve, *"First Love,"* Fathers and Children

> For no one can anticipate the time of disaster. Like fish taken in a cruel net, and like birds caught in a snare, so mortals are snared at a time of calamity, when it suddenly falls upon them.
>
> —Ecclesiastes 9:12 (NRSV)

> With quickfaring leap of the hoof [Actaeon] ran through the unfriendly forest, a hunter in terror of hunters. But in this new shape his dogs no longer knew their former master. . . . Deceived by the false appearance of a stag they devoured the dappled changeling body in senseless fury.
>
> —Nonnos, *Dionysiaca*, book 5

Of all the birds and beasts Turgenev hunted over five decades, his favorite quarry was the black grouse (*Lyrurus tetrix*): *Birkhuhn* (birch fowl) in German, *coq de bruyère* (heather cock) in French, *fagiano di monte* (mountain pheasant) in Italian, and *teterev* in Russian. Wily forest dwellers, black grouse fly rapidly and take off explosively—Turgenev spoke of their "thundering" up from the ground.[1] We know of his devotion to the bird from numerous sources, including letters, such as those he wrote to Fet, some of which we reviewed in chapter 2. His correspondence with Sergei Aksakov lays out specifics: for example, Turgenev personally bagged thirty-three black grouse in 1852, while he and his companions killed ninety-three during only four days of shooting in Zhizdra Province in 1856.[2]

In his fiction, Turgenev at times mentions black grouse in metaphorical contexts: the bird's mating vocalizations (*tokovan'e*) stand for indistinct human speech, as in both *A Gentry Nest* and *Virgin Soil*.[3] The species also appears prominently in nine of the *Notes of a Hunter* sketches for a variety of reasons: as a sign of environmental health and a luxurious gentry pursuit ("Khor' and Kalinych"); a relatively easy quarry for Ermolai ("Ermolai and the Miller's Wife"); and one of the most frequent enticements for the narrator to embark on hunting trips.[4]

Turgenev particularly savored Aksakov's commentary on black grouse. The penultimate passage in his first Aksakov review is a long excerpt from Aksakov's description of the bird's mating habits, and in the second review, Turgenev used the bird to pay Aksakov a glowing compliment: "If a black grouse could talk about himself, he would, I am sure, add not a word to what Mr. Aksakov has related about him."[5] In fact, the longest, most richly detailed chapter of Aksakov's *Orenburg-Province Hunter* is devoted to this species. Among many other things, we learn that though partridge are very hard to kill, only black grouse are tougher.[6] In the murmuring courtship call of the males, Aksakov asserts that "there is nothing pleasing to the ear about the notes themselves, yet in them one subconsciously senses and understands the harmony of life in nature as a whole."[7]

For Aksakov, the most noteworthy aspect of this polygamous species' behavior was its elaborate, flirtatious mating ritual, which takes place in the springtime:

> The males gather at a chosen site suitable for the deeds of heroism to be performed. This may be a clearing [*poliana*] in the forest, or a meadow on the edge of a wood or among trees on otherwise open ground, usually on higher ground. This site, unchanging, and regularly frequented, is known as a lek [*tok, ili tokovishche*]. Determined human efforts are required to compel the grouse to leave it and choose another . . . The blackcock sit on the upper branches, ceaselessly extending their necks downward, as though making low bows, curtsying and then straightening up, stretching their distended necks to the limit, hissing, muttering and calling, and letting their wings droop during their more energetic movements in order to maintain their balance . . . Furious fighting erupts: the males seize one another by the neck and drag one another about, pecking and scratching mercilessly, while blood spatters and feathers fly . . . and at the edge of the arena the lucky ones, or the nimblest, copulate with the females, who are utterly indifferent to the battles being fought for their favors.[8]

Bird courtship of this kind perhaps attracted Turgenev because even though it is primal and direct, it is also full of seemingly strange and superfluous rituals of dominance, fitness, attraction, and rejection. In other words, it is simultaneously very human and very unfamiliar. In contemplating the vernal spectacle of the lek, Turgenev, like Aksakov, may well have seen it as a profoundly significant phenomenon, linked to "the harmony of life in nature as a whole."

The black grouse's mating ground serves as a ready analogue for the numerous courtship scenes we find in Turgenev's work, but it gains special

FIGURE 6.1.   Black grouse (*Lyrurus tetrix*), male (right) and female (left). John Gould, *The Birds of Great Britain*, vol. 4 (London: Taylor and Francis, 1873).

resonance because the lek also functions as a simple showcase of nature's balance being spontaneously and conspicuously worked out in the wild. It is a stage on which birds enact the "disunity" and "harmony" of Turgenev's solipsism-love paradox.[9] The selfish pursuit of a mate—an individual creature's attempt to satisfy its own sexual or procreational *okhota*, injuring others in the process if need be—produces perhaps the most unselfish of all results: perpetuation of a species.

Turgenev's own mating habits notably diverged from the norms of his class and gender. As Victor Ripp has pointed out, his "most important erotic relationship," with Pauline Viardot, "was so unusual that it implies neurosis. . . . Turgenev's letters [to her] indicate an abnormal desire to appear submissive."[10] Turgenev's biographer, Leonard Schapiro, writes that "the sexual side of love was to play a small part in Turgenev's life," and notes only a few serious, if brief, love interests (among them Tat'iana Bakunina, Ol'ga Turgeneva, Mariia Savina), as well as a modest string of casual encounters with prostitutes and serf women.[11] His only child, Polina, was the result of a loveless liaison with one of the latter—Avdot'ia Ivanova—in the summer of 1841, as he confessed in an 1850 letter to Pauline Viardot: "I was young . . . it was nine years ago—I was bored in the country; I noticed a rather pretty seamstress my mother had taken into her service, I said two words to her, a visit was made, I paid, I left, and that was all, just as in the fairy tale about the wolf."[12]

In truth, Turgenev, a lifelong bachelor, shrank from wolfish competition among suitors, preferring to explore such contests in fictional works: "The Duelist," "A Quiet Spot" ("Zatish'e," 1854), "Iakov Pasynkov" (1855), and *Spring Torrents*, to name only a few examples. He instead deliberately and showily committed himself—for forty years—to the almost ritualized pursuit of an unattainable married woman. In the outdoor world, he had witnessed countless times the mating rituals of game birds and knew full well how hunters exploited their reproductive behavior to make kills while amorous quarry exposed itself to danger. "I have to say that I felt a little ashamed of killing birds in this distracted state, in the frenzied grip of the immutable law of nature, blind to everything and deaf to gunshots," Aksakov wrote about taking advantage of great snipe during their mating season.[13] If, as a hunter, Turgenev too was ashamed of employing such techniques, as a writer he does not hesitate to exploit the mating habits of people to reveal human capacities and deficiencies: our essential inability to escape the limbo between longing and fulfillment in every aspect of life, and our inevitable subjection to the physical limits of our animal selves, especially love and death. Elements of hunting and features of the hunter's quarry (chiefly the black grouse) make subtle appearances in Turgenev's most important works of the late 1850s and early 1860s—the period of his most impressive literary achievements—as a means of defamiliarizing these painful human dilemmas.

On the Eve

In Moscow en route to France in April 1859, Turgenev saw Sergei Aksakov a few days before the patriarch of Russian nature writing died. He then began his third novel in Vichy that June, finishing it at Spasskoe four months later.[14] He originally considered using "Insarov," the name of the male protagonist, as the title, but in the end called it *On the Eve* (*Nakanune*), which points to the work's cardinal themes far more suggestively. A typical nineteenth-century and Soviet interpretation of the title, thanks largely to Nikolai Dobroliubov's influential review article, "When Will the Real Day Come?" (the *Contemporary*, 1860), held that the text offered a picture of Russian society *on the eve* of major social reforms, especially the imminent abolition of serfdom, implemented in early 1861. Russian *nakanune*, however, evokes a much wider range of the novel's explorations. In modern usage, and as it did in Turgenev's time, *nakanune* simply means "the day before," or "just before," and it is frequently rendered in English as "on the eve." The etymology is straightforward: *nakanune* is originally a phrase, "on the canon" (*kanun* or *kanon*), with *kanun/kanon* being a term for the traditional set of prayers offered at the evening service immediately preceding an Orthodox Christian holiday.[15] The term thus connotes the moment at the end of today when believers pause to address God in the prescribed way as they prepare themselves spiritually for the holy day that will come tomorrow.

The word *nakanune* thus indicates a sacred balancing point in the novel's vast array of binary oppositions: today and tomorrow, quietism and action, Hamlet and Quixote, jest and seriousness, dalliance and devotion, health and illness, Bulgaria and Russia, and so on. Living on the borderline between today and tomorrow—between her old and new lives—the novel's heroine, Elena Stakhova, will offer two vital addresses to God, two "canons": one is a prayer, the other an un-prayer. She stands at the edge of these multiple dichotomies, placed by Turgenev in the position of a female black grouse at the lek, empowered to observe the proceedings and choose her course of action—and her mate. The agony of Elena's attempt to balance her alternatives, to achieve meaningful equipoise through intense moral observation and self-questioning, is presented by Turgenev with a depth and sympathy that make her one of the most fully realized female characters to appear in Russian fiction up to that time. In the end, however, as he so often does with male figures, Turgenev stymies both her mating and her mattering.

Among the first four novels, *On the Eve* contains perhaps the fewest overt hunting references, but it begins with one of the most extended and explicit dialogues on nature in any of Turgenev's works. Pavel Shubin, a jocose Russo-French sculptor, and Andrei Bersenev, a devoted student of philosophy, repose on the banks of the Moscow River in the estival warmth, shaded by a linden tree. Shubin, a Hamlet figure, lies on the grass face down (microscopically oriented, introspective), while Bersenev lies face up (telescopically oriented, extrospective). A long ecotropic description of nature's serene beauty on this calm summer day, akin to similar moments in *A Gentry Nest*, prefaces the two friends' discussion of the feelings that the natural world elicits from its observers.[16] In previous chapters, and in appendix 1, we have touched on some of their commentary. Bersenev believes that nature awakens a sense of both self-satisfaction and unease, which Shubin attributes to nature's unresponsiveness to human beings' admiration of the natural world. Nature's inability to return human affection, Shubin suggests, "quietly drives us into other, living [human] arms, but we don't understand nature and expect something from nature herself."[17] Bersenev agrees that nature can impel human beings to love other people, but insists that it also never stops "devouring us"—a thought to be taken up at length in "Enough!" ("Dovol'no!," 1862–64)—and therefore taunts us with the menacing mystery of death. At the outset, then, *On the Eve* establishes the natural environment as a space in which two unpredictable outcomes—love and death—coexist in a tense balance capable of eliciting both delight and revulsion.

Beyond this early dialogue, *On the Eve* offers little in the way of typical Turgenevian commentary on nature. Venatic equipoise has been subsumed here into a general exploration of social, national, and personal equilibrium, with relatively brief allusions to natural setting and no mention of field sport per se. Dmitrii Insarov's rugged practicality (including his Bulgarian jujitsu in defense of the women at Tsaritsyno) has some features we might associate with Turgenev's hunting ethos, and the narrator prominently invokes an ominous fishing metaphor near novel's end: "Death is like a fisherman who has caught a fish in his net and leaves it in the water for a time: the fish still swims, but the net is around it, and the fisherman will take it up—when he wishes."[18] Explicit references to hunting, however, are absent.

Thus the most striking reference to a form of *okhota* is an implicit one, connected with Uvar Ivanovich Stakhov during the boat excursion at Tsaritsyno in chapter 15: "Having noticed that in one part of the woods an echo repeated every sound especially clearly, he suddenly began calling like a quail. At first everyone gave a start, but they immediately felt genuine pleasure, especially since Uvar Ivanovich imitated the call very accurately."[19] This comports with Aksakov's assertion that "the Russian people are fond of the cry of the quail," which makes it popular as a cage bird, as Goncharov, too, noted in "Oblomov's Dream" (1849): "She charms the people's ear by singing, which is why under the roof of almost every home there hangs a string cage with a quail."[20] As a boy, Aksakov often assisted an old bird-catcher in attracting quail by means of "quail pipes" (*perepelinye dudki*), which imitated the male's mating call. The basic technique is clearly depicted in Vasilii Perov's famous painting *The Bird-Catcher* (*Ptitselov*, 1870), for which the landscape artist Aleksei Savrasov provided a forest background (figure 6.2).

Aksakov's frequent contact with quail informed his expert commentary on its reproductive habits, which are even more aggressive than those of the black grouse:

> As soon as the quail start calling, their amorous adventures begin; in other words, this cry is the expression of the irrepressible urge to mate . . . The male birds are furiously determined in their mating: they fling themselves upon a female time after time and one after another, but they do not fight among themselves . . . Such episodes usually ended with the more than satisfied female taking to her heels or flying away, pursued by several males . . . the ardor of the males reaches a wild level of intoxication [*do op'ianeniia, do bezumiia*].[21]

FIGURE 6.2. V. G. Perov, *The Bird-Catcher* (1870). By permission of Tret'iakov Gallery, Moscow.

These mating rituals resonate deeply with human interactions in *On the Eve*. Uvar Ivanovich's quail call—startling in the midst of a genteel outing—is an eruptive reminder of the primitive urge to mate and the competition for a female's favor. The call is all the more unexpected because it issues from the mouth of the novel's most inarticulate and sexually inert character, though in a way its earthy implications affirm Shubin's jocular epithet for Uvar: "power of the black soil" (*chernozemnaia sila*), which is repeated four times, including at the very end of the novel. Uvar's outburst is a crudely refreshing response to the Romantic apostrophe to nature ("Keep of this night, keep, beautiful nature, / At least the memory!") that echoes across the lake a moment earlier thanks to Zoia's performance of Lamartine's "Le lac" (published 1820) in Louis Niedermeyer's setting.[22] The quail call returns us to the atmosphere of courtship we experience in *A Gentry Nest*, when Lavretskii hears "something merry and wondrous in the ringing cry of the quail" as he makes his way home alone after the happy fishing party with Liza and her family.[23]

For Turgenev, mating is a moment when opposed elements come together, when the precise fulcrum of nature's balance is readily detectable, and the suitability of a potential mate is exposed. Uvar's quail call reminds us that, despite the trappings of a gentry picnic, Tsaritsyno functions as a lek, with Elena surrounded by the three principal suitors—Shubin, Bersenev, and Insarov—among whom she will choose a mate.[24] The drunken, sexually aggressive Germans who accost Elena's mother, Anna Vasil'evna, a few pages later—we recall here the "intoxication" Aksakov imputed to male quail—only heighten our sense that we are spectators at an arena of sexual assertion and competition. In chapter 15, we stand at the midpoint of the novel, "on the canon," and at the mating ground, where Elena is poised between her emotionally uncommitted past and her future love for Insarov, a man who will capture her affection in this chapter with a decisive physical display of moral courage. Anna Vasil'evna is threatened by a German "of enormous size, with a bull's neck and a bull's inflamed eyes" (evocative references to the sexual rapacity of male cattle), who then demands a kiss (*einen Kuss*) from Elena or Zoia.[25] When Insarov tosses this minotauric figure into the lake, he bests both Shubin (whose response to the cad is a witty and long-winded speech) and Bersenev (who says and does nothing). At home after the trip, as members of the group say their good-byes, "Elena for the first time shook Insarov's hand and, seated under her window, for a long time did not undress."[26] Given the way Turgenev eroticizes hands in subsequent scenes with Insarov and Elena, especially chapter 23, her physical gesture of pairing suggests a significant bond, just as the German's unwelcome "*Kuss*" represents far more than a kiss. At Tsaritsyno, her instinct has chosen a mate; in the following chapter, by presenting the reader a series of excerpts from her diary, Turgenev shows how her mind eventually catches up: "The word's been found—I've seen the light! O God! Have mercy on me . . . I'm in love!"[27]

Elena's attraction to Insarov is no simple matter of lust, but ultimately a deeply felt and deliberative response to his virtues, among them a Quixote-like earnestness and merciless, even cruel, opposition to predatory behavior. "Yes, he's not to be trifled with," she thinks, "and he knows how to come to someone's defense."[28] In thwarting a predator, Insarov has struck a chord with Elena, whose similar capacity for vigorous empathy, mocked by her callous father, Nikolai Artem'evich, has been well established: "'Lenochka!' he used to call out to her, 'Come quick. A spider is sucking the life out of a fly—liberate the unfortunate creature!' And Lenochka, very alarmed, would come running, free the fly, untangle its feet. 'Well, now let it bite you too, if you're so kind-hearted,' her father would remark ironically, but she did not listen to him."[29] Unlike the Slavophilically oriented Marfa Timofeevna in *A Gentry Nest*, who resigns herself to the inevitable suffering of flies captured by spiders, Elena has since girlhood embraced a sympathetic form of activism, saving dogs, kittens, fallen sparrows, even vermin. She, like Insarov, and like brave parent birds who sacrifice themselves to save their young, is a rescuer—an anti-predator, the opposite of such kite-like characters as Naum ("The Inn"), Varvara Pavlovna (*A Gentry Nest*), and Mar'ia Polozova (*Spring Torrents*). Elena's outlook is essentially Westernist in its assumption that injustice can be fought, that suffering is not inevitable, that it is wrong to let nature take its course when that course creates misery or verges on *proizvol*. Nikolai Artem'evich declares, "Her heart is so expansive that it embraces the whole of nature, down to the smallest cockroach or frog—in a word, everything except her own father."[30] Nikolai, however, is a man whose own imperiousness and cruelty (clearly displayed in his open affair with his mistress) call into question his ability to judge his daughter's heart, and in fact he completely misconstrues her relationship with nature. Elena does *not* embrace nature; she is an implacable foe of nature. Unlike the Slavophile characters in *A Gentry Nest*, she thoroughly rejects nature's indifference: "since childhood she had thirsted for action, for active goodness."[31] Insarov, too, seeks to foil predation, having grown up opposing what he sees as his native Bulgaria's single, national predator—the Turks. He and Elena are thus a fine match, given the alternatives available to her. As Ripp puts it, "The love of Elena for Insarov is not a marriage made in heaven but the result of a passionate process of elimination."[32] Elena has carefully chosen, and Insarov wins at the lek.

Unfortunately for Elena, Bersenev was right about the natural world's connection with death, and her attempts, however valiant, to fight that particular natural process are doomed to failure. Having clearly seen that Insarov's tuberculosis threatens his life, she actively and methodically prepares an opportunity for a sexual liaison with him during his recovery from a severe attack. Elena's assertive pursuit of premarital sex with the man she loves is an attempt to stave off mortality with a celebration of life and, possibly, procreation. Though it scandalized many readers, socialist critic Dobroliubov predictably applauded this scene at the time, calling it "charming, pure and profoundly moral."[33] The sexual bond, however, does nothing to avert death, and near the end Elena turns to her last, desperate bulwark against mortality: prayer. This is another crucial moment of being "on the canon," of keen awareness that a new tomorrow is about to begin.

In Venice, the evening before Insarov dies, Elena puts him to bed and turns to observe the outdoor environment from her liminal perch by their hotel window. The April sky touches her: "Oh, how quiet and tender was the night . . . surely all suffering, all grief must cease and fall asleep beneath this clear heaven, beneath these holy, innocent beams of light!"[34] The disjunction between the natural beauty she beholds and the equally natural destruction of her husband's body fills her with questions that she instinctively addresses to a supreme authority whose existence is, nonetheless, uncertain:

"O God!" thought Elena, "Why death, why separation, sickness and tears? And why this beauty, this sweet feeling of hope, why the reassuring awareness of a sturdy refuge, unfailing security, immortal protection [*pokrovitel'stvo*]? What is the meaning of this smiling, benevolent sky, this happy, reposing earth? Could it be that all this is only within us, and outside us is eternal cold and silence? Could it be that we are alone . . . alone . . . and that what's out there, everywhere, in all those inaccessible abysses and depths, everything, all of it, is alien to us? Why, then, this thirst for—and joy in—prayer?"[35]

At a similar moment in *A Gentry Nest*, when Liza Kalitina realizes that she has lost Lavretskii, she sees her anguish as a penalty exacted by God: she conceives her hopes of happiness as "criminal" and believes that she and Lavretskii "were swiftly punished" for them.[36] Activist Elena now echoes those conclusions of quietist Liza, but, unlike Liza, cannot conclude that she deserves God's retribution: "What if this is a punishment, . . . what if we must now pay in full for our guilt? My conscience was quiet, and is quiet now, but is that really proof of innocence? O God, are we really so criminal? Can it be that you, who created this night and this sky, that you want to punish us for having loved?"[37] Elena cannot comprehend how the maker of nature's reassuring beauty could also be a judge who would punish people for committing themselves to mutual love—punish them for mating.

It is here that Turgenev's narrator—not God, but wielding godlike omniscience—answers Elena's questions in a way that cruelly undermines everything the heroine of *On the Eve* represents: "Elena did not know that the happiness of each person is based on the unhappiness of another, that even a person's advantage and comfort require—just as a statue requires a pedestal—the disadvantage and discomfort of others."[38] This is possibly the most terrifying iteration of venatic equipoise in all of Turgenev's fiction. It presents a belief that could easily derive from his experience afield: the simple fact is that when a hunter succeeds, some creature dies, as we observed in chapter 2. At the level of individuals (as opposed to species or populations), hunting is a zero-sum game. Turgenev now enforces that merciless balance in Elena's life and amplifies the pathos by leaving her unaware of it. She does not know that her lifelong belief in the active pursuit of social good was baseless: why bother, after all, when any happiness achieved will be canceled out by misery elsewhere?

Here Turgenev characterizes the workings of human contentment as an expanded version of the "compensation" philosophy advanced in the early nineteenth century by Pierre-Hyacinthe Azaïs (*Des compensations dans les destinées humaines*, 1809), beloved by Lamartine and ridiculed by Herzen in *Who Is to Blame?*[39] Two of that novel's major characters have a conversation that conveys the essence of Azaïsian thinking:

"At times [frets Dmitrii Krutsiferskii] my own happiness terrifies me. Like the owner of enormous riches, I tremble in fear before what the future may hold. It's as if . . ."

"As if [Dr. Krupov responds] you'd have to pay for it later. Ha! What dreamers you are! Who was it who measured out your happiness? Whom will you have to pay? What a childish attitude. You yourself and Chance combined to create your happiness; therefore, it is yours. It would be ridiculous to punish you for it."[40]

Elena is a formidable woman whom Turgenev has endowed with a considerable degree of social, familial, and sexual agency, all of which have ultimately been undercut by a narrator who sides categorically with Azaïs, Liza Kalitina, and Krutsiferskii rather than with Herzen's mouthpiece of reason, the skeptical Dr. Krupov. As a desperate wife praying the evening before her husband will die of consumption, she is right, the narrator suggests, to suspect that happiness and freedom must always come at a great cost. On the other hand, what seems to be compensatory payment for earlier happiness could just as well be Elena's penalty for flouting the first, brutal rule of the lek: choose a healthy mate. This basic problem—physical frailty as an impediment to success in the natural world—continually plagued Turgenev as he coped with his own illness in the field, as we observed in chapter 2, and it lurks in the background of *On the Eve* as well.

To conclude this devastating chapter, Turgenev supplies a natural detail that confirms Elena's ignorance of the balance that dominates her life. Over the broad Venetian lagoon, she notices a lone gull ("probably scared up by a fisherman") and thinks to herself that it will be a good omen if the bird flies in her direction: "The gull circled in place, folded its wings—and, as if shot and wounded [*podstrelennaia*], with a plaintive cry fell somewhere far away, on the other side of a dark ship."[41] Here, Elena continues to follow her irrational instinct, by placing faith in prophetic signs, and we hope that she might deserve the same serene comfort that came to the narrator of "The Singers"—expressed through the image of a seagull bathed in the warm light of sunset—when he contemplated the singing of Iashka the Turk. That hope is dashed. True to her rational, activist self, she abandons superstition and embraces the reality of her predicament: "Elena shuddered, then felt ashamed for shuddering, and, without undressing, lay down on the bed alongside Insarov, who breathed deeply and rapidly."[42] Given the narrator's verdict on the relationship between human happiness and misery, she seems foolish for not having noticed that the bird fell as if "shot," as though by some unseen hunter responsible for reminding Elena that the ledger of her life must remain in balance.

The final chapter of *On the Eve* begins in Venice the day after Insarov's death. Elena, her voice and face "lifeless," arranges passage across the Adriatic Sea with Rendich the mariner, so that she might bury her husband's body on "Slav soil":

> He [Rendich] left. Elena crossed into the next room, leaned against the wall and stood there for a long time, as if turned to stone. Then she got down on her knees, but she was unable to pray. In her soul there were no feelings of guilt; she did not venture to ask God why he had shown no mercy, had taken no pity, had given no defense—why he had punished their fault beyond measure, if indeed there were a fault. Each of us is already guilty of living, and there is no great thinker, no benefactor of humanity, who might hope, by virtue of the benefit he brings, to have the right to live . . . But Elena was unable to pray: she had turned to stone.[43]

This un-prayer addresses her earlier supplication point for point. Long before that, in chapter 18, she and Insarov had first joined their lives at a roadside shrine on a rainy afternoon: "The quiet of bliss, the quiet of the calm harbor, of the goal attained, that heavenly peace, which imparts sense and beauty to death itself, had entirely flooded her with its surge of the divine. She desired nothing because she had everything."[44] That sense of serene refuge is now completely gone, because Elena's belief in the divine is shattered. In her earlier prayer in chapter 33, she had sensed protection (*pokrovitel'stvo*) because she sensed the existence of a protector (*pokrovitel'*), but the gesture of kneeling is all that is left of such faith now. Her last words in the novel, set forth in a short letter to her parents, evince a new outlook that embraces contingency: twice she repeats "I do not know what will become of me," and predicts, "I sought happiness—and perhaps I'll find death."[45] For her, the future is open, not written by a supreme judge who tracks the entries in some grand, invisible register of contentment.

"Turning to stone" here is synonymous with losing one's faith. Elena ends in the same state in which Evgenii Bazarov, Turgenev's most famous character, begins: she has become a materialist, a rationalist activist. Like Dr. Krupov, she is now a believer in personal agency and Chance, not in unseen hunters, not in protectors, not in cosmic fishermen who hold the net, not in heavenly ledgers, not in God. She has rejected Azaïs's notion that someone, or something, is keeping track of the felicific equipoise of individual human lives. The birds in the lek, not some force overseeing the lek, determine who mates with whom and whether those mates will reproduce.

Elena's existential question ("Why, then, this thirst for—and joy in—prayer?") is never answered in the text, but Turgenev implies that the desire to pray is generated by the same craving for mutual appraisal that leads to anthropotropism: the urge to personify, to cast our consciousness into the world around us and assume that the world watches us just as we watch it. This is Shubin's reasoning about nature at the start of the novel. It is also Feuerbach's answer to the question of God's origin. Strangely, Turgenev's narrator in *On the Eve*, unlike the novel's heroine, rejects the Feuerbachian view and forcefully affirms the existence of Azaïsian balance: "the happiness of each person is based on the unhappiness of another." This mystical assertion aligns with the fatalistic Slavophile worldview Turgenev had portrayed sympathetically in *A Gentry Nest* yet later denied as representing his own outlook. It is difficult to know whether we should see this as self-contradiction—or as balance.

"First Love"

If *On the Eve* examines the vagaries of human mating largely from a woman's perspective, the work Turgenev began immediately after finishing that novel regards the lek chiefly from the vantage point of the males. Written in St. Petersburg over a span of about three months in early 1860, the novella "First Love" tells the story of how the first-person narrator, Vladimir, falls in love with his summer neighbor, the young Princess Zinaida Zasekina, only to discover that his own father is having an extramarital affair with her. Turgenev claimed that the story was entirely autobiographical, a fictionalization of the summer of 1833, when his family rented a dacha near Moscow's Kaluga Turnpike, opposite the Pleasure Garden (Neskuchnyi sad), and he fell in love with Princess Ekaterina Shakhovskaia, an eighteen-year-old poet.[46] Perhaps because of the plot's intensely personal provenance, hunting motifs and courtship rituals are now far more explicit than in *On the Eve*, magnifying the brutal reality of competition for a mate and nudging Turgenev's characterization of nature from indifferent to fickle, even vindictive.

At the commencement of the action, Vladimir, who is idly preparing for his university entrance examinations, describes a favorite pastime: "It was my custom to wander about our garden every evening with my gun and watch out for [*karaulit'*] crows."[47] On this evening in late May, however, Vladimir will bag no birds: "the crows recognized me and only cawed at me sporadically from a distance." The crow (*vorona*) appears in Turgenev's other work chiefly as a wary observer of human activity or as a term of abuse.[48] In Aksakov's lengthy chapter on black grouse, he mentions that crows and magpies will take young birds as well as reveal the location of wounded grouse that have died before being found by dog or hunter.[49] The practice of shooting crows has several noteworthy connotations. First, Turgenev, in "Fifty Flaws," condemns killing non-game birds, including corvids: "When nothing has turned up in a long time, shoots at jackdaws, at small birds, at swallows—pointless cruelty!" (human flaw no. 36).[50] On the other hand, as Sergei Romanov points out in the entry on "Shooting" in his *Hunting Dictionary* (1877), crows serve as good target practice during the off season: "In winter it's sometimes useful . . . to drive with one's gun beyond turnpikes and to slaughterhouses, where there are always many crows and jackdaws."[51] Romanov classifies crows as predators (*khishchniki*) and discusses them in his entry on that topic, quoting Vaksel': "Crows and magpies are also shot, but they are so wary that only a rare bird will fly toward the hunter or allow him to approach."[52]

All these nuances gain fresh significance when, in the next paragraph, Vladimir stumbles upon a strange ritual:

A few steps from me—in a clearing [*poliana*], between some bushes of green raspberry—stood a tall, slender young woman in a striped pink dress and white headscarf. Around her there crowded four young men, and she was slapping them each in turn on the forehead with those small gray flowers whose name I don't know, but which are well known to children: these flowers look like little sacks and burst with a pop when you slap them on something hard. The young men were offering their foreheads so eagerly [*okhotno*]—and in the girl's movements (I could see her from one side) there was something so enchanting, commanding, caressing, mocking, and sweet that I almost cried out in surprise and pleasure and, it seemed, would have given anything in the world right there and then if only those charming little fingers would slap me, too, on the forehead. My gun slid down onto the grass, and I forgot everything. I devoured with my gaze this slender figure, and neck, and beautiful arms, and slightly disheveled blonde hair under the white scarf, and those half-closed intelligent eyes, and those lashes, and the tender cheek beneath them.[53]

What Vladimir witnesses here is nothing less than a human lek: in a clearing (*poliana*), the men stretch forward toward a young woman the way male black grouse, "as though making low bows" (in Aksakov's words), offer themselves for the approval of the female. The spectacle marks Vladimir's transition from observer (hunter concealed outside the lek) to participant, as his gun slips out of his hands and he succumbs to the loveliness of young Zinaida, almost to the point of intoxication or madness (*do op'ianeniia, do bezumiia*), like a mating quail. The process of metamorphosis here is, in its figurative way, Ovidian: the voyeuristic gaze has transformed a man into a grouse. Ovid's account of Actaeon—the hunter who became a stag as punishment for glimpsing the beauty of naked Diana—trembles just beneath the surface of these images. The rest of the novella will document Vladimir's rivalry with the other men competing for her attention, a situation foretold by his unusual hunt for predators (crows) rather than traditional game birds: he will vie with those who are also hunting Zinaida.

Turgenev's imagery superimposes metaphors of courtship and killing, blurring the distinction between hunter and hunted. All of the grouse at this figurative lek are, in a sense, "hunters," as they pursue a mate. In addition, Vladimir will, late in the tale, hunt among his fellow suitors, as he seeks to discover the "secret rival" who is rumored to have already been granted mating rights by Zinaida.[54] Another suitor, Malewski, gives Vladimir what sounds exactly like hunting advice: "Remember: in the garden, at night, by the fountain—that's where you need to keep watch [*karaulit'*]."[55] This is the same verb Vladimir had used to describe his crow hunting, when he clearly employed it in its secondary, colloquial meaning ("to watch for"), but now we perceive that the ambiguity inherent in his status as both his father's protégé and sexual competitor is hinted at by the primary meaning of *karaulit'*: "to watch over." This sense suggests the sentiment a solicitous son might direct toward his father, or, more likely still, the protective feeling that an honorable father should have for his child. As he sits in ambush, like a grouse hunter at the lek, waiting for Zinaida's clandestine lover to appear, Vladimir uses *karaulit'* twice more in its secondary (venatic) sense.[56]

Before he unmasks the rival, Vladimir, fingering his penknife, hears in his mind Aleko's vengeful lines from Pushkin's *The Gypsies*, a repetition of the way jealousy and infidelity are associated with that text in both *A Gentry Nest* and *Spring Torrents*.[57] When he does finally discover the secret paramour's identity, however, Vladimir reacts without hostility, as he balances the two senses of *karaulit'*: is he wary or protective? "Against my father himself I harbored no ill will," he writes. "On the contrary: it was as though he grew further in my eyes . . . Let psychologists explain this contradiction as they might."[58] Some measure of explanation can be found in Vladimir's identity as a hunter: he has succeeded in his hunt for the interloper, and he admires the mating success of his virile father at a lek full of determined rivals. Semyon Vengerov and Boris Zaitsev record that Turgenev, among his friends, frequently referred to his own father as "a great hunter before the Lord," using the biblical Nimrod allusion to hint at Sergei Turgenev's well-known skill as a seducer as well as his actual hunting prowess.[59]

Vladimir's father ("a man still young and very handsome") is a source of wonder for his son.[60] After all, Vladimir exists because his father successfully mated with his mother, even if it was simply to obtain her money, a fact he apparently made no attempt to conceal. His advice to young Vladimir is consonant with that brutally clear-eyed approach: "Take what you can for yourself, and yield to no one. Belong to yourself . . . do you know what can give a man freedom? . . . Will [*volia*], one's own will, and the power it bestows, which is better than freedom. Know how to want something [*khotet'*]—and you will be free, you will be in command."[61] This is precisely what the father achieves, even taking violent physical command of Zinaida by forcefully striking her arm with his riding crop near story's end when she attempts to resist his will. Such words and actions demonstrate that Vladimir's father lives out the self-serving freedom that Turgenev perceived, in the second Aksakov review, as the mysterious source of nature's balance. And yet, following a familiar pattern in Turgenev's fiction, the father—for all his youth, strength, beauty, and unapologetic assertion of moral freedom—suddenly dies of a stroke, a mere eight months after the episode with Zinaida. Ultimately, nature, in the form of death, is indifferent, even to the organisms who most closely follow her laws.

Zinaida, though objectified as a marriage target by her suitors, is not a passive figure. Turgenev depicts her as a nineteenth-century woman severely constrained by her economic, social, and gender status, but who, like her hidden lover, follows the dictates of her will, carving out considerable freedom and power within her circumscribed universe. In some ways, she resembles the female black grouse at the lek, observing the displays of the males who court her, and in other ways she imitates the Turgenevian conception of the nature goddess, though the balance she strikes is anything but impartial:

> In the whole of her tenacious, beautiful being there was some special, fascinating admixture of guile and unconcern, artificiality and simplicity, quietude and sportiveness. Over all that she did and said, over her every movement, there floated a subtle and easy charm; in all of it a peculiar, playful force proclaimed itself. And her face also ceaselessly changed and played: it expressed, at almost one and the same time, archness, pensiveness, and vehemence. The most varied feelings—light and swift as the shadows of clouds on a sunny, windy day—time and again ran over her eyes and lips.[62]

Another suitor, Lushin, sums up the litany of oxymorons more succinctly: "caprice [*kapriz*] and independence: those two words say it all."[63]

The paradoxical equilibrium of opposing forces within Zinaida, and among her suitors, is acted out in the ritual of "forfeits" (*fanty*) that she directs. A popular nineteenth-century practice throughout Europe, *fanty*, from German *Pfand* (pledge), was based on a balance of debts and credits—an accounting of the participants' behavior. As penalties for failure in an evening's various parlor games, players hand over slips of paper with trivial tasks written on them.[64] Now in the drawing room of her house, instead of the garden, Zinaida, who controls the collected forfeits, reenacts her dominant posture over the competing males by engaging in the particular variant known as "forfeits with a leader" (*fanty s vedushchim*): "I opened the door and stepped back in amazement. In the middle of the room, the princess stood on a chair and held in front of her a man's hat: around the chair crowded five men. They were trying to thrust their hands into the hat, but she raised it high and shook it vigorously."[65] As a penalty in some earlier game, Zinaida has placed in the hat a forfeit with "Kiss" written on it, and the men eagerly vie for a chance to obtain this token, which will grant them the right to offer her physical affection. The scene presents an indoor lek, with Vladimir, as he did before, watching from the periphery, though on this occasion, he is invited by Zinaida to enter and take his place among the suitors, where he has the good fortune to draw the "Kiss" forfeit. Zinaida's penalty is to receive a kiss on the hand from the bearer, and Vladimir awkwardly carries this out. As the games continue, Zinaida, as "leader," continues to dominate, devising humorous and humiliating penalties for the men. When she is required to imitate a statue, she literally stands on top of one of the suitors, imposing her superiority in bodily fashion.

Such physical manifestation of emotion—by people and by the natural environment—is a frequent occurrence in "First Love." Teenage Vladimir is carried away by the merriment of the courtship games: "I simply became intoxicated [*op'ianel*], as if from wine."[66] The term here is the same one used by Aksakov to describe the ardor of male quail as they contend for a mate.[67] At home after the party, exhilarated and unable to sleep, Vladimir watches the night sky filled with distant streaks of lightning that "trembled and twitched like the wing of a dying bird"—an image familiar to any wildfowler. "This mute lightning," he concludes, "these restrained blazes of light, seemed to answer those mute and secret impulses that were also flaring up inside of me."[68] Zinaida is "une femme capable de tout" who deals out pain as well as pleasure to Vladimir, sadistically twisting his hair and offering languorous kisses: "she amused herself with my passion, made a fool of me, pampered and tormented me."[69]

In spite of the pleasure she experiences as she "amuses herself," Zinaida, her name derived from "Zeus," bears some resemblance here to a Turgenevian goddess figure.[70] Near the midpoint of the tale, now deeply in love, Vladimir sometimes sits among the ruins of a tall stone greenhouse (*oranzhereia*) for hours at a time, surrounded by elements of the natural environment:

> Alongside me, white butterflies lazily fluttered among the dusty nettles. A bold sparrow landed not far away on a half-broken red brick and irritably cheeped, constantly turning his whole body about and spreading his little tail. The still-distrustful crows cawed occasionally, sitting high, high up on the denuded crown of a birch; the sun and wind quietly played in its fluid boughs. The serene and mournful sound of the bells in the Donskoi Monastery wafted in [*priletal*] at times—and I sat, and watched, and listened, and completely filled myself with some nameless sensation that had everything: sorrow, joy, foreboding, desire, and fear of life. But at that time I understood none of this and wouldn't have been able to put a name to what was fermenting within me, or might have given a single name to all of it: *Zinaida*.[71]

Mating competition—reflected even here, in the sparrow's territorial display—has instilled in Vladimir a sense of the balance of opposing forces within his own heart, affirmed by the oxymoronic pairs of emotions he feels and the equilibrium uniting the nonhuman life he observes. Heavens, earth, flora, fauna all come together in Zinaida. He is no longer a hunter—the crows at their safe distance remind us that he once was—but fully enveloped in his new identity as a young man in love, a devotee of his new goddess. The ruined greenhouse, a broken temple of nature, welcomes him as something like a worshipper, while the monastery bells toll in the background. His obsessive devotion is not reciprocated. Only Zinaida's capriciousness—her toying with her admirers, her very human exercise of *proizvol*—separates her from the impassive green goddess of the prose poem "Nature."

Fathers and Children

Turgenev's most complex and hotly debated fictional text, *Fathers and Children*, followed on the heels of "First Love" and was completed in the summer of 1861. The novel deepens many of the nature-related themes he had explored over the preceding decade and concentrates afresh on the hunting motifs he would largely abandon in his later fiction. In *Fathers and Children*, venatic equipoise becomes a life-or-death proposition, fatal when violated. Turgenev's depiction of courting in the novel is palpably primitive—out of human control, like disease or a merciless predator's attack, as the character Aleksei Petrovich had explicitly asserted in the final letter of the earlier story "A Correspondence" ("Perepiska," 1844–54): "Love is not a feeling at all; it is an illness, a well-known condition of body and soul. It does not develop gradually. It cannot be doubted and cannot be outwitted, though it does not always manifest itself in the same way. Usually it takes possession of a man without permission, suddenly, against his will—exactly like cholera or fever . . . It catches him, poor thing, as a kite [*korshun*] does a chick, and it carries him off wherever it likes, no matter how much he struggles or resists."[72] Evgenii Bazarov, the protagonist of *Fathers and Children*, is an embodied reminder that human coupling is a primal act, ultimately governed by subrational impulses, despite the decorous trappings of gentry culture and courtship. It is Esau (mating, *sparivanie*) peeking out from behind Jacob (courtship, *ukhazhivanie*). In this novel, Turgenev's frequent metaphorical association of human characters with animals and plants persistently illuminates an Ovidian subtext, in which ancient people and deities metamorphosed into flora and fauna, suggesting that the emotional and philosophical struggles of nineteenth-century Russians recapitulate the anxieties of classical antiquity, just as the younger characters in *Fathers and Children* recapitulate the anxieties of their parents.

Like the two young friends Shubin and Bersenev in *On the Eve*, Arkadii and Bazarov discuss the meaning of the natural world:

> "And is nature rubbish?" said Arkadii, pensively gazing into the distance at the dappled fields, beautifully and softly lit by the already sinking sun.
>
> "Nature is rubbish in the sense according to which you understand it. Nature is not a temple, but a workshop, and man is a laborer in it."[73]

Here, unlike Shubin and Bersenev, both of whom generally concur on the Romantic view of nature (*priroda*) as a unitary whole that has some sort of immanent meaning, Bazarov and Arkadii fail to agree even on the basics. To Bazarov, nature is simply the complete collection of organisms, not a thing of beauty that can inspire worship, as it does in Arkadii. If, as Bazarov implies, Arkadii views the natural world as a "temple," then Arkadii resembles young Vladimir in "First Love," who admires nature from the ruins of his greenhouse-shrine. Bazarov's dismissal of Pavel Petrovich's tragic history with his lost lover, the mercurial Princess R. ("What about the mysterious relations between a man and a woman? We physiologists know what sort of relations those are"), is in keeping with his self-proclaimed identity as a scientist and reinforces his materialistic vision of nature.[74]

In the first half of the novel, Bazarov's objectifying comments about women indicate a putatively scientific pose that underscores the emotionlessness of his materialism:

"Is she pretty?"

"Any pretty women around here?"

"She doesn't look like the rest of the skirts [*baby*]."

"She's got a pair of shoulders like I haven't seen in a long time."

"The only women who engage in freedom of thought are the ugly ones [*urody*]."

"What a sumptuous [*bogatoe*] body! . . . Straight to the anatomical theater with her."

"You could make whatever you wanted out of that girl; the other one's been around too much [*tertyi kalach*]."

"If a woman takes your fancy . . . try to attain your object; if you can't, well, there's no need, just walk away—it's not the end of the world [*zemlia ne klinom soshlas'*]."[75]

In the Weltanschauung of this young scientist, there is no love—only copulation. In fact, of all Turgenev's major characters, Bazarov may be the most prone to seeing human courtship as a lek, where participants unabashedly concern themselves with fitness and sexual coupling. It is a short distance from that kind of materialistic detachment to predation, which perhaps underlies Katia's comment about Bazarov to Arkadii late in the novel: "How can I put it? He's a predator, while you and I are domesticated [*ruchnye*]."[76] As we will see, Turgenev takes pains to present Bazarov as a nonhunter on the literal level, but he is equally careful to depict his nihilist hero as a hunter-predator on the metaphorical level—a hunter of women, as Costlow has shown. "It is hunting, predation, will—in all their etymological complexity—that haunt the scenes of Odintseva and Bazarov's encounter," and Costlow marshals compelling textual evidence that the Russian root *okhota* persistently appears in descriptions of that encounter.[77] Bazarov the metaphorical hunter will fail, in the end, largely because he lacks the balance of actual hunters, such as Nikolai Petrovich, and, above all, Arkadii. When love eventually infects him,

Bazarov's exaggeratedly clinical comments on women, and his dispassionate scientific outlook, become ironic to the point of ridiculousness.[78]

A key dialogue at the start of chapter 6 clearly schematizes the distinction between scientist and hunter:

> "You've got a little marsh here, along the aspen grove [said Bazarov].
> I scared up about five common snipe. You can kill them, Arkadii."
> "So you're not a hunter?" [asked Nikolai Petrovich.]
> "No."
> "You study physics then?" asked Pavel Petrovich, for his part.
> "Physics, yes, and the natural sciences in general."[79]

Bazarov clearly implies that Arkadii hunts, and his plain language ("You can kill them"), which avoids the idiomatic turns of phrase employed by Russian hunters, distances Bazarov from the practice of field sport, just as his reference to the "natural sciences" (*estestvennye nauki*) distances him from the notion of nature (*priroda*) as a living entity whose beauty prompts worshipful affection. Moreover, we know from the novel's first chapter that Arkadii's father, Nikolai Petrovich, is a hunter,[80] which establishes yet another bond between father and son, one of many details in the text suggesting that Nikolai and Arkadii are, in meaningful ways, the same person. Bazarov, the positivist-materialist, studies natural phenomena and can, for example, accurately identify the birds he sees. He even plunges into the nearby wetland, but he does not immerse himself in nature morally, spiritually, or aesthetically; he does not participate in it the way a hunter does. We eventually come to understand that Arkadii is a literal hunter and figurative scientist, while Bazarov is a figurative hunter and literal scientist.

The novel's dichotomous title is supported and echoed by innumerable binary oppositions in structure, ideology, and character, including the way Katia, Arkadii, Nikolai Petrovich, and Fenechka fall into the pro-nature camp, while Odintsova, Bazarov, and Pavel Petrovich are uninterested in the natural world: "Katia adored nature [*obozhala prirodu*], and Arkadii loved it, though he didn't dare admit that; Odintsova was indifferent to it, just as Bazarov was."[81] Turgenev makes it equally clear that the arts (especially literature and music) are closely associated with the nature-aligned characters, via Nikolai Petrovich's cello playing and devotion to poetry, Arkadii's love of music, and Katia's piano playing.[82] Nikolai Petrovich acknowledges the arts-nature linkage near the start of chapter 11: " 'But to reject poetry?' he again thought. 'To have no sympathy for [*ne sochuvstvovat'*] art, nature?' And he looked around, as though wishing to comprehend how it was possible not to sympathize with nature."[83] It comes as no surprise that the vivid description of the aspen grove that immediately follows Nikolai's questions here was borrowed almost verbatim from Turgenev's own language in a letter he wrote to Sergei Aksakov—the master of observing one's way into nature—nearly a decade before, while still in exile at Spasskoe-Lutovinovo.[84]

Bazarov expresses his contempt for art just as bluntly as he disparages nature: "Raphael isn't worth a brass farthing," and "I have no artistic sense—yes, I really have none."[85] For Bazarov, science is superior to all other forms of human perception and expression, including art, music, literature, philosophy, and love—the pillars of the Romantic "men of the forties"—and his devotion to science is expressed in terms that consistently belittle nature in its Romantic sense. For example, he reveres the agricultural chemistry of Justus von Liebig and considers a rare water beetle, *Dytiscus marginatus*, far more worthy of his attention than Pavel Petrovich's life-altering love affair with Princess R., which Bazarov regards simply as Pavel's failure to carry out his biological imperative as a male.[86] When Pavel Petrovich brings up Schiller and Goethe, Bazarov infamously responds that "a decent chemist is twenty times more useful than any poet."[87] As the action progresses, however, we begin to detect evidence that Bazarov is less than well served by science. When Arkadii seeks advice on scientific reading to replace his father's Pushkin volume, Bazarov recommends Ludwig Büchner's materialist treatise *Force and Matter* (*Kraft und Stoff*, 1855), which was a direct assault on the *Naturphilosophie* that Turgenev (and presumably his fictive contemporaries, the Kirsanov brothers) had imbibed from childhood.[88] It is telling, however, that both Bazarov and his pseudo-nihilist comrade get Büchner's title wrong, repeatedly calling it *Stoff und Kraft*, a hint that their supreme confidence in materialism rests on a shaky foundation.[89]

Given Turgenev's distaste for ingenious and figurative depictions of nature, we might expect that scientific observations and tabulations of the natural world would serve as a desirable extension of the ecotropic writing he so admired in Aksakov, but we see little evidence of this in his writings, including *Fathers and Children*. Quite the contrary: scientists, it seems, were not embracing a laudably ecotropic mode, but attempting to impose systems on the natural world, an undertaking that ignored the human hunger to celebrate beauty and to see humanity reflected in the nonhuman. As Newlin puts it, "A frog-dissecting, *Stoff-und-Kraft* materialism did not necessarily entail any genuine sympathy or respect for nature, or even a particularly deep knowledge of it; indeed, as Herzen had pointed out in the first of his *Letters on the Study of Nature* ('Empiricism and Idealism,' 1845), a purely data-driven, empiricist approach to the natural world tended to be both loveless and lifeless."[90] Strict materialism held no attraction for Turgenev, as his longtime friend, Iakov Polonskii, recalled: "He loved the word *nature* [*priroda*] and often used it, but couldn't abide the word *matter* [*materiia*]; he simply did not wish to recognize in it any particular substance or particular shade of the notion of nature. 'I haven't seen matter,' he'd argue, 'and you haven't seen it either. Why the devil then should I meditate over this word?'"[91] Similarly, in "Apropos of *Fathers and Children*" (1869), Turgenev explicitly disavowed "Bazarov's views on the arts," reinforcing the notion that nature and art are closely bound together in the novel.[92] In other words, scientists lack the hunter's eager, thoughtful, and reverent sense of venatic equipoise, which balances aesthetic sensitivity with attentive analysis of the nonhuman environment.

The ultimate failure of the scientific approach is Bazarov's surgical typhus poisoning while he performs an autopsy: his devotion to medical research, mixed with despondency over his inability to "attain his object" with Odintsova, gets him killed.[93] In chapter 27 of *Fathers and Children*, as Bazarov lies dying, Turgenev accurately and unflinchingly presents the symptoms of the disease: insomnia, anorexia, headache, fever, chills, cough, vertigo, nosebleed, and soon pyemia, hallucination, delirium, unconsciousness, and death.[94] (It is also tempting to speculate that Turgenev knew the etymology of *typhus* [Russian *tif*]: ancient Greek *tyfos*, meaning "vanity, conceit.")[95] Partially delirious now, the doomed nihilist pictures himself in a series of animal images, as though the natural sciences supply the visual vocabulary, while his fevered imagination insists on devising Ovidian metamorphoses. He calls Arkadii a fledgling and a jackdaw, describes himself as a "half-crushed worm," and declares that he won't "wag his tail" (*viliat' khvostom*) in the face of death.[96] Of all Bazarov's utterances in this scene, however, the most striking is his hallucination of *krasnye sobaki* (literally "red dogs"), clearly a representation of wildfowling: the "red dogs," which at first glance seem a surrealistic detail, are readily recognizable as *krasnye settera* (red setters), a common term for Irish setters in nineteenth-century Russia.[97] We can thus translate his statement as "While I was lying here, it seemed all the time that Irish setters were running around me, while you [Vasilii Ivanovich, Bazarov's father] performed a set over me, as if over a black grouse."[98] Bazarov explicitly sees himself as a black grouse, Turgenev's favorite quarry, and thereby invokes, once again, the rich behavioral lore connected with that bird.

Though Costlow has intriguingly framed Bazarov's hallucinatory transformation into prey as a reflection of the hunter Actaeon's ancient punishment by Diana in the context of classical myth, Aksakov's chapter on black grouse offers illuminating details on the way Russian hunters actually pursued the juvenile birds (*tetereviata*) in Turgenev's time.[99] For this form of hunting, sportsmen relied not on their marksmanship, but on their dogs: "A good dog with a superior sense of smell will not scratch for long at the traces but will circle and scout close to its master, soon picking up the scent of a covey, taking up a set—sometimes at distances of a hundred paces or more—and lead its master straight to the birds."[100] Turgenev comments in "Fifty Flaws" that it is in precisely this situation that ill-trained dogs will attack the juvenile birds: "Rushes from the set and seizes the game, which happens particularly often with young black grouse [*molodye tetereva*]" (canine flaw no. 7).[101] Female black grouse, Aksakov asserts, do their best to decoy the hunter away from their young, "But the fowler who knows these ploys will kill the mother straight away; then his dog will seek out all the young one by one, and a good shot . . . will bring them all down without fail . . . a dog will seek them all out if it has been trained to do so."[102] Older juveniles are readily shot while perched, almost suicidally refusing to budge: "nothing is easier than shooting every last one, as nothing will induce them to fly from the tree."[103] Some hunters employ blinds and place decoys for the easily duped grouse: "In this respect black grouse are so stupid that if you put a charred stump, a tussock, or a cap on a perch they will fly to join it, or so I am told."[104]

The mating grouse's toughness, stubbornness, fervor, obliviousness to lethal threats, and ultimate stupidity can all be seen as reinforcing key aspects of Bazarov's behavior, especially in his pursuit of Odintsova, whose refusal to couple with him is akin to the indifference Aksakov explicitly ascribes to female black grouse at the lek. Aksakov's descriptions of gun dogs as they take up a set for young grouse illustrate vividly the images of tracking and discovery evoked by Bazarov's hallucination. Dimly foreshadowed by the playful image of peasant boys chasing after him "like little dogs" (*sobachonki*) in chapter 10, the spectacle of the "red dogs" in chapter 27 of *Fathers and Children* has frightening implications.[105] The dogs' set (*stoika*) represents merely the moment of unmasking, the instant when the terrified bird is exposed; death will come later, through the agency of the patient hunter— like the patient fisherman in *On the Eve*—who inexorably follows the dog's lead, shotgun at the ready. Aksakov's account makes clear that experienced hunters are merciless, leaving no bird alive, especially in this specific form of the hunt, in which the sitting birds make easy targets. The Irish setters of Bazarov's delirium, less overtly harmful than the hounds of antiquity, are in their methodical way of informing on their victims more chillingly deliberate than Actaeon's bloodthirsty stag hounds. That Bazarov's own father is one of the gun dogs faintly echoes the disruptive role of Vladimir's father in "First Love": Vasilii Bazarov spoils Evgenii's ability to succeed at the lek by pointing to him, and death swiftly follows. This familial relationship helps clarify why, a few sentences later, Bazarov mentions the setters once more with such pointed intimacy: "And now I must return to *my dogs*. Strange! I want to focus my thought on death, and nothing comes of it."[106]

Albeit retrospectively, further poignancy is added to Bazarov's delirium when we recall that "The Partridges," in which the narrator is a wounded bird being searched out by a relentless hunting dog, was Turgenev's way of dramatizing his own wretchedness as he awaited, in the summer of 1882, his own death. In "The Partridges," Turgenev chooses not to describe the moment of extermination, and the narrator is suspended in the same dire limbo as Bazarov. In this connection we may also recall that Bazarov is the son of a metaphorical partridge, Arina Vlas'evna: "Vasilii Ivanovich compared her with a 'female partridge' [*kuropatitsa*]: the little bobbed tail of her short jacket really did impart something bird-like to her appearance."[107] Fittingly, she considers dogs to be "unclean animals."[108] What a horrifying biological devolution we witness, then, when Arina's beloved son—whom she calls a falcon (*sokol*) and whom Katia identifies as predatory (*khishchnyi*)—sees himself, in the end, as a black grouse, a fearful, dim-witted prey species much more akin to his skittish, partridge-like mother (or even quail-like Sitnikov) than to a raptor.[109]

Finally, Bazarov's hallucination of the Irish setters raises the question of their figurative master's identity. The vision may imply that our nihilist hero senses, entirely unscientifically, the existence of a deity who metaphorically employs setters to uncover his game. This would be a God who stalks his prey by stealth and flushes it before the sudden, fatal shot. The implication of a godlike hunter-figure prowling beyond the page—if there are gun dogs, there must be a hunter close behind—lends resonance to the novel's unexpectedly Christian concluding lines ("eternal reconciliation and life everlasting"), which allude to the Orthodox funeral canticle "Repose with the saints" ("So sviatymi upokoi") as well as to Pushkin's "indifferent nature" at the close of "Whether I wander down noisy streets."[110] On the other hand, the unseen hunter implied in Bazarov's delirium may simply be death itself, which employs his father as a spy, a reading that meshes with Vasilii Bazarov's use of the Latin phrase *ad patres* (to the fathers) as a euphemism for death in an anecdote he tells to his son and Arkadii.[111]

The utter incompatibility of Arkadii and Bazarov in the later chapters of *Fathers and Children* makes it difficult to remember that at the midpoint of the text they are competing with one another at the lek, rivals for the affection of the same woman—Anna Sergeevna Odintsova. By novel's end, however, Bazarov is dead and Arkadii is a happily married husband and father who recognized his ideal mate in Katerina Lokteva and withdrew from competition for her beguiling sister. In Bazarov's terms, his friend has achieved the purpose of a "man," a "male" of the human species.[112] Katia's role is crucial: though she is self-effacingly human, she functions as another goddess-like figure who instinctively grasps nature's balance. Turgenev intimately ties Katia to stoicism, while her widowed sister Anna seeks, but fails to find, the serenity promised by that philosophy.

In simple terms, stoical ethics held that a good life is achieved through recognition that the four primary passions—appetite, pleasure, fear, distress—are failures of the rational mind to come to correct conclusions and must therefore be discarded.[113] Living in harmony with nature was the key: "Stoic arguments about the goal of life lead to the conclusion that it is a life in agreement with nature, or a life of virtue—but they believed that such a life necessarily brings with it the inner state of tranquillity."[114] Striving to remove the irrationality of passion from one's life brought the stoic closer to harmony with nature's own equanimity and a state of *tranquillitas*, or, as it was called by Greek thinkers, *ataraxia*, "literally, freedom from trouble or anxiety."[115]

At the start of chapter 26, Turgenev playfully satirizes his Russian characters' attempts to live out the stoical prescription. By placing them in a carefully described "Greek portico [*portik*] made of Russian bricks," Turgenev strongly hints at the *stoa poikile*, or "painted portico" in the agora of ancient Athens, where Zeno and his disciples founded the new strain of Hellenistic thinking that took its name from the building they frequented.[116] The structure itself reflects the ideal of moderation espoused within its classical predecessor: even at midday, according to the narrator, it was cool inside the portico. Tellingly, Katia often visits this part of the estate, and it is here, we learn, that she seemingly takes the place of the mothballed statue of the "goddess of Silence" and communes with nature: "Surrounded by freshness and shade, she used to read, work, or surrender herself to that feeling of complete silence which is probably familiar to everyone and the charm of which consists in a barely conscious, mute watchfulness [*podkraulivan'e*] for the broad wave of life ceaselessly rolling around and within us."[117] Katia's meditative mood here invokes elements of Turgenev's venatic equipoise familiar from "A Journey to the Forest-Belt" and Lavretskii's experience "at the bottom of the river": unconsciousness, quietness, watchfulness, and holism.

Katia is the most successful of the novel's characters in approaching the Stoics' ideal of harmony with nature and suppression of passion. She is consistently merged with natural elements. At her first appearance, "She held in her hands a basket filled with flowers . . . Everything within her was still young and verdant."[118] She is closely tied to her pet borzoi, Fifi, who, in chapter 25, lies on the ground, stretched out "in what hunters call 'the hare's pose,'" while Katia and Arkadii feed sparrows in the garden.[119] Her deep devotion to music, in *Fathers and Children* an analogue of nature, is another significant piece of evidence, and her specific choice of Mozart's Sonata No. 14 in C minor (K. 457)—with its impassioned style—bespeaks her earthiness.[120] Katia is a vital conduit for musical art and in tune with nature, happily awash in the "broad wave of life." By novel's end, as the narrator reviews the fate of all the characters, it is Katia who achieves the true ataraxia that eludes her sister: "Katia was *the most serene of all*: she would look fondly around herself and one could see that Nikolai Petrovich had come to love her dearly."[121]

Anna Odintsova, unlike her sister, is a poor stoic because, though she professes to seek ataraxia, she is too frightened to achieve it through harmony with the natural world and therefore never attains it. *Spokoistvie*, the Russian equivalent of ataraxia, begins to be associated with her from her first appearance ("her bright eyes gazed serenely [*spokoino*] and intelligently—and it was serenely [*spokoino*], not pensively"), and forms of *spokoistvie*, which becomes her leitmotiv, will be applied to Odintsova nine times in this novel.[122] "Serenity," she tells herself, "is the best thing on earth," yet she thinks this merely to calm her nerves after Bazarov declares his love and embraces her with a "devouring look."[123] For Odintsova, the concept of serenity is a soothing pill, more tranquilizer than tranquillity. It is clear that her life is largely governed by fear, which compels her to seek order by asserting control wherever possible—at her estate, where "order reigned," and in her initial interactions with Bazarov: "I want to learn from you the Latin names of the wild plants and their properties . . . Order is needed in all things."[124] In spite of Fifi's amiable personality, Odintsova is presented in chapter 16 as "standing on the path and scratching Fifi's ears with the tip of her open parasol," as though she prefers to shield herself, maintaining a safe distance from the realm of gazehounds.[125] She also dislikes Katia's beloved portico, having once encountered there a grass snake (*Natrix natrix*)—like Bazarov, a predator of frogs—and, most significantly, she is frightened of the chaos embodied by Bazarov himself: "I am afraid of this man."[126] For Odintsova, nature is to be named, tamed, and kept away; for Katia, nature is to be joined, even emulated.

Arkadii, who, like Katia, "adored nature," specifically invites Katia to the portico—the temple—in order to propose marriage to her. She receives his halting preamble to the proposal with considerable equanimity: "Katia said nothing in reply, but stopped looking at Arkadii . . . Katia kept her eyes lowered. It seemed that she didn't even understand what he was leading up to, and she was waiting for something . . . She sat in the same position . . ."[127] Katia's assent to the match is notably dispassionate, and she seems amused at herself for succumbing to mild emotion: "After long reflection, barely smiling, she said, 'Yes' . . . she innocently began to cry, quietly laughing at her own tears."[128] Katia, something like a worshipper or goddess in the stoic temple, thus reaches a quiet contentment that resembles ataraxia. Arkadii, for his part, achieves the kind of complete and enduring success at the mating ground that eludes Rudin, Lavretskii, Insarov, and Bazarov: "Someone who has never seen such tears in the eyes of a beloved being," declares the narrator after Katia's assent, "has yet to experience the degree to which, utterly overwhelmed by gratitude and shame, a person can be happy on this earth."[129]

The congruities of characterization in *Fathers and Children* are completed when, in a double wedding ceremony, Katia happily marries Arkadii, and Fenechka happily marries his father, Nikolai Petrovich. Just as the Kirsanov father and son are tightly linked, so are the brides, Fenechka and Katia: "After her husband and [her son] Mitia, Fenechka (Fedos'ia Nikolaevna) adored no one so much as her daughter-in-law [Katia], and when Katia sat down at the piano, she was happy to remain with her all day long."[130] Equally associated with nature, the two women share other traits as well. When Fenechka and Nikolai Petrovich are becoming acquainted, she hides from him—just as Katia "hides" in her music—in a field of rye overgrown with wormwood and cornflowers, merging with the natural landscape and looking out at him timidly "like a small animal."[131] And just as Katia is associated with flowers and that which is "young and verdant," Fenechka too is a vision of fertility and the bloom of youth: "There comes a time in the lives of young women when they suddenly begin to flower and blossom out, like summer roses; such a time had come for Fenechka."[132] This is the moment Bazarov sees her in a lilac arbor with a freshly gathered bouquet of red and white roses still wet with dew.

Bazarov and Pavel Petrovich are congruent too: both are "dead" by novel's end (one literally, the other figuratively), and both project their frustrated longing for love upon Fenechka—Bazarov because of Odintsova's unattainability, Pavel Petrovich because of the Princess R.'s. Ultimately, both—to use Bazarov's expression—have "bet on the card of a woman's love," lost, and "sunk to the point of being no good for anything."[133] Bazarov's commitment to physiology and the "natural sciences" has utterly failed him. He begins as a confident scientist ("People are like trees in a forest: no botanist would study each individual birch"), but unbidden love transforms him into a frustrated young swain who vandalizes individual trees out of spite: "In conversations with Anna Sergeevna he more than ever expressed his indifferent contempt for everything Romantic, but when he was alone, he indignantly acknowledged the Romantic within himself. Then he would set out into the forest and walk with long strides, breaking off the branches he happened upon and in an undertone cursing her and himself."[134] Bazarov, in fact, is associated with arboreal imagery as much as the main female characters are linked to flowers. He acts as an expert arborist to Nikolai Petrovich early on, and later confesses to Arkadii that an aspen growing on the edge of a cellar-pit on the Bazarovs' modest estate reminds him vividly of his childhood belief in the magical properties of place. That tree is also a link to the aspen grove seen by Nikolai Petrovich when he rues having been given *Kraft und Stoff* by Arkadii—an aspen grove that overlooks the marsh where the adult Bazarov now captures frogs for medical experimentation instead of meditating, like Nikolai, on the magic of natural and artistic beauty.[135] Spitefully confiding in Arkadii, Bazarov sees himself as "self-broken" (*samolomannyi*), as a tree might be, and grows insolent when his Romantically inclined friend notices the way a maple leaf falls to the ground and compares it to a beautiful butterfly.[136] Later, Arkadii muses with Katia on the etymology of the Russian word for ash tree (*iasen'*) and notes that she, unlike Bazarov, does not reproach him for speculating on the metaphorical significance of the natural world.[137]

In chapter 21, when Bazarov abandons his parents after a three-day visit, the first in as many years, his mother finally masters her grief and offers reassurance to her despairing husband: " 'What's to be done, Vasia? A son's a like a slice that's been cut off. He's like a falcon: he flies in when he wants, flies away when he wants. But you and I are like stump-mushrooms in the hollow of a log. We sit side by side and never budge. Only I'll stay here with you, never changing, just as you will with me.' Vasilii Ivanovich removed his hands from his face and embraced his wife, his friend, as tightly as he used to hug her in his youth. She comforted him in his sorrow."[138] Here Arina Vlas'evna uses the word *opënki*, a broad term for various mushroom species that grow on the stumps left behind when trees are broken or felled—an apt arboreal metaphor for the way their son has irretrievably broken away, leaving his mother and father rooted to the stump of his boyhood home, where they endure in a place of brokenness. In the final paragraph of his pioneering 1856 article on mushroom gathering, Aksakov had described the order in which more than a dozen varieties of Russia's edible mushrooms appear over the course of a year, and it is the *opënki* that mature last, the final mushrooms to be had before winter comes.[139] The image of the two old mushrooms grieving for their departed falcon will be echoed on the last page of *Fathers and Children*, when they will grieve again, endlessly—kneeling, weeping, praying, and gazing at "the mute stone under which their son lies buried."[140]

When the Bazarovs wave good-bye to their son in chapter 21, what should be an unbearably painful scene represents, in the broader context of Turgenev's writings on the place of humanity in the natural world, a moment of profound contentment. Arina and Vasilii have successfully mated, nested, and grown old together. They love each other. Their never-ending mutual consolation refutes the universal solipsism Turgenev had asserted in his second review of Aksakov's hunting treatise, that nature requires every organism to "take possession of its surroundings as its own property."[141] Instead, Bazarov's steadfast parents offer a lived example of "that selfsame universal, endless harmony, in which, conversely, all that lives lives for another and only in another attains its reconciliation or its resolution, and all lives merge into a single, universal life—this is one of those 'open' secrets that we all see and do not see."[142] Arina and Vasilii, in the way they love one another, model how Turgenev directed his readers to love the natural world: "If it is only 'through love' [as Goethe wrote] that one can draw near to nature, then this love must be unselfish, like any authentic feeling: love nature not by virtue of what she means in relation to you, a person, but because she, in and of herself, is sweet and dear to you—and you will understand her."[143]

Conclusion

"I'm a Sportsman": Deviations and Doubts

> There was nothing else on earth that exhilarated me as much as hunting: I knew of no higher pleasure than the excitement you experience on a hunt. Nonetheless, misgivings about the legitimacy of this pleasure crept into my soul.
>
> —Vladimir Chertkov, "An Evil Pastime," 1890

In Tom Stoppard's epic, three-part play about mid-nineteenth-century Russian writers and intellectuals, *The Coast of Utopia* (2001), Turgenev is one of the main characters. He makes his first appearance onstage as a diffident fledgling poet: "He is twenty-three and well over six feet tall, with a surprisingly light, high voice."[1] The scene is Premukhino, family estate of the Bakunins. Turgenev has just begun chatting with Tat'iana Bakunina during a friendly stroll through the gardens:

Tatiana: Are you a writer?

Turgenev: No. But I thought I was. (*He "shoots" at birds flying over. Laughs.*) I'm a sportsman. (*Pause.*) But I'd still like to write a decent poem one day. Tomorrow, for example. It's lovely here. I'd like to stay.[2]

In that autumn of 1841, Turgenev was recently returned from Berlin, where he had finished three years of graduate study in philosophy. Stoppard insightfully introduces him as a seasoned hunter who is secondarily a writer, and a self-doubting writer, at that. The young sportsman's unlikely ascent to the pinnacle of literary prominence lay less than a decade ahead, but in just over two decades he would find himself one of his country's most beleaguered and debated literary figures, a target of ire from Russians of all political stripes. In this later period, the early, consistent preoccupations—including nature and humanity's place in it—persisted, though Turgenev explored them in unaccustomed ways, and at times his agility seemed to falter.

The precarious balance of ideological positions he had maintained in his fiction was perceived as offensively off-kilter by most readers of *Fathers and Children*, which the left generally took as a trivializing parody of the novel's nihilist hero, and the right saw as a denigration of traditional gentry institutions. Turgenev's esteem among Russian readers slipped further still in the wake of his next novel, *Smoke* (1865–67), which achieved nowhere near the success of his previous large-scale works and merely intensified the storm of criticism in which he found himself. Nonetheless, in the mid-to-late 1860s Turgenev entered a time of personal contentment perhaps unrivaled in his life. In May 1863 he began the process of settling in Baden-Baden (where the Viardots had taken up residence following Pauline's retirement from the operatic stage), acquired probably the finest gun dog he ever owned (Pégase), and enjoyed a period of comparatively good health.[3] Frequent hunting trips and salutary fellowship with friends were, however, accompanied by an overall decline in the quantity and quality of his fiction, a decline frequently seen as having been caused by geographical retreat from his turbulent homeland and literary retreat from his customary realism. In his last years, Turgenev may at times seem to have lost interest in nature, but I believe that interest was merely expressing itself in altered forms. At the same time, another important change was gradually making itself felt: the intensification of his guilt about hunting.

Mutations

In the years between *Fathers and Children* and *Smoke*, Turgenev completed only three stories: "Phantoms" ("Prizraki," 1855–63), "The Dog" ("Sobaka," 1864), and "Enough!" (1862–64). The first two inaugurate his newfound attraction to paranormal subjects, initially essayed in "Faust" eight years earlier. The supernatural and mysterious would now dominate the thematic complex of his short fiction for the last twenty years of his life.

It is difficult to classify the plotless and deliberately fragmentary dozen pages of monologue that constitute "Enough!" Nabokov certainly exaggerates when he says that it contains a declaration of Turgenev's "decision to give up literature."[4] As Turgenev himself put it in an 1878 letter to his editor at the *Herald of Europe* (*Vestnik Evropy*), Mikhail Stasiulevich, "Enough!" was "a subjective mess" (*sub"ektivishchina*)—full of "memories and impressions so personal that there was no need to share them with the public."[5] These "impressions" return us to the despondent musing on humanity's impermanence in Day One of "Journey to the Forest-Belt." In chapter 16 of "Enough!" Turgenev's first-person narrator clearly acknowledges the superiority of natural beauty to anthropogenic beauty (art): beauty exists in nature, but only where human beings, despite their precious gifts of consciousness and liberty, are absent. Such, the narrator argues, is the case with an exquisite butterfly, which will be beautiful again a thousand years from now, whereas artistic beauty—generated by individuals, not species—is gone forever as soon as it is destroyed:

> Unconsciously and inexorably obedient to her laws, she [nature] does not recognize art, just as she does not recognize freedom, does not recognize good; from time immemorial advancing and ephemeral, she tolerates nothing immortal, nothing immutable. . . . Man is her child, but what is human, what is artistic, is inimical to her, precisely because it attempts to be immutable and immortal. Man is the child of nature, but she is a universal mother and she has no favorites: all that exists in her bosom came into being only at the expense of another and must in its time yield its place to another—she creates by destroying, and it is all the same [*vsë ravno*] to her what she creates and what she destroys— provided that life does not come to an end, and provided that death is not deprived of its rights.[6]

The voice of Goethe's "Nature" rings out clearly here, but the implications for artistic creation are far bleaker and more in line with the despair of Leopardi. In "Enough!" Turgenev expands the cheerless pronouncements near the end of *On the Eve* by suggesting that the entirety of nature's creative energy—not just the sphere of human happiness—is a closed system: all things come into being "at the expense of" other things. "Where can we poor humans, poor artists," Turgenev's narrator continues, "contend with this deaf-mute force that is blind from birth and that does not even rejoice in its victories, but moves on, goes forward, devouring everything?"[7]

It might be tempting to modify Nabokov's verdict and see "Enough!" as Turgenev's giving up on the *natural*—a refusal to lavish his literary care on an omnipotent, indifferent, atemporal force against which human beings and their works are helpless. That view seems supported by Turgenev's marked turn late in life toward the *super*natural—in such stories as "An Unfortunate Girl" ("Neschastnaia," 1869) and "Knock . . . Knock . . . Knock . . ." ("Stuk . . . Stuk . . . Stuk. . . . ," 1871) and by his overriding concern with what Marina Ledkovsky calls "telepathy and forebodings, . . . visionary dreams, the fatal power of heredity, and magnetism" in "A Strange Story" ("Strannaia istoriia," 1870), "The Dream" ("Son," 1877), "Father Aleksei's Tale" ("Rasskaz ottsa

Alekseia," 1877), "The Song of Triumphant Love" ("Pesn' torzhestvuiush-chei liubvi," 1881), and "Klara Milich" (1883).[8] Even one of his finest late works, "King Lear of the Steppes" ("Stepnoi korol' Lir," 1870), not on its face a supernatural story, features a nearly superhuman Lear figure in the character of Martyn Kharlov.

It is not the case, however, that Turgenev, in the last twenty years of his life, lost his adroitness in treating the natural environment or abandoned the ideal of venatic equipoise. In many of the fantastic works from this period, there is considerable attention to natural detail, but from unaccustomed per-spectives, as in the descriptions of both Russian and far-flung landscapes in "Phantoms":

> We soared aloft like woodcock swooping toward a birch tree, and again we were carried in a straight line. Instead of grass, the tops of trees flashed past beneath our feet. It was wondrous to see the forest from above, with its bristly spine lit by the moon. It resembled some huge, slumbering beast and accompanied us with a broad and ceaseless rus-tling that sounded like an unintelligible growl. From time to time we happened upon a small clearing; to one side of it, a jagged band of shadow loomed beautiful and black . . . At times a hare would plain-tively cry out below; above, an owl whistled, also plaintively; the air smelled of mushrooms, budding flowers, lovage-herb; the moonlight simply poured forth in all directions, cold and stern; the "Stack-Poles" glittered just above our heads.[9]

Familiar game species—woodcock, hare—are present, but natural scenes of fauna, forest, and sky are encased in the narrator's bizarre vision of flying above the earth, as he is embraced by Ellis, a mysterious feminine appa-rition "seemingly woven out of semi-transparent milky mist."[10] With her help, the narrator now possesses the power of flight, like the woodcock Tur-genev so often described in fiction and killed in life. The fantastical context defamiliarizes these natural images, which undeniably partake of the same comprehensive vividness on display in earlier works. Clearly new, though, is Turgenev's willingness to perceive the natural landscape from aloft, to adopt the avian vantage point—an early step, perhaps, in the heightened sympathy for birds discernible in his late works.

The treatment of nature in *Smoke*, however, suggests a deviation from Turgenev's usual deftness and equanimity with the subject. A follow-up to *Fathers and Children*, *Smoke* is a more satiric novel that takes keener aim at Slavophilism and the reactionary conservatism of smug Russian aristocrats. Particularly noteworthy are the parodic jabs at Turgenev's former friend,

Aleksandr Herzen—through the figure of Stepan Gubarev and the chattering adherents of his Slavophilic socialism—and the explicit endorsement of Westernism, chiefly through the interminable pronouncements of Sozont Potugin.[11] A semiautobiographical hunter and sententious advocate of what he calls "civilization," Potugin provoked a good deal of outrage among readers not only for political reasons, but also because his connection to the plot seemed tenuous, even though the author considered him an integral part of the text from its inception.[12] As an observer of the natural world, Potugin—clearly a spokesman for many of Turgenev's own views—is often a conduit for the facile anthropotropism that pervades *Smoke*.

Potugin's hunting and animal analogies, in comparison to what we find in Turgenev's earlier work, are ungainly. He tells the protagonist, Grigorii Litvinov,

> Once I was making my way with gun and dog along a forest . . . into some marshland to go after snipe; other hunters had told me a great deal about this marsh. I look, and sitting there in a clearing in front of a little hut is a merchant's steward, fresh and hale as a hulled nut; he's smirking about something—what, I don't know. And I asked him, "Where's that marsh around here I've heard tell about, and are there any snipe in it?" "Certainly, certainly!" he sang out right away, with an expression on his face as though I'd just given him a ruble. "My pleasure, sir. The marsh is first-rate. As far as any wild birds, well, Good Lord! Lots and lots of them." I set off, and not only did I find no wildfowl, but the marsh itself had dried up. Be so good as to tell me: Why does a Russian lie? Why does a political economist lie, and also about wildfowl?"[13]

For Potugin, who is conspicuously unconcerned with the ruin of the wetland itself, the tale of the hunting trip is merely a didactic tool for denouncing human vice. He now devises awkward natural similes in yet another anecdote, this one boasting of how he got the better of a brash young radical whom Potugin calls a *"v'iunosha,"* a showy portmanteau of *v'iun* (loach) and *iunosha* (young man). Like Bazarov and Litvinov himself, this *v'iunosha* studies "the natural sciences"; Potugin gleefully "baits" and "catches" him.[14] Even though Potugin forces his hapless interlocutor to admit that his sexual looseness flouts the natural behavior of animals because, as the *v'iunosha* protests, "beasts are no rule for man"—human exceptionalism with which Turgenev would take issue—the entire anecdote once again comes off as a convenient instrumentalization of the natural world.[15] The same can be said of Potugin's unsubtle description of how he first made the acquaintance of

Irina Ratmirova, the novel's heroine: "Here's a simile for you: a tree stands before you, and there's no wind. How can a leaf on a lower branch touch a leaf on a higher branch? It's impossible. But a storm comes along, everything mixes together—and those two leaves touch."[16]

Such obvious nature-rhetoric is particularly troubling when it issues from a character who can plausibly be seen as the author's mouthpiece, but even more distressing is that Turgenev himself, in the novel's structure, displays a similarly obtrusive penchant for turning nature into a tool. For all their loveliness, his rich descriptions of the landscape surrounding Baden-Baden exist to soothe the protagonist after wrenching developments in the plot, when Litvinov wanders the Black Forest hills to clear his mind.[17] Like the narrator's tree-gazing in "Kas'ian from Krasivaia Mech'," this is an example of nature transformed into a palliative for human beings. To be charitable, perhaps Turgenev, as in *Notes of a Hunter*, is implying the foolishness of such an attitude toward the organic world: after all, Litvinov is tragically unable to resist the pull of his former love for Irina, and the lesson could be that those who exploit nature for personal solace may end up punished by their own natural longings. Once Litvinov derails his life in order to reunite with Irina, the novel's narrator (echoing "Enough!") observes, "Nature does not deal in logic, our human logic; she has her own, which we do not understand and do not acknowledge until she runs over us, as with a wheel."[18] On the other hand, many further instances of natural description in *Smoke* display a heavy-handed anthropotropism: the trapped butterfly that blatantly symbolizes Litvinov's predicament, the explicit comparison of deceptive local bankers to flowers damaged by the scythe, and the name "Osinina" for Irina's family, transparently derived from *osina*, or aspen, the quivering tree whose inconstancy was disparaged by the narrator of "The Tryst."[19] Finally, the symbolic role of heliotrope (*Heliotropium europaeum*), as a token exchanged between Litvinov and Irina, dominates the entire novel. This weedlike flower's strong scent and habit of turning toward the sun have prompted a number of Russian critics to speculate about the reason for its prominence in the text—it might reflect Litvinov's inability to turn away from Irina over the years, might be a reference to Ovid's account of the myth of Clytie and Helios, and so on—but none have come to convincing conclusions.[20] What remains clear is that heliotrope, already a feature of the plot in Turgenev's earliest plans for the novel,[21] in no way functions as a phytotropic element of setting, but solely as an emblem of human concerns.

After *Smoke*, Turgenev fruitfully returned to vital themes and descriptive modes from the *Notes of a Hunter* cycle. "The Brigadier" (1867), for instance, employs the device of a wayfaring hunter-narrator, much like the

Kostomarovo landowner in *Notes of a Hunter*, to tell a story that unfolds just after St. Peter's Day—the start of hunting season. The opening chapter consists of a single long paragraph in which we are given a meticulous, fondly elegiac reminiscence of the natural beauty that once engulfed the sleepy estates of "Great-Russian Ukraine," and chapters 4–8 contain a fishing interlude similar to the one in "Raspberry Water."[22] In 1871–72, Turgenev created a sequel to "Chertopkhanov and Nedopiuskin" ("The End of Chertopkhanov"), and in late 1873 returned to two stories he had begun to draft for *Notes of a Hunter* decades earlier. He now completed these and added them to the cycle in 1874: "A Living Relic" and "It's Clattering!"[23]

In fact, "A Living Relic" is one of Turgenev's most moving treatments of the natural environment, as well as a curtain call for major characters and themes from earlier works. The dying, visionary heroine, Luker'ia, a young peasant woman confined to her bed by debilitating illness (possibly scleroderma),[24] defends nature with a fierceness equal to Kas'ian's and observes the environment with a sensory acuity superior to the ecstatic hunter's in "Forest and Steppe":

> I, thank God, can see fine and hear everything—everything. A mole digging underground—even that I can hear. And I catch every smell, no matter how faint it might be! If buckwheat blooms in the field or a linden tree in the garden—I don't need to be told: I'm the first one to smell it. Only a little breeze has to make its way from there. . .
>
> . . . I watch, I listen. The bees in the apiary buzz and hum; a dove lands on the roof and starts to coo; a little brood-hen stops by with her chicks to peck at crumbs; or a sparrow or butterfly will arrive—it's a delight to me. Year before last some swallows even built a nest over there in the corner and raised their young. How fascinating it was! One would fly in, alight on the nest, feed the little babies, and then disappear. You look, and there's another swallow to replace the first one. Sometimes it doesn't fly in but only flashes past the open door, and the babies, well, all at once they peep and open their beaks wide . . . I waited for them the next year too, but they told me that a hunter from hereabouts shot them with his gun. What did he have to be so selfish for? One whole swallow's no bigger than a beetle . . . what wicked gentlemen you hunters are![25]

In a variation on the "Scandinavian legend" in *Rudin*, the birds that enter Luker'ia's dwelling have no need to fly off to find their nest: they build it indoors, confident of their safety, perhaps because Luker'ia is a gentle and welcoming invalid in repose. She attains the kind of serene watchfulness previously associated in Turgenev's work with hunters, like the narrator of "Journey to the Forest-Belt," but in this late tale it is the hunters who disturb and destroy her serenity as well as the lives of the birds she loves to watch. Luker'ia achieves a balance of sensory, spiritual, existential, and environmental forces not through hunting but through her status as half alive, half dead—partly of this world, partly of the next. In her dreams, her illness takes the form of a "little ruddy [*ryzhen'kii*] dog," echoing Bazarov's Irish setters, and Death itself is personified as a tall, imposing female figure—a form akin to the green goddess of "Nature."[26] Secure in her kenotic outlook, Luker'ia reaches an unselfish oneness with *priroda* that makes her the antithesis of such self-obsessed characters as Chulkaturin in "Diary of a Superfluous Man" or the "Hamlet" of the Shchigry District. In a subtle hint that she, like the swallows, is somehow a hunter's victim, she dies soon after St. Peter's Day, as she had predicted.

Turgenev's last and longest novel, *Virgin Soil* (*Nov'*, 1870–76), is both a reaffirmation of nature's indifference and a welcome return to form after *Smoke*. The work took shape during the early 1870s, a period when Turgenev rarely visited Russia, though he spent the summer of 1876 completing most of the manuscript during nearly six weeks of intensive work at Spasskoe-Lutovinovo.[27] Despite early negative reaction in Russia when *Virgin Soil* first appeared, in January and February of 1877, its depiction of the "going-to-the-people" movement, known as *narodnichestvo*, proved prescient, and the novel eventually enjoyed considerable popularity among Russian readers and abroad.[28] From his first sketches in 1870, Turgenev intended the work to explore characters who "seek within the real . . . something great and significant, but this is nonsense: real life is prosaic and must be so."[29] The main character, Aleksei Nezhdanov, is just such a "romantic of realism" (*romantik realizma*): vigorous, intelligent, but also a sensitive idealist and secret poet who kills himself after failing as both a revolutionary and a lover.[30] As Schapiro points out, his is "the tragedy of a Hamlet who longs to be a Don Quixote."[31] In this he is a mutation of Bazarov, the putative realist who had "resentfully recognized the romantic in himself," and *Virgin Soil* in many ways functions as a worthy sequel to *Fathers and Children*.[32]

Turgenev intimately associates Nezhdanov with the natural world's seductive beauty. As a newly hired tutor at a rural estate, he is immediately drawn to the "old-fashioned [*pradedovskii*], black-earth garden" there:

The entire garden was vaguely shining green with the first beauty of spring's blossoming; there was still no sign of the intense summertime buzzing of insects. Young leaves murmured; somewhere chaffinches were singing; two turtle-doves were cooing all the while in one and the same tree; a cuckoo called, shifting from one place to another; and from far away, beyond the millpond, came the friendly din of rooks, which resembled the creaking of a multitude of cartwheels. And over all this young, secluded, peaceful life, bright clouds sailed by, puffing out their breasts like large, lazy birds. Nezhdanov watched, listened, and drew in the air through parted, chilled lips.[33]

Having gazed for a time at the garden, he keeps his windows open all day, allowing the fresh air to stream in and enjoying the nightingale trills of evening. Later in May, he lingers in the nearby birch wood, where "he thought of nothing, entirely giving himself over to that special springtime sensation to which—in the hearts of both young and old—there is always sorrow attached: the agitated sorrow of longing in the young, the immovable sorrow of regret in the old."[34] Nezhdanov observes and imbibes the environment much as Lavretskii did in *A Gentry Nest*: deeply, naturally, unconsciously. By June, against a vivid natural backdrop, he realizes that he has fallen in love with the novel's heroine, Marianna Sinetskaia, a niece of the estate's owner:

> There were high, playful clouds about the blue sky, a strong and steady wind; the dust on the road had been killed by yesterday's rain; the brittle-willows rustled, shined, and streamed—everything was in motion, everything was in flight. A quail call was borne along as a liquid whistling from the distant hills through verdant ravines precisely as if this cry had wings and was flying upon them; rooks were shining in the sun; some dark fleas were moving along the straight edge of the bare horizon: these were peasants re-plowing the upturned fallow earth . . . he shuddered when he saw the roof of the house, the top floor, the window of Marianna's room. "Yes," he said to himself, and his heart warmed, "[Markelov]'s right—she's a good woman—and I love her."[35]

Here, even as Turgenev invokes the primal mating urge associated with the quail call in *On the Eve*, he makes subtle reference to the novel's title and its epigraph by means of the flea-like peasants working the land in the far distance: "Virgin soil must not be turned up by a shallow-skimming wooden ard, but by a deeply drawing plow."[36] Never simply geotropic, the concept of "virgin soil" (derived from the Russian lexical root *nov-*, "new") has a number of human implications in the text, but here it seems to hint at the new feelings being plowed up in young Nezhdanov and Marianna.

Nezhdanov's dreamy relationship with nature is, however, a sign of his "romantic" essence, and the persistent bond he shares with the environment is characterized by a soft, sentimental devotion that ultimately disqualifies him from revolutionary activity. The textual evidence quoted above, which later evolves into more-explicitly metaphorical accounts of natural beauty, strongly suggests that Nezhdanov is doomed. Consider, for example, the ensuing outdoor set-piece in which Marianna invites Nezhdanov to meet her secretly in an old grove of weeping birches:

> The wind was not letting up; long clusters of branches waved and tossed about like plaits that had been let down; as before, high clouds were being carried along quickly; and when one of them flew across the sun, the surrounding landscape would come to a halt—and turn not dark, but monochromatic. But as soon as it flew past, suddenly everywhere bright patches of color would restlessly sway once again: they would intermingle, become variegated, and mix with patches of shadow . . . The sound and motion stayed the same, but a kind of festive joy was being added to them. With the same joyous force passion bursts into a darkened, agitated heart . . . And this is precisely what Nezhdanov brought into his breast.[37]

The link between what Nezhdanov feels during this assignation and the state of the natural world—for example Marianna's pliancy and the metaphor of the trees letting down their hair—is too close, and the narrator's final comment—which brazenly unmasks the simile uniting the agitated birch grove and the hero's emotions—is too neat, too simplistically anthropotropic. We are being made privy here to Nezhdanov's way of seeing and interpreting his natural surroundings—as emblems of his own moods; these are the idyllic impressions of a "romantic of realism," an admirer of old-fashioned gardens and weeping groves who is too ready to perceive them as reflections of his inner life. A few pages later, part 1 of *Virgin Soil* is brought to a close when the couple leaves the birch wood: "They went home together pensive and happy; young grass fawned at their feet; young foliage rustled all around; patches of color and shadow slid briskly along their clothing—and both of them smiled at the troubled play of the leaves, at the merry gusts of wind, at the fresh brilliance of the foliage, at their own youthfulness, and at each other."[38] The passage is ominous: for Turgenev, nature is indifferent, not a sensitive barometer of human emotion.

To Nezhdanov, the natural world is "something great and significant," but, as Turgenev wrote in his plan for *Virgin Soil*, "this is nonsense: real life is prosaic and must be so." The character who best embodies the sensible and prosaic is Vasilii Solomin, manager of a writing-paper factory and a figure Turgenev, in his plan for the novel, intended to be "a real expert of the

American type who goes about his business just as serenely as a peasant plows and sows . . . A vulgar nature [*natura*], laconic, without aesthetic principle, but strong and brave, not prone to boredom, restrained. His religion is the triumph of the lower class, in which he desires to participate. A Russian revolutionary."[39] On the last page of the novel, another *narodnik*, Paklin, declares that Russia needs "strong, gray, monochromatic, popular [*narodnye*] people" and describes Solomin—the true hero of *Virgin Soil*—as having "a heart that is pained the same way ours is and hates the same things we hate, but his nerves are quiet and his whole body behaves as it should . . . a fine fellow! A man with an ideal, but no phrasemonger; educated, but from the people; simple, but canny . . . What more could you ask?"[40] It is stable, methodical Solomin, a man who has achieved equipoise, who ends up wedding Marianna, a mere two days after Nezhdanov shoots himself. The monochromatic and shadow-tinged features that persist in the natural scenes shared by Marianna and Nezhdanov presage that the "strong, gray" man, who wears a "gray work-jacket" will succeed colorful, naively naturegazing Nezhdanov.[41]

Solomin does not see the natural world as a storehouse of metaphors or sympathetic stirrings. When Marianna complains near the middle of the novel that a cruel relative, Anna Zakharovna, has maliciously linked Marianna to her disgraced father by saying that "the apple doesn't fall far from the apple tree," Solomin reassures her: "I don't know who Anna Zakharovna is, or about this apple tree you mentioned, but really, some stupid woman says something stupid to you and you can't bear it? How are you going to live?"[42] As we saw in chapter 5, Rudin, to impress Natal'ia Lasunskaia, had dramatically compared himself to an apple tree overburdened with fruit. In *Virgin Soil*, Solomin is the anti-Rudin—to him, apple trees are simply trees—while Nezhdanov is an extension of Rudin, a believer in natural emblems. In his farewell note to Solomin and Marianna, Nezhdanov writes, "I just glanced out the window: among the quick-rushing clouds there stood a single beautiful star. No matter how fast they rushed by, they couldn't cover it up. This star reminded me of you, Marianna!"[43] The imagery here echoes Lavretskii's and Lemm's Romantic celestial emblem ("pure stars") for another ultimately unattainable heroine: Liza Kalitina.[44]

In a long paragraph, Turgenev thoroughly describes the ugliness of Solomin's factory: "On all sides one was struck by laxity, filth, soot . . . what a stench, what stuffiness everywhere!" The grounds are littered with garbage, shaggy mongrels, pigs, and a sooty, wailing four-year-old boy; Nezhdanov responds, "I confess that all this disorder surprises me."[45] It is outside this repulsive but productive temple to anti-nature, where dead trees are rendered into writing paper, that Nezhdanov will kill himself. In the suicide scene, Turgenev invokes stark contrasts of setting to illuminate his characters' outlooks on nature:

> The day was gray, the sky hung low, and a damp breeze stirred the tips of the grass and rocked the leaves of the trees; the factory rattled and rumbled less than it did at that time on other days; from its yard came the smell of coal, tar, and tallow. Watchfully and suspiciously, Nezhdanov peered around and went straight to the old apple tree that had attracted his attention on the very day of his arrival, when he had looked out the window of his little apartment. The trunk of this apple tree was overgrown with dry moss; the rough, bare branches, hung here and there with red-green leaves, rose upward, contorted into the likeness of aged, pleading arms bent at the elbow. Nezhdanov stood firmly on the dark soil surrounding the apple tree's roots . . . there was no other human being in sight. . . .
>
> . . . It was as though the whole place was deserted, had turned away from him, had withdrawn forever and left him at the whim [*proizvol*] of fate. Only the factory dully droned and reeked, and aloft small, prickly droplets of cold drizzle started to fall.
>
> Then Nezhdanov, looking up through the crooked branches of the tree under which he was standing, at the low, gray, apathetically blind [*bezuchastno-slepoe*], damp sky, gave a yawn, shrugged, and thought, "There's nothing else left—can't go back to Petersburg, to prison." He tossed down his cap and, already aware in his entire body of a kind of sickly-sweet, powerful, agonizing desire to stretch, pressed the revolver to his chest and pulled the trigger.[46]

This lonely, decrepit apple tree—clearly a figure for both the man now standing upon its roots and his romantic illusions—has outlived its time and now displays only a few spots of color. The overwhelming sky is gray—a hue pointedly associated with Solomin—and it melds with the factory to dominate the scene. When he looks up, Nezhdanov finally glimpses the truth: not an idyll of empathetic nature, but a blind and uncaring vault that does not, cannot, participate in his life. What he sees beyond the tree is that to be deserted and subject to nature's *proizvol* is the inevitable state of all that lives in the organic world. At last cognizant of his irrelevance, Nezhdanov mortally wounds himself and unites Solomin and Marianna by inviting them to join hands over his chest as he dies. In a final nod to the dead man's obsolete view of nature, the champions of the monochromatic (*odnotsvetnyi*) place token flowers (*tsvety*) near the corpse, as Nezhdanov had requested in one of his Romantic poems, doubtless written on the kind of paper such hideous factories produce.[47]

In *Virgin Soil*, hunting appears prominently only once, in the long description of a painting that hangs in fusty Fomushka and Fimushka Subochev's gentry nest, where "time seemed to have stopped for them and no 'novelty' [*novshestvo*] penetrated the boundary of their 'oasis.'"[48] It is an oil portrait of Fomushka himself as a young man, resplendent in full coursing regalia, galloping on a bay horse across a snowy landscape after unseen game.[49] The portrait, like its owners, and like the mode of hunting it depicts, is now nothing more than an early nineteenth-century curio, just as irrelevant as Nezhdanov himself.

Misgivings

In the last dozen years of his life, even as he gravitated further toward the uncanny in the stories and experimented with new approaches to nature themes in the novels, Turgenev tended to reserve explicitly hunting-oriented topics for a range of nonfiction genres, as we have seen in earlier chapters. These include a memoiristic encomium to Pégase ("Pégase," 1871) and a pragmatic code of hunting norms ("Fifty Flaws," 1876). Such examples signal Turgenev's continued embrace of the venatic life, and indeed he hunted until he was no longer physically capable of taking the field, at least through the end of 1881.[50] It is nonetheless undeniable that late in life—what Eva Kagan-Kans calls "his twilight years when he was more and more enveloped in an atmosphere of unrelieved gloom"[51]—Turgenev produced more written evidence than ever before that he was aware of the moral objections to hunting, that with the passage of time the voices of Kas'ian and Luker'ia, as it were, had grown more insistent.

Turgenev's heightened sense of conscience could well have been part of a larger trend among the educated classes in his homeland. The Russian Society for the Protection of Animals (RSPA) was founded in October 1865, and ten years later, Dostoevsky prominently endorsed it in a moving essay for the January 1876 issue of *Diary of a Writer*.[52] The RSPA and similar organizations in Russia chiefly promoted anticruelty measures to protect domestic animals, but certain hunting practices, including the coursing of wolves, were also opposed.[53] While Turgenev never mentioned the RSPA in writing, one can safely assume that he was aware of its activities, especially in view of the prominent notices—including Dostoevsky's—that it received in the Russian press on its ten-year anniversary in 1875, an occasion marked by the publication of a two-hundred-page history of the organization by one of its prominent members, Vladimir Iversen.[54]

We can only speculate about whether and how Turgenev might have been influenced by Dostoevsky's or Iversen's work, but in March-April 1876, he too addressed the issue of animal cruelty by translating his friend Gustave Flaubert's freshly completed "La légende de Saint Julien l'Hospitalier." Turgenev tackled the project with remarkable intensity: "I look upon nothing else in my entire literary career," he wrote to Stasiulevich at the time, "with more pride than upon this translation. It was a *tour de force* to make Russian grapple with French and not end up vanquished. Whatever readers may say, I'm pleased with myself and pat myself on the back."[55] The second of Flaubert's *Trois contes*, "Saint Julien" is a neo-hagiographic account, based on the extraordinary stained-glass images at Rouen Cathedral, of the life of the medieval hunter-warrior Saint Julian, whose sadistic slaughter of animals verges on the grotesque.

Flaubert's treatment of his hero at times portrays the same kind of human-animal transmutation and yearning for communion with nature that we have noted in Turgenev's own work. Offended as a boy by a mouse who distracts him in church, Julian kills the rodent, then gleefully crushes the life out of a pigeon with his own hands. His father now declares him ready to hunt, gives him a hunting manual, and young Julian devotes himself to his new passion with sanguinary relish. His mastery of coursing, hounding, falconry, snaring, trapping, and baiting enables him to kill deer, fox, wolves, wild bulls, bear, boar, quail, hares, rabbit, geese, otter, duck, woodcock, cranes, badger, peacock, jays, blackbirds, porcupines, polecats, lynx, wild goat, and beaver: "He would come home at night covered with earth and blood, with thistles in his hair and smelling of wild beasts. He grew to be like them. And when his mother kissed him, he responded coldly to her caress and seemed to be thinking of deep and serious things."[56] Julian is cursed by a stag to kill his own father and mother, does so, and is then shunned by people and animals alike: "He gazed with yearning at the colts in the pastures, the birds in their nests, the insects on the flowers; but they all fled from him at his approach and hid or flew away."[57] Though Julian is revered in the West as a "hospitaller" for his eventual willingness to offer boundless hospitality— even, in the end, embracing a hideous leper (Jesus in disguise) to warm him with his naked body—Turgenev changes Flaubert's epithet for the saint from "hospitalier" to "the Merciful [*milostivyi*]." This small but significant alteration suggests that Julian is venerable not only for generosity to strangers, but for eventually learning to show mercy to animals. Flaubert's text seemingly prompted Turgenev to interrogate his own moral code as a hunter: it was during his early work on the translation of "Saint Julien" that he compiled "Fifty Flaws," with its injunctions against cruelty to both dogs and quarry.

The Flaubert tale may also have helped stimulate the creation of "The Quail" (1882), one of Turgenev's final works, which functions as a Russian transposition of Saint Julian's story. Like young Julian, the narrator is a boy who is introduced to hunting by his father and is excited by killing:

> [My father] often took me with him . . . this was a tremendous pleasure for me! . . . I would imagine myself to be a hunter! . . . When a shot rang out and a bird fell, I would always jump up and down and even shout— what great fun it was! The wounded bird would writhe and beat its wings on the grass or in Trésor's mouth—she would bleed, but for me it was still such fun, and I felt no pity [*zhalost'*] at all. What wouldn't I have given to be able to shoot a gun myself and kill partridges and quail! . . . Sometimes, far off, in a stubble field or among young shoots of grain, you could see bustards sticking up; there, I thought: after killing such a big thing my life would be complete [*posle etogo i zhit' ne nado*]![58]

When a brave mother quail feigns a broken wing to decoy the hunter, his dog, and the narrator away from her young, she cannot escape the jaws of Trésor. The boy's pity is awakened when the fatally wounded quail, now trembling in his father's hand, seems to think, "Why must I die? What for? I was doing my duty, trying to save my little ones by leading the dog away— and I was caught! What a poor thing I am! A poor thing! It's not fair! Not fair!"[59] The remorseful narrator now buries the quail and plants a cross, made of twigs, over her grave. That night, he dreams of the mother quail, ascended to heaven, who now "has a little golden crown on her head, to reward her for having suffered for the sake of her children!"[60] This brush with the quail's saintly self-sacrifice completely removes the boy's "passion for hunting," though he later takes up shooting as an adult. Even so, one last incident convinces the grown-up narrator to abandon hunting for good: he and a companion begin to slaughter a brood of black grouse, but the sight of the wounded mother grouse returning to the nest to help her young is too much to bear. The narrator breaks cover and claps his hands to shoo the birds away. "Here I suddenly seemed to be such a wicked man," the story concludes. "From that day it became harder and harder to kill and spill blood."[61]

Turgenev had written "The Quail" in the autumn of 1882, at Sof'ia Tolstaia's invitation, and the tale ultimately appeared in *Stories for Children by I. S. Turgenev and Count L. N. Tolstoy* (*Rasskazy dlia detei I. S. Turgeneva i grafa L. N. Tolstogo*), published in early 1883. The collection featured artwork by four famous Russian painters: Viktor Vasnetsov, Vladimir Makovskii, Vasilii Surikov, and Il'ia Repin. Both Surikov and Vasnetsov supplied illustrations for Turgenev's contribution. Surikov's depicts the grief-stricken boy, caressing the quail in his hands, as his father looks on, gesturing as if in explanation. Trésor, unconcerned, continues his search among the shrubs in the background (figure C.1).

Vasnetsov gently captures the troubled narrator's dream of the mother quail's apotheosis and his guilt at having been party to her death (figure C.2).[62]

FIGURE C.1. V. I. Surikov, illustration for "The Quail" (1882). *Rasskazy dlia detei I. S. Turgeneva i gr. L. N. Tolstogo*. Moscow: Izdanie P. A. Bers i L. D. Obolenskogo, 1883.

Courtesy Russian National Library, Moscow.

Figure C.2. V. M. Vasnetsov, illustration for "The Quail" (1882). *Rasskazy dlia detei I. S. Turgeneva i gr. L. N. Tolstogo.* Moscow: Izdanie P. A. Bers i L. D. Obolenskogo, 1883.

Courtesy Russian National Library, Moscow.

Though "The Quail," as we observed in chapter 3, bears similarities to the account of a mother partridge that Turgenev related to Pauline Viardot in 1849,[63] we cannot take Vasnetsov's and Surikov's images as representations of Turgenev himself. The story is only partially autobiographical: Turgenev, unlike Tolstoy, never stopped hunting for any reason other than physical disability.

In these late works, we detect a suspicion that certain nonhunters, enlightened by spiritual striving or the innocence of youth—Kas'ian, Luker'ia, Saint Julian, the narrator of "The Quail"—can see the natural world as clearly as hunters and may even be better observers because they have been morally freed of the desire to kill what they admire—freed from the *okhota* that leads sportsmen to hunt. Aksakov himself had likewise, in his final decade, expressed misgivings about declining fish and bird populations as well as vanishing habitat, and he conveys a sense of shame at having killed inordinate numbers of birds. Tolstoy, too, famously renounced hunting and became a vegetarian just after *Stories for Children* was published. Aging Russian hunters in the 1800s were thus not immune to a certain degree of contrition about their earlier devotion to blood sport.[64]

Guilt about hunting could also have been increased by a gradual realization that the precious relationship between hunting and nature observation, established at midcentury by Aksakov and Turgenev, was something of a platitude by the 1870s. In *Anna Karenina*, when Sergei Koznyshev tells his half-brother Konstantin Levin that "hunting and similar sports are good because they put one in touch with nature," Tolstoy's implication is that such a view, or at least the arrogance of making such a sweeping generalization, is repugnant.[65] Koznyshev is Tolstoy's spokesman for the bankrupt conventional thinking of Russian intellectuals, the antithesis of Levin's spontaneity and instinctive embrace of the natural world. The fond hunting memoirs Vaksel' and Fet wrote in the 1880s are motivated in part by a desire to look back and document a time when shooting was a newly discovered gateway to the wonders of the organic world, when Turgenev himself, writing in 1852, had called hunting "the pastime that brings us close to nature."[66] The fresh, luminous vision of hunting as a way to commune with nature, advanced by the narrator of "Forest and Steppe," had, three decades later, become a received notion among the clever, self-satisfied men of Koznyshev's set—a race of Jacobs who either aped or gawked at the ruggedness of Esau. Perhaps in part because of this, Turgenev in the 1870s takes greater pains to keep his writing about nature and hunting separate, which might help explain the impetus for his late experiments in venatic nonfiction and his comment in 1880: "I can't admire nature when I'm hunting—that's all nonsense: you admire her when you lie down or sit down to rest after the hunt."[67]

Picturing Turgenev the Hunter

In this context we can return at last to Dmitriev-Orenburgskii's 1880 portrait of Turgenev the hunter (figure I.1). Standing alone with his shotgun, this figure exudes zeal for the hunt and comfort in the outdoors. If, however, we step back and examine the finished painting for which that solo portrait served as a study (figure C.3), the effect is decidedly different.

This enormous canvas depicts a pheasant and hare shoot organized for Grand Duke Nikolai Nikolaevich of Russia (1831–91), third son of Tsar Nicholas I (whom Turgenev detested), in the countryside south of Paris, probably in early December 1879.[68] In the background we see the chateau of Chambaudoin, which would be destroyed in 1942, near Pithiviers in the Loiret. This full scene offers a sorrowful counterpoise to the Turgenev portrait: there is no evidence of the inner fire of *okhota* so evident in the solo study. Instead, we witness not the inspiration for or process of shooting, but its result, which conveys neither the joyous essence of *okhota* nor the opportunity it afforded hunters to merge with the natural world: next to a rutted road, we have over two dozen dead birds and five dead hares arranged on the ground, and a mass of at least thirty people chatting among themselves, impervious to their surroundings, with only Turgenev, in precisely the same

Figure C.3. N. M. Dmitriev-Orenburgskii, *Une chasse au faisan, offerte au grand-duc Nikolaï Nikolaïévitch par le baron Ury de Gunzbourg en 1879* (1880). Courtesy Musée Tourguéniev, Bougival.

pose as the solo portrait, gazing at the viewer. The tallest of all the assembled figures, he strikes me as very much alone in this crowd, looking somewhat lost in the large-scale enterprise of which he is merely a part. Gone is the adventurous spark of Turgenev's shooting in its heyday: one hunter, with his dog, perhaps with a guide, matching wits with elusive quarry in natural seclusion—the vision advanced by Shishkin's *Landscape with Hunter* (figure 2.4). In place of all this, and subverting the politically progressive character that Russian shooting had by then developed, we are confronted by the bloody aftermath of a royal amusement.

If Dmitriev-Orenburgskii's full canvas seems static and ruefully detached from the natural world, then Aleksei Bogoliubov's depiction of Turgenev, created at the same time in 1880, seems to show the comical figure of an old man indulging himself in a young man's sport (figure C.4).

This is one of three watercolors painted by Bogoliubov that also depict the Chambaudoin hunt, so it serves as a contemporaneous variant of the Dmitriev-Orenburgskii solo portrait. As Patrick Waddington describes it, here "Turgenev comes out older, squatter, and much portlier."[69] The title (*"Today I'm more pleased with myself"*), handwritten by the artist beneath the image, serves as a caption to what Bogoliubov, in his memoir of Turgenev, calls a "caricature."[70] Tellingly, Bogoliubov's proposal that this rendering accompany the first posthumous edition of *Notes of a Hunter* was not accepted.[71] Its depiction of a silly-looking old sportsman may well have been deemed fatally incongruous with the cycle's delicate artistry and by-then-venerable status. *Notes of a Hunter* was, instead, frequently published with the Dmitriev-Orenburgskii solo portrait.[72]

As we scrutinize the legacy of Turgenev's own work and others' representations of the man himself, we are left to wonder about what picture we ultimately form of James's "Nimrod of the north," Belinskii's painter of "Russian nature," Goncharov's shotgun-wielding troubadour, Fet's zealous correspondent, Aksakov's literary partner, Goncourt's lovable barbarian.[73] Though many have tried, it is impossible to distill a *triple extrait*—to use Turgenev's own metaphor—of such a profoundly self-questioning, learned, multifaceted hunter-writer, but Stoppard succeeds better than most. As portrayed by Jason Butler Harner in the 2007 New York production of *The Coast of Utopia*, young Turgenev scans the sky, aims an invisible shotgun aloft, and boyishly imitates the report of his weapon. "I'm a sportsman. But I'd still like to write a decent poem one day. Tomorrow, for example. It's lovely here. I'd like to stay." This small piece of stage business, set forty years before the creation of their paintings, might seem beneath the dignity of Dmitriev-Orenburgskii's portrait, more in keeping with Bogoliubov's comic figure. And it

FIGURE C.4. A. P. Bogoliubov, *"Today I'm More Pleased with Myself"* (1880). Courtesy State Russian Museum, St. Petersburg.

is true that, on the night I saw the play, the moment drew general laughter from the audience, who seemed amused that a sophisticated Russian intellectual would mime a hunter's passion on first acquaintance with a potential mate like Tat'iana Bakunina. But the instinctive gesture also paradoxically captured the seriousness of Turgenev's dedication to hunting, the deep meaning this ancient, recently innovated practice held for him, the fraught interplay of his identities as hunter and writer, his yearning for a nest, and his unrestrainable responsiveness to the beauty of the organic world around him—a world for which he never escaped the pang of unreciprocated adoration. It was an impressive feat of theatrical dexterity that foretold a young writer's future course and united the essential features of his hunting nature.

APPENDIX 1

Turgenev on Nature's Indifference: A Chronology

Steno (1834)

                    . . . Oh!
What is the meaning of life? The meaning of Death? You,
O heaven, I question, but you are silent,
Clear, in cold grandeur!

                                        (PsspS1:335)

Andrei (1845)

                    . . . My God!
How indifferent, how deaf is nature!
How burdensome to the striving, living
Soul is her rightful freedom,
Her order, eternity and calm!

                                        (PsspS1:335)

Filippo Strozzi (1847)

O, mother of ours—eternal earth!
Just as indifferently do you swallow up
Your children's sweat, tears, and blood,

Shed for a righteous cause,
As you do the morning droplets of dew!
And you, living, moving, resounding air,
You too just as indifferently bear forth
A final sigh, final prayers,
Final oaths before death,
As you do the song of a young shepherd.

*(PsspS*1:398)*

Letter to Pauline Viardot, Paris, 30 May (11 June) 1849

[A peasant's pulling his shirt up over his head in despair at his crops' failure was] a last, mute protest by man against the cruelty of beings like himself or against the brutal indifference of nature. That's what she is—she is indifferent; there is a soul in us, and perhaps to some extent around us . . . it is a weak radiance that old night eternally seeks to swallow up. That does not keep wicked nature from being admirably beautiful—and the nightingale can bring us delightful ecstasies while some poor, unfortunate, half-crushed insect dies painfully in the bird's gizzard.

*(PsspP*1:287)*

Letter to Pauline Viardot, Courtavenel, 16 (28) July 1849

Thousands of worlds, in abundance strewn about the most distant depths of space, are nothing more than the infinite expansion of life, of that life that is to be found everywhere, that penetrates everywhere, that forces in each drop of water an entire world of plants and insects to be born, with no aim and no necessity. It is the product of an irresistible, involuntary, instinctive movement which cannot do otherwise; this is not premeditated creation. But what is this life? Ah! I know nothing, but I know that at this moment it is everything, it is in full flower, at its peak strength. I do not know if this will continue long, but I know that at this moment it is thus: it makes the blood flow in my veins without any effort by me, and it makes the stars appear in the sky, like pimples on the skin, and this costs it nothing extra and benefits it no more greatly. This indifferent, powerful, voracious, selfish, pervasive thing is life; it is nature, it is God. Call it what you like, but do not worship it. Please understand me: when it is beautiful, when it is good (which does not always happen), worship it for its beauty, for its goodness, but do not worship it for its glory or its grandeur! . . . For, in the first place, there is for it nothing great and nothing small; in the second place, there is no more glory in the act of creation than there is in a tumbling rock, in flowing water, in a stomach that digests; all of this can only follow the Law of its existence, and this is Life.

(PsspP1:311)

"Diary of a Superfluous Man" (1850)

I am dying . . . Live, you who are alive!
And may youthful life play
At the crypt's entrance,
And may indifferent nature
Shine with eternal beauty![1]

(PsspS4:215)

"Journey to the Forest-Belt" (1850–57)

From the depths of the age-old forests, from the immortal bosom of the waters, the same voice rises up: "I care nothing for you," says nature to man. "I reign, while you busy yourself with how to escape death" . . . It is difficult for man, the creature of a single day, born yesterday and today already doomed to death—it is difficult for him to bear the cold gaze of eternal Isis apathetically fixed upon him.

(PsspS5:130)

Second Review of S. T. Aksakov's *Notes of an Orenburg-Province Hunter* (1852)

Without question, in her entirety she [nature] constitutes one great, well-proportioned whole—every point within her is united with every other point—but at the same time her aspiration is that precisely each point, each separate unit within her, exist exclusively for itself, consider itself the center of the universe, turn to its own advantage everything around it, negate the independence of those surroundings and take possession of them as its own property. To the mosquito that sucks your blood, you are food, and he makes use of you just as calmly and without shame as the spider into whose net he has toppled does him, just as a root that digs in the dark makes use of the earth's moisture. Direct your attention for a few moments to the fly that freely flits from your nose to a lump of sugar, to a drop of nectar in the heart of a flower—and you will understand what I mean; you will understand that the fly is resolutely on her own just as much as you are on your own. How, from this disunity and fragmentation by means of which everything seems to live only for itself, how there emerges that selfsame universal, endless harmony, in which, conversely, all that lives lives for another and only in another attains its reconciliation or its resolution, and all lives merge into a single, universal life—this is one of those "open" secrets that we all see and do not see.[2]

(PsspS4:516–17)

On the Eve (1859)

Knock as much as you like on nature's door, but she won't answer with a comprehensible word, because she's mute. She'll resound and whine like a string, but don't expect a song from her. . . . She also threatens us: she reminds us of terrible . . . yes of unattainable mysteries. Must she not swallow us up, does she not ceaselessly devour us? In her are both life and death, and death in her speaks as loudly as life.

(PsspS6:165, 166)

Letter to A. A. Fet, Paris and Courtavenel, 27, 31 August (8, 12 September) 1860

I predict that you will frequently see me as a guest at your place [Fet's new estate of Stepanovka]—with Flambeau (who is turning out to be an excellent dog) or with some other companion of the canine sort. Let's live a few more peaceful years before the end—and then let

Indifferent nature
Shine with eternal beauty.[3]

(PsspP4:233–34)

Fathers and Children (1861)

However passionate, sinful, and rebellious the heart concealed in that grave, the flowers growing upon it serenely look at us with their innocent eyes, which speak not only of eternal tranquillity, of that great tranquillity of "indifferent" nature; they also speak of eternal reconciliation and life everlasting.

(PsspS7:188)

"The Tit" (1863)

In your little song of greeting,
Can it be that my hearing is captivated

Only by the indifferent play
Of unanswering nature?

(PsspS12:298)

"Enough: Fragment from the Notes of a Deceased Artist" (1864)

In the end, nature is irresistible; she has no reason to hurry, and sooner or later she will take what is hers. Unconsciously and inexorably obedient to her laws, she does not recognize art, just as she does not recognize freedom, does not recognize good; from time immemorial advancing and ephemeral, she tolerates nothing immortal, nothing immutable. . . . Man is her child, but what is human, what is artistic, is inimical to her, precisely because it attempts to be immutable and immortal. Man is the child of nature, but she is a universal mother and she has no favorites: all that exists in her bosom came into being only at the expense of another and must in its time yield its place to another—she creates by destroying, and it is all the same to her what she creates and what she destroys—provided that life does not come to an end, provided that death is not deprived of its rights. . . .

. . . Where can we poor humans, poor artists, contend with this deaf-mute force that is blind from birth and that does not even rejoice in its victories, but moves on, goes forward, devouring everything? How can one withstand these heavy, crude, endlessly and indefatigably approaching waves?

(PsspS7:228–29)

Smoke (1865–67)

But nature does not deal in logic, our human logic; she has her own, which we do not understand and do not acknowledge until she runs over us, as with a wheel.

(PsspS7:373)

Letter to Pauline Viardot, Spasskoe, 23 June (5 July) 1868

Having seated myself on a bench (as in the first letter of my story "Faust"), I involuntarily thought of Viardot; flooded with the purest light, filled with fragrance, beauty and evident serenity, the land around me was a true field of carnage: everything furiously, violently devoured everything else: I saved the life of one small ant who, despite desperate opposition, was dragged and rolled along the sand, turning tigerlike summersaults, by a large ant: no sooner had I saved the little one than he seized with the same ferocity a little half-dead fly; this time I didn't interfere. Destroy or be destroyed; there's no alternative: so we'll destroy!

(PsspP9:23)

"The Blackbird I" (1877)

[The sounds made by a blackbird in the garden] breathed eternity . . . breathed all the freshness, all the indifference, all the force of eternity. The voice of nature herself could be heard in them—that beautiful, instinctive voice that never began and will never end.

(PsspS10:176)

"Nature" (1879)

"I [Nature] am contemplating how to give more power to the leg-muscles of the flea, that it might better evade its enemies. The balance of attack and defense has been upset . . . I must restore it."

"What?" I murmured in reply. "That's what you're thinking about? But aren't we human beings your favorite children?" . . .

"All creatures are my children . . . I care for them equally—and I destroy them equally . . . I know neither good nor evil . . . Reason is no law to me—and what is justice? I gave you life, and I will take it away and give it to others, both worms and humans . . . it's all the same to me . . . Now go defend yourself and stop bothering me!"

(PsspS10:164–65)

Letter to Zh. A. Polonskaia, Bougival, 27 May (8 June) 1882

Everything around me is green, in bloom, birds are singing, etc. But all this is beautiful and nice when you're healthy, while I [a very sick man] can't help remembering "indifferent" nature.

(PsspP13.1 [1968]: 269)

APPENDIX 2

[On S. T. Aksakov's *Notes of an Orenburg-Province Hunter*]

In Moscow a few days ago, S. T. A[ksako]v's *Notes of an Orenburg-Province Hunter* came out; he is the same author, we will note incidentally, to whom we are already obliged for a splendid book on fishing.[1] We congratulate Russian literature and our readers on the appearance of the present *Notes*. Such books appear in Russia all too rarely. One who has not yet made the acquaintance of S. T. A[ksako]v's new work cannot imagine the degree to which it is entertaining, or what a charming freshness wafts from its pages. Moreover, readers will not think that *Notes of an Orenburg-Province Hunter* has value merely for hunters: anyone who simply loves nature in all her variety, in all her beauty and strength; anyone who cherishes a display of universal life—in the midst of which man himself stands as a living link, higher, but tightly bound to the other links—will not be able to tear himself away from Mr. A[ksako]v's work; it will become his desktop book, and he will read and re-read it with delight; the naturalist will be enraptured with it. . . . We will allow ourselves the pleasure, in an upcoming issue of the *Contemporary*, to speak in detail about this work that was written with so much love and such knowledge of the subject; and we will speak about that love "on location," since we will be in the country, in the natural world of which this love serves as such a faithful and poetic reflection, and we ourselves will be indulging in sport; for now, we will limit ourselves only to a request that readers not confuse this capital book, which simultaneously enriches both the specialized literature to which it belongs and Russian literature in general—not confuse this book with the trifling and foolish booklets on hunting that have lately appeared.[2]

To prove to readers that there is nothing exaggerated in our praise for Mr. A[ksako]v's book, we offer the following excerpts.[3]

Here is a description of a woodland river from which no master would turn away. (It must be added that Mr. A[ksako]v divides all game into four main categories: marshland, aquatic, woodland, and steppe, and at the beginning of each section paints a general picture of the game's habitat.)

[. . .]

And here is a description of a spring and "simple watermills":[4]

[. . .]

Here is an excerpt "from the inner" life of the forest:

[. . .]

Here is the steppe in spring and autumn:

[. . .]

But the author knows how to speak about subjects other than nature alone: listen to how the wild geese fly to their feeding ground, and how the black grouse performs his courtship ritual:

[. . .]

Here is an example of mastery and distinction in his description of the exterior of that pretty bird, the partridge:

[. . .]

But we might never finish if we wanted to adduce here all that is wonderful in Mr. A[ksako]v's book. I repeat that we will have more to say before long—and we will speak in detail. Now, however, it remains for us to wish this book, which does honor to readers in general and hunters in particular, the most brilliant success and the widest possible distribution. It is impossible to read this book without some kind of gratifying, clear, and complete feeling, similar to those feelings that nature herself arouses in you; we know of no higher praise than this.

APPENDIX 3

S. Aksakov's *Notes of an Orenburg-Province Hunter*. MOSCOW, 1852

(Letter to one of the editors of the *Contemporary*)

"There is a time for business and an hour for amusement"

From the book called *Ordainer, or A New Rule and Establishment of Order for the Falconer's Way*[1]

Over the course of last summer you reminded me more than once, dear N[ikolai] A[lekseevich],[2] of my promise to speak in greater detail in your journal about S. A[ksako]v's wonderful book; until this very day I was unable to keep my word: as a true hunter—a hunter body and soul—I have barely allowed the gun to leave my hands all this time, and have not touched my pen at all.

But now winter is upon us; on the second of October the first frost hit, then on the third of October a blizzard started in the morning and still hasn't let up; the fields suddenly turned white; there's no way to hunt for any length of time; outside, in the words of the Russian song, the snow "carouses, spins and gets in your eyes";[3] a week ago I was still shooting woodcock by the dozen, but now you'd have a hard time killing a pair; these cruel, early cold snaps have "given them a shove," as hunters put it. The arrival of "Winter the Enchantress"[4] is always hard and mirthless, but her appearance is especially sad when she comes unexpectedly, so early, as she did this year. We had no autumn; she killed autumn—autumn with all its quiet beauty, with its "magnificent withering" . . .[5] It's terrible to think that in early October winter has already started. . . . Sharply standing out against the deathly whiteness of the victorious snow, the fresh and not yet faded green of the birches, and especially of the poplars, seems somehow false and mocking. Sitting within the four walls of my room, I recalled my promise: I was unable to hunt, but my thoughts were still occupied with hunting; I eagerly took up the pen and here write for the *Contemporary* a critique of *Notes of an Orenburg-Province Hunter*—a book that has not left my desk since the moment of my arrival in the country.

Nonetheless, to tell the truth, I write not a critique, for in Mr. A[ksako]v's book there is nothing, or almost nothing, to criticize. The little mistakes, omissions, and misfires to be found in it have all, or nearly all, been enumerated and noted in Issue 8 of the *Muscovite* in the very sensible article signed with the initials V. V.[6] These very same initials appear in the same journal beneath a series of small stories about hunting in the environs of Moscow—stories distinguished by fidelity of tone, simplicity of exposition and demonstrating that the author is a passionate and experienced hunter. Mr. A[ksako]v's chief error (on measuring gunpowder) he himself attempted to correct by means of a special announcement printed in the *Moscow Gazette*. For our part, we will only add that *Notes of an Orenburg-Province Hunter* is not a book like Elzéar Blaze's *Chasseur au chien d'arrêt*, which is considered the classic work on French hunting.[7] Mr. A[ksako]v's *Notes* is not a hunting book in the strict sense; it cannot serve as a complete manual for the beginning hunter, though valuable remarks and pieces of advice are to be found on nearly every page. The author himself perceives this. Here's what he says at the very start of his book: "I first thought I would begin my wildfowling notes by speaking in detail about all aspects of hunting, not only of shooting and game, its haunts and habits in the province of Orenburg, but also of hunting dogs, shotguns, and various accessories and broadly of the technical aspects. Now that I have set to work on it I realize that since I set aside my gun the technical side has greatly advanced and that I have little detailed knowledge of the current state of affairs."[8]

Indeed, in the twenty-five years that have passed since the estimable Mr. A[ksako]v stopped hunting,[9] everything—the dogs, the guns and the firearm accessories—has changed; French and Courland dogs no longer enjoy their former fame; Marklov dogs were about to triumph and then utterly died out;[10] English dogs, especially full- and half-blood pointers,[11] have climbed in popularity; half-bloods are nearly best in our climate. With regard to setters, which were on the point of pleasing their masters with their rapid search, tirelessness, and imperviousness to cold, opinions are starting to become divided. English guns from Manton, Mortimer, and Purdey have replaced not only the Morgenroths and Starbuses, but even the Lepages; German, Viennese and Prague guns have entirely fallen into disuse; they have only the advantage of a low price for their quite durable finish to commend them; but if not our Tula pieces, then guns from War- saw, Beckers, of course cost more than they do.[12] Twenty-five years ago the question had not yet arisen (and I openly confess that for me it remains not entirely answered)—of whether one should consider the invention of breech-loading guns (à la Robert or Lefaucheux) to be a step forward in the art or, on the contrary, a frivolous and fruitless endeavor.[13] Are they destined to supplant muzzle-loading guns or not? Guns using the Robert system offer many advantages, but there are also many disadvantages; about all this you will find not a word from Mr. A[ksako]v. Elzéar Blaze has devoted an entire chapter to this question.[14] He concludes by rejecting Robert-system guns, but Count Langel, author of the book *Hygiène des chasseurs*, is in favor of them.[15] Furthermore, who among our hunters will now start using clumsy, heavy cartridges instead of the elegant and durable powder-flasks and shot- guns of Dickson and other English masters?[16] Unbearable wadding—instead of tidy and fashionable plasters![17] As regards percussion caps, though the author has never shot with them (see *Notes of an Orenburg-Province Hunter*, p. 222—in our time this seems simply incredible!), he nonetheless does them full justice (he does not consider powder flasks and shotguns handy and sticks to the old-fashioned bandolier); but he does not, and could not, say a word about the latest improvements in this area; he does not mention English dark percussion caps or the French ones engraved with the letter G. (Gévelot), which, in addition to never misfiring (English ones, with a reinforced bottom, can even be put into water just before the shot), also do not come apart, like the Austrian percussion caps bearing the letters *S. B.*, for the famous factory of Sellier & Bellot, or like our homegrown anony- mous caps, which misfire even in dry weather and continually wound the shooter's hand or cheek with their fragments.[18] Incidentally, with regard to percussion-cap bags, I have long shared the opinion of many experienced hunters about them; all such bags hitherto devised have indeed turned out to be unsatisfactory; finally, last year, there appeared an apparatus of Eng- lish invention that absolutely attained its goal. This apparatus consists of a small, circular chamois bag on a belt, with a matching lid on a spring; you reach for a percussion cap, and the lid yields to the pressure of your fingers, then immediately snaps shut by itself, as soon as you've got the cap. This is extraordinarily convenient and very simple, like the egg of Columbus or

Pascal's wheelbarrow.[19] The rules proposed by the author for training dogs are quite correct; it's pleasant for us to see that even twenty-five years ago Mr. A[ksako]v did not approve of spiked collars and other tricks from the German dog-training that prevailed in his time. Indeed, train the dog at home to be obedient, to come when her name is called, to obey the command "back!" Jokingly make her bring you a piece of paper or a glove (but by no means a stone or a key, as Mr. A[ksako]v advises), and set out with her into the field: if she has blood and, this is the chief thing, breeding,[20] your dog will quickly understand what you require of her. This year I experienced this in practice: for the first time I went hunting with a young half-blood English dog (though she was the daughter of an excellent mother) whom I had trained at home; and, though she, due to the meekness of her temperament, for a whole six months was afraid of the sound of a gunshot and would always simply slink some distance behind me, as soon as she decided one fine day to hurl herself upon a green sandpiper that had been killed ten paces from her, her progress amazed even me; after about fourteen days she was already working like an experienced dog: standing stock still, giving up retrieved game splendidly; in a word, she had completely taken the place of her (unfortunately) aging mother . . .[21]

But let us return to Mr. A[ksako]v's book. It follows, from everything I've said, that its technical section is rather weak and incomplete—it has, to use a grandiloquent term, dropped behind the current state of the art; but, I repeat, the author himself does not deny this and, besides, the technical section of his notes consists of thirty-four pages for which devotees of hunting must nonetheless be grateful to Mr. A[ksako]v, especially for the excellent advice on shooting (pp. 31–33). His first rule—"Never think about missing"—reminds me of the proverb of an old muscovite hunter, the long-deceased L. I. Tatarinov, whom I used to know in my early youth. "Shooters," he used to say, "fall into three groups: eekers, poppers, and smackers. Eekers just say 'Eek' when game jumps up; poppers shoot and miss; smackers shoot and hit the mark. A popper can become a smacker, but you'll never make a smacker out of an eeker."[22]

After these thirty-four pages of introduction, the book proper begins.

And what a lovely thing this book is! How much freshness, grace, observation, understanding and love of nature it contains! . . . But I observe that I'm descending into exclamations, and in criticism, they say, that just won't do. Allow me to discuss my observations in detail.

Mr. A[ksako]v's book can be examined from two points of view: the point of view of the hunter, and the point of view of the naturalist [*estestvoispytatel'*]. I shall begin with the first.

I am certain that any hunter who has a chance to read Mr. A[ksako]v's *Notes* will in particular be attracted and touched by the author's sincere and ardent love for his subject—the noble pursuit of hunting—and by the honesty of his passion. Some will object that in essence hunting is trifling nonsense, a "momentary" amusement, and does not merit such forceful expressions; but besides the fact that, in my opinion, without sincere devotion to the subject no one will succeed even with trifles, I could adduce striking proof that in human life and in the history of humanity hunting occupies a prominent place. Everyone knows what the right to hunt signified in the European world not only during the middle ages, but also up to the most recent times (the abolition of previous hunting laws—"game laws" in English—constituted one of the most important reforms carried out by Earl Grey as recently as 1831),[23] and this is why I will not persist regarding the decrees of Henry IV,[24] or regarding the fact that so many noteworthy people have been passionate hunters, etc. I will simply observe that hunting should in all fairness be considered one of man's most important undertakings. Besides Nimrod in the Bible[25] or other Asiatic hunter-kings whose depictions have been preserved in the remnants of the most ancient palaces and temples, it is worth recalling the passage in canto 11 of *The Odyssey* in which Ulysses, among the specters of ancient heroes he has summoned from Hades at Circe's urging, sees the mythical giant Orion:

> After him [Minos], I was aware of gigantic Orion
> in the meadow of asphodel, rounding up and driving together
> wild animals he himself had killed in the lonely mountains,
> holding in his hands a brazen club, forever unbroken.[26]

From time immemorial, Russians, too, have loved to hunt. This is confirmed by our folksongs, our tales, and all our legends. And where can you hunt better than in Russia? There's room and there's quarry.[27] Monomakh in his *Testament* left us a description of his battles with aurochs and bear;[28] the worthy father of a great son, one of the wisest Russian tsars, Aleksei Mikhailovich, passionately loved to hunt.[29] Everyone has heard of his *Ordainer, or A New Rule and Establishment of Order for the Falconer's Way*;[30] less well known are his letters to one of his boyars, reported by the archeographical commission.[31] In them, the Tsar tells him about his "trips." In general, hunting is inherent in Russians: give a peasant a gun, even if it's held together with string, and a little handful of powder, and he'll go roaming about, wearing only his bast sandals, in marshes and forests, from dawn till dusk. And don't think that he'll shoot just ducks: with this same gun, he'll go lie in wait for bear on their "oats,"[32] ram down the muzzle not a bullet, but some sort of homemade, knocked-together slug—and he'll kill that bear; actually, he won't kill it so much as let the bear maul him a bit, and then he'll rest up and drag himself home half-alive and, if he recovers, he'll go back after the same bear with the same gun. True, it will sometimes happen that the bear will attack him again, but, you see, it was a Russian who came up with the saying "Scared of beasts? Stay out of the woods." It is with this general, widespread passion of the Russian—a passion whose innermost roots, perhaps, should be sought in his half-Eastern origin and primordial nomadic habits—that Mr. A[ksako]v's book could not be more in keeping: it breathes that passion and is permeated by it. I myself have never been to Orenburg Province, but I am glad that Mr. A[ksako]v hunted there—in those majestic steppes, abounding with game, so wonderfully described by him;[33] it was they, I think, that imparted to his passion its fascinating sincerity and strength, and to his brush its freedom and breadth.

Here I should, as promised, say a few words on how naturalists will view Mr. A[ksako]v's work. I myself, as you know, do not have the honor of belonging to their community; but I passionately love nature, especially in her living manifestations, and therefore I will allow myself to say a few words about *Notes of an Orenburg-Province Hunter* from this point of view as well. Man cannot fail to be fascinated by nature; he is connected to her by a thousand unbreakable threads: he is her son; the sympathy that is awakened in one's soul by lower creatures—so similar to man in their outward appearance, inner structure, organs of sensation and feeling—is somewhat reminiscent of that lively interest each of us takes in the development of an infant.[34] We all indeed love nature—at least, no one can say that he positively does not love her; but even in this love there tends to be a great deal of egoism. To wit: we love nature in relation to us; we gaze at her as if she is on a pedestal of our own making. It is because of this, by the way, that time and again, in so-called "natural descriptions," we find either comparisons with the dynamics of human emotion ("and the whole crag, unscathed, laughs," and so on)[35] or the simple and clear transmission of external phenomena is replaced by disquisitions about those phenomena.[36]

Meanwhile, an outlook of that sort is utterly discordant with the true meaning of nature, with her basic tenor. Without question, in her entirety she constitutes one great, well-proportioned whole—every point within her is united with every other point—but at the same time her aspiration is that precisely each point, each separate unit within her, exist exclusively for itself, consider itself the center of the universe, turn to its own advantage everything around it, negate the independence of those surroundings and take possession of them as its own property. To the mosquito that sucks your blood, you are food, and he makes use of you just as calmly and without shame as the spider into whose net he has toppled does him, just as a root that digs in the dark makes use of the earth's moisture. Direct your attention for a few moments to the fly that freely flits from your nose to a lump of sugar, to a drop of nectar in the heart of a flower—and you will understand what I mean; you will understand that the fly is resolutely on her own just as much as you are on your own. How, from this disunity and fragmentation by means of which everything seems to live only for itself, how there emerges that selfsame universal, endless harmony, in which, conversely, all that lives lives for another and only in another attains its reconciliation or its resolution, and all lives merge into a single, universal life—this is one of those "open" secrets that we all see and do not see. It's tempting to speak of this— but it would lead me too far astray; I will content myself by reminding you of Goethe's famous pages on nature, and cite two or three words said by him:

> Nature places abysses between all beings, and they all strive to devour one another. She disunites all in order to unite all . . .
> Her crown is love. Only through love can one draw near to her . . .
> It seems that she only troubles herself in order to create individuals— and individuals mean nothing to her. She ceaselessly builds and cease- lessly destroys . . .[37]

If it is only "through love" that one can draw near to nature, then this love must be unselfish, like any authentic feeling: love nature not by virtue of what she means in relation to you, a person, but because she, in and of her- self, is sweet and dear to you—and you will understand her.

Returning to Mr. A[ksako]v's book, I cannot refrain from doing him proper justice. He looks upon nature (both animate and inanimate) not from some exclusive point of view, but as one should look at her: clearly, simply, and with complete sympathy; he does not complicate things unnecessarily, use cunning or add extraneous motives and goals; he observes intelligently, conscientiously and keenly; he only wants to learn, to see. And before such scrutiny, nature opens up and allows him to "peep in" at her. You will laugh at this, but I assure you that once I had read, for example, the chapter on the black grouse, it actually seemed to me that it would be impossible to live better than a black grouse. . .

The author brought to the depiction of this bird the same completeness, that roundedness of each separate life, of which we spoke above, etc., etc.[38] If a black grouse could tell us about himself, he would, I am sure, not add a word to what Mr. A[ksako]v has told us about him. One should say the same about the goose, the duck, the woodcock—in a word, about all the bird species with which he acquaints us. Germans consider the goose—that much-regarded and wary bird—to be stupid; the Russian, on the contrary, has observed that even thunder attracts the attention of a goose; indeed, with every thunderclap he twists his head and looks heavenward. Though that makes him not the least bit smarter, he shares this lot with many philosophers. Joking aside, I cannot get my fill of admiring Mr. A[ksako]v's avian "physiologies." I do not intend at all to compare him with Buffon and I dare not deny the great merits of "the father of natural history," but I must confess that such glittering rhetorical descriptions as, for example, the description, familiar to us all since childhood, of a horse—"The horse is man's noblest conquest," etc.—in essence do very little to acquaint us with the animals to which they are dedicated.[39] It truly seems to me that eloquent designs of this kind present the writer far fewer difficulties than authentic, warm, living descriptions, just as it is incomparably easier to tell the hills that they are "heavenward flights of dust," the crag that it "laughs," the lightning that it is a "phosphorescent snake,"[40] than it is to convey to us poetically the majesty of the crag above the sea, the tranquil immensity of the mountains, or the sharp flash of lightning . . . This is understandable: nothing can be more difficult for a man than to detach himself from his very being and to think himself into the phenomena of nature . . . Without budging from your spot, roar with all the thunders of rhetoric, and this will not cost you a great deal of effort; try to understand and express what takes place within even something as simple as a bird that falls silent just before the rain, and you will see that this is not easy.

For all the aforementioned reasons, I imagine that any naturalist will read and re-read Mr. A[ksako]v's book with genuine pleasure. The late Audubon would, I think, have been deeply moved by it.[41] Do you know, for example, that accurate depiction of the external appearance and color of birds is considered one of the greatest difficulties in natural history? Observe how well they all turned out for Mr. A[ksako]v. I am all the more certain of the success of *Notes of an Orenburg-Province Hunter* among naturalists because their science has recently taken a more positive and practical turn, or, more precisely, a turn directed toward the living observation and study of nature, rather than toward the compilation of those sometimes poetic and profound, but nearly always murky and indeterminate hypotheses, with which Schelling used to turn heads at the beginning of the present century.[42]

I will say a few more words about the style of Mr. A[ksako]v's *Notes*. I am extraordinarily fond of his style. This is authentic Russian speech: genial and direct, supple and adroit. There is nothing pretentious and nothing superfluous, nothing strained and nothing sluggish—his freedom and precision of expression are equally remarkable. This book was eagerly written and is eagerly read.[43] I have already remarked more than once on how masterfully Mr. A[ksako]v is able to write descriptions (several excerpts appeared in the April issue of *Sovremennik*).[44] I would now like to draw your attention to the following circumstance. There can sometimes be subtly developed, nervous, irritably poetic personalities who possess some particular outlook on nature, a particular sense of her beauty; they take note of many nuances, many often barely perceptible particulars, and occasionally they succeed in expressing them extremely felicitously, neatly, and gracefully, though the larger outlines of the picture either escape them or they lack sufficient strength to grasp and hold on to them.[45] One could say that they mostly have access to the scent of nature, and their words are fragrant. Their particulars are winning as regards the general impression. Mr. A[ksako]v is not among such personalities, and of this I am very glad. Here too he does not use cunning, does not take note of anything out of the ordinary, anything of the sort that only "the few" reach; but what he sees, he sees clearly, and with a firm hand and power-ful brush paints a well-composed and generous picture. It seems to me that descriptions of this sort are more to the point and more faithful: in nature herself there is nothing cunning or tricky; she never shows off in any way, never coquettes; in her very caprices she is genial. No poets with genuine and strong talents ever "struck a pose" before the face of nature; they did not try, as they say, to "eavesdrop" or "spy" on her secrets; in great and simple words they transmitted her simplicity and greatness: she did not irritate them, she ignited them; but in this flame there was nothing painful. Recall Pushkin's and Gogol's descriptions or even the celebrated passage in *King Lear* where Edgar describes for blind Gloucester the steep sea-cliff that supposedly falls away precipitously at his very feet:

> Come on, sir; here's the place. Stand still. How fearful
> And dizzy 'tis to cast one's eyes so low!
> The crows and choughs that wing the midway air
> Show scarce so gross as beetles. Halfway down
> Hangs one that gathers samphire—dreadful trade!
> Methinks he seems no bigger than his head.
> The fishermen that walk upon the beach
> Appear like mice; and yond tall anchoring bark,
> Diminish'd to her cock; her cock, a buoy
> Almost too small for sight. The murmuring surge
> That on th' unnumb'red idle pebble chafes
> Cannot be heard so high. I'll look no more . . .[46]

A mere two or three features; the poet wishes neither to say something out of the ordinary nor to find in the picture that appears before his eyes particular, as-yet-unnoticed details; with the true instinct of genius he keeps to the single chief sensation—the sensation of the height from which Edgar gazes and the diminution of all objects below; and is it possible meanwhile to add anything? The ancient Greeks looked upon nature with similar simplicity; one could adduce a multitude of evidence for this . . . However, they had in going before us a great advantage: in their fortunate mouths poetry for the first time began to speak in a sonorous and sweet voice about man and nature. (I confess that I am unable to find sympathy for literatures predating the Greeks.) That is why nothing can compare with immortal youth, with the freshness and force of first impressions, which fly to us from the songs of Homer. I just mentioned Pushkin: the relationship of this poet—who was truly ancient in spirit—to nature was just as simple and natural [*estestvennyi*] as that of the ancients, and, for all the boldness of his poetic images, utterly sensible. Who doesn't know his "Cloud"? I will not deny myself the pleasure of copying out this entire poem:

> Last cloud of the scattered storm!
> Alone, you speed through bright azure,
> *Alone, you cast a doleful shadow,*
> *Alone, you sadden exultant day.*
>
> You recently covered the sky all around,
> And lightning menacingly entwined you,
> *And you loosed mysterious thunder*
> *And watered the greedy earth with rain.*
>
> Enough—go hide! The time has passed,
> The earth has refreshed itself and the storm has swept by,
> And the wind, caressing the little leaves of trees,
> *Drives you from the becalmed heavens.*[47]

Wonderful! . . . In a word, when you describe nature's phenomena the point is not to say everything that may enter your head: say what should enter each person's head, but in such a way that your depiction is as forceful as what you depict, and neither you nor we listeners will have anything more to wish for.

But should our amazed sympathy for such images and such sounds not render us unfair to those semi-feminine poetic personalities that I mentioned above, then the felicitous, ingratiating poetry of Tiutchev and Fet will find an echo in our heart. I wanted only to say that Mr. A[ksako]v did not set out on their road, and, I repeat, his manner couldn't possibly contribute more to the amiably intelligent, clear and manly tone of the entire book.

My letter has turned out to be quite long, but nonetheless how much more I would like to say to you: to convey my own observations, to speak about the so-called "successes and failures" of hunters, about hunters' superstitions, legends, and popular beliefs. But I'm afraid of wearying both your attention and the attention of the reader. I will set all that aside for another letter, which you will receive shortly.[48] I will limit myself now to the wish that hunting, the pastime that brings us close to nature, will teach us patience, and sometimes even composure in the midst of danger, and will impart health and strength to our bodies as well as courage and freshness to our spirits; this pastime enjoyed by our forefathers on the banks of broad Russian rivers, and by that hero of folk ballads, the bowman Robin Hood, in the merry green oak-woods of Old England, and by many other good people the world over—long may it prosper still in our homeland! Oberon's magic horn will not cease to sound for those "who have ears," and Weber is not the last great musician who will be inspired by the poetry of the hunt![49] I just said that hunting brings us close to nature: only the hunter sees her at all times of the day or night, in all her beauty, in all her horror. Let us sincerely thank Mr. A[ksako]v for his book and wish that others would follow his trail and relate to us all those multifarious kinds of hunting that he has not touched upon. I close with the words of Aleksei Mikhailovich's *Ordainer*: "O hunters assiduous and most wise, the more you read this book of the fair and glorious hunt, so a multitude of good and clever things will you see and learn. If you will read with wisdom, you will find every consoling goodness . . ." and "When you hunt, enjoy yourselves, comfort yourselves with this good amusement, so very diverting and pleasing and merry, that sorrow and sadness of any kind may not overcome you."[50]

P.S. I have heard that a second edition of *Notes of an Orenburg-Province Hunter* is in preparation[51]—the book's success anticipated my praises; so much the better!

October–November 1852
Village of Spasskoe[52]

APPENDIX 4

"The Hunter's Fifty Flaws and Fifty Flaws of a Gun Dog"

I. S. Turgenev

In submitting the following notes on a hunter's and a dog's flaws[1]—notes suggested to me by many years' experience—I am far from thinking that I have "exhausted my task," as they say, and I wish only to point out the most major among these flaws. If it should occur to someone to ask me why I have not enumerated the hunter's and dog's virtues, then I will answer that such virtues are implied by the flaws themselves: one need only take their opposite.

Hunter's Flaws

1. Does not like to get up early.
2. Tires quickly while hunting.
3. Is impatient, easily irritated, becomes annoyed with himself, loses his composure and inevitably begins to shoot poorly.
4. Walks poorly, fails to circle, halfheartedly seeks game, is insufficiently persistent in an action once it has been undertaken.
5. Marks time too long in one place.
6. Does not know how to dress appropriately for the time of year.
7. Does not take the necessary precautions against rain, wind, and so forth.
8. Becomes bored and dejected when there is little game.

9. Is unobservant, fails to pay attention to the habits of his quarry, to the local conditions and to the time—or he wants to prove himself more stiff-necked than everything around him: the quarry, the dog, the weather, and nature herself.

10. Does not *constantly* keep his eyes trained on the dog.

11. Drills the dog too much, does not trust her, forces her to search in the manner that seems best to him and confuses her.

12. Hurries, babbling "Apporte! Cherche!" [Fetch! Seek!] when he wants the dog to find some killed or wounded game more quickly, and fails to lead the dog to the designated spot *wordlessly*.

13. Yells at the dog, whistles, and cries out after, for example, she has given chase to a hare and now no longer hears and is indeed no longer capable of hearing.

14. Senselessly punishes the dog, or fails to punish her at all; is inconsistent or illogical in his behavior toward her.

15. Shoots his dog in the rump as she gives chase—unpardonable barbarity!

16. Does not look after the dog's food himself, with the result that his dogs are for the most part poorly fed. Oatmeal is an excellent feed, but only on condition that it be thoroughly boiled.

17. Is indecisive; is easily embarrassed. When game appears suddenly, one has to fire . . . but he merely sighs.

18. Is grudging with cartridges; stingy. This should be his very last concern.

19. Shoots too quickly from both barrels and without taking aim, so that, if he hits the quarry, he tears it to shreds.

20. Aims too long and allows the game to get too far off; tries to "direct" the gun, which is no good for anything.

21. Does not "have the butt," that is, does not know how to raise the gun quickly and nimbly, or brings it up badly: he rests one corner of the butt against his shoulder.

22. When he cannot see the quarry (for example, in a thicket), he cannot figure out how to shoot.

23. Is insufficiently quick in shooting, which is especially important when you find yourself on a narrow path in the forest.

24. During a battue, does not know how to look about in both directions vigilantly and precisely.

25. When loading the gun after firing, does not keep the dog at his side and lets her loose; black grouse and partridge take wing, flushed by the dog, while the hunter is left merely to gnash his teeth.

26. Shoots worse at game running or flying from left to right than from right to left.

27. Does not know how to shoot ahead of game at a long distance; does not know how to raise the gun when aiming at a bird flying straight at him or to lower his aim when firing at game that has flown from over his head and is moving into the distance.

28. Shoots at 100 or at 200 paces. There are those who muck about even at 300, or at 400 paces, and with small shot besides.

29. During a battue, shoots incautiously now in the direction of the beaters, now in the direction of his companions.

30. Is not ashamed to shoot at a lying hare or sitting bird.

31. Incautiously carries the gun cocked, with the barrel directed toward his companions; whereas it is well to recall the wise saying of a French sportsman: "Mere umbrellas have gone off on occasion."

32. If stumbling with his gun, does not immediately examine it to determine whether there is dirt in the muzzle, which can cause the barrel to explode.

33. Cannot refrain from shooting at game when, for whatever reason, shooting at it is not permissible; or he shoots at game that is heading toward his companion.

34. Shoots without permission using someone else's dog.

35. Lies in wait under a bush and, as soon as his companion finds something, immediately runs out to take a shot.

36. When nothing has turned up in a long time, shoots at jackdaws, at small birds, at swallows—pointless cruelty!

37. Does not know how to mark where shot game will fall.

38. Complains of his bad luck to companions who have nothing to do with it.

39. Makes noise and engages in conversation where he should be silent.

40. Is superstitious: attaches importance to omens, tries to explain "good fortune," "misfortune," etc.

41. In times of misfortune assumes a crushed or insulted air, which is unpleasant for his companions, and in the event of "good fortune" ridicules or poses.

42. Is envious, cannot bear his companion's success, tries to take over his best spots.

43. Keeps his gear in a disorderly or dirty state.

44. Does not look after the greasing and good repair of his footwear, which often results in his feet becoming chafed.

45. Eats and drinks too much during a hunt.

46. Sleeps during a hunt. For such a marksman it would be far more seemly to stay home.
47. Is afraid of the damp, the wind, or hot weather.
48. During hot spells ceaselessly drinks water, which, in the first place, is harmful and, in the second place, does not in the slightest slake one's thirst.
49. Is untruthful in his hunting stories—a universally familiar, quite widespread flaw, though a harmless, at times amusing one.
50. Does not permit his companions to boast or even to tell a fib or two in his presence . . . an inhumane trait!

Flaws of a Gun Dog

1. Has an untrustworthy or poor scent.
2. Searches slowly or entirely along a straight line, or tramples one place rather than "circling" or "sweeping" to the right and left.
3. Searches too quickly, full tilt, as setters often do; it looks fine, but sometimes leaves one's quarry off to the side, out of danger.
4. Puts off her suit, that is, gradually distances herself from the hunter.
5. In a forest, does not search close by.
6. Follows the trail at too slow an advance, which is especially disadvantageous when one is hunting partridge; this bird runs very quickly, as is well known.
7. Rushes from the set and seizes the game, which happens particularly often with young black grouse and hares, or tries to catch game as it takes off.
8. Tells lies—that is, makes false sets.
9. Has an uneasy set, moves forward bit by bit, stirs, especially as the hunter approaches.
10. Has no set at all or has a very short set—cannot contain herself.
11. Has too dead a set and cannot put up game when given the command "Pille!" [Take!], as is sometimes necessary (for example, when one is hunting woodcock in a thicket).
12. Does not leave her set when her master calls, which tends to be particularly unpleasant in dense and thick shrubbery; it may happen that the hunter is forced to search out his dog for a whole hour.
13. Does not know how to find wounded or killed game. This tends to happen almost exclusively with dogs who have the gift of excellent scent. It is true that hunters themselves are for the most part to blame for this, when they hurry the dog, etc. (see hunter's flaw no. 12).

14. Chases (silently or barking) after a bird or after a hare, puts up a bird, and again gives chase.
15. Having seen where a bird goes down, rushes there and puts it up.
16. Is not "appellish" [*appelista*]—does not return at the whistle.
17. Having heard a shot, no matter how far off, runs there.
18. After a shot is made, does not wait to be commanded to raise the game and rushes off to raise it herself.
19. When foreseeing punishment, does not give herself into the hunter's hands, does not approach him, but circles nearby.
20. Bites when punished.
21. Is envious, searches poorly and generally behaves improperly when another dog is in the field.
22. Hinders her fellows.
23. When another dog is searching, continually stops and looks at her: "Did *she* find anything?"
24. Even when there is no other dog present, time and again stops, twirls her tail and looks around: "Is anything there?"
25. Does not immediately give the game to her master.
26. "Slobbers up" [*muslit*] the game, that is, takes it all the way into her mouth and seems to chew it.
27. Crushes game—there go the guts!
28. Eats game (for the most part due to hunger).
29. Quickly tires and begins, as they say, to "shine your spurs," that is, to walk right behind the hunter. Dogs with fat paws tire more rapidly than others.
30. Is afraid of hot weather or strong wind.
31. Is afraid of the cold: shivers, presses close, shifts from one foot to the other. Is afraid of the damp in marshes and early hoar-frost.
32. Does not go into the water after killed game.
33. If the game has fallen on the opposite side of a stream, swims across, seizes the game, but does not bring it back across.
34. Does not bring killed game or other retrieved objects all the way back to her master, but drops them several paces away from him.
35. Is afraid of a shot and either runs off to the side or sneaks along about fifty paces behind the hunter.
36. Runs back home from the field.
37. Fights with other dogs; takes away their game by force.
38. Has an aversion to game of some well-known kind (most often waterfowl) and does not proffer it.

39. Is too sensitive to a wound; cannot bear a paw-prick or contusion.

40. Does not remain behind when given the command "Back!"

41. When on leash, instead of walking at the hunter's heels, strains forward, pulls the leash and drags the hunter behind.

42. Chews through the rope when tied.

43. Does not stay when the hunter has given her the command "Couche!"—moves away from him (in order to sneak up on some ducks, for instance).

44. Misbehaves and does not believe the hunter when he (for instance) makes her search for a bird that has moved.

45. Misbehaves by refusing food and thereby deprives herself of strength for the hunt.

46. In a cart or carriage does not lie quietly during the journey but constantly climbs up.

47. When happy, jumps up on the hunter and makes holes in his clothing with her claws.

48. Passionately loves to seek out hedgehogs and barks at them.

49. Performs astonishingly firm and handsome sets for larks.

50. Does not understand that during a battue a dog must hold herself quietly and not make noise: scratches, shakes her head noisily or suddenly starts to sneeze violently.

Notes

Introduction. The Hunting Writer

Epigraph note: L. N. Tolstoy, *Polnoe sobranie sochinenii*, vol. 23 (Moscow: Gosudarstvennoe izdatel'stvo khudozhestvennoi literatury, 1957), 29.

1. See M. P. Alekseev, "Turgenev—propagandist russkoi literatury na zapade," in *Russkaia literatura i ee mirovoe znachenie* (Leningrad: Nauka, 1989), 268–307; Nicholas Žekulin, "Turgenev as Translator," *Canadian Slavonic Papers* 50, nos. 1–2 (March–June 2008): 155–76; Orlando Figes, *The Europeans: Three Lives and the Making of a Cosmopolitan Culture* (New York: Henry Holt, 2019), 302–3.

2. V. G. Belinskii, "Vzgliad na russkuiu literaturu 1847 goda," *Polnoe sobranie sochinenii*, vol. 10 (Moscow: Izdatel'stvo Akademii Nauk SSSR, 1956), 347.

3. Quoted from K. N. Lomunov, "Turgenev i Lev Tolstoi: Tvorcheskie vzaimootnosheniia," in *I. S. Turgenev v sovremennom mire*, ed. S. E. Shatalov (Moscow: Nauka, 1987), 123, 125–26. The two statements are quoted from a letter to Fet (11, 12 March 1877) in L. N. Tolstoi, *Polnoe sobranie sochinenii*, vol. 62 (Moscow-Leningrad: Gosudarstvennoe izdatel'stvo, 1953), 315, and from A. Sergeenko, *Kak zhivet i rabotaet gr. L. N. Tolstoi* (Moscow: Tipo-litografiia tovarishchestva I. N. Kushnerev, 1898), 53.

4. K. K. Arsen'ev, "Priroda v proizvedeniiakh Turgeneva," in *Sobranie kritcheskikh materialov dlia izucheniia proizvedenii I. S. Turgeneva*, vol. 1, ed. V. Zelinskii (Moscow: Tipo-litografiia V. Rikhter, 1906), 127.

5. Vladimir Nabokov, *Lectures on Russian Literature*, ed. Fredson Bowers (New York: Harcourt, Brace, Jovanovich, 1981), 69.

6. Daniyal Mueenuddin, preface to Ivan Turgenev, *A Sportsman's Notebook*, trans. Charles and Natasha Hepburn (New York: Ecco, 2020), xxv.

7. Hugo Tauno Salonen, *Die Landschaft bei I. S. Turgenev* (Helsinki: Kirjapaino-Osakeyhtiö Sana, 1915); Michael Nierle, *Die Naturschilderung und ihre Funktion in Versdichtung und Prosa von I. S. Turgenev*, Studien zur Geschichte der russischen Literatur des 19. Jahrhunderts, Frankfurter Abhandlungen zur Slavistik 11 (Bad Homburg: Verlag Gehlen, 1969).

8. *PsspS4*:182. Turgenev refers to Nicholas Saunderson (1682–1739), a blind English mathematician whose remark about the connection between color and sound was noted by a number of writers, including Madame de Staël; see *PsspS4*:595.

9. *PsspS7*:296.

10. *PsspS10*:176. "Drozd (I)" was one of the prose poems published posthumously in 1930.

11. V. I. Dal', ed., *Tolkovyi slovar' zhivogo velikorusskogo iazyka v chetyrekh tomakh*, 3rd ed., vol. 2 (St. Petersburg–Moscow: M. O. Vol'f, 1905), column 1266; M. Vasmer, *Etimologicheskii slovar' russkogo iazyka v chetyrekh tomakh*, trans. O. N. Trubachev, 3rd ed. (St. Petersburg: Terra, 1996), 3:49; *Virgin Soil* (*Nov'*, 1870–76), *PsspS9*:155.

12. Dal', *Tolkovyi slovar'*, vol. 1, column 1302; Vasmer, *Etimologicheskii slovar'*, 2:28.

13. Dal', *Tolkovyi slovar'*, vol. 3, column 1147; Vasmer, *Etimologicheskii slovar'*, 3:362, 490–91.

14. A. P. Evgen'eva, ed., *Slovar' russkogo iazyka v chetyrekh tomakh*, Akademiia Nauk SSSR, Institut russkogo iazyka, vol. 3, 2nd rev. ed. (Moscow: Izdatel'stvo Russkii iazyk, 1983), 437.

15. Ia. P. Polonskii, "I. S. Turgenev u sebia v ego poslednii priezd na rodinu (Iz vospominanii)," quoted from S. M. Petrov and V. G. Fridland, eds., *I. S. Turgenev v vospominaniiakh sovremennikov* (Moscow: Khudozhestvennaia literatura, 1983), 2:362. See also chapter 6.

16. Ian Helfant, "S. T. Aksakov: The Ambivalent Proto-ecological Consciousness of a Nineteenth-Century Russian Hunter," *Interdisciplinary Studies in Literature and Environment (ISLE)* 13, no. 2 (Summer 2006): 57–71.

17. Thomas Newlin, "At the Bottom of the River: Forms of Ecological Consciousness in Mid-Nineteenth-Century Russian Literature," *Russian Studies in Literature* 39, no. 2 (Spring 2003): 81.

18. *PsspS*4:522.

19. I. S. Aksakov to I. S. Turgenev, Abramtsevo, 22 January 1853, *Russkoe obozrenie* 29 (September 1894): 8–9.

20. N. A. Nekrasov, "Literaturnyi maskarad nakanune novogo (1852) goda: Zametki novogo poeta," *Polnoe sobranie sochinenii*, vol. 12.2 (St. Petersburg: Nauka, 1995), 270–71. Panaev's verbal caricature of Turgenev appeared as part of a "literary masquerade" he coauthored with Nekrasov for the January 1852 issue of the *Contemporary*. In 1851, Turgenev had published his last two *Notes of a Hunter* stories—"Bezhin Meadow" and "Kas'ian from Krasivaia Mech'"—in the journal. As we will see in chapter 3, it was Panaev, coeditor of the *Contemporary*, who actually devised the title *Notes of a Hunter*.

21. G. B. Kurliandskaia, *Esteticheskii mir I. S. Turgeneva* (Orel: Izdatel'stvo gosudarstvennoi teleradioveshchatel'noi kompanii, 1994), 137.

22. *Novoe vremia*, 8 (20), September 1883, no. 2704, quoted in *PsspS*10:441.

23. K. K. Arsen'ev, "Peizazh v sovremennom russkom romane," in his *Kriticheskie etiudy po russkoi literature*, vol. 2 (St. Petersburg: Tipografiia M. M. Stasiulevicha, 1888), 316.

24. Perov painted two portraits of Turgenev: one in 1871, one the following year; see Patrick Waddington, *A Catalogue of Portraits of Ivan Sergeyevich Turgenev (1818–83)* (Wellington: Whirinaki, 1999), 30–32.

25. Nikolai Dmitrievich Dmitriev-Orenburgskii (1838–98) painted his portrait of Turgenev from life, in Paris, during several sittings in January 1880, as a study for a larger canvas, *Une chasse au faisan, offerte au grand-duc Nikolaï Nikolaïévitch par le baron Ury de Gunzbourg en 1879*, now held by the Musée Tourguéniev, Bougival. See Waddington, 48–49; *PsspP*12.2 (1967): 510; *Literaturnaia mysl'*, 1923, no. 1, 246, note 2; *Explication des ouvrages de peinture, sculpture, architecture, gravure, et lithographie des artistes vivants exposés au Palais des Champs-Élysées le 2 mai 1881* (Paris: Charles de Morgues frères, 1881), 70, item 749.

26. Jane Costlow, "Odintseva's Bath and Bazarov's Dogs: The Dismantling of Culture in *Fathers and Children*," in *Worlds within Worlds: The Novels of Ivan Turgenev* (Princeton, NJ: Princeton University Press, 1990), 107.

27. A similar observation has recently been made about the early twentieth-century US ecologist Aldo Leopold by his biographer, Curt Meine: "Aldo Leopold would never have become the seminal thinker he became, had he not been a hunter. It was in fact his lifelong passion for wildlife (which included, but was not limited to, hunting) that made him the thinker he was." Jeffrey Kramer and Curt Meine, "Reconciling the Land Ethic and the Hunting of Wildlife," Center for Humans and Nature, https://www.humansandnature.org/does-hunting-make-us-human-reconciling-the-land-ethic-and-the-killing-of-wildlife.

28. Natal'ia Kudel'ko dubs this the "Aksakov-Turgenev tradition" (aksakovsko-turgenevskaia traditsiia): N. A. Kudel'ko, "'Okhota pitala i literaturu': I. S. Turgenev i ego literaturnye posledovateli ob osobennostiakh natsional'noi okhoty," Spasskii vestnik 10 (2004): 115–16.

29. Cheryll Glotfelty, "Introduction: Literary Studies in an Age of Environmental Crisis," in The Ecocriticism Reader: Landmarks in Literary Ecology, ed. Cheryll Glotfelty and Harold Fromm (Athens: University of Georgia Press, 1996), xviii–xix.

30. Camilo Gomides, "Putting a New Definition of Ecocriticism to the Test: The Case of 'The Burning Season,' a Film (Mal)Adaptation," Interdisciplinary Studies in Literature and Environment (ISLE) 13, no. 1 (Winter 2006): 16.

31. Jane T. Costlow and Amy Nelson, "Integrating the Animal," in Other Animals: Beyond the Human in Russian Culture and History, ed. Costlow and Nelson (Pittsburgh: University of Pittsburgh Press, 2010), 2.

32. Michael Lundblad, "From Animal to Animality Studies," PMLA 124, no. 2 (March 2009): 500.

33. Lundblad, 500.

34. Garry Marvin and Susan McHugh, "In It Together: An Introduction to Human-Animal Studies," in Routledge Handbook of Human-Animal Studies, ed. Marvin and McHugh (New York: Routledge, 2014), 7–8.

35. Costlow and Nelson, "Integrating the Animal," 3.

36. Dym, PsspS7:276.

1. Catching Nature by the Tail

Epigraph notes: Letter of 3 (15) January 1857, Paris, PsspP3:180; PsspS5:178. Turgenev began the story 30 June (12 July) 1857 and completed it 15 (27) November 1857.

1. See, for example, G. B. Kurliandskaia, "O filosofii prirody v proizvedeniiakh Turgeneva," Voprosy russkoi literatury 2, no. 17 (1971): 46–49; Eva Kagan-Kans, "Turgenev, the Metaphysics of an Artist, 1818–1883," Cahiers du Monde russe et soviétique 13, no. 3 (July–September 1972): 382–83; S. G. Borzenko, "Turgenev i priroda (Filosofskie motivy v pis'makh I. S. Turgeneva)," Voprosy russkoi literatury 28 (1976): 32; Galina A. Time, Nemetskaia literaturno-filosofskaia mysl' XVIII–XIX vekov v kontekste tvorchestva I. S. Turgeneva (geneticheskie i tipologicheskie aspekty), Vorträge und Abhandlungen zur Slavistik, Bd. 31 (Munich: Verlag Otto Sagner, 1997), 8.

2. See Wsewolod Setschkareff, Schellings Einfluß in der russischen Literatur der 20er und 30er Jahre des XIX. Jahrhunderts (Leipzig: Veröffentlichungen des Slavischen Instituts an der Friedrich-Wilhelms-Universität Berlin, 1939), 6–22; and Aileen Kelly, The Discovery of Chance: The Life and Thought of Alexander Herzen (Cambridge, MA: Harvard University Press, 2016), 69–74.

3. Kelly, *Discovery of Chance*, 15.

4. Isaiah Berlin, "German Romanticism in Petersburg and Moscow," in *Russian Thinkers*, 2nd ed. (London: Penguin, 2008), 160.

5. "Avtobiografiia," *PsspS*11:203.

6. "Pis'ma iz Berlina," dated 1 March 1847 (New Style), *PsspS*1:291.

7. "Pis'ma iz Berlina," *PsspS*1:291.

8. "Iakov Pasynkov," *PsspS*5:60. In *On the Eve* (*Nakanune*), Bersenev's father has written an unpublished treatise entitled *"Appearances or Transfigurations of the Spirit in the World*, a work in which Schellingianism, Swedenborgianism and Republicanism were blended in a most original fashion": *PsspS*6:198. When Bersenev begins to explain his keen interest in Schelling to Elena Stakhova, the artist Shubin interrupts: "For God's sake! You don't really want to give Elena Nikolaevna a lecture on Schelling do you? Have mercy!": *PsspS*6:175.

9. *Rudin*, *PsspS*5:259; "Sobaka," *PsspS*10:129–30.

10. For a comprehensive overview of Turgenev's literary treatment of dogs see A. D. Briggs, "One Man and His Dogs: An Anniversary Tribute to Ivan Turgenev," *Irish Slavonic Studies* 14 (January 1993): 1–20.

11. Kagan-Kans, "Turgenev, the Metaphysics of an Artist," 384.

12. *PsspS*1:197–235; *PsspS*5:90–129.

13. Peter Thiergen, " 'Priroda do otvratitel'noi stepeni ravnodushna': Alexandre Herzen et le scepticisme de son époque face à la nature," *Revue des études slaves* 78, no. 2–3 (2000): 261–63. See also Paul Carus, "Goethe's Nature Philosophy," *Open Court* 21 (1907): 227–37.

14. Though in Turgenev's day the essay was assumed to be Goethe's own work, authorship of the fragmentary "Die Natur" has been disputed, and modern scholars by and large attribute it to Georg Christoph Tobler (1757–1812). Goethe, however, clearly believed "Die Natur" to represent his own views; see Robert J. Richards, *The Tragic Sense of Life: Ernst Haeckel and the Struggle over Evolutionary Thought* (Chicago: University of Chicago Press, 2009), 111 note 93. The basic observations in "Die Natur" seem to have originated in Orphic hymns, appropriated by Anthony Ashley-Cooper, 3rd Earl of Shaftesbury, and made their way from his writings to Goethe; see Mark O. Kistler, "The Sources of the Goethe-Tobler Fragment 'Die Natur,' " *Monatshefte* 46, no. 7 (December 1954): 383–89, and Henry F. Fullenwider, "The Goethean Fragment 'Die Natur' in English Translation," *Comparative Literature Studies* 23, no. 2 (Summer 1986): 170–77.

15. *The Maxims and Reflections of Goethe*, trans. and ed. Bailey Saunders (New York: Macmillan, 1906), 207–12.

16. See George A. Wells, "Goethe and Evolution," *Journal of the History of Ideas* 28, no. 4 (October–December 1967): 538.

17. Margarita Odesskaia has suggested that certain ideas of French naturalist Georges-Louis Leclerc, Comte de Buffon (1707–88), may have anticipated or influenced the Goethean concept of nature's indifference; see Odesskaia, *"Zapiski okhotnika* I. S. Turgeneva: Problema zhanra," *Litteraria Humanitas* 7 (Alexandr Sergejevič Puškin v evropských kulturních souvislostech) (Brno: Masarykova univerzita, 2000), 199–200.

18. *Maxims and Reflections of Goethe*, 213; my italics.

19. Robert Louis Jackson, "The Root and the Flower, Dostoevsky and Turgenev: A Comparative Aesthetic," in *Dialogues with Dostoevsky: The Overwhelming Questions* (Stanford, CA: Stanford University Press, 1993), 164.

20. For more on Schelling and Goethe's *Naturphilosophie* see Phillip R. Sloan, "'The Sense of Sublimity': Darwin on Nature and Divinity," *Osiris* 16, *Science in Theistic Contexts: Cognitive Dimensions* (2001): 252–54.

21. Odesskaia, "*Zapiski okhotnika* I. S. Turgeneva," 201.

22. A. S. Pushkin, "Brozhu li ia vdol' ulits shumnykh," *Polnoe sobranie sochinenii*, vol. 3 (Leningrad: Nauka, 1977), 130.

23. A. I. Gertsen, "Pis'mo II: Nauka i priroda—Fenomenologiia myshleniia," *Pis'ma ob izuchenii prirody*, *Sobranie sochinenii v tridtsati tomakh*, vol. 3 (Moscow: Izdatel'stvo Akademii Nauk SSSR, 1954), 130. Quoted from Alexander Herzen, *Selected Philosophical Works*, trans. L. Navrozov (Moscow: Foreign Languages Publishing House, 1956), 138, 137 (translation modified).

24. A. I. Gertsen, *Kto vinovat? Sobranie sochinenii v tridtsati tomakh*, vol. 4 (Moscow: Izdatel'stvo Akademii Nauk SSSR, 1955), 126, 321; see Thiergen, "'Priroda do otvratitel'noi stepeni ravnodushna,'" 271.

25. A. I. Gertsen, "Pered grozoi," *Sobranie sochinenii v tridtsati tomakh*, vol. 6 (Moscow: Izdatel'stvo Akademii Nauk SSSR, 1955), 23–24, 37. Quoted from Herzen, *Selected Philosophical Works*, 352, 366. See also Berlin, "German Romanticism," 222–23.

26. A. I. Gertsen, "LVII god respubliki, edinoi i nerazdel'noi," *Sobranie sochinenii v tridtsati tomakh*, vol. 6 (Moscow: Izdatel'stvo Akademii Nauk SSSR, 1955), 56. Quoted from Herzen, *Selected Philosophical Works*, 384 (translation modified).

27. A. I. Gertsen, "Consolatio" (1849), *Sobranie sochinenii v tridtsati tomakh*, vol. 6 (Moscow: Izdatel'stvo Akademii Nauk SSSR, 1955), 99–100. Quoted from Herzen, *Selected Philosophical Works*, 427 (translation modified).

28. As we will see in chapter 4, Herzen's precepts in *Letters on the Study of Nature* and *From the Other Shore* significantly influenced Turgenev's own thought about the workings of the natural world.

29. A. I. Gertsen, "Robert Ouen," *Byloe i dumy*, *Sobranie sochinenii v tridtsati tomakh*, vol. 11 (Moscow: Izdatel'stvo Akademii Nauk SSSR, 1957), 246–47. Quoted from Herzen, "Robert Owen," in *My Past and Thoughts*, trans. Constance Garnett, rev. Humphrey Higgens, vol. 3 (New York: Knopf, 1968), 1245.

30. Leonard Schapiro, *Turgenev: His Life and Times* (Cambridge, MA: Harvard University Press, 1982), 31; Herzen to N. Kh. Ketcher, 1 March 1844, *Sobranie sochinenii v tridtsati tomakh*, vol. 22 (Moscow: Izdatel'stvo Akademii Nauk SSSR, 1961), 176; Kelly, *Discovery of Chance*, 412; N. S. Nikitina, ed., *Letopis' zhizni i tvorchestva I. S. Turgeneva (1818–1858)* (St. Petersburg: Nauka, 1995), 138–46. On Turgenev's and Herzen's similar views of nature see Kurliandskaia, "O filosofii prirody," 50.

31. Letters to Pauline Viardot, Paris, 30 May (11 June) 1849, *PsspP*1:287; and Courtavenel, 16 (28) July 1849, *PsspP*1:311.

32. "Poezdka v Poles'e," *PsspS*5:130.

33. "Priroda," *PsspS*10:165.

34. Giacomo Leopardi, *Operette Morali: Essays and Dialogues*, trans. Giovanni Cecchetti (Berkeley: University of California Press, 1982), 195–97, 199.

35. Leopardi, 199.

36. Letter to Pauline Viardot, Spasskoe, 23 June (5 July) 1868, *PsspP*9:23.

37. Letter to Pauline Viardot, Paris, 30 May (11 June) 1849, *PsspP*1:287.

38. *Nakanune*, *PsspS*6:162.

39. "Gamlet i Don Kikhot," *PsspS*5:341. Quoted from Elizabeth Cheresh Allen's translation in "Hamlet and Don Quixote," in *The Essential Turgenev* (Evanston, IL: Northwestern University Press, 1994), 557–58 (translation modified).

40. "Zapiski ruzheinogo okhotnika Orenburgskoi gubernii S. A—va," *PsspS*4:516–17; for a complete translation see appendix 3.

41. *Ottsy i deti*, *PsspS*7:119.

42. Letter of 16 (28) July 1864 to Valentine Delessert, Baden-Baden, *PsspP*6:43.

43. Spinoza, *Ethics*, trans. Samuel Shirley (Indianapolis: Hackett, 1992), Part 5, Proposition 19. On Goethe's debt to Spinoza see Franz Rosenzweig, *Philosophical and Theological Writings*, trans. and ed. Paul W. Franks and Michael L. Morgan (Indianapolis: Hackett, 2000), 60–61.

44. "Geschichte und Naturbeschreibung der merkwürdigsten Vorfälle des Erdbebens welches an dem Ende des 1755sten Jahres einen großen Theil der Erde erschüttert hat" (1756), quoted in *Immanuel Kants kleinere Schriften zur Naturphilosophie*, vol. 2, ed. Otto Buek (Leipzig: Verlag der Dürr'sche Buchhandlung, 1907), 321.

45. Jackson, "Root and the Flower," 164–69.

46. Jackson, "Root and the Flower," 167, 169.

47. Sergei Aksakov, *Zapiski ob uzhen'e ryby*, *Sochineniia*, vol. 4 (Moscow: Gosudarstvennoe izdatel'stvo khudozhestvennoi literatury, 1956), 10; quoted from *Notes on Fishing*, trans. Thomas Hodge (Evanston, IL: Northwestern University Press, 1977), 6. Aksakov's sentiment is uncannily akin to Thoreau's, expressed at almost the same time: "The surliness with which the woodchopper speaks of his woods, handling them as indifferently as his axe, is better than the mealy-mouthed enthusiasm of the lover of Nature" (drafted 1845–47): Henry David Thoreau, *A Week on the Concord and Merrimack Rivers* (Boston: James Munroe, 1849), 112–13.

48. "Breter," *PsspS*4:42.

49. "Gamlet Shchigrovskogo uezda," *PsspS*3:265–6.

50. Andrew Durkin, "A Guide to the Guides: Writing about Birds in Russia in the Nineteenth Century," *Russian Studies in Literature* 39, no. 3 (Summer 2003): 12.

51. For example, the adjective *strastnyi* (passionate) is used ten times in Turgenev's *Zapiski okhotnika*; four of those ten occurrences (40 percent) are in the phrase *strastnyi okhotnik* (passionate hunter); no other *strastnyi* phrase occurs more than once. Aksakov, in his *Zapiski ruzheinogo okhotnika*, uses the adjective *strastnyi* a total of twenty-two times: twelve times with *okhotnik* (55 percent), three times with *okhota* (14 percent), and only seven times (32 percent) with other nouns.

52. Aaron M. Moe, *Zoopoetics: Animals and the Making of Poetry* (Lanham, MD: Lexington Books, 2014), 10; Moe, "Toward Zoopoetics: Rethinking Whitman's 'Original Energy,'" *Walt Whitman Quarterly Review* 31 (2013): 2.

53. I have in mind something related to what Thomas Newlin calls the "ecological thinking" he sees arising in mid-nineteenth-century Russian literature: "Simply put, it shows a basic appreciation for nature as such—that is, for the real, actual natural world, in its sometimes messy and seemingly 'desolate' 'charm' and variety": Newlin, "At the Bottom of the River: Forms of Ecological Consciousness in

Mid-Nineteenth-Century Russian Literature," ed. Rachel May, *Russian Studies in Literature* 39, no. 2 (Spring 2003): 71–90: 74.

54. "Asia," *PsspS*5:178. It must be added that humans are of course incapable of pure zootropic writing, since the mere representation of any creature in a text, simply embodying it in human language, is turning the animal to some form of human use; see introduction and Garry Marvin and Susan McHugh, "In It Together: An Introduction to Human-Animal Studies," in *Routledge Handbook of Human-Animal Studies* (New York: Routledge, 2014), 7–8.

55. My use of *ecotropism* is related, but not identical, to the poet John Campion's in his manifesto entitled "Toward an Ecotropic Poetry": http://worldatuningfork. com/wp-content/uploads/2013/ 05/Toward-An-Ecotropic-Poetrywidermargins. pdf.

56. As a term, *anthropotropism* is already in limited theological use, coined in German by Abraham Heschel in his *Die Prophetie* (Kraków: Nakładem Polskiej Akademji Umiejętności, 1936); the term *Anthropotropismus*, opposed to *Theotropismus*, first appears on 141. See Robert Erlewine, *Judaism and the West* (Bloomington: Indiana University Press, 2016), 119: "In the anthropotropic turn, the breach with the everyday is such that a turning [*Wendung*] takes place on the part of the divine and is directed toward [*Richtung*] a particular human being." *Anthropotropism* is also used in studies of technology: "Science fiction author and media theory professor Paul Levinson (1998) has defined remediation as the 'anthropotropic' ('anthropo-' for 'human' and 'tropic' for 'toward') process by which new media technologies improve upon or remedy prior technologies in their rendering of human performance": Terje Hillesund and Claire Bélisle, "What Digital Remediation Does to Critical Editions and Reading Practices," in *Digital Critical Editions*, ed. Daniel Apollon, Claire Bélisle, and Philippe Regnier (Champaign: University of Illinois Press, 2014), 133. Hillesund and Bélisle refer here to Paul Levinson, *Soft Edge: A Natural History and Future of the Information Revolution* (London: Routledge, 1998): "'anthropotropic' theory—evolution of media towards human performance" (p. xvi) . . . the 'anthropotropic' evolution of media . . . the evolution of media towards more human function" (p. 81).

57. In an article originally published in 2003, Robert L. Jackson commented, "*Proizvol* has roughly three distinct though related meanings in Russian: one's own choice, desire; self-will (*svoevolie*); arbitrariness": "Breaking the Moral Barrier: Anna Karenina's Night Train to St. Petersburg," in Robert L. Jackson, *Close Encounters: Essays on Russian Literature* (Boston: Academic Studies Press, 2013), 103. This third sense, which will be my focus, has been translated in more recent English-language scholarship as "arbitrariness," "arbitrary power," "arbitrary rule," "misconduct," "excess," "capricious official power," "petty despotism," "arbitrary authority," "arbitrary will," "capricious behavior," "unconstrained autocracy," "caprice," "arbitrary exercise of power," and so on.

58. Jane Costlow, *Heart-Pine Russia: Walking and Writing the Nineteenth-Century Forest* (Ithaca, NY: Cornell University Press, 2013), 27; quotation corrected from published version via personal communication with the author.

59. *Biuffon dlia iunoshestva, ili Sokrashchennaia istoriia trekh tsarstv prirody* sochinennaia Petrom Blanshardom, vol. 1 (Moscow: Tipografiia S. Selivanovskogo, 1814), 117–18, which is a Russian translation of an adaptation of Buffon's magisterial *His-*

toire naturelle: Le Buffon de la jeunesse, ou Abrégé d'histoire naturelle. . . . Rédigé par Pierre Blanchard, 4th ed., vol. 1 (Paris: Chez Leprieur, 1809).

60. Letter to M. A. Bakunin and A. Efremov, 3, 8 (15, 20) September 1840, Marienbad, *PsspP*1:168.

61. F. I. Buslaev, *Moi dosugi*, vol. 2 (Moscow: Sinodal'naia tipografiia, 1886), 80; quoted from *PsspS*6:420.

62. For the sources, production techniques, textual history, and iconography of Ambodik's volume see Anthony Hippisley's introduction to the facsimile edition: N. M. Maksimovič-Ambodik, *Emvlemy i simvoly (1788): The First Russian Emblem Book*, ed. and trans. Anthony Hippisley (Leiden: Brill, 1989), xiii–xlvii. Maksimovich-Ambodik's book plays an important role in *A Gentry Nest* (1858–59), as we will see in chapter 5.

63. Quoted from Hippisley's translation of Maksimovich-Ambodik, 23.

64. "Zapiski ruzheinogo okhotnika Orenburgskoi gubernii S. A—va" (1852), *PsspS*4:516.

65. "Zapiski ruzheinogo okhotnika Orenburgskoi gubernii S. A—va," *PsspS*4:518. Turgenev here objects to a pronouncement originally published as the opening sentence of Buffon's entry on "Le cheval": "La plus noble conquête que l'homme ait jamais faite est celle de ce fier et fougueux animal qui partage avec lui les fatigues de la guerre et la gloire des combats." Comte Georges Louis Leclerc de Buffon, *Histoire naturelle, générale et particulière, avec la description du Cabinet du roi*, vol. 4 (Paris: De l'Imprimerie royale, 1753), 174. Turgenev first mocked Buffon's encomium to the horse in "Lebedian'," from the *Notes of a Hunter* cycle: "Any hunter who values shooting and gun dogs is a passionate admirer of the noblest animal in the world: the horse" (*PsspS*3:172–73). In the opening paragraph of "Pégase" ("Pegaz," 1871), Turgenev openly disputed Buffon's claim: "The dog, much more than the horse, deserves the title of 'man's noblest conquest,' to use Buffon's famous expression" (*PsspS*11:157). Pushkin, in his draft article "O proze" (1822), not published until a year after Turgenev's death, had objected to precisely the same passage: "D'Alembert once said to La Harpe: do not speak of Buffon to me. Buffon writes, 'The noblest of all man's conquests was this proud, fiery, etc., animal.' Why not simply say—'the horse'? . . . Precision and brevity—these are the two virtues of prose. It demands matter and more matter—without it brilliant expressions serve no purpose." Quoted from *Pushkin on Literature*, ed. and trans. Tatiana Wolff, rev. ed. (Stanford, CA: Stanford University Press, 1986), 43.

66. "Asia," *PsspS*5:163, 169, 174, 176, 186.

67. "Asia," *PsspS*5:162, 173.

68. Raphael based the fresco on Poliziano's late fifteenth-century retelling (in *Stanze per la giostra*) of Ovid's account in *Metamorphoses*, Book 13; see *The Stanze of Angelo Poliziano*, trans. David L. Quint (University Park: Penn State University Press, 1979), 59–61, and Duncan T. Kinkead, "An Iconographic Note on Raphael's *Galatea*," *Journal of the Warburg and Courtauld Institutes* 33 (1970): 313–15. On Turgenev's intense admiration for Raphael see Irene Pearson, "Raphael as Seen by Russian Writers from Zhukovsky to Turgenev," *Slavonic and East European Review* 59, no. 3 (July 1981): 364–68.

69. *Ottsy i deti*, *PsspS*7:26.

70. *Ottsy i deti*, *PsspS*7:21–2.

71. *Ottsy i deti*, *PsspS*7:165.

72. Bill Freedman and Brian Douglas Hoyle, "Finches," *Grzimek's Animal Life Encyclopedia*, 2nd ed., vol. 11 (Detroit: Gale, 2004), 323–39. The chaffinch's Russian name, *ziablik*, is related to its migratorial habits, "possibly from *ziabnut'* [to suffer from the cold], because the chaffinch appears with the first snowmelt and departs only with the onset of winter": Max Vasmer, *Etimologicheskii slovar' russkogo iazyka v chetyrekh tomakh*, trans. O. N. Trubachev, 3rd ed. (St. Petersburg: Terra, 1996), 2:111.

73. The final line of MacLeish's "Ars Poetica" (1926): "A poem should not mean / But be."

74. As Mikhail Gershenzon put it, "For his entire life, Turgenev consciously preached that truth about Don Quixote: the strength, wisdom, beauty, and happiness of *the undivided spirit, the unbowed will [volia]*. . . . He envied Don Quixote; he considered himself a Hamlet and, most importantly, experienced all the torments of Hamlet's malady": Gershenzon, *Mechta i mysl' I. S. Turgeneva* (Moscow: Knigoizdatel'stvo v Moskve, 1919), 79.

75. Jackson, "Root and the Flower," 170.

76. Don Pablo to Don Bal'tazar, *Neostorozhnost'*, *PsspS*2:19.

77. *The Rape of the Lock* (1712–17), canto V, line 43.

2. The Gun before the Lyre

Second epigraph note: Henry James, *Partial Portraits* (London: Macmillan, 1894), 305.

1. I. A. Goncharov to S. A. Tolstaia, 11 November 1870, in Goncharov, *Sobranie sochinenii v vos'mi tomakh*, vol. 8 (Moscow: Khudozhestvennaia literatura, 1980), 385.

2. Thomas Brooks, *The Crown and Glory of Christianity* (1662), in *The Complete Works of Thomas Brooks*, vol. 4 (Edinburgh: James Nichol, 1847), 91.

3. V. S. Pritchett, *The Gentle Barbarian: The Work and Life of Turgenev* (New York: Ecco, 1977). In 1872, Goncourt called Turgenev "that gentle giant, that lovable barbarian" (Tourguéniev, le doux géant, l'aimable barbare); Edmond de Goncourt and Jules de Goncourt, *Pages from the Goncourt Journals*, trans. and ed. Robert Baldick (New York: NYRB Classics, 2007), 197.

4. See, for example, the striking similarity between Turgenev's loving description (through the hunter-narrator) of awaiting woodcock at their roding grounds (*stoiat'na tiage*) after sunset on a May evening in "Ermolai i mel'nichikha" (*PsspS*3:29–30) and Aksakov's account of precisely the same activity in his *Zapiski ruzheinogo okhotnika*, *Sobranie sochinenii*, vol. 4 (Moscow: Gosudarstvennoe izdatel'stvo khudozhestvennoi literatury, 1956), 444–45.

5. John M. MacKenzie, *The Empire of Nature: Hunting, Conservation, and British Imperialism* (Manchester: Manchester University Press, 1988), 10. See also Andrew Durkin's discussion of the sportsman's "self-handicapping," in Andrew R. Durkin, *Sergei Aksakov and Russian Pastoral* (New Brunswick, NJ: Rutgers University Press, 1983), 73.

6. Among the handful of works that seek to address Turgenev's hunting in earnest are V. A. Gromov's "Ruzh'e i lira Turgeneva," *Okhotnich'i prostory* 20 (1964): 190–200; "Na okhote v Spasskom," *Okhotnich'i prostory* 25 (1967): 218–24; and Richard Freeborn's "The Hunter's Eye in *Zapiski okhotnika*," *New Zealand Slavonic Journal*, no. 2 (1976): 1–9. Also noteworthy is Vasilii Shapochka's non-scholarly compendium, *Okhotnich'i tropy Turgeneva* (Orel: Veshnie vody, 1998).

7. See Durkin, *Sergei Aksakov*, 72–73. It is probable that the basic German term for "hunt," *Jagd*, is also derived from an Indo-European root that can mean both "to chase" and "to wish for"; see Porkorny, "Indogermanisches Etymologisches Wörterbuch," *Indo-European Etymological Dictionary*, 2 February 2002, Department of Comparative Indo-European Linguistics at Leiden University, 16 July 2005. See also Thomas Newlin's provocative linking of lust (and other forms of desire) with *okhota* in his "The Thermodynamics of Desire in Turgenev's *Notes of a Hunter*," *Russian Review* 72, no. 3 (2013): 367–68.

8. O. A. Egorov, *Ocherk istorii russkoi psovoi okhoty (XV–XVIII vv.)* (St. Petersburg: Izdatel'stvo Dmitrii Bulanin, 2008), 300–301.

9. Egorov, 280, 285. *Okhotnik* is first used to mean "hunter" in a legal document dating to 1495, while *okhota* is first used to mean "hunting" in a document dated 1596.

10. Egorov, 281. The older, more traditional term for hunting was *potekha* (modern Russian "amusement"), while the older term for hunter was *lovets* ("catcher").

11. B. Munsche, *Gentlemen and Poachers: The English Game Laws 1671–1831* (Cambridge: Cambridge University Press, 1981), 32. For what follows, my chief sources on ancient hunting practices are Denison Bingham Hull, *Hounds and Hunting in Ancient Greece* (Chicago: University of Chicago Press, 1964), and J. K. Anderson, *Hunting in the Ancient World* (Berkeley: University of California Press, 1985). A late eighteenth-century, early nineteenth-century form of Russian hawking is described at length by S. T. Aksakov in "Okhota s iastrebom za perepelkami," in his *Rasskazy i vospominaniia okhotnika o raznykh okhotakh* in S. T. Aksakov, *Sobranie sochinenii v chetyrekh tomakh*, vol. 4 (Moscow: Gosudarstvennoe izdatel'stvo khudozhestvennoi literatury, 1956), 480–503.

12. For clarity, I shall hereafter refer to *psovaia okhota* as "coursing" and *gon'ba* as "hounding."

13. For a comprehensive discussion of how borzois were employed in wolf coursing see chapter 2 of Ian Helfant's *That Savage Gaze: Wolves in the Nineteenth-Century Russian Imagination*, the Unknown Nineteenth Century (Boston: Academic Studies Press, 2018), 33–69.

14. A. V. Kamernitskii, *Okhota s sobakami na Rusi (X–XX vv.)*, Seriia Mir okhoty (Moscow: Veche, 2005), 8, 64.

15. Kamernitskii, 64.

16. This digest of coursing techniques is drawn from Egorov; Kamernitskii; Fedosiuk, "Okhota," in his *Chto neponiatno u klassikov, ili Entsiklopediia russkogo byta XIX veka*, 2nd ed. (Moscow: Izdatel'stvo Nauka, 1998); and *Slovar' okhotnika*, compiled by Natsional'nyi fond Sviatogo Trifona, http://ebftour.ru/slovar ohotnika.htm.

17. L. P. Sabaneev, *Sobaki okhotnich'i: Borzye i gonchie* (Moscow: Terra, 1992), 150.

18. Pushkin, *Polnoe sobranie sochinenii v desiati tomakh*, vol. 4 (Leningrad: Izdatel'stvo nauka, Leningradskoe otdelenie, 1978), 170.

19. A. A. Fet, *Stikhtovoreniia i poemy*, Biblioteka poeta, bol'shaia seriia, 3rd ed. (Leningrad: Sovetskii pisatel', Leningradskoe otdelenie, 1986), 131.

20. N. A. Nekrasov, *Polnoe sobranie sochinenii i pisem v piatnadtsati tomakh*, vol. 1, AN SSSR IRL (Leningrad: Nauka, Leningradskoe otdelenie, 1981), 49.

21. Nekrasov, himself a hunter, frequently included sporting scenes in his work: e.g. *Korobeiniki* (Chast' 4, "Ai barynia! Barynia! [Pesnia]"), "Iz poemy *Mat'*" (Chast'

3, "Pis'mo: Varshava, 1824 god"), and *Komu na Rusi zhit' khorosho* (Chast' 1, glava 5, "Pomeshchik"); see N. A. Nekrasov, *Polnoe sobranie sochinenii i pisem v piatnadtsati tomakh*, vol. 4 (Leningrad: Nauka, Leningradskoe otdelenie, 1982), 63–66, 254–59, and vol. 5 (Leningrad: Nauka, Leningradskoe otdelenie, 1982), 68–83. Nekrasov likewise treated coursing in the 1844 feuilletons "Nechto o dupeliakh, o doktore Pufe i o psovoi okhote" and "Zhurnal'nye otmetki [17 September 1844]" (Nekrasov, *Polnoe sobranie sochinenii i pisem v piatnadtsati tomakh*, vol. 12.1, 133–38, 147–53) as well as in the 1844 vaudeville *Peterburgskii rostovshchik* (Rostomakhov's song in scene 10; Nekrasov, *Polnoe sobranie sochinenii i pisem v piatnadtsati tomakh*, vol. 6, 155–56). See also M. V. Bulgakov, "Russkie pisateli-okhotniki: Nikolai Alekseevich Nekrasov (1821–1877)," *Okhota i okhotnich'e khoziaistvo*, 2008, no. 8, 38–41.

22. *War and Peace* (*Voina i mir*, vol. 2, part 4, chapters 3–5). For a venatically informed analysis see Ian Helfant, "Harnessing the Domestic to Confront the Wild: Borzoi Wolf Hunting and Masculine Aggression in *War and Peace*," in *That Savage Gaze*, 1–32.

23. Turgenev, "Piat'desiat nedostatkov ruzheinogo okhotnika i piat'desiat nedostatkov legavoi sobaki," *PsspS*10:274. See appendix 4.

24. L. N. Vaksel', *Karmannaia knizhka dlia nachinaiushchikh okhotit'sia s ruzh'em i legavoi sobakoiu*, 3rd ed. (St. Petersburg: Tipografiia Eduarda Pratsa, 1870), 119.

25. *PsspS*10:274. Rarely, a few peasant beaters were also employed to flush game, a modest version of the coursing battue (*oblava*).

26. S. T. Aksakov, *Notes of a Provincial Wildfowler*, trans. Kevin Windle (Evanston, IL: Northwestern University Press, 1998), 277.

27. Turgenev, "Zapiski ruzheinogo okhotnika Orenburgskoi gubernii. S. A—va," *PsspS*4:510–11. Sabaneev asserted in the mid-1890s that Turgenev, in the late 1850s to 1860s, owned some of the first pointers in Russia. L. P. Sabaneev, *Sobaki okhotnich'i: Legavye* (Moscow: Terra, 1992), 427, 462.

28. In 1852, Aksakov jokingly described the transition: "formerly in Russia broken German was used, and now Russians mangle French." Aksakov, *Zapiski ruzheinogo okhotnika*, 161. Windle's translation of Aksakov's treatise omits the early chapters on hunting equipment and dogs.

29. Aksakov, *Zapiski ruzheinogo okhotnika*, 160, 162.

30. "Le bon chien fait le bon chasseur, le bon chasseur fait le bon chien": Elzéar Blaze, *Chasseur au chien d'arrêt* (Paris: Librairie de Moutardier, 1836), 331, 339.

31. Egorov, *Ocherk istorii russkoi psovoi okhoty*, 293.

32. Kamernitskii, *Okhota s sobakami na Rusi*, 105–6.

33. L. P. Sabaneev, *Okhotnich'i zveri* (Moscow: Terra, 1992), 135 (written 1878).

34. Egorov, *Ocherk istorii russkoi psovoi okhoty*, 293.

35. Ian Helfant, "That Savage Gaze: The Contested Portrayal of Wolves in Nineteenth-Century Russia," in *Other Animals: Beyond the Human in Russian Culture and History*, ed. Jane Costlow and Amy Nelson (Pittsburgh: University of Pittsburgh Press, 2010), 65–68.

36. One occasional exception is the hare. "According to him [N. I. Trubetskoi's huntsman at Bellefontaine], we'll have to wipe out 300 to 400 hares, since the neighbors have been complaining about them a great deal": Turgenev's letter to Louis Viardot, 27 August 1857, *PsspP*3:253, 382. Elzéar Blaze, Turgenev's favorite French hunting writer, joked about a conversation he had with an acquaintance

who, citing Pythagoras and the abbé de Saint-Pierre, disputed the right of humans to kill animals. "We must," quips Blaze, "eat partridges, or partridges will eat us." Though he goes on to say that killing these birds spares crops, the reasoning is forced and the tone jocular. Blaze was debating with Antoine Deschamps de Saint-Amand (1800–69), a gifted poet and disciple of Hugo; see Blaze, *Chasseur au chien d'arrêt*, 45–46.

37. B. I. Markov, *Moskva okhotnich'ia* (Moscow: Tsentropoligraf, 1997), 192–93.

38. In his second review (1852) of *Notes of an Orenburg-Province Hunter*, Turgenev particularly stresses the utility of Aksakov's treatise to *estestvoispytateli* (*PsspS*4:518–19).

39. Pushkin, *Polnoe sobranie sochinenii*, vol. 6, 104. The dog's name is taken from the protagonist of Charles Nodier's gothic adventure novel, *Jean Sbogar* (1818).

40. *Anna Karenina* (especially part 6, chapters 8–13). Five years after Turgenev's death, Anton Chekhov would succinctly express the hunterly link between Tolstoi and Turgenev, both acknowledged masters of natural description: "I am convinced that as long as there exist in Russia forests, ravines, and summer nights, and as long as sandpipers call and lapwings cry . . . neither Turgenev nor Tolstoi will be forgotten": A. P. Chekhov to D. V. Grigorovich, 12 January 1888, in Chekhov, *Polnoe sobranie sochinenii i pisem v tridtsati tomakh, Pis'ma*, vol. 2 (Moscow: Nauka, 1975), 175.

41. O. V. Filiushkina, "K voprosu o proiskhozhdeniia *Zapisok okhotnika*," *Spasskii vestnik* 9 (2002): 133–34.

42. I. F. Rynda, "Cherty iz okhotnich'ei zhizni I. S. Turgeneva," in *Cherty iz zhizni Ivana Sergeevicha Turgeneva* (St. Petersburg: Tipografiia A. S. Suvorina, 1903), 36. Rynda's account of Turgenev's early hunting habits is drawn from personal interviews with L. V. Krivtsov (a contemporary of Turgenev and former country neighbor), the daughters and grandson of Afanasii Alifanov, and Turgenev's valet, M. Peregrinov. It is clear that Krivtsov had intimate knowledge of Turgenev's hunting life, and Alifanov—as Turgenev's lifelong hunting guide at Spasskoe and environs—was in a unique position to observe his master's forays in the field; see *PsspP*2:105–6. Several of the biographical details in this paragraph are drawn from Rynda's "Cherty."

43. In Turgenev's first-person, partially autobiographical story "Perepelka" ("The Quail," 1882), the narrator claims that his father forbade him to shoot birds until he turned twelve (*PsspS*10:119).

44. Nikolai Chernov, *Spassko-Lutovinovskaia khronika (1813–1883)* (Tula: IPO Lev Tolstoi, 1999), 52. On Kupferschmidt (1805–79) see also *PsspP*2:301; Filiushkina, 135; and L. N. Tolstoi, *Polnoe sobranie sochinenii*, vol. 83 (Moscow: Gosudarstvennoe izdatel'stvo Khudozhestvennaia literatura, 1938), 61. See Ian Helfant's discussion of the Moscow Hunting Society in *That Savage Gaze*, 36–38.

45. Chernov, *Spassko-Lutovinovskaia khronika*, 55; Rynda, "Cherty," 40

46. See Turgenev's autobiographical "Memorial," *PsspS*11: 198, and *PsspS*3: 452–53.

47. Rynda, "Cherty," 40.

48. I. S. Turgenev, *Pervoe sobranie pisem I. S. Turgeneva: 1840–1883 gg.* (St. Petersburg: Tipografiia M. M. Stasiulevicha, 1884), 92, note 1.

49. Rynda, "Cherty," 42.

50. See *PsspS*11:405.

51. Rynda, "Cherty," 40.

52. On Varvara Petrovna's gift see Rynda, 41. The oft-repeated tale of Turgenev's sorrow at the death of a *gustopsovaia borzaia* named Swan (Lebed') comes from N. Nikol'skii, "Iz zapisei o Turgeneve-okhotnike," *Okhotnich'i prostory* 6 (1956): 357–58. Nikol'skii says that he found among the effects of his late father a note about Turgenev transcribed by the elder Nikol'skii in 1891 from the words of one Vasilii Ivanovich Kononykin, "who in his youth often hunted with Ivan Sergeevich," but there is no mention of any Kononykin in any of the authoritative reference works on Turgenev, or in any of Turgenev's letters. There is likewise no epistolary trace of Lebed', despite Turgenev's habit of frequently mentioning his favorite dogs by name in his correspondence. Even if the third-hand Kononykin story is true, which seems less than likely, it never alleges that Turgenev hunted with borzois, merely that he owned some at one time.

53. *PsspS4:509*.

54. "Votre occupation favorite?—La chasse!" in 1869, but in 1880, Turgenev answered the same question with "Prendre du tabac" (*PsspS12:371*).

55. Letter to S. T. Aksakov, 17 October 1852, Spasskoe, *PsspP2:152*.

56. Letter to Louis Viardot, ca. November 1843–early February 1844, St. Petersburg, *PsspP1:202*. Viardot published his account of this hunt in the summer of 1844 (in *Illustration* 24, 31 August, 7 September), then as part of a booklet published in Paris (*Quelques chasses en Russie*, 12 ff.) in 1845, then as part of his popular book, *Souvenirs de chasse* (1846), which underwent numerous editions during his lifetime. See J. Douglas Clayton's introduction to his translation of Louis Viardot, *"Hunting in Russia" and "The Story of Dmitry"* (Ottawa: Slavic Research Group at the University of Ottawa, 2008), xv.

57. Quoted from *Letopis' zhizni i tvorchestva I. S. Turgeneva (1818–1858)*, ed. N. S. Nikitina (St. Petersburg: Nauka, 1995), 88.

58. Unfortunately, Louis Viardot seems to have left us no reminiscences of hunting with Turgenev. He rendered anonymous the Russian hunters who appear in his hunting memoirs, and decoding their identities is impossible; see *PsspP1:479*. See also Clayton's introduction to Viardot, *"Hunting in Russia" and "The Story of Dmitry,"* ix–xxiv.

59. D. I. Kolbasin, "Na okhote s Turgenevym," *Iuzhnyi sbornik v pol'zu postradavshikh ot neurozhaia* (Odessa: Shul'tse, 1892), otdel 1, 139–47. In the description that follows, I will be citing from "Zabytye vospominaniia o Turgeneve-okhotnike: Publikatsii, predisloviia i primechaniia V. Gromova. Na okhote s Turgenevym," *Okhotnich'i prostory*, Moscow, 1966, no. 24, 190–204.

60. For this portrait, originally entitled *The Hunter* (*Okhotnik*), Kramskoi had his fellow painter N. K. Bodarevskii (1850–1921) pose in hunting costume. The work was included in the first traveling exhibition of the Wanderers (Peredvizhniki), 1871. See N. Marchenko and K. V. Zelenoi, *Litsa i sud'by: Portret XVIII–nachala XIX veka v sobranii Natsional'nogo khudozhestvennogo muzeia Respubliki Belarus'* (Minsk: Izdatel'stvo Chetyre chetverti, 2002), 90.

61. Kolbasin, "Na okhote s Turgenevym," 198–99.

62. Without mentioning the dog by name, Turgenev discusses Bouboule's remarkable progress in his second review of Aksakov's *Orenburg-Province Hunter*; see appendix 3, paragraph 4.

63. Kolbasin, "Na okhote s Turgenevym," 197–98.

64. Letter of 10 (22) February 1854, St. Petersburg, *PsspP2*:285. As Nicholas Žekulin has pointed out, Turgenev's physical complaints during this period are difficult to identify; Žekulin, "Ivan Turgenev," in *Russian Novelists in the Age of Tolstoy and Dostoevsky*, ed. J. Alexander Ogden and Judith E. Kalb, Dictionary of Literary Biography, vol. 238 (Detroit: Gale, 2001), 357. Leonard Schapiro has noted (*Turgenev: His Life and Times* [Cambridge, MA: Harvard University Press, 1982], 129) that the problem is compounded by the continuing reluctance of scholars editing Turgenev's correspondence to publish the specifics, which are decorously omitted: e.g., "Details of a medical nature have been left out" (*PsspP3*:250, editor's note; letter to Botkin, 6 [18] August 1857, Boulogne).

65. Kolbasin, "Na okhote s Turgenevym," 199–201.

66. Kolbasin, 201–2.

67. This paragraph is based on Rynda, "Cherty," 44–49.

68. Letter of 8 (20) September 1858 to his daughter Polina, Spasskoe, *PsspP3*:335.

69. The following details and quotations are drawn from A. A. Fet, *Moi vospominaniia: 1848–1889*, chast' I (Moscow: Tipografiia A. I. Mamontova, 1890), chiefly 254–80. Nekrasov's hunting trip with Turgenev at Spasskoe in late September 1854, which might otherwise have generated rich details of Turgenev's hunting practice, was unfortunately hamstrung by Nekrasov's ill health, poor weather, and unreliable peasant guides; see Bulgakov, "Russkie pisateli-okhotniki," 38–41; *Letopis' zhizni i tvorchestva I. S. Turgeneva (1818–1858)*, 269–70.

70. "This day has enormous significance for hunters and they always wait for it impatiently. It is momentous because in all provinces of Russia, except the northern ones, starting on this holiday, hunting is permitted for all kinds of game, which, for its part, has had time to raise its young": S. I. Romanov, *Slovar' ruzheinoi okhoty* (Moscow–St. Petersburg: Izdanie Nikolaia Ivanovicha Mamontova, 1877), 295. "At last June arrives, and St. Peter's Day approaches, the day shooting is permitted": N. A. Osnovskii, "Petrov den': Iz vospominanii okhotnika," *Sovremennik* 48 (1854), 178.

71. Fet asserts that Lev Tolstoy used to make fun of Turgenev's devotion to this dog and claims that when Pauline Viardot met the dog as a puppy, she said "bouboule, bouboule," and the name stuck. Fet, *Moi vospominaniia*, 255.

72. Fet offers a lyrical depiction of their afternoon rest in the forest: "I can't keep from recalling our bivouacs in the forest. On a sweltering, absolutely windless July day, the open burn zones [*gari*] where the black grouse predominantly held, are reminiscent in their temperature of a red-hot stove. But the guide brings us to the bottom of a gully overgrown and overshadowed by tall woods. There among the twining roots of century-old firs grows an unbroken green carpet of round leaves, and when you part them with the butt of your gun or a branch, there shows black before you a moisture shining like polished steel. This is the forest brook. Its water is so cold that your teeth start to chatter, and you can imagine what a joy is its pure stream to a hunter wearied by thirst." Fet, *Moi vospominaniia*, 265.

73. *Letopis' zhizni i tvorchestva I. S. Turgeneva (1818–1858)*, 432, 434; *PsspP3*:341, 342 (letters to Druzhinin and Nekrasov).

74. Letter to A. A. Fet of 18 (30) June 1859, Vichy (*PsspP4*:56); letter to A. A. Fet of 22 July (3 August) 1859, Bellefontaine (*PsspP4*:71); letter to A. A. Fet of 1 (13) August 1859, Courtavenel (*PsspP4*:77).

75. Pietsch, a German artist and critic who befriended Turgenev in 1847, described summers in Baden-Baden: "Starting in mid-August a special form of rest-lessness would descend upon [Turgenev] and in equal measure upon his dog Pégase, about whom it was said that the master loved his four-legged friend more tenderly than he did people: they could hardly wait for the first day of hunting, at which time it was impossible to hold them back. With Louis Viardot, who all his life was an equally passionate hunter, and with two dogs, Turgenev would board a carriage that would take them away to a place booked for hunting, or to the estate of one of their friends. Having traveled at sunrise an incalculable number of leagues, they would return to the villa only in the evening, always with a rich bag": *Vossische Zeitung*, 1883, nos. 425–29, quoted from S. M. Petrov and V. G. Fridland, eds., *I. S. Turgenev v vospom-inaniiakh sovremennikov*, vol. 2 (Moscow: Khudozhestvennaia literatura, 1983), 253.

76. The final line of Schiller's "Das Siegesfest" ("The victory celebration"), in Tiutchev's translation ("Pominki," 1851). The German text that follows is Turgenev's parody of the final stanza of the original poem. In Schiller's "Only the gods remain forever," Turgenev replaces "gods" with his comic catalogue of game.

77. Letter to A. A. Fet, 18 (30) June 1859, Vichy, *PsspP4*:56–57.

78. Letter to A. A. Fet, 22 July (3 August) 1859, Bellefontaine, *PsspP4*:71.

79. Letter to A. A. Fet, 29 June (11 July), 1860, Bad Soden, *PsspP4*:218 (all ellipses here are Turgenev's). The ailing writer had arrived in Soden, just west of Frankfurt, and settled into the Hotel de l'Europe to take the waters for six weeks; see his letter to Herzen, *PsspP4*:196.

80. Letter to A. A. Fet, 16 (28) July 1860, Courtavenel, *PsspP4*:221.

81. *Ottsy i deti*, *PsspS7*:33.

82. Letter to L. N. Vaksel', 29 January (10 February) 1853, Spasskoe, *PsspP2*:196.

83. Letter to Annenkov, 28 September (10 October) 1854, *PsspP2*:297.

84. Letter of 16 (28) August 1873 to Flaubert, Bougival, *PsspP12*:205.

85. D. N. Sadovnikov, "Vstrechi s I. S. Turgenevym: 'Piatnitsy' u poeta Ia. Polon-skogo v 1880 godu," *Russkoe proshloe*, 1923, no. 3, 100.

86. V. A. Gromov, "Rasskaz mtsenskogo starozhila (Novye materialy ob I. S. Tur-geneve)," *Okhota i okhotnich'e khoziaistvo* 8 (1960): 50.

87. By the standards of the gentry hunters of his day, the size of Turgenev's hunt-ing retinue and the bountiful dining during long trips were not unusual. See, e.g., Vaksel''s notes on the requisites for an extended hunting foray: "When departing to hunt for a significant length of time, it's necessary to take along if not a cook, then at least a man who knows how to boil and fry, a supply of various grains, strong bouil-lon, dried mushrooms, tea, oats for the dogs and finally bedding. It doesn't hurt to stock up on Persian powder as well (Persian powder doesn't kill bedbugs, but merely stuns them.) . . . In the field, one must always have along a man who knows the local-ity and can, in addition, carry spare charges, game, and so on." Vaksel', *Karmannaia knizhka*, 3rd ed., 217–18.

3. "A Different Kind of Game"

Epigraph note: "Les i step'," *PsspS3*:354; A. I. Gertsen, "O romane iz narodnoi zhizni v Rossii (Pis'mo k perevodchitse 'Rybakov')," *Sobranie sochinenii*, vol. 13 (Mos-cow: Izdatel'stvo Akademii Nauk, 1958), 177.

1. In this chapter I will, unless otherwise noted, limit myself to discussing the *Notes of a Hunter* cycle in its original form, before Turgenev added three additional tales in the 1870s.

2. M. P. Alekseev, "Zaglavie *Zapiski okhotnika*," in *Turgenevskii sbornik*, vol. 5 (Leningrad: Izdatel'stvo Nauka, Leningradskoe otdelenie, 1969), 214–16; M. M. Odesskaia, "Ruzh'e i lira: Okhotnichii rasskaz v russkoi literature XIX veka," *Voprosy literatury*, no. 3 (May–June 1998): 240–43.

3. Alekseev, "Zaglavie *Zapiski okhotnika*," 214–15.

4. Odesskaia, "Ruzh'e i lira," 240–42.

5. One of the earliest Russian hunting sketches in this period was published by Kukol'nik in the inaugural issue of *Zhurnal konnozavodstva i okhoty*, a monthly that began publication in 1842: "Starina: Zimniaia i letniaia potekha na zveri," *Zhurnal konnozavodstva i okhoty* 1, no. 3 (March 1842): 29–38; see A. I. Akopov, *Otechestvennye spetsial'nye zhurnaly 1765–1917: Istoriko-tipologicheskii obzor* (Rostov: Izdatel'stvo Rostovskogo universiteta, 1986), 63. Nekrasov's "A Landowner of Twenty-Three Souls," with its long passages on hunting dogs, appeared in the May 1843: "Pomeshchik dvadtsati trekh dush," *Literaturnaia gazeta*, no. 12 (21 May 1843): 227–34. See also scene 10 of Nekrasov's vaudeville "Peterburgskii rostovshchik" (*Literaturnaia gazeta*, 31 August 1844, no. 34), in which the character Rostomakhov, who believes that the dog is "nature's most wondrous creation, superior to man," sings a song on the glories and expenses of coursing with hounds: Nekrasov, *Polnoe sobranie sochinenii i pisem v piatnadtsati tomakh*, vol. 6 (Leningrad: Nauka, Leningradskoe otdelenie, 1983), 154–55. Khomiakov's tendentious 1845 article for *Moskvitianin* entitled "Sport, Hunting" ("Sport, okhota"), is his translation from, and jingoistic commentary on, hunting sketches published the previous year in an unspecified British journal: Khomiakov, *Polnoe sobranie sochinenii*, vol. 1 (Moscow: Tipografiia Bakhmeteva, 1861), 434–44.

6. Odesskaia, "Ruzh'e i lira," 241; on the 1843 hunting trip with Louis Viardot see *PsspP*1:202.

7. Alekseev, "Zaglavie *Zapiski okhotnika*," 210–12; *PsspS*3:404.

8. Odesskaia, "Ruzh'e i lira," 249, 252.

9. N. A. Osnovskii, *Zamechaniia Moskovskogo okhotnika na ruzheinuiu okhotu s legavoiu sobakoiu*, 2nd ed. (Moscow: Tipografiia Vedomostei Moskovskoi Gorodskoi Politsii, 1856).

10. S. I. Romanov, *Slovar' ruzheinoi okhoty* (Moscow–St. Petersburg: Izdanie Nikolaia Ivanovicha Mamontova, 1877), 260.

11. Thomas Newlin, "At the Bottom of the River: Forms of Ecological Consciousness in Mid-Nineteenth-Century Russian Literature," ed. Rachel May, *Russian Studies in Literature* 39, no. 2 (Spring 2003): 73. For Rule''s role in Osnovskii's manual see Osnovskii, *Zamechaniia Moskovskogo okhotnika*, 17 note, 21 note. Romanov asserts that "the greater part of the zoological conclusions contained in the book belong, in all probability, not to Mr. Osnovskii, but to the well-known professor, K. F. Rul'e, with whose help this book was compiled" (Romanov, *Slovar' ruzheinoi okhoty*, 261).

12. L. P. Sabaneev, *Sobaki okhotnich'i: Legavye* (Moscow: Terra, 1992), 133.

13. Letter to L. N. Vaksel', late May 1852, Moscow, *PsspP*2:137.

14. Letter to Louis Viardot, 28 January (9 February) 1853, Spasskoe, *PsspP*2:193.

15. *Karmannaia knizhka dlia nachinaiushchikh okhotit'sia s ruzh'em i legavoi soba-koiu.* The *Pocket Book* was so significantly enlarged in its fourth edition (1876) that Vaksel' changed the title to *Handbook (Rukovodstvo).*

16. L. N. Vaksel', *Karmannaia knizhka dlia nachinaiushchikh okhotit'sia s ruzh'em i legavoi sobakoiu,* 3rd ed. (St. Petersburg: Tipografiia Eduarda Pratsa, 1870), vii–viii.

17. Romanov, *Slovar' ruzheinoi okhoty,* 48.

18. "*Karmannaia knizhka dlia nachinaiushchikh okhotit'sia s ruzh'em i legavoi sobakoi* L'va Vakselia" (review), *Sovremennik* 6 (June 1856): 55–64. See V. A. Gromov, "Pisateli-okhotniki i *Karmannaia knizhka* L. N. Vakselia," *Okhotnich'i prostory* 17 (1962): 260–67.

19. "*Karmannaia knizhka . . .* L'va Vakselia," 57.

20. "*Karmannaia knizhka . . .* L'va Vakselia," 58, 59.

21. "*Karmannaia knizhka . . .* L'va Vakselia," 58.

22. "*Karmannaia knizhka . . .* L'va Vakselia," 58, 64.

23. Sergei Aksakov, *Notes on Fishing,* trans. Thomas Hodge (Evanston, IL: Northwestern University Press, 1997), 5.

24. In a letter to I. P. Borisov, 28 January (9 February) 1865, Paris, Turgenev writes "He is such a fine dog that the entire universe is astonished at him—crowned heads . . . pay homage to him and offer enormous sums for him. He searches out any wounded beast or bird so well that he is truly becoming a legend . . . Ask any urchin in the Grand Duchy of Baden if he's heard of Pégase, the dog belonging to a local Russian, and he won't know anything about the Russian, but he'll know Pégase!" (*PsspP*6:98).

25. "Piat'desiat nedostatkov ruzheinogo okhotnika i piat'desiat nedostatkov legavoi sobaki," *Zhurnal okhoty* 4, no. 6 (1876): 1–5; *PsspS*10:272–77.

26. Elzéar Blaze, *Chasseur au chien d'arrêt* (Paris: Librairie de Moutardier, 1836), 331, 339.

27. See Aksakov's comments in Aksakov, *Notes of a Provincial Wildfowler,* trans. Kevin Windle (Evanston, IL: Northwestern University Press, 1998), on great snipe (p. 33), black-tailed godwits (44), redshanks (54), coots (142), curlews (174–75), and plovers (180).

28. The scientific name for wormwood, *Artemisia absinthium,* honors the goddess Diana (Artemis); this aromatic herb has been used since antiquity as an antihelminthic, and in more recent times as the key flavoring in absinthe. See Belinda Rowland and Rebecca Frey in *Gale Encyclopedia of Alternative Medicine,* 2nd ed., 4 vols., ed. Jacqueline Longe (Detroit: Gale, 2005), accessed online. A crucial botanical component of Turgenev's natural descriptions, wormwood (*polyn'*) can be associated with bitterness (e.g., Sanin's disgust at the start of *Veshnie vody; PsspS*8:255) or, as we will see later in this chapter, hallucinogenic disorientation (e.g., the narrator's impending confusion in the initial paragraph of "Bezhin lug"; *PsspS*3:87).

29. "Kuropatki," *PsspS*10:187.

30. See Turgenev's 28 July (9 August) 1849 letter from Courtavenel (*PsspP*1:322–23) to Pauline Viardot in which he explained that partridges excel at playing dramatic scenes: they can pretend to be wounded to lead dogs and hunters away from their nestlings. Two days before, Turgenev's dog Sultan (borrowed from Louis Viardot) had seized such a mother bird, but the dog was such a "perfect gentleman" (original in English) that the bird was unharmed, and Turgenev let "this courageous mother who was too good an actress" have her freedom.

31. Thomas H. Hoisington, "The Enigmatic Hunter in Turgenev's *Zapiski ochotnika*," *Russian Literature* 42 (1997): 51.

32. Dale E. Peterson, *Up from Bondage: The Literatures of Russian and African American Soul* (Durham, NC: Duke University Press, 2000), 93. See the survey of early Russian field guides and hunting treatises in Andrew R. Durkin, "A Guide to the Guides: Writing about Birds in Russia in the Nineteenth Century," *Russian Studies in Literature* 39, no. 3 (Summer 2003): 7–12.

33. Patrick Waddington, *A Catalogue of Portraits of Ivan Sergeyevich Turgenev (1818–83)* (Wellington: Whirinaki, 1999), 6. Several other caricatures of Turgenev by Vaksel' are known; see *PsspP2*:582, and Waddington, 6–7. Vaksel' likewise sketched Lev Tolstoi, in 1854; see E. Tsakni, "Neizvestnyi portret Tolstogo," *Literaturnoe nasledstvo*, vols. 37–38 (Moscow: Izdatel'stvo AN SSSR, 1939), 698–99.

34. In "O razvitii revoliutsionnykh idei v Rossii," Herzen uses the phrase "le chef-d'œuvre de J. Tourguêneff *Récits du Chasseur*": A. I. Gertsen, *Sobranie sochinenii*, vol. 7 (Moscow: Izdatel'stvo Akademii Nauk, 1954), 97.

35. A. I. Gertsen, "1831–1863" (1863), *Sobranie sochinenii*, vol. 17 (Moscow: Izdatel'stvo Akademii Nauk, 1959), 102; quoted from *A Herzen Reader*, ed. and trans. Kathleen Parthé (Evanston, IL: Northwestern University Press, 2012), 195.

36. A. I. Gertsen, "O romane iz narodnoi zhizni v Rossii (Pis'mo k perevodchitse 'Rybakov')" (1857), *Sobranie sochinenii*, vol. 13 (Moscow: Izdatel'stvo Akademii Nauk, 1958), 177.

37. *The Discovery of Chance: The Life and Thought of Alexander Herzen* (Cambridge, MA: Harvard University Press, 2016), 169.

38. "Vmesto vstupleniia," in *Literaturnye i zhiteiskie vospominaniia*, *PsspS11*:8–9; quoted from "Instead of an Introduction," *Literary Reminiscences and Autobiographical Fragments*, trans. David Magarshack (Chicago: Ivan R. Dee, 2001), 102–3.

39. Edmond de Goncourt and Jules de Goncourt, *Pages from the Goncourt Journals*, trans. and ed. Robert Baldick (New York: NYRB Classics, 2007), 198; translation modified. See also N. M. Gut'iar, *Ivan Sergeevich Turgenev: Biografiia* (Iur'ev: Tipografiia K. Mattisena, 1907), 165.

40. Leonard Schapiro, *Turgenev: His Life and Times* (Cambridge, MA: Harvard University Press, 1982), 66.

41. "Andrei Kolosov," *PsspS4*:9; "Tri portreta," *PsspS4*:81.

42. *PsspS4*:78.

43. "Ermolai i mel'nichikha," *PsspS3*:25; "Zhivye moshchi," *PsspS3*:326–27.

44. *PsspS3*:172, 212; see Odesskaia's discussion of the hunter's natural tendency to encounter a multiplicity of human types and settings: M. M. Odesskaia, "*Zapiski okhotnika* I. S. Turgeneva: Problema zhanra," *Litteraria Humanitas* 7 (Alexandr Sergejevič Puškin v evropských kulturních souvislostech) (Brno: Masarykova univerzita, 2000), 204–5.

45. Henrietta Mondry, *Political Animals: Representing Dogs in Modern Russian Culture*, Studies in Slavic Literature and Poetics (Leiden: Brill Rodopi, 2015), 38. The great economic value placed on hunting dogs in the nineteenth century led to stories of landowners' having their precious puppies breastfed by lactating serf women (pp. 31–37) and setting their hounds on misbehaving serf children, which served as the basis (46–48) for one of Ivan Karamazov's tales of human depravity in book 5, chapter 4 ("Bunt") of Dostoevskii's *Brothers Karamazov* (*Brat'ia Karamazovy*).

46. Newlin, "At the Bottom of the River," 80.

47. For a useful summary of the intertwined histories of Turgenev's and Aksakov's *Notes* see V. V. Borisova, "'Zapiski okhotnika' I. S. Turgenev versus 'Zapiski ruzheinogo okhotnika Orenburgskoi gubernii' S. T. Aksakova," in *Turgenev i liberal'naia ideia v Rossii*, ed. G. M. Rebel', M. V. Volovinskaia, and V. Ia. Iasyreva (Perm': PGGPU, 2018), 172–77. Borisova (173) even speculates that Nekrasov deliberately chose Panaev's title for Turgenev's *Notes of a Hunter* because it tapped into enthusiasm for Aksakov's recently published *Notes on Fishing* and that Aksakov deliberately changed the title of his hunting treatise so that it would not be identical to Turgenev's simple *Notes of a Hunter* (*Zapiski okhotnika*) and could better "underscore his own priorities."

48. *PsspS3*:19; S. T. Aksakov, *Sobranie sochinenii v chetyrekh tomakh*, vol. 4 (Moscow: Gosudarstvennoe izdatel'stvo khudozhestvennoi literatury, 1956), 444–45.

49. Borisova, "'Zapiski okhotnika,'" 180.

50. M. O. Gershenzon, *Mechta i mysl' I. S. Turgeneva* (Moscow: Knigoizdatel'stvo v Moskve, 1919), 70.

51. Dale E. Peterson, "The Completion of *A Sportsman's Sketches*: Turgenev's Parting Word," in *The Poetics of Ivan Turgenev*, ed. David Lowe (Washington, DC: Kennan Institute, 1989), 55.

52. M. K. Kleman, "Programmy 'Zapisok okhotnika,'" *Uchenye zapiski Leningradskogo gosudarstvennogo universiteta* 76, no. 11 (1941): 88–126; *PsspS3*:373–84.

53. I am treating "Death" ("Smert'") as a setting. When Turgenev added three more tales to *Notes of a Hunter* in the 1870s, he departed from the earlier person-vs.-setting approach to chapter titles.

54. "Pevtsy," *PsspS3*:216.

55. N. A. Petrovskii, *Slovar' russkikh lichnykh imen*, 6th ed. (Moscow: Russkie slovari, 2005), 157.

56. Fourteen names are derived from or related to animals: Khor' (=*Mustela putorius*); Pichukov (<*pichuga*=small bird); Zverkov (<*zver'*=beast); Ovsianikov (<*ovsianik*=bear that destroys oat crops); Karasikov (<*karas'*=*Carassius auratus*); Blokha (=order Siphonaptera); Penochkin (<*penochka*=genus *Phylloscopus*); Biriuk (=solitary wolf [regional]); Kasatkin (<*kasatka*=*Hirundo rustica*); Kulik (=suborder Charadrii); Gornostaev (<*gornostai*=*Mustela erminea*); Bobrov (<*bobr*=*Castor fiber*); Kozel'skii (*kozel*=*Capra hircus*); Khriak (=male *Sus scrofa*). Five names are related to plants and trees: Dubovshchina (<*dub*=genus *Quercus*); Suchok (=twig/knot); Losniakova (<*losniak*=*Liparis loeselii*); Sitnikov (<*sitnik*=genus *Juncus*); Chertopkhanov (<*chertopolokh*=genus *Carduus*). One name is derived from natural features: Tuman (=fog). Borderline cases: Kobyliatnikoff (<*kobyliatnik*=horseflesh eater; appears in French transliteration); Krupianikov (<*krupenik*=buckwheat pudding). For a sense of the relative abundance of nature-based names in *Notes of a Hunter*, recall that, of the 112 most common Russian surnames Unbegaun compiled from the 1910 St. Petersburg address book, only nineteen (17 percent) derive from names for animals, plants, or natural features: B. O. Unbegaun, *Russian Surnames* (Oxford: Oxford University Press, 1972), 412–13.

57. I. A. Goncharov, "Luchshe pozdno, chem nikogda," *Sobranie sochinenii*, vol. 8 (Moscow: Khudozhestvennaia literatura, 1980), 143. Goncharov's essay was written ca. 1869–79 and published in 1879.

58. Henry James, *Partial Portraits* (London: Macmillan, 1894), 314–15.

59. Gershenzon, *Mechta i mysl' I. S. Turgeneva*, 74–86; Hoisington, "Enigmatic Hunter," 51–52.

60. "Malinovaia voda," *PsspS3*:36–37. Turgenev revisits the theme of impoverished country folk fishing for sustenance in the story "Brigadier" ("Brigadir," 1867); *PsspS8*:43.

61. "Odnodvorets Ovsianikov," *PsspS3*:63. This and other references to the narrator's grandfather could well be based on Turgenev's own maternal grandfather, Petr Ivanovich Lutovinov, who was passionately devoted to coursing and hounding; see O. V. Filiushkina, "K voprosu o proiskhozhdeniia *Zapisok okhotnika*," *Spasskii vestnik* 9 (2002): 133–34.

62. "Odnodvorets Ovsianikov," *PsspS3*:64.

63. "Odnodvorets Ovsianikov," *PsspS3*:66.

64. "Odnodvorets Ovsianikov," *PsspS3*:61, 66.

65. "Chertopkhanov i Nedopiuskin," *PsspS3*:275.

66. "Chertopkhanov i Nedopiuskin," *PsspS3*:276–77. Turgenev had described this same postmortem treatment of a hare in "Ded" (*PsspS1*:60), the fourth poem of his *Derevnia* cycle. Olga Filiushkina connects the image with Turgenev's maternal grandfather, P. I. Lutovinov. Filiushkina, "K voprosu o proiskhozhdeniia *Zapisok okhotnika*," 133, 134–35.

67. "Chertopkhanov i Nedopiuskin," *PsspS3*:286, 288–89.

68. "Burmistr," *PsspS3*:124.

69. "Burmistr," *PsspS3*:127.

70. Iu. G. Oksman plausibly suggests that the dateline was included to align "The Steward" with the scathing critique of Russian society in Belinskii's celebrated letter to Gogol', which was dated "15 July 1847, Salzbrunn" (*PsspS3*:471).

71. A. I. Gertsen, "Consolatio," *S drugogo berega*, *Sobranie sochinenii*, vol. 6, 99, quoted from Herzen, *Selected Philosophical Works*, trans. L. Navrozov (Moscow: Foreign Languages Publishing House, 1956), 427.

72. Peter Thiergen, "'Priroda do otvratitel'noi stepeni ravnodushna': Alexandre Herzen et le scepticisme de son époque face à la nature," *Revue des études slaves* 78, no. 2–3 (2000): 269, 277.

73. L. I. Skokova, "Chelovek i priroda v *Zapiskakh okhotnika* Turgeneva," *Voprosy literatury* 6 (November–December 2003): 342.

74. Chertopkhanov i Nedopiuskin," *PsspS3*:281.

75. "Moi sosed Radilov," *PsspS3*:55.

76. "Gamlet Shchigrovskogo uezda," *PsspS3*:269.

77. "Smert'," *PsspS3*:197–98.

78. "Smert'," *PsspS3*:198, 201, 206; Pushkin, "Brozhu li ia vdol' ulits shumnykh," *Polnoe sobranie sochinenii*, vol. 3 (Leningrad: Nauka, 1977), 130.

79. "Smert'," *PsspS3*:205; Pushkin, *Polnoe sobranie sochinenii*, vol. 4, 9.

80. "Mémoire sur l'alternance ou sur ce problème: La succession alternative dans la reproduction des espèces végétales vivant en société, est-elle une loi générale de la nature?," *Annales des sciences naturelles* 5 (1825): 353–81.

81. "Smert'," *PsspS3*:200, 203, 207.

82. "Smert'," *PsspS3*:200.

83. "Svidanie," *PsspS3*:245.

84. Based on such details, Skokova offers a plausible opposing interpretation, suggesting that "Nature and the girl constitute a single whole in Turgenev's description. The writer seems to underscore that the girl is part of nature, that she is just as natural and beautiful as primeval nature itself": Skokova, "Chelovek i priroda," 345. Such a reading does not exclude the possibility that, on one level, Akulina embodies nature, and, on another, that Viktor does, a contradiction that contributes to the story's rich ambiguity.

85. "Svidanie," *PsspS3*:245.

86. "Svidanie," *PsspS3*:248.

87. "Gamlet Shchigrovskogo uezda," *PsspS3*:268; "Biriuk," *PsspS3*:161.

88. "Svidanie," *PsspS3*:240.

89. "Svidanie," *PsspS3*:240–41.

90. "Malinovaia voda," *PsspS3*:37–38.

91. "Ermolai i mel'nichikha," *PsspS3*:29.

92. "Kas'ian s Krasivoi Mechi," *PsspS3*:118. Turgenev actually owned property on the Krasivaia Mech', having inherited from his mother the village of Kadnoe Men'shoe there; *PsspS3*:469.

93. "Kas'ian s Krasivoi Mechi," *PsspS3*:110.

94. Turgenev's comments to his translator, Henri-Hippolyte Delaveau, for the 1858 French translation of *Notes*, also strongly indicate that Kas'ian was a religious sectarian and "wanderer" (*strannik*); *PsspS3*:467–68.

95. "Kas'ian s Krasivoi Mechi," *PsspS3*:114.

96. "Kas'ian s Krasivoi Mechi," *PsspS3*:110.

97. "Kas'ian s Krasivoi Mechi," *PsspS3*:115.

98. "Kas'ian s Krasivoi Mechi," *PsspS3*:116.

99. Newlin, "At the Bottom of the River," 80; letter to Pauline Viardot, Paris, 1 May 1848 (*PsspP1*:261–62). Jane Costlow offers a concurring interpretation: "The syntax of interruption and question in this story asks us to confront just how it is that the aesthetic appreciation of nature can coexist so blithely with hunting—or with the spectacle of poverty and destruction we have just been privy to." Jane Costlow, *Heart-Pine Russia: Walking and Writing the Nineteenth-Century Forest* (Ithaca, NY: Cornell University Press, 2013), 36.

100. "Bezhin lug," *PsspS3*:87, 90, 104.

101. See S. T. Aksakov, "Neskol'ko slov o sueveriiakh i primetakh okhotnikov," *Rasskazy i vospominaniia okhotnika o raznykh okhotakh, Sobranie sochinenii v chetyrekh tomakh* vol. 4 (Moscow: Gosudarstvennoe izdatel'stvo khudozhestvennoi literatury, 1956), 561–68; excerpts translated in Aksakov, *Notes on Fishing*, 175–77.

102. "Bezhin lug," *PsspS3*:100.

103. "Bezhin lug," *PsspS3*:105.

104. See Patricia Carden, "Finding the Way to Bezhin Meadow: Turgenev's Intimations of Mortality," *Slavic Review* 36, no. 3 (September 1977): 455.

105. "Pevtsy," *PsspS3*:208.

106. For compelling links between classical literature and the tale's dissonant conclusion see Leslie O'Bell, "The Pastoral in Turgenev's 'Singers': Classical Themes and Romantic Variations," *Russian Review* 2 (April 2004): 285–86.

107. "Циркают ястреба, когда они чего-нибудь испугаются": *PsspS3*:215. Now normally spelled *tsyrkat'* (цыркать), this onomatopoetic verb was classified as a southernism by Dal': V. I. Dal', ed., *Tolkovyi slovar' zhivogo velikorusskogo iazyka v chetyrekh tomakh*, 3rd ed., vol. 4 (St. Petersburg–Moscow: M. O. Vol'f, 1909), column 1261. In modern usage, the word tends to refer to the sounds made by insects (especially crickets and grasshoppers) as well as birds (most often tits).

108. "Pevtsy," *PsspS3*:222.

109. Skokova, "Chelovek i priroda," 340; Borisova, "'Zapiski okhotnika,'" 177, 179. The passage in question is "Светлеет воздух, видней дорога, яснеет небо, белеют тучки, зеленеют поля" (The air brightens, the road's more visible, the sky grows clearer, the clouds shine white, the fields glow green): *PsspS3*:355.

110. "Les i step'," *PsspS3*:358.

111. The joyous tone of "Forest and Steppe," with its eager embrace of *volia*, is identical to that of a poem, "Before the Hunt" ("Pered okhotoi"), Turgenev had written two years earlier and published in the January 1847 issue of *Sovremennik*: "Светлое небо, здоровье да воля— / Здравствуй, раздолье широкого поля!" (Radiant sky, health and freedom— / Greetings to you, wide open meadow!); *PsspS1*:64.

112. Aksakov, *Sobranie sochinenii*, vol. 4, 9; quoted from Aksakov, *Notes on Fishing*, 3.

113. Aksakov, *Sobranie sochinenii*, vol. 4, 11; quoted from Aksakov, *Notes on Fishing*, 7.

4. Thinking Oneself into Nature

Epigraph note: Diary entry for 17 April 1906, L. N. Tolstoi, *Polnoe sobranie sochinenii*, vol. 55 (Moscow: Gosudarstvennoe izdatel'stvo khudozhestvennaia literatura, 1937), 216.

1. S. T. Aksakov to I. S. Aksakov, 29 December 185, quoted in V. V. Borisova, E. Nikitina, and T. A. Terent'eva, eds., *Letopis' zhizni i tvorchestva S. T. Aksakova (1791–1859 gg.)* (Ufa, 2011), 154. Aksakov's biographer, S. I. Mashinskii, mistakenly gives the year as 1849 in *S. T. Aksakov: Zhizn' i tvorchestvo*, 2nd ed. (Moscow: Khudozhestvennaia literatura, 1973), 263.

2. S. T. Aksakov to I. S. Aksakov, 2 (14) January 1851, quoted in *PsspS4*: 669. Sergei Aksakov's eyesight was so poor at this point in his life that he could no longer read, so he wrote by dictating to amanuenses, and readings aloud of his work were performed by others.

3. S. T. Aksakov to I. S. Turgenev, 12 (24) January 1852, *Russkoe obozrenie* 28 (August 1894): 462–63; *Letopis' zhizni i tvorchestva I. S. Turgeneva (1818–1858)*, ed. N. S. Nikitina (St. Petersburg: Nauka, 1995), 177.

4. *Letopis' zhizni i tvorchestva S. T. Aksakova*, 155.

5. Turgenev to Aksakov, 2 (14) February 1852, St. Petersburg, *PsspP2*:117.

6. See appendix 2 for the complete text of this review.

7. *PsspS4*:508.

8. Leonard Schapiro, *Turgenev: His Life and Times* (Cambridge, MA: Harvard University Press, 1982), 93; *Letopis' zhizni i tvorchestva S. T. Aksakova*, 161, 162. Four days later, Ivan Aksakov wrote to praise Turgenev's Gogol obituary for being part of the "friendly, unison choir of two generations": quoted in N. Pakhomov, "Istoriia odnoi druzhby (I. S. Turgenev i sem'ia Aksakovykh)," *Okhotnich'i prostory* 28 (1970): 193.

9. Letter to the Viardots, 1 (13) May 1852, St. Petersburg, *PsspP2*:135.

10. Letter to S. T., I. S., and K. S. Aksakov, 6 (18) June 1852, Spasskoe, *PsspP2*:137–38, 139.

11. Ivan Turgenev, "Gogol' (Zhukovskii, Krylov, Lermontov, Zagoskin)," *PsspS11*:67.

12. On the secret visit to Moscow see Orlando Figes, *The Europeans: Three Lives and the Making of a Cosmopolitan Culture* (New York: Henry Holt, 2019), 162.

13. V. A. Gromov, "Rasskaz mtsenskogo starozhila (Novye materialy ob I. S. Turgeneve)," *Okhota i okhotnich'e khoziaistvo* 8 (1960): 50; *Letopis' zhizni i tvorchestva I. S. Turgeneva (1818–1858)*, 207–15.

14. Letter to S. T., I. S., and K. S. Aksakov, 6 (18) June 1852, Spasskoe, *PsspP2*:138.

15. S. T. Aksakov to I. S. Turgenev, 7 (19) October 1852, Abramtsevo, *Russkoe obozrenie* 28 (August 1894): 480. Ivan Aksakov took active part in encouraging Turgenev to finish the review ("Be healthy, hunt, and write"): I. S. Aksakov to I. S. Turgenev, 29 May (10 June) 1852, *Russkoe obozrenie* 28 (August 1894): 472.

16. *PsspS4*:671.

17. Aksakov, *Sobranie sochinenii*, vol. 4, 627.

18. *Russkoe obozrenie* 28 (August 1894): 471. E. L. Voitolovskaia echoes this in her "I. S. Turgenev o S. T. Aksakove," *Leningradskii gosudarstvennyi pedagogicheskii institut imeni A. I. Gertsena: Uchenye zapiski* 170 (1958): 122.

19. *PsspS4*:500.

20. *PsspS4*:500.

21. See appendix 3 for the complete text of this review.

22. *Moskvitianin* 4, otdelenie V (February 1853): 227, 229, quoted in *PsspS4*:672.

23. *PsspS4*:513, 517, 519, 521. While enlarging his *Notes on Fishing* for its second edition in 1854, Aksakov playfully quoted, without attribution, Turgenev's description of his style; see S. T. Aksakov, *Notes on Fishing*, trans. Thomas Hodge (Evanston, IL: Northwestern University Press, 1997), 51, 212 (note 25).

24. *PsspS4*:516, 518. Jane Costlow discusses Turgenev's contempt for "rhetorical" art of this kind in the painting of Karl Briullov and the Romantic prose of Aleksandr Bestuzhev-Marlinskii: Costlow, *Worlds within Worlds: The Novels of Ivan Turgenev* (Princeton, NJ: Princeton University Press, 1990), 25. Given the Benediktov passages of which Turgenev disapproves, we might speculate that the bad Hugo poetry he has in mind could be something like these two stanzas from "Extase" (1828) in *Les orientales*: "I walked the shore alone, one starlit night. / No sea-sails, and no sky-clouds were in sight. / My eyes delved further than the real world goes. / The woods, the hills, and nature all around / Appeared to question with a muffled sound / The skies' flames, the seas' flows. / And, bowing down their crowns of golden fire, / The endless legions of the starry choir— / A thousand varying voices in accord— / And, curling the white spray down from their crest, / All the blue waves who never submit or rest— / Cried: "It is God the Lord!" Quoted from E. H. Blackmore and A. M. Blackmore, *Selected Poems of Victor Hugo: A Bilingual Edition* (Chicago: University of Chicago Press, 2001), 25–27. If the source of Turgenev's particular irritation at Hugo, whom he detested until they met in 1876 (see *PsspP1*:566, *PsspP3*:517), is the then-pious French poet's invocation of nature as a glorification of God, he could not say such a thing in print, so perhaps his "everywhere you see the author, not nature" is a veiled way of saying that in Hugo's poetry, everywhere you see God, not

nature. Elizabeth Cheresh Allen's study offers general support for such an interpretation: "Lacking faith in an ultimate sacred order that imparts meaning to events, Turgenev creates his own order and thereby espouses his own faith, a faith in aesthetic inventiveness that brings the only salvation Turgenev can envision—secular salvation." Elizabeth Cheresh Allen, *Beyond Realism: Turgenev's Poetics of Secular Salvation* (Stanford, CA: Stanford University Press, 1992), 54. Perhaps significantly, Aksakov never mentions God or the divine in *Notes of an Orenburg-Province Hunter* except in set phrases such as "God only knows how," and so on. For more on Turgenev's intense dislike for Hugo see Figes, *Europeans*, 408–9.

25. *PsspS*4:519.

26. Two years later, for example, in an article on Tiutchev's work, he wrote of "the captivating though somewhat monotonous grace" of Fet and asserted that "[Tiutchev's] feeling for nature is unusually subtle, alive and true; but he, speaking a language that is not quite accepted in good society, does not exploit it, does not set about putting together and coloring his figures. Mr. Tiutchev's comparisons of the human world with the world of nature—a kindred world to him—tend not to be stiff and cold, do not offer a schoolmasterly tone, do not try to serve as an explanation of some ordinary thought that has appeared in the author's head and been taken by him for his own discovery." "Neskol'ko slov o stikhotvoreniiakh F. I. Tiutcheva," *Sovremennik* 4 (1854): 23–26; *PsspS*4:524, 527.

27. 28 December 1852 (8 January 1853), Spasskoe, *PsspP*2:178. In Turgenev's speech on the 1880 dedication of the Pushkin monument in Moscow, he quotes Mérimée, who outlines in similar terms the difference between the Russian and French approaches to writing verse: "Your poetry seeks truth above all, whereas beauty then appears by itself. Our [French] poets, by contrast, proceed along a completely opposite path. They worry above all about the effect, the wit, the brilliance of their work, and if, in addition to all that, the opportunity to avoid violating verisimilitude presents itself to them, then they will take it into the bargain, if you will" (*PsspS*12:344). Quoted from "Speech Delivered at the Dedication of the Monument to A. S. Pushkin in Moscow," trans. Elizabeth Cheresh Allen, in *The Essential Turgenev* (Evanston, IL: Northwestern University Press, 1994), 843.

28. *PsspS*4:516–17. Turgenev rightly suspected that this passage, in which he skirts Spinozan ("*deus sive natura*," the view that God and nature are interchangeable) and Goethean pantheism, would be cut by the censor, yet he also believed that it constituted the chief interest of this review for nonhunters. See Turgenev's letters to Annenkov, 10 (22) January 1853 (*PsspP*4:672) and Sergei Aksakov, 5 and 9 (17 and 21) February 1853 (*PsspP*2:203); see also Schapiro, *Turgenev*, 22–23. Victor Ripp suggests that "Turgenev's logical uncertainty" in this passage of the Aksakov review "reflects the [curiously intimate] condition of the Slavophile-Westernizer polemic in general": Victor Ripp, *Turgenev's Russia: From "Notes of a Hunter" to "Fathers and Sons"* (Ithaca, NY: Cornell University Press, 1980), 51.

29. Though it had been censored, Turgenev was at pains to share the passage privately with Aksakov, in a letter of 5, 9 (17, 21) February 1853, Spasskoe, *PsspP*2:204–5. The passage was never actually published in Turgenev's lifetime; it is still omitted from the first reprint of the Aksakov review: Turgenev, *Sochineniia*, vol. 1 (Moscow: Tipografiia E. Lissner i Iu. Roman, 1880), 293–307. It first appeared in print over a decade after Turgenev's death: *Vestnik Evropy* 1 (1894): 342–44; see *PsspP*2:509.

30. A. I. Gertsen, "Publichnye chteniia g-na professora Rul'e," *Sobranie sochinenii v tridtsati tomakh*, vol. 2 (Moscow: Izdatel'stvo Akademii Nauk SSSR, 1954), 142; quoted from Aileen Kelly, *The Discovery of Chance: The Life and Thought of Alexander Herzen* (Cambridge, MA: Harvard University Press, 2016), 178–79.

31. A. I. Gertsen, "Pis'mo II: Nauka i priroda—Fenomenologiia myshleniia," *Pis'ma ob izuchenii prirody, Sobranie sochinenii*, vol. 3 (Moscow: Izdatel'stvo Akademii Nauk SSSR, 1954), 131–32, quoted from Alexander Herzen, *Selected Philosophical Works*, trans. L. Navrozov (Moscow: Foreign Languages Publishing House, 1956), 138, my italics.

32. Herzen goes on to differentiate still further human and nonhuman interactions with nature: "The animal is never at discord with nature; it is the last link in the development of individual life that combines with the general life of nature without conflict; the dual nature of man lies precisely in the fact that he, in addition to his positive existence, cannot but take a negative attitude to material life. He remains at discord not only with external nature but even with himself. This disharmony torments him and it is this suffering that impels him onward": Gertsen, "Pis'mo II: Nauka i priroda," 136–37, quoted from Herzen, *Selected Philosophical Works*, 139.

33. Charles Darwin, *On the Origin of Species by Means of Natural Selection*, 3rd ed. (London: John Murray, 1861), 524.

34. Turgenev, "Gamlet i Don Kikhot," *PsspS*5:341, quoted from Elizabeth Cheresh Allen's translation (altered) in *The Essential Turgenev*, 557–58. Though Turgenev had begun formulating his famous Hamlet-Quixote dichotomy as early as 1847–48, he did not write up the article until 1857–59; it was published in the January 1860 issue of *Sovremennik*. See *PsspS*5:507–9.

35. *PsspS*4:517.

36. *PsspS*4:517. Nicholas Žekulin rightly stresses that it is human beings, among all living things, who are capable of conceptualizing and loving nature; see *"De gustibus disputandum est*: Turgenev's (Dis)agreements with His Hero Bazarov," in *Tusculum slavicum: Festschrift für Peter Thiergen*, ed. Elisabeth von Erdmann, Aschot Isaakjan, Roland Marti, and Daniel Schümann (Zürich: Pano Verlag, 2005), 299, 305.

37. G. B. Kurliandskaia, "O filosofii prirody v proizvedeniiakh Turgeneva," *Voprosy russkoi literatury* 2, no. 17 (1971): 51.

38. *PsspS*4:500.

39. *PsspS*4:516.

40. *PsspS*4:509.

41. Aksakov, *Notes of a Provincial Wildfowler*, trans. and ed. Kevin Windle (Evanston, IL: Northwestern University Press, 1998), 131.

42. *PsspS*4:519. Turgenev's turn away from the German Idealists by the late 1840s is well documented. See Michael Nierle, *Die Naturschilderung und ihre Funktion in Versdichtung und Prosa von I. S. Turgenev*, Studien zur Geschichte der russischen Literatur des 19. Jahrhunderts (Bad Homburg: Verlag Gehlen, 1969), 29; and Turgenev's letter to Gertsen of 23 October (4 November) 1862, Paris, *PsspP*5:124.

43. *PsspS*4:519.

44. *PsspS*4:516.

45. The first part of this quotation is my translation from the "Gun Dog" ("Legavaia sobaka") chapter of Aksakov's *Notes of an Orenburg-Province Hunter* (Aksakov, *Sobranie sochinenii*, vol. 4, 164); the second part is from "Hares," quoted from *Provin-*

cial Wildfowler, 283. In "Legavaia sobaka," Aksakov goes on to claim that shooting has two chief advantages over coursing, hounding, and falconry: the wide variety of species that can be bagged with a shotgun, and "in shooting, success depends on the art and stamina of the shooter" rather than on the "energy and eagerness of dogs or predatory birds."

46. *PsspS*4:511–13. Turgenev's only criticism of Aksakov's *Notes of an Orenburg-Province Hunter* was that the book was sadly out of date with regard to the latest in firearm technology and dog breeding; he was quick to point out, however, that Aksakov himself openly admitted this shortcoming (*PsspS*4:513).

47. *PsspS*4:510.

48. Blaze, for example, declares that only deficient hunters shoot juvenile partridges in September before they fully fledge: such sportsmen are akin to cowardly soldiers who stab children to bloody their swords. He jestingly recalls a recruit who bragged, "I have cut off the arm of an Austrian at the Battle of Wagram." After Blaze retorts that it would have been better to cut off his head, the young man replies, "Doubtless true, but that was already done!" *Chasseur au chien d'arrêt* (Paris: Librairie de Moutardier, 1836), 153.

49. Blaze describes hares and rabbits, as well as seven species of bird (partridge, quail, pheasant, rail, woodcock, snipe, duck); Aksakov discusses hares and forty-two species of bird.

50. *PsspP*2:152; italics in the original.

51. *PsspS*4:517.

52. Thomas Newlin, "At the Bottom of the River: Forms of Ecological Consciousness in Mid-Nineteenth-Century Russian Literature," ed. Rachel May, *Russian Studies in Literature* 39, no. 2 (Spring 2003): 74–75.

53. Voitolovskaia, "I. S. Turgenev o S. T. Aksakove," 123.

54. *PsspS*4:514.

55. *PsspS*4:514.

56. *PsspS*4:514.

57. *PsspS*4:514–15. Newlin, "At the Bottom of the River" (81, 89 note 21), argues that Turgenev's conservationist views are more naïve than Aksakov's similar sentiments.

58. See Ian Helfant, "S. T. Aksakov: The Ambivalent Proto-ecological Consciousness of a Nineteenth-Century Russian Hunter," *Interdisciplinary Studies in Literature and Environment (ISLE)* 13, no. 2 (Summer 2006): 57–71.

59. *PsspS*4:520.

60. *PsspS*4:520.

61. *PsspS*4:521.

62. *PsspS*4:672.

63. Letter to L. N. Vaksel', 25 May (6 June) 1853, Spasskoe, *PsspP*2:234.

64. S. T. Aksakov to I. S. Turgenev, 29 October (10 November) 1852, Abramtsevo, *Russkoe obozrenie* 28 (August 1894): 484.

65. I. S. Aksakov to I. S. Turgenev, 22 January (3 February) 1853, Abramtsevo, *Russkoe obozrenie* 29 (September 1894): 8–9.

66. S. T. Aksakov to I. S. Turgenev, end of January (beginning of February) 1853, *Russkoe obozrenie* 29 (September 1894): 10–11. See also Andrew Durkin, *Sergei Aksakov and Russian Pastoral* (New Brunswick, NJ: Rutgers University Press, 1983), 71.

67. M. M. Odesskaia, "Ruzh'e i lira: Okhotnichii rasskaz v russkoi literature XIX veka," *Voprosy literatury* 3 (May–June 1998): 249.

68. N. A. Nekrasov, *Komu na Rusi zhit' khorosho?*, chast' 1, glava 5, "Pomeshchik," in Nekrasov, *Polnoe sobranie sochinenii i pisem v piatnadtsati tomakh*, vol. 5 (Leningrad: Nauka, Leningradskoe otdelenie, 1982), 83.

69. S. I. Romanov, *Slovar' ruzheinoi okhoty* (Moscow–St. Petersburg: Izdanie Niko-laia Ivanovicha Mamontova, 1877), 565–66 (entry on Turgenev's *Notes of a Hunter*). See also V. A. Gromov, "Pisateli-okhotniki i *Karmannaia knizhka* L. N. Vakselia," *Okhotnich'i prostory* 17 (1962): 263.

70. L. P. Sabaneev, *Okhotnich'i zveri* (Moscow: Terra, 1992), 135.

71. The only other fiction Turgenev completed during his exile was a sketch of the provincial types with whom he had mixed while living in the provinces: "Dva priiatelia," begun 15 (27) October and finished 20 November (2 December) 1853, the very last weeks of the author's seclusion: *PsspS4*:625 and *Letopis' zhizni i tvorchestva I. S. Turgeneva (1818–1858)* (St. Petersburg: Nauka, 1995), 249.

72. Turgenev began "The Inn" 18 (30) October 1852, finished it 14 (26) Novem-ber 1852: *PsspS4*:612.

73. Voitolovskaia, "I. S. Turgenev o S. T. Aksakove," 121.

74. A conspicuous exception is Robert L. Jackson, "Turgenev's 'The Inn': A Philo-sophical Novella," *Russian Literature* 16, no. 4 (1984): 411–19.

75. Letter from S. T. Aksakov to Turgenev, 10 (22) March 1853, *Russkoe obozrenie* 9 (1894): 26.

76. Letter from S. T. Aksakov to Turgenev, 14 (26) March 1853, *Russkoe obozrenie* 9 (1894): 31–32.

77. Letter to S. T., K. S., and I. S. Aksakov, 2 (14) April 1853, *PsspP2*:217.

78. *PsspS4*:613.

79. *PsspS4*:516.

80. *PsspS4*:278.

81. Jackson, "Turgenev's 'The Inn,'" 413.

82. *PsspS4*:320.

83. Thomas Newlin, "The Thermodynamics of Desire in Turgenev's *Notes of a Hunter*," *Russian Review* 72 (July 2013): 367–69.

84. *PsspS4*:282.

85. *PsspS4*:283. Compare Auden and Isherwood's proverb in their play *The Dog beneath the Skin* (1935): "Happy the hare at morning, for she cannot read / The Hunt-er's waking thoughts": Christopher Isherwood and W. H. Auden, *The Dog beneath the Skin, or Where Is Francis?* (London: Faber and Faber, 1935), 91.

86. *PsspS4*:305.

87. *PsspS4*:290.

88. *PsspS4*: 307, 314, 315.

89. *PsspS4*:274.

90. V. E. Flint et al., *A Field Guide to Birds of Russia and Adjacent Territories*, trans. Natalia Bourso-Leland (Princeton, NJ: Princeton University Press, 1984), 57.

91. Mark Cocker and Richard Mabey, *Birds Britannica* (London: Random House, 2005), 117.

92. V. I. Dal', ed., *Tolkovyi slovar' zhivogo velikorusskogo iazyka v chetyrekh tomakh*, 3rd ed., vol. 2 (St. Petersburg–Moscow: M. O. Vol'f, 1905), column 436.

93. Quoted from N. M. Maksimovič-Ambodik, *Emvlemy i simvoly (1788): The First Russian Emblem Book*, ed. and trans. Anthony Hippisley (Leiden: Brill, 1989), 23.

94. Aksakov, *Provincial Wildfowler*, 95, 182, 197, 234. In *Childhood Years of a Bagrov Grandson* (*Detskie gody Bagrova-vnuka*, 1856–57), Aksakov reiterates that the kite is a threat to helpless young domestic fowl: "What a lot of chores and cares I had! Every day I had to . . . watch . . . the brood-hen clucking as she guarded her tiny chicks, watch the kites circling, hovering above them": *Sobranie sochinenii*, vol. 4, 503–4.

95. *PsspS7:*399, *PsspS8:*111, 267. In his correspondence Turgenev only mentions kites twice, both times, curiously, in letters to Iakov Polonskii, nearly twenty years apart. In one, he asserts that it was kites who devoured Prometheus's flesh (24 December 1856 [8 January 1857], *PsspP3:*560), and in the other he insultingly compares Nekrasov to an "old, wretched kite" (13 [25] May 1875, *PsspP14:*94).

96. *PsspS4:*263.

97. *PsspS4:*260.

98. *PsspS11:*261.

99. *PsspS11:*256, 269, 306. According to Viardot, Turgenev refused to dictate the tale in Russian but instead used a combination of French, German, and Italian. The final text of the transcription, however, is entirely in French.

100. *PsspS11:*258. The modern Russian translation in *PsspS11* misleadingly gives *sterviatnik* (vulture), while Grigorovich renders "oiseau de proie" as *korshun*, in keeping with Turgenev's original intention.

101. *PsspS4:*317.

102. *PsspS11:*256.

103. *PsspS4:*517.

104. Letter to Pauline Viardot, 28 July (9 August) 1849, Courtavenel, *PsspP1:* 322–23.

105. *PsspS10:*142.

106. Quoted in *Letopis' zhizni i tvorchestva I. S. Turgeneva (1818–1858)*, 154.

107. *PsspS4:*518.

108. *PsspS4:*500.

109. *PsspS4:*516.

5. Nature and Nidification

First epigraph note: N. M. Maksimovich-Ambodik, *Emvlemy i simvoly* (St. Petersburg: Imperatorskaia Tipografiia, 1788), 205, quoted from N. M. Maksimovič-Ambodik, *Emvlemy i simvoly (1788): The First Russian Emblem Book*, ed. and trans. Anthony Hippisley (Leiden: Brill, 1989).

1. Leonard Schapiro, *Turgenev: His Life and Times* (Cambridge, MA: Harvard University Press, 1982), 90, 115. "The Master's Own Office" ("Sobstvennaia gospodskaia kontora"), a short fragment from the novel, was published in 1859 (*PsspS5:* 385–86).

2. Letter to K. S. Aksakov, 16 (28) October 1852, Spasskoe, *PsspP2:*150.

3. Letter to P. V. Annenkov, 28 October (9 November) 1852, Spasskoe, *PsspP2:*155. Turgenev employed the phrase *"triple extrait"* in his fiction only once, fifteen years later, in *Smoke*, but in very similar fashion. Sozont Potugin, the author's Westernizer-mouthpiece, proclaims his disgust with the Slavophiles' veneration of the Russian

peasantry: "I'm not about to start sniffing this *triple extrait de mougik russe* [triple extract of Russian peasant]" (я этого triple extrait de mougik russe нюхать не стану): *PsspS7*:329.

4. M. O. Gershenzon, *Mechta i mysl' I. S. Turgeneva* (Moscow: Knigoizdatel'stvo v Moskve, 1919), 70; see chapter 3.

5. Aksakov to Turgenev, 9 (21) March 1853, and Turgenev to Aksakov, 2 (14) April 1853, *Letopis' zhizni i tvorchestva I. S. Turgeneva (1818–1858)*, ed. N. S. Nikitina (St. Petersburg: Nauka, 1995), 231, 234. Quotation from letter to S. T., K. S., and I. S. Aksakov, 2 (14) April 1853, *PsspS2*:217.

6. *Rasskazy i vospominaniia okhotnika o raznykh okhotakh. S pribavleniem stat'i "O solov'iakh" I. S. Turgeneva*; see Aksakov, *Sobranie sochinenii*, vol. 4 (Moscow: Gosudarstvennoe izdatel'stvo khudozhestvennoi literatury, 1956), 636–37; V. V. Borisova, E. Nikitina, and T. A. Terent'eva, eds., *Letopis' zhizni i tvorchestva S. T. Aksakova (1791–1859 gg.)* (Ufa, 2011), 193.

7. On the problem of how to translate the word *Poles'e*, and on the fitful evolution of Turgenev's story, see Jane Costlow, *Heart-Pine Russia: Walking and Writing the Nineteenth-Century Forest* (Ithaca, NY: Cornell University Press, 2013), 19–22.

8. *PsspS5*:432–33.

9. The earliest stirrings of the *Poles'e* theme appear in a footnote Turgenev had included in his story "Pevtsy" from *Zapiski okhotnika* explaining what the *Poles'e* was; in an early draft of the note, he promised to write further on the theme some day; see *PsspS3*:221 and *PsspS4* (1963): 432.

10. *PsspS5*:434. According to V. A. Gromov, the 1860 inclusion of "Poezdka" in *Zapiski okhotnika* was Osnovskii's doing; see Dale E. Peterson's discussion in "The Completion of *A Sportsman's Sketches*: Turgenev's Parting Word," in *The Poetics of Ivan Turgenev*, ed. David Lowe (Washington, DC: Kennan Institute, 1989), 53. In the West, "Journey to the Forest-Belt" has recently received fine commentary from Robert Louis Jackson, Thomas Newlin, and Jane Costlow. See Jackson, "The Root and the Flower, Dostoevsky and Turgenev: A Comparative Aesthetic," in *Dialogues with Dostoevsky: The Overwhelming Questions* (Stanford, CA: Stanford University Press, 1993), 164–66; Newlin, "At the Bottom of the River: Forms of Ecological Consciousness in Mid-Nineteenth-Century Russian Literature," *Russian Studies in Literature* 39, no. 2 (Spring 2003): 82–85; and Costlow, "Walking into the Woodland with Turgenev," in *Heart-Pine Russia*, 17–39.

11. "Poezdka v Poles'e," *PsspS5*:135.

12. "Poezdka v Poles'e," *PsspS5*:139.

13. Letter to P. V. Annenkov, 9 (21) March 1857, Paris, *PsspP3*:210. Fragments of the "Third Day" can be found in *PsspS7* (1964): 301–2.

14. "Poezdka v Poles'e," *PsspS5*:147.

15. Jackson, "Root and the Flower," 167.

16. Newlin, "At the Bottom of the River," 84.

17. Costlow, "Walking into the Woodland with Turgenev," in *Heart-Pine Russia*, 32, 34.

18. *PsspS5*:437, reprinted from *PsspS7* (1964): 420.

19. The word *koromyslo* (also *koromysel*), of disputed etymology, occurs in its entomological sense only two other times in Turgenev's nonepistolary writing: once in chapter 22 of *Veshnie vody*, as Sanin sees *koromysla* fly by while he waits in a

German forest for his dueling opponent to arrive (*PsspS*8:301), and once in the prose poem "Nasekomoe" (see below). In his letters, Turgenev uses the term only four times and always in the folk-colloquial expression *"dym koromyslom"* (literally "smoke like a shoulder pole"), which means something like "fearful commotion": see Sophia Lubensky, *Russian-English Dictionary of Idioms* (New York: Random House, 1995), 225. Aksakov uses *koromysel* (his preferred form) twice: once as a type of bait in *Notes on Fishing*, and once in "Sobiranie babochek," his memoir of collecting butterflies while at Kazan' University, in a passage on the insect collection of another student, Vasilii Tim'ianskii: S. T. Aksakov, *Sobranie sochninenii v chetyrekh tomakh*, vol. 2 (Moscow: Gosudarstvennoe izdatel'stvo khudozhestvennoi literatury, 1955), 186. For a prominent appearance in Russian poetry see Konstantin Bal'mont's "Koromyslo" (published 1903).

20. Turgenev's original *devitsy* (maidens) I render as "damsels" because, in modern French usage, *demoiselle*—the early nineteenth-century source of English "damselfly"—refers to a damselfly (Zygoptera), while the more general French term *libellule* covers both dragonflies (Anisoptera) and damselflies. Nonetheless, Turgenev's *koromyslo* is obviously a large and robust green hawker, not a slender damselfly.

21. I. I. Shangina, *Russkii traditsionnyi byt: Entsiklopedicheskii slovar'* (St. Petersburg: Izdatel'stvo Azbuka Klassika, 2003), 397.

22. Shangina, 11, 397.

23. R. S. Pavliuk and A. Iu. Kharitonov, *Nomenklatura strekoz (Insecta, Odonata) SSSR: Poleznye i vrednye nasekomye Sibiri* (Novosibirsk: Nauka, 1982), 19.

24. Turgenev uses the general term for dragonfly, *strekoza*, only twice in his extant writings: once in a letter to Annenkov of 14 and 18 September 1852 to describe the scratching sound of his pen (*strekozinnyi pisk*) (*PsspP*2:144), and once in the second paragraph of *Nakanune*, to describe the ungraceful appearance of Bersenev, as he lies on his back, chatting with Shubin: "his awkwardness was evident in the very position of his arms, of his torso, tightly wrapped in a short, black frock-coat, of his long legs with upraised knees like the hind legs of a dragonfly" (*PsspS*6:161).

25. "Poezdka v Poles'e," *PsspS*5:130, 140. The editors of Turgenev's works remind us that Isis was a personification of nature "expounded in early-nineteenth-century academic dictionaries of mythology and found in both European and Russian poetry" (*PsspS*5:436). "Poezdka" contains the only mention of Isis in all of Turgenev's works and extant correspondence.

26. Costlow, "Walking into the Woodland with Turgenev," in *Heart-Pine Russia*, 31.

27. "Poezdka v Poles'e," *PsspS*5:139.

28. Shangina, *Russkii traditsionnyi byt*, 397; "Бабий ум—бабье коромысло: и криво, и зарубисто, и на оба конца," V. I. Dal', *Poslovitsy russkogo naroda* (Moscow: Gosudarstvennoe izdatel'stvo khudozhestvennoi literatury, 1957), 351. For a verse celebration of the *koromyslo* see Samuil Marshak, "Vchera i segodnia" (published 1925).

29. "Priroda," *PsspS*10:165.

30. Diane Morgan, *From Satan's Crown to the Holy Grail: Emeralds in Myth, Magic, and History* (London: Praeger, 2007), 46. See also John Sinkankas, *Emerald and Other Beryls* (Phoenix: GeoScience, 1981), 69, 95; "Ceremony of the Scarab," in *Dictionary of Gems and Gemology*, ed. Mohsen Manutchehr-Danai (Berlin, Heidelberg: Springer, 2009), online. The adjectival and noun forms of "emerald" (*izumrud*) appear twelve

times in Turgenev's fiction, including in two of the *Notes of a Hunter* tales: "Ermolai i mel'nichikha" and "Kas'ian s Krasivoi Mechi." Significantly, in the latter, emeralds adorn the first sentence of the narrator's underwater simile for the forest: "leaves on the trees at times shine through like emeralds, at times thicken into golden, almost black greenery" (*PsspS*3:115). In the 1846 poem "Na okhote—letom," just as in "Poezdka v Poles'e," emerald is associated with a hunter's safe woodland repose: "Ласково приняли нас изумрудные, свежие тени" ("Fresh, emerald shadows tenderly accepted us") (*PsspS*1:59). Emerald is mentioned in Turgenev's correspondence only three times, including this relevant sentence in a letter of 18 (30) August 1862 to Fet, describing Baden-Baden: "A wondrous place; heaps of greenery; old, shady trees covered with emerald moss, good weather, lovely vistas, kind friends, good health—what more could I ask?" (*PsspP*5:105).

31. "Nasekomoe," *PsspS*10:151.

32. "Nasekomoe," *PsspS*10:151.

33. Stacey A. Combes, "Neuroscience: Dragonflies Predict and Plan Their Hunts," *Nature* 517 (15 January 2015): 279.

34. H. E. Ewing, "The Speed of Insects in Flight," *Science* 87, no. 2262 (6 May 1938): 414. *Aeshna mixta*, a European species, made seven meters per second.

35. "Poezdka v Poles'e," *PsspS*5:147.

36. Richard Freeborn, "The Hunter's Eye in *Zapiski okhotnika*," *New Zealand Slavonic Journal* 2 (1976): 1–9.

37. *PsspS*5:466.

38. Alfred, Lord Tennyson, *The Princess: A Medley* (published 1847), part 5, line 147, in *The Works of Alfred Lord Tennyson*, vol. 4 (London: Macmillan, 1888), 89.

39. *PsspS*5:207.

40. *PsspS*5:232–33.

41. N. A. Ostrovskaia reliably recorded Turgenev as saying, "Most often I'm haunted by an image, and for a long time I can't seize it. Strangely enough, it's often a secondary character who becomes clear to me, then the main character. In *Rudin*, for example, it was Pigasov who presented himself before all the others, and the way he started arguing with Rudin, the way Rudin dressed him down—and after that Rudin too took shape": N.A. Ostrovskaia, "Iz vospominanii o Turgeneve," in *I. S. Turgenev v vospominaniiakh sovremennikov*, vol. 2 (Moscow: Khudozhestvennaia literatura, 1983), 66. A. V. Polovtsev offers a similar reminiscence of Turgenev's method: "At first one of the future characters, which I almost always base on real people, starts to float around in my imagination. Often the figure who engrosses you is not the main character, but one of the secondary ones without whom there would be no main character." "Vospominaniia ob I. S. Turgeneve," *Tsar'-Kolokol: Illiustrirovannyi vseobshchii kalendar' na 1887 god* (Moscow, 1886), 77, quoted from *I. S. Turgenev v vospominaniiakh sovremennikov*, vol. 2, 443.

42. *PsspS*5:212.

43. On *Pigasii* see N. A. Petrovskii, *Slovar' russkikh lichnykh imen*, 4th ed. (Moscow: Russkie slovari, 1995), 238. Russian *Pegas* comes from the French form *Pégase*, which was also the name of one of Turgenev's favorite hunting dogs in Germany in the 1860s; see Turgenev's memoir on the animal in *PsspS*11:157–63.

44. *Zapiski ruzheinogo okhotnika Orenburgskoi gubernii*, *Sobranie sochinenii*, vol. 4, 242. Another Russian term for the lapwing, *chibis*, which derives from the same

perception of syllables in the bird's call, gives its name to Masha Chibisova, a young dancer under Stiva Oblonskii's lecherous patronage in *Anna Karenina*; she debuts in part 4, chapter 7.

45. Sergei Aksakov, *Notes of a Provincial Wildfowler*, trans. and ed. Kevin Windle (Evanston, IL: Northwestern University Press, 1998), 81. "Последняя спица в колеснице, во всей болотной птице" (literally "The last spoke in the chariot, and of all the marshland birds"): *Zapiski ruzheinogo okhotnika, Sobranie sochinenii*, vol. 4, 240.

46. *PsspS5*:229.

47. *PsspS5*:230.

48. *PsspS5*:231.

49. *PsspS5*:217.

50. *PsspS5*:259.

51. *PsspS5*:227.

52. *PsspS5*:228–29.

53. Goethe, "Erlkönig," in *The Collected Works*, vol. 1, ed. Christopher Middleton (Princeton, NJ: Princeton University Press, 1983), 87.

54. *PsspS5*:249.

55. *PsspS5*:266.

56. For analysis of Turgenev's antipathy toward Rudin's form of wordy self-statement see "Rhetoric and Sincerity: Turgenev and the Poetics of Silence," in Jane Costlow, *Worlds within Worlds: The Novels of Ivan Turgenev* (Princeton, NJ: Princeton University Press, 1990), 11–29.

57. See also Costlow's discussion of the *besedka* at the Kirsanovs' estate in *Fathers and Children*: "Odintseva's Bath and Bazarov's Dogs: The Dismantling of Culture in *Fathers and Children*," in *Worlds within Worlds*, 119–20.

58. *PsspS5*:269.

59. "A hunter's booth or stand for ducks or black grouse": V. I. Dal', ed., *Tolkovyi slovar' zhivogo velikorusskogo iazyka v chetyrekh tomakh*, 3rd ed., vol. 1 (St. Petersburg–Moscow: M. O. Vol'f, 1903), column 208.

60. *PsspS5*:277.

61. *PsspS5*:277–78.

62. *PsspS3*:197–98. Turgenev paraphrases chapter 1, stanza 19 of Pushkin's *Evgenii Onegin* here.

63. *PsspS5*:280, 283. For further commentary on the symbolic potential of Avdiukha's Pond see Joseph L. Conrad, "Turgenev's Landscapes: An Overview," *Russian Language Journal* 41, no. 140 (Fall 1987): 126.

64. *PsspS5*:282.

65. S. T. Aksakov, *Notes on Fishing*, trans. Thomas Hodge (Evanston, IL: Northwestern University Press, 1997), 35–36.

66. *PsspS5*:293.

67. See *PsspS5*:494; S. M. Solov'ev, *Sochineniia v vosemnadtsati knigakh*, book 1 (Moscow: Golos, 1993), 147–48.

68. Bertram Colgrave and R. A. B. Mynors, eds., *Bede's Ecclesiastical History of the English People* (Oxford: Clarendon, 1969), 183–85.

69. *PsspS5*:245, 260, 285. Recall that in "The Duelist" ("Breter"), Küster's second speaks of shooting Luchkov "like a partridge" in their final confrontation (*PsspS4*:78).

70. *PsspS5*:311.

71. *PsspS5*:321; my italics.

72. M. P. Alekseev, "Pis'ma I. S. Turgeneva," *PsspP1*:28.

73. V. V. Vysotskaia, "Dva tipa prostranstva v proizvedeniiakh Turgeneva: 'Gnezdo' i 'bezgnezdov'e,' " *Spasskii vestnik* 13 (2006): 121–30; O. M. Barsukova-Sergeeva, "Simvolika gnezda i bezdny v romanakh I. S. Turgeneva," *Russkaia rech'* 1 (January–February 2004): 8–15.

74. For representative examples of the former expression see *PsspP3*:139 (1856), *PsspP3*:158–59 (1856), *PsspP4*:243 (1860), *PsspP6*:46 (1864); for examples of the latter see *PsspP3*:251 (1857), *PsspP4*:63 (1859). Note the almost identical phrase ("Что за охота лепиться к краешку чужого гнезда?"), which appears in Bersenev's thoughts as he cedes his place to Insarov in the wooing of Elena Stakhova: *Nakanune*, *PsspS6*:264. To Schapiro, such passages are indicative of "extreme loneliness, of Turgenev's realization that there was something missing from his life, which Pauline could not supply": Schapiro, *Turgenev*, 245.

75. Letter to M. N. Tolstaia, 7 (19) November 1859, Spasskoe, *PsspP3*:170.

76. Letter to V. P. Botkin, 18 (30) September 1864, Baden-Baden, *PsspP6*:49, 266.

77. *PsspS10*:178; "Bez gnezda" was one of the prose poems published posthumously in 1930.

78. Letter to M. N. Tolstaia, 7 (19) November 1859, Spasskoe, *PsspP4*:105.

79. Aksakov, *Provincial Wildfowler*, 54, 56, 82, 113, 174–75, 205–6, 228.

80. Aksakov, *Provincial Wildfowler*, 27, 45.

81. "Perepelka," *PsspS10*:122.

82. *PsspS3*:50.

83. "Groza promchalas'," *PsspS1*:45; "Odin, opiat' odin ia. Razoshlas'. . .," *PsspS1*:52; "Malinovaia voda," *PsspS3*:31; "Chertopkhanov i Nedopiuskin," *PsspS3*:279.

84. *PsspS6*:6–7.

85. *PsspS6*:49.

86. *PsspS6*:50.

87. *PsspS6*:138.

88. Jane Costlow, "Gossip, Silence, Story: Language in *A Nest of Gentry*," in *Worlds within Worlds*, 37.

89. *PsspS6*:120.

90. Dal', *Poslovitsy*, 412, 608.

91. V. I. Dal', *O pover'iakh, sueveriiakh i predrassudkakh russkogo naroda*, 2nd ed. (St. Petersburg–Moscow: M. O. Vol'f, 1880), http://www.rodon.org/dvi/opsiprn.htm. The only other important magpie references in Turgenev's fiction occur in "Poezdka v Poles'e," when Efrem hurls an insult at Kondrat before fleeing ("Hey, you white-sided magpie, get along, while your tail is still whole!": *PsspS5*:142) and chapter 10 of "Stepnoi Korol' Lir" (1869–70), when the narrator compares the Fool character, Suvenir Bychkov, to a magpie (*PsspS8*:178); in his notes on the character, Turgenev called him "a gossip [*spletnik*], curious as a magpie": *PsspS10* (1965): 380.

92. Jane Costlow, "Gossip, Silence, Story: Language in *A Nest of Gentry*," in *Worlds within Worlds*, 37; *PsspS6*:132.

93. *PsspS6*:132.

94. Letter to Pauline Viardot, 28 November (10 December) 1846, St. Petersburg, *PsspP*1:216. "Sovremennye zametki," *PsspS*1:286–87.

95. "Охоча соро́ка до нахо́дки (т.е. воро́вка)": Dal', *Poslovitsy*, 575.

96. When *A Gentry Nest* was published, memory of Gertsen's well-known 1846 story, "The Thieving Magpie" ("Soroka-vorovka"), was still fresh. In this tale, a troupe of serf actors belonging to a Russian provincial prince performs the play on which Rossini's opera is based: *La pie voleuse* (published 1815), by Théodore Baudouin d'Aubigny and Louis-Charles Caigniez. The lead actress, drawing on the way her tyrannical master pressures her for sex, effectively portrays the heroine Annette's horror at the way the judge ("bailli de Palaiseau") attempts to force himself upon her. Eventually, as a means of punishing the prince, the serf actress has an affair with someone else and becomes pregnant. Ruing her own enserfment and that of her newborn child, she soon dies. See Gertsen, "Soroka-vorovka," *Sobranie sochinenii*, vol. 4 (Moscow: Izdatel'stvo Akademii nauk SSSR, 1955), 213–35.

97. *PsspS*6:53.

98. *PsspS*8:358, 373, 377. *Spring Torrents* is in many ways a reimagining of *A Gentry Nest* in which one love triangle with a decent man, worthy woman, and femme fatale (Lavretskii-Liza-Varvara) is reflected in another (Sanin-Gemma-Mar'ia), and two cuckolds are profiled (Lavretskii, Ippolit Polozov). In both works, infidelity is expressed through references to Pushkin's *The Gypsies*: Ernest's mockery of Lavretskii and desire to learn the song setting of "Staryi muzh, groznyi muzh" in *A Gentry Nest* (*PsspS*6:52), and Mar'ia Nikolaevna's mockery of Polozov in *Spring Torrents* ("A gypsy woman once foretold a violent death for me, but that's rubbish. I don't believe it. Imagine Ippolit Sidorych with a dagger?!": *PsspS*8:362). Echoes of Zemfira's attitude are readily detectable in the liberties valued by Varvara Pavlovna, and especially in Mar'ia Nikolaevna's statements to Sanin: "Do you want to know what I love more than anything? . . . Freedom [*svoboda*], most of all and above all . . . Now you can perhaps understand why I married Ippolit Sidorych; with him I am free, absolutely free, free as the air, as the wind . . . And I knew this before the wedding; I knew that with him I'd be a Cossack on the loose [*vol'nyi kazak*]! . . . It's impossible to put chains on me, and I don't put them on others. I love freedom and refuse to recognize obligations—and not just for myself" (*PsspS*8:365–66, 367).

99. "Postoialyi dvor," *PsspS*4:302. For Aksakov, the pike was the piscine incarnation of greed: see *Notes on Fishing*, 128–29.

100. *Veshnie vody, PsspS*8:379.

101. *Dym, PsspS*7:354. In the early stages of his infatuation with Irina, Litvinov had been portrayed as a captive bird: "He tried to break free of the enchanted circle in which he agonized and tirelessly struggled, like a bird fallen into a trap" (*PsspS*7:283).

102. *PsspS*6:152.

103. "I am fundamentally and incorrigibly a Westernizer, and I never have and never do conceal it. Nonetheless, in spite of this, I took special pleasure in depicting in the character of Panshin (in *A Gentry Nest*) all the comic and vulgar sides of Westernism. I made the Slavophile Lavretskii 'crush him on every point' [in their chapter 33 debate]. Why did I do this, I, who consider Slavophile teachings false and fruitless? Because *in this instance, as I conceived it, that's precisely the way life turned out*, and I wanted above all to be sincere and truthful" (Turgenev's italics): "Po povodu *Ottsov i detei*" (published 1869), *PsspS*11:88–89.

104. "Luna plyvet vysoko nad zemleiu" is Turgenev's original composition (1840), in imitation, as he himself noted, of Heine's "Der Mond ist aufgegangen": *PsspS6*:17, 418.

105. *PsspS6*:69.

106. *PsspS6*:70.

107. *PsspS6*:84.

108. *PsspS6*:64–65.

109. Newlin, "At the Bottom of the River," 71–90; Costlow, "History and Idyll in *A Nest of Gentry*," in *Worlds within Worlds*, 69.

110. *PsspS6*:65.

111. *PsspS6*:101.

112. The nightingale who falls in love with the beautiful rose and sings in vain to her all night was a commonplace in Persian poetry that symbolized the poet and his indifferent beloved; see A. S. Pushkin, "Solovei i roza" (1827), and A. V. Kol'tsov, "Solovei: Podrazhanie Pushkinu" (1831).

113. Cf. the naïve Romantic idealism—fed by German philosophy and refracted through Kozlov's poem "K drugu V. A. Zh[ukovskomu]" (1822) and Schubert's "Die Gestirne" (1816)—of the narrator's youthful enchantment with the "eternal" stars in Turgenev's story "Iakov Pasynkov" of three and a half years earlier: *PsspS5*:62, 65.

114. *PsspS6*:10, 19, 33, 37, 76–77, 153. Significantly, *baibak*, the word for steppe marmot (*Marmota bobak*), is also a colloquialism for "lazybones."

115. *PsspS6*:40.

116. *PsspS6*:66.

117. Maksimovich-Ambodik, *Emvlemy i simvoly*, 77; quoted from N. M. Maksimovič-Ambodik, *Emvlemy i simvoly (1788): The First Russian Emblem Book*, ed. and trans. Anthony Hippisley (Leiden: Brill, 1989). The examples that follow are all taken from this edition.

118. Among other relevant emblems in Ambodik: "Burning laurel" ("Lavr v ogne") (no. 643: "I cannot burn and keep silence") and "Laurel sapling" ("Lavrovaia otrasl'"—cf. the manor house called *Lavriki*) (no. 230: "With God's help").

119. *PsspS6*:136.

120. *PsspS6*:106.

121. Quoted in Newlin, "At the Bottom of the River," 76.

122. *PsspS6*:141.

6. Life at the Lek

Second epigraph note: Nonnos, *Dionysiaca*, vol. 1, trans. W. H. D. Rouse, Loeb Classical Library (Cambridge, MA: Harvard University Press, 1940), 191.

1. Letter to P. V. Annenkov, 26 July (7 August) 1853, Spasskoe, *PsspP2*:245. This is the letter in which Turgenev explains his recent hunting expedition to the ancient reaches of the Forest-Belt with the peasant guide Egor, along the banks of the Desna River—a crucial moment in the evolution of "Journey to the Forest-Belt."

2. Letters to S. T. Aksakov, 17 (29) October 1852, Spasskoe, *PsspP2*:152, and 9 (21) July 1856, Spasskoe, *PsspP3*:114.

3. See *A Gentry Nest*, chapter 19 ("he [a one-armed peasant] mumbled like a black grouse"; *PsspS6*:62) and *Virgin Soil*, chapter 30 ("he [a schismatic prophet] kept hammering away at the same thing, like a black grouse!"; *PsspS9*:326).

4. Within the extended *Zapiski okhotnika* cycle, the black grouse appears in "Khor' i Kalinych" (opening paragraph), "Ermolai i mel'nichikha," "Bezhin lug," "Kas'ian s Krasivoi Mechi," "Burmistr" (opening paragraph), "Smert'" (opening paragraph), "Chertopkhanov i Nedopiuskin" (opening paragraph), "Zhivye moshchi" (opening paragraph), and "Stuchit!" (opening sentence).

5. *PsspS*4:518.

6. Sergei Aksakov, *Notes of a Provincial Wildfowler*, trans. Kevin Windle (Evanston, IL: Northwestern University Press, 1998), 186.

7. Aksakov, *Provincial Wildfowler*, 230.

8. Aksakov, *Provincial Wildfowler*, 231–32.

9. Turgenev's second review of *Notes of an Orenburg-Province Hunter*, *PsspS*4:517. See chapter 4.

10. Victor Ripp, *Turgenev's Russia: From "Notes of a Hunter" to "Fathers and Sons"* (Ithaca, NY: Cornell University Press, 1980), 159–60.

11. Leonard Schapiro, *Turgenev: His Life and Times* (Cambridge, MA: Harvard University Press, 1982), 11, 22, 27–29, 109–11, 295–301. Orlando Figes generally imputes to Turgenev a more forthright sex drive and concludes that his relationship with Pauline Viardot was sexual; see Figes, *The Europeans: Three Lives and the Making of a Cosmopolitan Culture* (New York: Henry Holt, 2019), 118, 212–13, 358–60, 417–19.

12. Letter to Pauline Viardot of 18 (20) September 1850, Turgenevo, *PsspP*2:55; see also Figes, *Europeans*, 149. "The fairy tale about the wolf" is probably an allusion to Charles Perrault's version of the Red Riding Hood tale, "Le Petit Chaperon Rouge," first published in 1679, which bears an explicit moral advising young women to beware of wolves, clearly a metaphor for sexually predatory men; see Francisco vaz da Silva, "Teaching Symbolism in 'Little Red Riding Hood,'" in *New Approaches to Teaching Folk and Fairy Tales*, ed. Christa C. Jones and Claudia Schwabe (Boulder, CO: Utah State University Press, 2016), 175. In 1862, the publisher Pierre-Jules Hetzel invited Turgenev to edit a Russian edition of nine of Perrault's fairy tales, which appeared in 1866; Turgenev may have translated two of the tales himself. See *PsspP*5:86, 448.

13. Aksakov, *Provincial Wildfowler*, 33.

14. Aksakov died in Moscow on 30 April (12 May) 1859; see V. V. Borisova, E. Nikitina, and T. A. Terent'eva, eds., *Letopis' zhizni i tvorchestva S. T. Aksakova (1791–1859 gg.)* (Ufa, 2011), 247. In his 22 October (3 November) 1859 letter to Ivan Aksakov, Turgenev described receiving while abroad the news of Sergei Timofeevich's death and being "profoundly upset" by it (*PsspP*4:100).

15. V. I. Dal', ed., *Tolkovyi slovar' zhivogo velikorusskogo iazyka v chetyrekh tomakh*, 3rd ed., vol. 2 (St. Petersburg–Moscow: M. O. Vol'f, 1905), column 210; M. Vasmer, *Etimologicheskii slovar' russkogo iazyka v chetyrekh tomakh*, trans. O. N. Trubachev, 3rd ed., vol. 3 (St. Petersburg: Terra, 1996), 39.

16. *PsspS*6:164–65.

17. *PsspS*6:166.

18. *PsspS*6:299. The passage could well be an adaptation of Ecclesiastes 9:12: "For no one can anticipate the time of disaster. Like fish taken in a cruel net, and like birds caught in a snare, so mortals are snared at a time of calamity, when it suddenly falls upon them" (NRSV).

19. *PsspS6*:218.

20. Aksakov, *Provincial Wildfowler*, 203. Russians traditionally hear the call as "Pod'-polot'" ("Go and weed!"), a summons to practical labor ironically out of keeping with the sloth and inertia of Uvar Ivanovich. See I. A. Goncharov, *Oblomov, Sobranie sochinenii*, vol. 4 (Moscow: Khudozhestvennaia literatura, 1979), 104.

21. Aksakov, *Provincial Wildfowler*, 204–5.

22. For the important role of "Le lac" in *On the Eve* see Jane Costlow, "On the Eve and the Sirens of Stasis," in her *Worlds within Worlds: The Novels of Ivan Turgenev* (Princeton, NJ: Princeton University Press, 1990), 87–90.

23. *PsspS6*:84.

24. The first time the three suitors are gathered (in chapter 11), they are, significantly, accompanied by the calling of hidden quail as they walk together along a field of tall rye (*PsspS6*:204). In chapter 22, a fourth suitor, the ridiculous Mr. Kurnatovskii, is foisted upon Elena by her venal and hypocritical father, but Kurnatovskii is the least suited of all, as Shubin tells her: "both [Insarov and Kurnatovskii] are practical men, but look at their differences: one is a real, living person who's been given an ideal by life; the other doesn't even have a sense of duty, but simply an official uprightness and empty efficiency [*del'nost'*]": *PsspS6*:249.

25. *PsspS6*:219–20.

26. *PsspS6*:223.

27. *PsspS6*:228.

28. *PsspS6*:227.

29. *PsspS6*:183.

30. *PsspS6*:190.

31. *PsspS6*:183.

32. Ripp, *Turgenev's Russia*, 175.

33. N. A. Dobroliubov, "Kogda zhe pridet nastoiashchii den'?," *Sobranie sochinenii v trekh tomakh*, vol. 3 (Moscow: Gosudarstvennoe izdatel'stvo khudozhestvennoi literatury, 1952), 49.

34. *PsspS6*:290.

35. *PsspS6*:290.

36. *PsspS6*:126, 139.

37. *PsspS6*:291.

38. *PsspS6*:291.

39. A. I. Gertsen, *Kto vinovat?, Sobranie sochinenii*, vol. 4 (Moscow: Izdatel'stvo Akademii Nauk SSSR, 1955), 99; Michel Baude, "Un protégé de Madame de Staël: Pierre-Hyacinthe Azaïs," *Revue d'Histoire littéraire de la France*, 66ᵉ Année 1 (January–March 1966): 149.

40. Gertsen, *Kto vinovat?*, 129–30; quoted from Herzen, *Who Is to Blame?*, trans. Michael R. Katz (Ithaca, NY: Cornell University Press, 1984), 197. Krutsiferskii's worry is echoed in Lavretskii's lament after he loses Liza Kalitina, as we observed in chapter 5: "So it is in the lottery, too: turn the wheel a bit more and the beggar, perhaps, would become a rich man" (*PsspS6*:136).

41. *PsspS6*:291. This gull is a precursor of the doomed, wandering bird in "Bez gnezda," written almost twenty years later.

42. *PsspS6*:291.

43. *PsspS6*:297.

44. *PsspS6*:236.

45. *PsspS6*:298.

46. See Schapiro, *Turgenev*, 2, and *Letopis' zhizni i tvorchestva I. S. Turgeneva (1818–1858)*, ed. N. S. Nikitina (St. Petersburg: Nauka, 1995), 23.

47. *PsspS6*:307.

48. See *A Gentry Nest* (*PsspS6*:59), "The Singers" (*PsspS3*:210), "Kas'ian of Krasivaia Mech'" (*PsspS3*:112), and "Lone Wolf" (*PsspS3*:160); Lavretskii sees crows at the beginning of chapter 18, on his way to Vasil'evskoe (*PsspS6*:59).

49. Aksakov, *Provincial Wildfowler*, 234, 238.

50. *PsspS10*:274. The jackdaw (*galka; Coloeus monedula*, formerly *Corvus monedula*) and Eurasian crow (*vorona; Corvus corone*) are closely related.

51. S. I. Romanov, *Slovar' ruzheinoi okhoty* (Moscow–St. Petersburg: Izdanie Nikolaia Ivanovicha Mamontova, 1877), 475–76.

52. Romanov, *Slovar'*, 514; L. N. Vaksel', *Karmannaia knizhka dlia nachinaiushchikh okhotit'sia s ruzh'em i legavoi sobakoiu*, 3rd ed. (St. Petersburg: Tipografiia Eduarda Pratsa, 1870), 167.

53. *PsspS6*:307. Ripp rightly notes that Turgenev's not bothering to find a precise name for the gray flowers is unusual in his fiction, though I suspect that the ignorance here is deliberate, serving to reinforce our sense of the narrator's immaturity—he is an inexperienced, teenage incarnation of Turgenev; see Ripp, *Turgenev's Russia*, 182. Thomas Newlin analyzes the mating ritual of the woodcock (*val'dshnep*), known as "roding" (*tiaga*), and, using examples from *Notes of a Hunter*, convincingly links it to human longing and sexual desire; see Thomas Newlin, "The Thermodynamics of Desire in Turgenev's *Notes of a Hunter*," *Russian Review* 72 (July 2013): 370.

54. *PsspS6*:330.

55. *PsspS6*:349.

56. *PsspS6*:350.

57. *PsspS6*:349. The Frenchman Ernest links Lavretskii to the "old husband, fearsome husband" of Zemfira's song, and Mar'ia Polozova mocks her husband in similar fashion; see also chapter 5.

58. *PsspS6*:356. Vladimir's willingness to accept his father's liaison with Zinaida bears some resemblance to *snokhachestvo*—the Russian peasant tradition of granting a father sexual rights to his son's new bride—which Bazarov powerfully invokes in his debate with Pavel Petrovich in *Fathers and Children* (*PsspS7*:53).

59. "He was a mighty hunter before the Lord; therefore it is said, 'Like Nimrod a mighty hunter before the Lord'" (Genesis 10:9, NRSV); see S. A. Vengerov, "Turgenev (Ivan Sergeevich)," *Entsiklopedicheskii slovar' Brokgauz-Efron*, vol. 34 (St. Petersburg: Tipografiia aktsionernogo obshchestva Brokgauz-Efron, 1902), 97; Boris Zaitsev, *Zhizn' Turgeneva* (Paris: YMCA-Press, 1949), 8.

60. *PsspS6*:304.

61. *PsspS6*:324.

62. *PsspS6*:326.

63. *PsspS6*:332.

64. For a general discussion of forfeits as played in nineteenth-century Russia see Iur'ev and Vladimirskii, eds., *Pravila svetskoi zhizni i etiketa: Khoroshii ton* (St. Petersburg: Tipografiia i Litografiia V. A. Tikhanova, 1889), 214–17. Turgenev mentions

forfeits in only one other work, "Iakov Pasynkov" (1855), also as a parlor game that appears in the context of courtship among young people. In that story, forfeits are described as being payable by compliments, kisses, searching for a particular object, making a guess, or dancing (*PsspS5*:64).

65. *PsspS6*:318. The sexual metaphor of the men's hands thrusting into Zinaida's hat verges, uncharacteristically for Turgenev, on blatancy.

66. *PsspS6*:320.

67. Aksakov, *Provincial Wildfowler*, 205.

68. *PsspS6*:322–23.

69. *PsspS6*:326, 335–36.

70. N. A. Petrovskii, *Slovar' russkikh lichnykh imen*, 6th ed. (Moscow: Russkie slovari, 2005), 140.

71. *PsspS6*:327–28.

72. *PsspS5*:47.

73. *PsspS7*:43.

74. *PsspS7*:34.

75. *PsspS7*:61, 65, 69, 71, 75, 83, 87.

76. *PsspS7*:156.

77. Jane Costlow, "Odintseva's Bath and Bazarov's Dogs: The Dismantling of Culture in *Fathers and Children*," in *Worlds within Worlds*, 129.

78. Nicholas Žekulin underscores the irony of how Bazarov's inexorable love for a particular woman completely undermines his materialistic ideology; see "*De gustibus disputandum est*: Turgenev's (Dis)agreements with His Hero Bazarov," in *Tusculum slavicum: Festschrift für Peter Thiergen*, ed. Elisabeth von Erdmann, Aschot Isaakjan, Roland Marti, and Daniel Schümann (Zürich: Pano Verlag, 2005), 301–3.

79. *PsspS7*:27.

80. *PsspS7*:8.

81. *PsspS7*:86. The archaic, primary meaning of Russian *obozhat'* (to adore) was the same as modern *obozhestvliat'*: to make a god out of (someone or something). The root *Bog* in *obozhat'* thus hints more strongly than English *adore* that Arkadii and Katia view nature as tantamount to a deity.

82. *PsspS7*:43, 46, 77, 82. See the discussion in Žekulin, "*De gustibus disputandum est*," 295–96.

83. *PsspS7*:54.

84. Turgenev to Aksakov, 12, 16 (24, 28) May 1853, *PsspP2*:230–31; *Letopis' zhizni i tvorchestva (1818–1858)*, 238.

85. *PsspS7*:52, 78.

86. *PsspS7*:29, 34. For a roughly contemporaneous English description of this impressive beetle, the "Marginated Dytiscus," see Thomas Brown, *The Zoologist's Textbook*, vol. 1 (Glasgow: Archibald Fullarton, 1833), 517.

87. *PsspS7*:28.

88. "The contradiction of several of Hegel's and Schelling's constructs by facts uncovered by the natural sciences prompted Büchner (in the preface to the first edition of *Kraft und Stoff*) to speak with indignation of the *Naturphilosophen* and express the hope that 'the time of learned ostentation, philosophical quackery and intellectual hocus-pocus has passed' ": "Biukhner (Büchner)," in *Entsiklopedicheskii slovar'*

Brokgauz i Efron: Biografii, vol. 2 (Moscow: Nauchnoe izdatel'stvo Bol'shaia Rossiis-kaia Entsiklopediia, 1992), 795–96.

89. *PsspS7*:45. The book had been translated into Russian as *Sila i materiia* by N. Polilov in 1860 (2nd ed., 1907). Given the widespread notoriety of Büchner's treatise at the time, I suspect that Bazarov and Arkadii's mistake with the title was deliberately included by Turgenev.

90. Thomas Newlin, "At the Bottom of the River: Forms of Ecological Consciousness in Mid-Nineteenth-Century Russian Literature," *Russian Studies in Literature* 39, no. 2 (Spring 2003): 75. Newlin goes on to quote Gertsen: "A discerning eye . . . will easily see that something is not quite right in all the spheres of the natural sciences. They lack something, something that the abundance of facts cannot make up for. Their truths have some blank spots. Every branch of the natural sciences keeps us painfully aware that there is in nature something intangible, something we cannot grasp." Gertsen, *Sobranie sochinenii*, vol. 3 (Moscow: Izdatel'stvo Akademii Nauk SSSR, 1954), 95.

91. Ia. P. Polonskii, "I. S. Turgenev u sebia v ego poslednii priezd na rodinu (Iz vospominanii)," quoted from S. M. Petrov and V. G. Fridland, eds., *I. S. Turgenev v vospominaniiakh sovremennikov*, vol. 2 (Moscow: Khudozhestvennaia literatura, 1983), 362.

92. *PsspS*11:90.

93. *PsspS7*:87.

94. William A. Petri Jr., "Epidemic Typhus," *Merck Manual Professional Version*, https://www.merckmanuals.com/professional/infectious-diseases/rickettsiae-and-related-organisms/epidemic-typhus.

95. "Typhus," in *Oxford English Dictionary*, 3rd ed., https://www-oed-com.ezproxy.wellesley.edu.

96. *PsspS7*:178, 183. This expression means "to leave someone or someplace suddenly and quickly (often in order to avoid someone's company, doing an unpleasant chore etc.)"; "to (try to) evade something" (to "weasel" one's way out of something); and "to ingratiate oneself before someone, be subservient, try desperately to please someone": Sophia Lubensky, *Russian-English Dictionary of Idioms* (New York: Random House, 1995), 755.

97. See L. P. Sabaneev, "Irlandskii setter (krasnyi setter)," in *Sobaki okhotnich'i: Legavye*, vol. 1 (Moscow: Terra, 1992), 182, 186, 187–88, 191–92, 194, 201, 205, 214–15, 217.

98. For more on the translation of *krasnye sobaki* see Thomas P. Hodge, "The 'Hunter in Terror of Hunters': A Cynegetic Reading of Turgenev's *Fathers and Children*," *Slavic and East European Journal* 51, no. 3 (Fall 2007): 463. Note that Nikolai Shcherban', a friend and journalist who helped deliver the manuscript of *Fathers and Children*, records Turgenev as having explained to Vasilii Botkin, "Bazarov is delirious. It's not just 'dogs' that appear to him, but specifically 'red' ones, because his brain is inflamed with an onrush of blood": N. V. Shcherban', "Iz vospominanii ob I. S. Turgeneve (1861–1875)," in *I. S. Turgenev v vospominaniiakh sovremennikov*, vol. 2 (Moscow: Khudozhestvennaia literatura, 1983), 38. This remark helps explain why Turgenev might have specifically chosen red-coated Irish setters—among all the breeds of gun dog he knew so well—to perform a set over the black grouse in Bazarov's hallucination.

99. Costlow, "Odintseva's Bath," 133–37.

100. Aksakov, *Provincial Wildfowler*, 234–35; translation modified.

101. *PsspS*10:275; see appendix 4.

102. Aksakov, *Provincial Wildfowler*, 235.

103. Aksakov, *Provincial Wildfowler*, 236.

104. Aksakov, *Provincial Wildfowler*, 242.

105. *PsspS*7:44.

106. *PsspS*7:178; my italics.

107. *PsspS*7:171.

108. "[Arina Vlas'evna] was afraid of mice, grass-snakes, frogs, sparrows, leeches, thunder, cold water, drafts, horses, goats, redheads, and black cats and considered crickets and dogs unclean animals" (*PsspS*7:113). Noteworthy in this context is Arina Vlas'evna's distaste for red-haired people (*ryzhie liudi*), reminding us of Bazarov's Irish setters. In her fear of grass snakes and drafts, Arina resembles Odintsova (*PsspS*7:84, 164).

109. *PsspS*7:100, 128, 156.

110. *PsspS*7:188, 469; A. S. Pushkin, "Brozhu li ia vdol' ulits shumnykh," *Polnoe sobranie sochinenii*, vol. 3 (Leningrad: Nauka, 1977), 130.

111. *PsspS*7:111.

112. *PsspS*7:34.

113. See A. A. Long and D. N. Sedley, eds., *The Hellenistic Philosophers*, vol. 1 (Cambridge: Cambridge University Press, 1987), 419–20. Martha Nussbaum labels this aspect of the stoic project as "the extirpation of the passions." See Martha C. Nussbaum, *The Therapy of Desire: Theory and Practice in Hellenistic Ethics*, vol. 2 (Princeton, NJ: Princeton University Press, 1994), 359 ff.

114. Gisela Striker, "Ataraxia: Happiness as Tranquillity," *Monist* 73, no. 1 (January 1990): 99.

115. Striker, "Ataraxia," 97.

116. Turgenev explicitly addresses stoical ethics through the character of Baburin, who is fascinated by Zeno's teachings in the later story "Punin i Baburin" (1872–74): *PsspS*9:33, 445. See also Chauncey E. Finch, "Turgenev as a Student of the Classics," *Classical Journal* 49, no. 3 (December 1953): 119–20.

117. *PsspS*7:164.

118. *PsspS*7:77.

119. *PsspS*7:154.

120. *PsspS*7:82. Turgenev calls the piece "Mozart's C minor Sonata-Fantasia," a reference to both the Piano Sonata No. 14 in C minor, K. 457 (1784) and the Fantasia in C minor, K. 475 (1785), which were originally published together.

121. *PsspS*7:185; my italics.

122. *PsspS*7:68.

123. *PsspS*7:98, 99.

124. *PsspS*7:76, 83.

125. *PsspS*7:159.

126. *PsspS*7:100; Patrick T. Gregory and Leigh Anne Isaac, "Food Habits of the Grass Snake in Southeastern England: Is *Natrix natrix* a Generalist Predator?," *Journal of Herpetology* 38, no. 1 (March 2004): 88–95.

127. *PsspS7*:165–67.

128. *PsspS7*:167.

129. *PsspS7*:167.

130. *PsspS7*:186.

131. *PsspS7*:40. Note also that some of the imagery from "The Tryst" (cornflowers, rustic outdoor meeting place) is repeated here, but this time things end well for the serf girl, and she is lovingly pursued, not ignored, by her male partner. Katia, when she played the piano, *"hid*, retreated into herself . . . She wasn't so much shy as distrustful" (*PsspS7*:82; italics in the original). Katia engages in sincere, self-revelatory music making, like Lemm, and unlike Varvara Pavlovna, in *A Gentry Nest*.

132. *PsspS7*:135.

133. *PsspS7*:34.

134. *PsspS7*:78–79, 87.

135. *PsspS7*:41, 118.

136. *PsspS7*:119, 121–22.

137. *PsspS7*:155.

138. *PsspS7*:128–29.

139. S. T. Aksakov, "Zamechaniia i nabliudeniia okhotnika brat' griby," *Sobranie sochinenii*, vol. 4 (Moscow: Gosudarstvennoe izdatel'stvo khudozhestvennoi literary, 1956), 597.

140. *PsspS7*:188. In its humble way, the fungal image supports Costlow's suggestion that Bazarov's parents are analogues of Ovid's Baucis and Philemon, who are transformed into an oak and a linden: see Costlow, "Odintseva's Bath," 133.

141. *PsspS4*:516.

142. *PsspS4*:517.

143. *PsspS4*:517.

Conclusion. "I'm a Sportsman"

Epigraph: "Zlaia zabava (Mysli ob okhote)" (St. Petersburg: Tipografiia A. S. Suvorina, 1890), 3. Lev Tolstoi provided a brief, approving preface for this pamphlet. For a full discussion see Ian Helfant, *That Savage Gaze: Wolves in the Nineteenth-Century Russian Imagination*, the Unknown Nineteenth Century (Boston: Academic Studies Press, 2018), 99–103.

1. Tom Stoppard, *Voyage* (*The Coast of Utopia*, Part 1) (New York: Grove, 2002), 48.

2. Stoppard, *Voyage*, 48.

3. Leonard Schapiro, *Turgenev: His Life and Times* (Cambridge, MA: Harvard University Press, 1982), 192–93.

4. Vladimir Nabokov, *Lectures on Russian Literature*, ed. Fredson Bowers (New York: Harcourt, Brace, Jovanovich, 1981), 67.

5. Letter to M. M. Stasiulevich, 8 (20) May 1878, Paris, *PsspP*16.1:111.

6. *PsspS7*:228–30. See also appendix 1.

7. *PsspS7*:230.

8. Marina Ledkovsky, *The Other Turgenev* (Würzburg: Jal Verlag, 1973), 14.

9. "Prizraki," *PsspS7*:196–97. "Stack-Poles" (*stozhary*) is a traditional Russian folk name for the Pleiades.

10. "Prizraki," *PsspS7*:193.

11. On Turgenev's late rift with Gertsen see Nicholas Žekulin, "Ivan Turgenev," in *Russian Novelists in the Age of Tolstoy and Dostoevsky*, ed. J. Alexander Ogden and Judith E. Kalb, Dictionary of Literary Biography, vol. 238 (Detroit: Gale, 2001), 362–63; Aileen M. Kelly, "What Is History?," in her *The Discovery of Chance: The Life and Thought of Alexander Herzen* (Cambridge, MA: Harvard University Press, 2016), 412–51.

12. Patrick Waddington, "Turgenev's Notebooks for *Dym*," *New Zealand Slavonic Journal* (1989–90): 60–64.

13. *Dym, PsspS7*:327–28.

14. *Dym, PsspS7*:328.

15. *Dym, PsspS7*:328.

16. *Dym, PsspS7*:309.

17. *Dym, PsspS7*: 295–96, 347, 383.

18. *Dym, PsspS7*:373.

19. *Dym, PsspS7*:279, 344, 388. See chapter 3.

20. See A. A. Bel'skaia's thorough summary of scholarship on the topic in "Oboniatel'nyi segment khudozhestvennogo mira romana I. S. Turgeneva *Dym*," *Kul'tura i tekst* 7 (2004): 113–24.

21. Waddington, "Turgenev's Notebooks for *Dym*," 44, 58.

22. "Brigadir," *PsspS8*:39, 43–47.

23. *PsspS3*:507, 511–12, 516. For a detailed discussion of these late additions to *Zapiski okhotnika* see Dale E. Peterson, "The Completion of *A Sportsman's Sketches*: Turgenev's Parting Word," in *The Poetics of Ivan Turgenev*, ed. David Lowe (Washington, DC: Kennan Institute, 1989), 53–62.

24. Richard M. Ellis, Rupak Moitra, and Nigel North, "Turgenev's 'Living Relic': An Early Description of Scleroderma?," *Journal of the Royal Society of Medicine* 98, no. 8 (2005): 372–74.

25. "Zhivye moshchi," *PsspS3*:330–31.

26. "Zhivye moshchi," *PsspS3*:334.

27. Schapiro, *Turgenev*, 269.

28. Žekulin, "Ivan Turgenev," 365–66; Schapiro, *Turgenev*, 269–71.

29. From Turgenev's July 1870 plan for *Nov'*, *PsspS9*:399.

30. *Nov'*, *PsspS9*:384, and the plan for *Nov'*, *PsspS9*:399.

31. Schapiro, *Turgenev*, 265.

32. *Ottsy i deti*, *PsspS7*:87.

33. *Nov'*, *PsspS9*:171.

34. *Nov'*, *PsspS9*:176, 184.

35. *Nov'*, *PsspS9*:263.

36. *Nov'*, *PsspS9*:133. The source of the epigraph, ostensibly "From the notes of a certain proprietor-agronomist," remains unknown (*PsspS9*:492).

37. *Nov'*, *PsspS9*:265.

38. *Nov'*, *PsspS9*:270.

39. Plan for *Nov'*, *PsspS9*:399.

40. *Nov'*, *PsspS9*:387–78.

41. *Nov'*, *PsspS9*:271.

42. *Nov'*, *PsspS9*:290.

43. *Nov'*, *PsspS9*:379.

44. *Dvorianskoe gnezdo, PsspS6*:69–70.

45. *Nov', PsspS9*:223.

46. *Nov', PsspS9*:375–76. He had first glimpsed the tree from his lodging at the factory in chapter 27: "Nezhdanov went to the window and looked at the little garden . . . A single ancient apple tree especially attracted his attention for some reason. He shuddered, stretched, opened his traveling-bag—and withdrew nothing from it; he fell into thought" (*PsspS9*:305).

47. *Nov', PsspS9*:202, 377, 380.

48. *Nov', PsspS9*:237.

49. *Nov', PsspS9*:243.

50. Turgenev kept hunting in France, and crossed the English Channel to shoot partridge at Six Mile Bottom, Cambridgeshire, in October 1881, as he had in the autumns of 1878 and 1880; see Patrick Waddington, *Turgenev and England* (New York: New York University Press, 1981), 226, 229, 280; and *Letopis' zhizni i tvorchestva I. S. Turgeneva (1876–1883)*, ed. N. N. Mostovskaia (St. Petersburg: Nauka, 2003), 214–15, 355, 415–16.

51. Eva Kagan-Kans, "Fate and Fantasy: A Study of Turgenev's Fantastic Stories," *Slavic Review* 28, no. 4 (December 1969): 546.

52. F. M. Dostoevskii, "Rossiiskoe obshchestvo pokrovitel'stva zhivotnym," *Dnevnik pisatelia*, January 1876, *Polnoe sobranie sochinenii*, vol. 22 (Leningrad: Izdatel'stvo Nauka, Leningradskoe otdelenie, 1981), 26–27, 330–31; Amy Nelson, "The Body of the Beast: Animal Protection and Anticruelty Legislation in Imperial Russia," in *Other Animals: Beyond the Human in Russian Culture and History*, ed. Jane T. Costlow and Amy Nelson (Pittsburgh: University of Pittsburgh Press, 2010), 95–98.

53. Helfant, *That Savage Gaze*, 98–99.

54. V. E. Iversen, *Pervoe desiatiletie (1865–1875) Rossiiskogo obshchestva pokrovitel'stva zhivotnym: Istoricheskii ocherk ego deiatel'nosti* (St. Petersburg: Tipografiia A. M. Kotomina, 1875).

55. Letter of 29 March (10 April) 1877 to M. M. Stasiulevich, Paris, *PsspP15.2*:111. The translation was first published in *Vestnik Evropy*, 1877, no. 4, 603–28, under the title "The Catholic Legend of Julian the Merciful." Turgenev's translation of "Hérodias," the third of the *Trois contes*, appeared in *Vestnik Evropy* the following month. On Turgenev's vigorous promotion of Flaubert in Russia, and his work on the *Trois contes*, see Orlando Figes, *The Europeans: Three Lives and the Making of a Cosmopolitan Culture* (New York: Henry Holt, 2019), 301–2, 390–91.

56. Quoted from Gustave Flaubert, "The Legend of Saint Julian the Hospitaller," in *The Complete Works of Gustave Flaubert*, vol. 8 (London: M. Walter Dunne, 1904), 12; see *PsspS10*:200.

57. Quoted from "The Legend of Saint Julian the Hospitaller," 32; see *PsspS10*:215.

58. "Perepelka," *PsspS10*:118–19.

59. "Perepelka," *PsspS10*:120.

60. "Perepelka," *PsspS10*:121.

61. "Perepelka," *PsspS10*:122.

62. Tolstoi later wrote in *What Is Art?* (*Chto takoe iskusstvo?*, 1897), "One of our painters is Vasnetsov. He painted images in the Kiev Cathedral; everyone praises him

as the founder of some sort of new, elevated kind of Christian art. He worked on these images for decades. He was paid tens of thousands of rubles, and all these images are a foul imitation of an imitation of imitations which contains not a single spark of feeling. And this same Vasnetsov drew a picture for Turgenev's "The Quail," . . . a picture that depicts a sleeping boy with pouting upper lip and, over him, as in a dream, the quail. And this picture is a genuine work of art." L. N. Tolstoi, *Polnoe sobranie sochinenii*, vol. 30 (Moscow: Gosudarstvennoe izdatel'stvo khudozhestvennoi literatury, 1951), 146.

63. Letter of 28 July (9 August) 1849 to Pauline Viardot, Courtavenel, *PsspP*1:322–23.

64. See Ian Helfant, "S. T. Aksakov: The Ambivalent Proto-Ecological Consciousness of a Nineteenth-Century Russian Hunter," *Interdisciplinary Studies in Literature and Environment (ISLE)* 13, no. 2 (Summer 2006): 65–68; and Ronald LeBlanc, "Tolstoy's Way of No Flesh: Abstinence, Vegetarianism, and Christian Physiology," in *Food in Russian History and Culture*, ed. Musya Glants and Joyce Toomre (Bloomington: Indiana University Press, 1997), 84, 98 note.

65. L. N. Tolstoi, *Anna Karenina*, part 3, chap. 2, *Polnoe sobranie sochinenii*, vol. 18 (Moscow-Leningrad: Gosudarstvennoe izdatel'stvo Khudozhestvennaia literatura, 1934), 256.

66. From the concluding paragraph of Turgenev's second review of Aksakov's hunting treatise, *PsspS*4:522.

67. D. N. Sadovnikov, "Vstrechi s I. S. Turgenevym: 'Piatnitsy' u poeta Ia. Polonskogo v 1880 godu," *Russkoe proshloe* 3 (1923): 100.

68. For an analysis of the complete canvas and its tortuous route to Bougival in 2006 see A. Guski and A. Seljak, "Portraits d'un chasseur: Tourguéniev et Nikolaï D. Dmitriev-Orenbourgsky. Essai sur un tableau disparu," *Cahiers Ivan Tourguéniev, Pauline Viardot, Maria Malibran* 25 (2001): 193–201. On Turgenev's relations with Dmitriev-Orenburgskii see L. I. Kuz'mina, "Turgenev i khudozhnik N. D. Dmitriev-Orenburgskii," in *Turgenevskiii sbornik: Materialy k Polnomu sobraniiu sochinenii i pisem I. S. Turgeneva*, vol. 3, ed. N. V. Izmailov and L. N. Nazarova (Leningrad: Izdatel'stvo Nauka, Leningradskoe otdelenie, 1967), 264–71.

69. Patrick Waddington, *A Catalogue of Portraits of Ivan Sergeyevich Turgenev (1818–83)* (Wellington: Whirinaki, 1999), 49.

70. N. V. Ogareva, "Turgenev v poslednie gody zhizni: Iz vospominanii i pisem A. Bogoliubova, 1873–1883," *Literaturnoe nasledstvo* 76 (1967): 462.

71. This would have been either the first (1883) or second (1884) editions of Glazunov's ten-volume set; see Waddington, *Catalogue of Portraits*, 49; Ogareva, "Turgenev v poslednie gody zhizni," 462, 481; *PsspS*3:440.

72. Guski and Seljak, "Portraits d'un chasseur," 194; Kuz'mina, "Turgenev i khudozhnik N. D. Dmitriev-Orenburgskii," 270–71.

73. Henry James, *Partial Portraits* (London: Macmillan, 1894), 305; V. G. Belinskii, "Vzgliad na russkuiu literaturu 1847 goda," in V. G. Belinskii, *Polnoe sobranie sochinenii*, vol. 10 (Moscow: Izdatel'stvo Akademii Nauk SSSR), 1956, 347; I. A. Goncharov to S. A. Tolstaia, 11 November 1870, in Goncharov, *Sobranie sochinenii v vos'mi tomakh*, vol. 8 (Moscow: Khudozhestvennaia literatura, 1980), 385; Edmond de Goncourt and Jules de Goncourt, *Pages from the Goncourt Journals*, trans. and ed. Robert Baldick (New York: NYRB Classics, 2007), 197.

Appendix 1

Appendix note: See Eva Kagan-Kans, "The Abyss of Nature," in *Hamlet and Don Quixote: Turgenev's Ambivalent Vision* (The Hague: Mouton, 1975), 83–87; Peter Thiergen, "'Priroda do otvratitel'noi stepeni ravnodushna': Alexandre Herzen et le scepticisme de son époque face à la nature," *Revue des études slaves* 78, nos. 2–3 (2000): 267–70; Robert Louis Jackson, "The Root and the Flower, Dostoevsky and Turgenev: A Comparative Esthetic," in *Dialogues with Dostoevsky: The Overwhelming Questions* (Stanford, CA: Stanford University Press, 1993), 162–87.

1. Turgenev quotes the final quatrain of Pushkin's "Brozhu li ia vdol' ulits shumnykh": A. S. Pushkin, *Polnoe sobranie sochinenii*, vol. 3 (Leningrad: Nauka, 1977), 130.

2. See appendix 3 for a complete translation of the review.

3. Pushkin, vol. 3, 130.

Appendix 2

Appendix note: First published in *Sovremennik*, 1852, no. 4, section 6, 325–31, unsigned. Censor's permission, 6 April 1852. Translation taken from *PsspS4*:500–508. Aksakov's hunting treatise was published in March 1852. This brief review by Turgenev, one of the first devoted to the new book, served as a placeholder until he could complete the expansive second review, published in January 1853; see appendix 3.

1. The first edition of Aksakov's *Notes on Fishing* (*Zapiski ob uzhen'e ryby*) had appeared in February 1847.

2. Perhaps a reference to such shoddy hunting manuals as Patfainder [Pathfinder], *Egerskie zapiski, ili Nachertanie, kak nakhodit' dich', v kakikh mestakh, v kakoe vremia goda i razlichnye sposoby streliat' ptits i zverei . . .*, which had been published in two volumes a year earlier (Moscow, 1851) to negative reviews; see *PsspS4*:670.

3. Turgenev now introduces a series of eight long extracts from Aksakov's book.

4. "Mel'nitsy-kolotovki" in the original. I follow Kevin Windle's translation here; see Sergei Aksakov, *Notes of a Provincial Wildfowler* (Evanston, IL: Northwestern University Press, 1998), 88.

Appendix 3

Appendix note: First published in *Sovremennik*, 1853, no. 1, signed "I. T." Censor's permission, 31 December 1852. Turgenev sent the manuscript to Nekrasov from Spasskoe in a letter of 16 (28) December 1852; see *PsspP2*:172–73. The review is translated here from *PsspS4*:509–22; for a detailed discussion see chapter 4. This is the second of Turgenev's reviews of Aksakov's hunting treatise. The first, much shorter, notice had appeared in *Sovremennik* eight months earlier; see appendix 2.

1. Turgenev here pays tribute to Aksakov by borrowing this epigraph verbatim from the first of two epigraphs that Aksakov placed under the title of his *Notes on Fishing* (*Zapiski ob uzhen'e*) in 1847. For details on the original provenance of the quotation, in the reign of Tsar Aleksei Mikhailovich, see Sergei Aksakov, *Notes on Fishing*, trans. Thomas Hodge (Evanston, IL: Northwestern University Press, 1997), 209, note 1.

2. Turgenev addresses the letter to Nikolai Alekseevich Nekrasov (1821–78), editor-in-chief of *Sovremennik* and a devoted hunter.

3. From a Russian folksong known in many variants that usually begins "На улице то дождь, то снег" ("Outside, now rain, now snow"); see *PsspS4*:673.

4. A reference to the final line of chapter 7, stanza 29 of Pushkin's *Evgenii Onegin*: "Winter the enchantress is on her way" (Идет волшебница зима).

5. A reference to a line in stanza 7 of Pushkin's unfinished poem "Autumn" ("Osen'"): "I love nature's magnificent withering" (Люблю я пышное природы увяданье).

6. Turgenev refers to the review by N. N. Vorontsov-Vel'iaminov in *Moskvitianin*, 1852, no. 8, April, book 2, section 5, 106–20.

7. *Chasseur au chien d'arrêt* (Paris: Librairie de Moutardier, 1836) by Elzéar Blaze (1786–1848).

8. Unless otherwise noted, quotations from Aksakov's treatise are taken, with occasional small alterations, from Sergei Aksakov, *Notes of a Provincial Wildfowler*, trans. Kevin Windle (Evanston, IL: Northwestern University Press, 1998).

9. Failing eyesight had forced Aksakov to give up hunting by the 1830s.

10. Marklov dogs (*marklovskie sobaki*), similar to modern German shorthaired pointers, represented an attempt to breed a peculiarly Russian gun dog in the 1820s or 1830s. One "Baron Marklovskii" or possibly "Marklov" imported the original pair into Russia from Courland, and their descendants became popular with Russian hunters for two or three decades before inbreeding led to the fall of the breed. Details of the breed and its origins are scant. See A. V. Kamernitskii, *Okhota s sobakami na Rusi (X–XX vv.)*, Seriia Mir okhoty (Moscow: Veche, 2005), 108–10.

11. [Turgenev's note:] Pointer (from "to point") is the name given to English dogs with short hair; setter (from "to set") is the name given to long-haired dogs. In addition, these two breeds are differentiated by body shape, search, and especially set: the pointer stands, having stretched out and raised his head as if "pointing"; the setter crouches and sometimes lies down. Both breeds search at a full run, but the pointer moves at a handsome gallop, while the setter runs as fast as his legs can carry him; the scent of pointers is much keener and "higher"; the setter tends to stop suddenly, abruptly; it must be confessed that he often passes—or rather flies—right by the game. Setters are generally fiery and of no use at all in the forest, but in a marsh they "sweep" gloriously. The chief reproach leveled at pointers is that they are sensitive to cold and, like setters, are reluctant to give up retrieved game. For this the English keep a special kind of dog, "retrievers," that is, searchers [*otyskateli*].

12. Joseph Manton (1766–1835) was a well-known English gunsmith; Mortimer: London-based family of Scottish gunsmiths active from the mid-1700s to the late 1800s; Purdey: London-based family of gunsmiths active from 1814 to the present; Hans Morgenroth: Nuremburg-based gunsmith active from ca. 1600; Peter Starbus: Swedish gunsmith active in Amsterdam and Stockholm in the late 1700s; Jean Lepage (1779–1822): well-known French gunsmith; Becker: Warsaw-based family of gunsmiths active from 1840.

13. Jean Antoine Robert was a Paris-based inventor who devised a breechloading system for metallic cartridges in 1831; Casimir Lefaucheux (1802–52) was a French

gunsmith who pioneered breechloading firearms and self-contained cartridge systems.

14. Blaze, chapter 2 ("Armement du chasseur"), 7–34.

15. Le Comte de Langel, *Guide et hygiène des chasseurs* (Paris: Arthus-Bertrand, Bohaire & Madame Huzard, n. d. [after 1836]).

16. Dickson: a family of Scottish gunsmiths based in Edinburgh and active from 1820 to the present.

17. Turgenev uses the term *fliast* (from German *Pflaster*), which S. I. Romanov's *Slovar' ruzheinoi okhoty* (Moscow–St. Petersburg: Izdanie Nikolaia Ivanovicha Mamontova, 1877), 509, describes as a round gun-wad stamped out of felt or cardboard.

18. Jules-Félix Gévelot (1826–1904) of Paris founded an ammunition factory that served both sporting and military customers. Sellier & Bellot was founded in Prague in 1825 by Frenchman Louis Sellier, who was soon joined by partner Jean Maria Nicolaus Bellot; the company was a mass producer of percussion caps in the nineteenth century and remains a major ammunition manufacturer today. While not an Austrian factory per se, Sellier & Bellot was chartered by Franz I, emperor of Austria.

19. Turgenev refers to the popular myth that Columbus challenged his critics to make an egg stand on its end, then accomplished the feat by flattening it with a tap on the table. Turgenev also (mistakenly) believed that Blaise Pascal invented the wheelbarrow; in his letter to Nekrasov of 16 (28) December 1852 that accompanied the manuscript of his Aksakov review, he wrote, "By the way, in one place I mention Pascal's wheelbarrow—you know that Pascal invented this evidently quite simple machine" (*PsspP*2:173).

20. [Turgenev's note:] I know that many will be up in arms against this sense of *breeding*; how many times have I had to listen to tales of an extraordinary peasant dog, a half-mongrel, etc. But the exception proves the rule: one non-purebred dog in a hundred can succeed, but the others are good for nothing. In precisely the same way, a different gun bought in Tula for twenty-five paper rubles can hit the mark wonderfully, especially until the drill-traces are cleaned out of the muzzle . . . But what does this prove? In my own time I have seen only one peasant dog with extraordinary scent; she really did look like a mongrel. But, even with all her qualities, she couldn't stand still more than twenty seconds, and her owner had to "manage somehow" and keep up with her. On the other hand, I am prepared to admit that far from all the dog breeds fit for fowling have been researched properly. In France I have seen wire-haired poodle-crosses or poodles (barbets)—of a kind utterly distinct from gun dogs—who appeared to be magnificent for marshland or riverside hunting.

21. Here Turgenev refers to two of his favorite dogs: Diana (d. 1858), and her daughter Bouboule (Bubul'ka), who had her first hunting trials in July of 1852. See the discussion of this outing, described in detail by Dmitrii Kolbasin, in chapter 2.

22. Tatarinov's original Russian terms are *akhal*, *pukal*, and *shlëpal*.

23. Charles Grey, 2nd Earl Grey (1764–1845), was prime minister of Great Britain from 1830 to 1834. His administration passed the Game Act of 1831, still in force today, which protects the hare and certain species of game birds by establishing open and closed hunting seasons and requiring licenses for hunters; Britons of any social class, as long as they were licensed, could now legally hunt.

24. Turgenev probably refers here to Henry IV of France (ruled 1589–1610), who placed metal identity-bands on the legs of his falcons and is credited as the inventor

of modern bird-banding; see Harold B. Wood, "The History of Bird Banding," *Auk* 62 (1945): 257.

25. Genesis 10:9: "Like Nimrod a mighty hunter before the Lord" (NRSV); "*ispolin lovets pred Gospodem*" (Old Church Slavonic); "*sil'nyi zverolov, kak Nimrod, pred Gospodom*" (Russian).

26. Canto 11, ll. 572–75 of *The Odyssey of Homer*, trans. Richmond Lattimore (New York: Harper Collins, 1975), 183.

27. [Turgenev's note:] Fairness demands mention that, unfortunately, the quantity of our game is quickly diminishing; the reasons for this are of two kinds. The first is comforting: draining of marshes, and so on. But the second is not so pleasant: destruction of forests and the tendency of Russian hunters not to take pity on "little mothers" [*matki*—reproducing females]; the habit of baiting and netting partridge in winter is also extraordinarily harmful. [Aksakov wrote elsewhere about this latter practice, of which he approved, in "Lovlia shatrom teterevov i kuropatok," in *Rasskazy i vospominaniia okhotnika o raznykh okhotakh, Sobranie sochinenii v chetyrekh tomakh*, vol. 4 (Moscow: Izdatel'stvo khudozhestvennoi literatury, 1956), 515–23.]

28. Vladimir II "Monomakh" (1053–1125), grand prince (reigned 1113–25) of Kievan Rus'; Turgenev refers to his *Testament* (*Pouchenie*), written to his children ca. 1117 and preserved in the Laurentian Codex of the Russian Primary Chronicle.

29. Tsar Aleksei Mikhailovich Romanov (1629–76; reigned 1645–76): son of Tsar Mikhail, first of the Romanov monarchs. Aleksei Mikhailovich was an avid hunter who commissioned a well-known falconing treatise, quoted for the epigraph of this review. His son was Peter I (reigned 1682–1725), the Great.

30. [Turgenev's note:] See Novikov's *Ancient bibliotheca*, 2nd ed., part 3, 430. [Full citation: *Drevniaia rossiiskaia vivliofika, soderzhashchaia v sebe sobranie drevnostei rossiiskikh, do istorii, geografii i genealogii rossiiskie kasaiushchikhsia* N. Novikova, 2nd ed., chast' III (Moscow: V Tipografii Kompanii Tipograficheskoi, 1788), 430–32.]

31. Turgenev refers to "Tsar Aleksei Mikhailovich's Letters to the Steward Matiushkin" ("Pis'ma tsaria Alekseia Mikhailovicha k stol'niku Matiushkinu"), published in *Akty, sobrannye v bibliotekakh i arkhivakh Rossiiskoi imperii arkheologicheskoiu ekspeditsieiu imp. Akademii nauk, 1645–1700*, vol. 4 (St. Petersburg: V Tipografii II Otdeleniia Sobstvennoi E. I. V. Kantseliarii, 1836), 138–41.

32. Turgenev later intended to contribute to Aksakov's planned *Hunter's Miscellany* (*Okhotnichii sbornik*) "a story on how the peasants shoot bears on oat-fields in the Forest-Belt"; letter from Turgenev to S. T., K. S., and I. S. Aksakov, 23–24 April (5–6 May) 1853, *PsspP*2:224. When Aksakov's proposed miscellany was denied publication permission by the censor, Turgenev kept the bear story and later developed it into an episode in "A Journey to the Forest-Belt" (published 1857). See chapter 5.

33. [Turgenev's note:] See *Notes of an Orenburg-Province Hunter*, 231.

34. On rendering the gender of "nature" (*priroda*) in this context, I cite Jane Costlow's comments on translating a similar statement by Dmitrii Kaigorodov: "Russian's grammatical gender poses real dilemmas in the translation of passages like this, where the feminine gender of nature (*priroda*) and the 'masculine' *chelovek* (human, or 'man') will seem more marked in an English rendering than they are in the Russian. While translating the Russia[n] pronoun as 'her' may seem to anthropomorphize (or sexualize) nature, using 'it' is even more awkward, given the kind of mutual 'converse' and communion . . . evoke[d] here." Jane Costlow, "Dmitrii Kaigorodov

and the Ethics of Attentiveness: Knowledge, Love and Care for *Rodnaia Priroda*," in *Understanding Russian Nature: Representations, Values and Concepts*, ed. Arja Rosenholm and Sari Autio-Sarasmo, Aleksanteri Papers 4 (Saarijärvi: Gummerus Printing, 2005), 63, note 2.

35. A quotation from V. G. Benediktov's poem "The Crag" ("Utes," 1835).

36. [Turgenev's note:] Victor Hugo (e.g. *Orientales*) serves as a prime example of that sort of poetry. It would be difficult to count how many times this false manner has found itself imitators and devotees while at the same time not a single one of his images will survive: everywhere you see the author instead of nature; and man is only strong when he is guided by her. [Hugo's *Les orientales* (1829): a collection of virtuosic poems devoted largely to contrasting the Greeks and Ottoman Turks.]

37. The entire passage from "Meanwhile . . ." to the end of the Goethe quotations was removed by the censor before publication; Turgenev later sent the deleted text to Aksakov in his letter of 5, 9 (17, 21) February 1853 (*PsspP2*:203). The three Goethe quotations appeared in Turgenev's own Russian translation from Goethe's "Die Natur" (1782 or 1783), a work modern scholars generally attribute to Georg Christoph Tobler (1757–1812). "Open secrets" seems to be a reference to the second paragraph of Goethe's short discourse: in Gertsen's 1844 translation, it runs, "She eternally speaks with us, but does not reveal her secrets." A. I. Gertsen, "Pis'mo II: Nauka i priroda—Fenomenologiia myshleniia," *Pis'ma ob izuchenii prirody, Sobranie sochinenii v tridtsati tomakh*, vol. 3 (Moscow: Izdatel'stvo Akademii Nauk SSSR, 1954), 139. Turgenev's censored passage remained unpublished in Russia until 1894; see chapter 4.

38. This sentence was removed by the censor; see preceding note.

39. Turgenev here parodies a pronouncement of French naturalist Georges-Louis Leclerc, Comte de Buffon (1707–88) of the kind that appeared in early nineteenth-century children's literature, e.g., "Of all the quadrupeds domesticated by man, the most sublime is the horse. This proud and fiery animal shares with him martial labors and the glory of battle. The horse, being as intrepid as her rider, scorns all hazards": *Biuffon dlia iunoshestva, ili Sokrashchennaia istoriia trekh tsarstv prirody sochinennaia Petrom Blanshardom*, vol. 1 (Tipografiia S. Selivanovskogo, 1814), 117–18, a translation of *Le Buffon de la jeunesse, ou Abrégé d'histoire naturelle. . . .* Rédigé par Pierre Blanchard, 4th ed., vol. 1 (Paris: Chez Leprieur, 1809).

40. "Heavenward flights of dust" is an inexact quotation of "Flights of dust into the heavens" (Побеги праха в небеса) in V. G. Benediktov's "Mountain Peaks" ("Gornye vysi," 1836). The crag that "laughs" and the "phosphorescent snake" (actually "fiery snake"—"ognennyi zmei") are to be found in Benediktov's "The Crag" ("Utes").

41. John James Audubon (b. 1785), the celebrated French American artist and ornithologist, had died in January 1851. His *Birds of America* was first published in London from 1827 to 1838; the second edition was published in New York from 1839 to 1844.

42. Friedrich Wilhelm Joseph Schelling (1775–1854): German Idealist philosopher who developed his *Naturphilosophie* in the last few years of the eighteenth century and first decade of the nineteenth; see chapter 1.

43. Here Turgenev offers a playful pun on *okhota* (hunt, hunting) by repeating the related adverb *okhotno*, which also means "gladly, willingly."

44. Turgenev refers to his brief initial review of Aksakov's book; see appendix 2.

45. Turgenev alludes here to the poets F. I. Tiutchev (1803–73) and A. A. Fet (1820–92), whom he mentions by name later in the review; he also alludes to himself. In a letter of 28 December 1852 (9 January 1853) to Sergei Aksakov's son Ivan, Turgenev wrote of the soon-to-be-published book review: "There are several thoughts in it about how nature is described in which I do not spare myself" (*PsspP2*:178).

46. Turgenev's own, non-metrical translation of an excerpt from Shakespeare's *King Lear*, act 4, scene 6, ll. 15–26. Turgenev inserted a footnote after his Russian version of the third line ("that hover there in the air in the middle distance"—которые вьются там в воздухе на средние расстояния): " '. . . that wing the midway air . . .' Untranslatable."

47. "The Cloud" ("Tucha," 1835) is written in rhymed couplets of amphibrachic tetrameter; Turgenev's italics.

48. Turgenev's plan to write a third review of Aksakov's hunting notes, though mentioned here and in two other letters (to Nekrasov and I. S. Aksakov), never came to fruition; see *PsspP2*:173, 178.

49. *Oberon*: 1826 opera by Carl Maria von Weber (1786–1826), based on an epic poem (1780) by Christoph Martin Wieland (1733–1813). Oberon, King of the Elves, gives to a knight and his squire a magic horn with which they can summon him. Weber's earlier opera *Der Freischütz* (1821) had been set within a German hunting milieu.

50. *Drevniaia rossiiskaia vivliofika*, 431, 432.

51. See S. T. Aksakov's letter to I. S. Turgenev, Abramtsevo, 7 (19) October 1852: "My *Hunter's Notes* were sold out long ago, and I am forced to embark on a second edition." *Russkoe obozrenie* 28 (August 1894): 480.

52. Spasskoe-Lutovinovo, in the Mtsensk region, Orel oblast', about two hundred miles south of Moscow, was the country seat of Turgenev's mother's family and was inherited by Turgenev following her death in 1850. He was exiled there from May 1852 to November 1853.

Appendix 4

1. "Piat'desiat nedostatkov ruzheinogo okhotnika i piat'desiat nedostatkov legavoi sobaki" was first published in *Zhurnal okhoty* 4, no. 6 (1876): 1–5; *PsspS*10:272–77. Rather than deprive the dog of animacy by means of the pronoun *it*, I have chosen throughout to use feminine pronouns to reflect the feminine grammatical gender of the Russian word for *dog* (*sobaka*) and the fact that Turgenev predominantly used female hunting dogs.

BIBLIOGRAPHY

Akopov, A. I. *Otechestvennye spetsial'nye zhurnaly 1765–1917: Istoriko-tipologicheskii obzor*. Rostov: Izdatel'stvo Rostovskogo universiteta, 1986.

Aksakov, S. T. *Notes of a Provincial Wildfowler*. Translated and edited by Kevin Windle. Evanston, IL: Northwestern University Press, 1998.

———. *Notes on Fishing*. Translated and edited by Thomas P. Hodge. Evanston, IL: Northwestern University Press, 1997.

———. *Sobranie sochinenii v chetyrekh tomakh*. 4 vols. Moscow: Gosudarstvennoe izdatel'stvo khudozhestvennoi literatury, 1955–56.

———. *Zapiski okhotnika Orenburgskoi gubernii*. S politipazhami, latinskimi nazvaniiami ptits i primechaniiami g. prof. K. F. Rul'e. 3rd ed. Moscow: Tipografiia L. Stepanovoi, 1857.

Aksakov, S. T., K. S. Aksakov, and I. S. Aksakov. "Pis'ma S. T., K. S. i I. S. Aksakovykh k I. S. Turgenevu, 1851–1861." Edited by L. N. Maikov. *Russkoe obozrenie* 28 (August 1894): 449–88; 29 (September 1894): 5–38; 29 (October 1894): 478–501; 30 (November 1984): 7–30; 30 (December 1894): 571–601.

Aksakov, V. S. *Dnevnik 1854–1855 gg*. Moscow: Izdatel'stvo AST/Astrel'/Liuks, 2004.

Alekseev, M. P., ed. *I. S. Turgenev: Stat'i i materialy*. Orel: Knizhnoe izdatel'stvo, 1960.

———. *Russkaia kul'tura i romanskii mir*. Leningrad: Izdatel'stvo Nauka, 1985.

———. *Russkaia literatura i ee mirovoe znachenie*. Leningrad: Nauka, 1989.

———. "Zaglavie *Zapiski okhotnika*." In *Turgenevskii sbornik*. Vol. 5, 210–18. Leningrad: Izdatel'stvo Nauka, Leningradskoe otdelenie, 1969.

———, ed. *"Zapiski okhotnika" I. S. Turgeneva (1852–1952): Sbornik statei i materialov*. Orel: Izdatel'stvo Orlovskaia pravda, 1955.

Alekseev, M. P., and N. V. Izmailov, eds. *Turgenevskii sbornik: Materialy k "Polnomu sobraniiu sochinenii i pisem" I. S. Turgeneva*. Vol. 1. Moscow-Leningrad: Nauka, 1964.

Allen, Elizabeth Cheresh. *Beyond Realism: Turgenev's Poetics of Secular Salvation*. Stanford, CA: Stanford University Press, 1992.

Anderson, J. K. *Hunting in the Ancient World*. Berkeley: University of California Press, 1985.

Apollon, Daniel, Claire Belisle, and Philippe Regnier, eds. *Digital Critical Editions*. Champaign: University of Illinois Press, 2014.

Arkhangel'skii, A. *Priroda v proizvedeniiakh S. T. Aksakova*. Moscow: Tipografiia Obshchestvennaia Pol'za, 1916.

Arsen'ev, K. K. *Kriticheskie etiudy po russkoi literature*. Vol. 2. St. Petersburg: Tipografiia M. M. Stasiulevicha, 1888.

——. "Priroda v proizvedeniiakh Turgeneva." In *Sobranie kritcheskikh materialov dlia izucheniia proizvedenii I. S. Turgeneva* 1, edited by V. Zelinskii, 127–37. Moscow: Tipo-litografiia V. Rikhter, 1906.

Arustamova, A. A. "Ritmicheskoe voploshchenie motivov liubvi i gnezda v romane I. S. Turgeneva 'Dvorianskoe gnezdo.'" *Vestnik Permskogo universiteta* 1 (1996): 107–13.

Bagrii, Anna. "Izobrazhenie prirody v proizvedeniiakh I. S. Turgeneva." *Russkii filologicheskii vestnik*, nos. 1–2 (1916): 267–87.

Balykova, L. A. *Biblioteka Ivana Sergeevicha Turgeneva*. Vol. 1, *Knigi na russkom iazyke*. Orel: Izdatel'stvo OGTRK, 1994.

Barsukova-Sergeeva, O. M. "Simvolika gnezda i bezdny v romanakh I. S. Turgeneva." *Russkaia rech'* 1 (January 2004): 8–15.

Baude, Michel. "Un protégé de Madame de Staël: Pierre-Hyacinthe Azaïs." *Revue d'histoire littéraire de la France, 66ᵉ Année* 1 (January–March 1966): 149–52.

Bede. *Bede's Ecclesiastical History of the English People*. Edited by Bertram Colgrave and R. A. B. Mynors. Oxford: Clarendon, 1969.

Belekhova, S. P., and A. G. Volkhovskaia. *S ruzh'em i liroi: Russkaia literatura i okhota. Al'bom-katalog po materialam vystavki*. Moscow: Tipografiia Print-Studio, 2017.

Belevich, N. "Iz vospominanii 'deda' (otryvok)." *Okhota*, no. 21 (1892): 2–3.

Belinskii, V. G. *Polnoe sobranie sochinenii.* Vol. 10. Moscow: Izdatel'stvo Akademii Nauk SSSR, 1956.

Bel'skaia, A. A. "Oboniatel'nyi segment khudozhestvennogo mira romana I. S. Turgeneva *Dym*." *Kul'tura i tekst* 7 (2004): 113–24.

Berlin, Isaiah. "An Episode in the Life of Ivan Turgenev." *London Magazine* 4, no. 7 (July 1957): 14–24.

——. *Russian Thinkers*. 2nd ed. London: Penguin, 2008.

Bialyi, G. A. "Lev Tolstoi i *Zapiski okhotnika* Turgeneva." *Vestnik Leningradskogo universiteta* 3, no. 4 (1961): 55–63.

Blaze, Elzéar. *Chasseur au chien d'arrêt*. Paris: Librairie de Moutardier, 1836.

——. *The Sportsman and His Dog; or, Hints on Sporting*. Edited and translated by Herbert Byng Hall. London: John and Daniel A. Darling, 1850.

Bogdanov, B. V., ed. *Dusha moia, vse mysli moi v Rossii: I. S. Turgenev v Spasskom-Lutovinove*. Moscow: Planeta, 1989.

Bogoliubov, A. P. *Zapiski moriaka-khudozhnika*. Samara: Izdatel'skii dom Agni, 2014.

Borisova, V. V. "'Zapiski okhotnika' I. S. Turgeneva versus 'Zapiski ruzheinogo okhotnika Orenburgskoi gubernii' S. T. Aksakova." In *Turgenev i liberal'naia ideia v Rossii*, edited by G. M. Rebel', M. V. Volovinskaia, and V. A. Iasyreva, 172–80. Perm': PGGPU, 2018.

Borisova, V. V., E. P. Nikitina, and T. A. Terent'eva, eds. *Letopis' zhizni i tvorchestva S. T. Aksakova (1791–1859 gg.)*. Ufa, 2011. https://aksakov.do.am/index/letopis/0-21.

Borzenko, S. G. "Turgenev i priroda: Filosofskie motivy v pis'makh I. S. Turgeneva." *Voprosy russkoi literatury* (L'vov: Izdatel'stvo L'vovskogo universiteta) 28 (1976): 31–37.

Briggs, A. D. P. "One Man and His Dogs: An Anniversary Tribute to Ivan Turgenev." *Irish Slavonic Studies* 14 (1993): 1–20.

Brodskii, N. L. "Proza *Zapisok okhotnika.*" *Turgenev i ego vremia* (Moscow-Petrograd: Gosudarstvennoe izdatel'stvo) 1 (1923): 193–99.

Brooks, Thomas. *The Complete Works of Thomas Brooks.* Vol. 4. Edinburgh: James Nichol, 1847.

Brostrom, Kenneth N. "The Heritage of Romantic Descriptions of Nature in Turgenev." Edited by Paul Debreczeny. *American Contributions to the Ninth International Congress of Slavists* (Slavica: Columbus) 2: *Literature, Poetics, History* (1983): 81–96.

Brown, Thomas. *The Zoologist's Textbook.* Vol. 1. Glasgow: Archibald Fullarton, 1833.

Buek, Otto, ed. *Immanuel Kants kleinere Schriften zur Naturphilosophie.* Vol. 2. Leipzig: Verlag der Dürr'sche Buchhandlung, 1907.

Buell, Lawrence. *The Environmental Imagination.* Cambridge, MA: Harvard University Press, 1995.

Buffon, Comte Georges-Louis Leclerc de. *Biuffon dlia iunoshestva, ili Sokrashchennaia istoriia trekh tsarstv prirody* sochinennaia Petrom Blanshardom. Vol. 1. Moscow: Tipografiia S. Selivanovskogo, 1814.

——. *Histoire naturelle, générale et particulière, avec la description du Cabinet du roi.* Vol. 4. Paris: De l'Imprimerie royale, 1753.

——. *Le Buffon de la jeunesse, ou Abrégé d'histoire naturelle. . . .* Rédigé par Pierre Blanchard. 4th ed. Vol. 1 Paris: Chez Leprieur, 1809.

Bulgakov, M. V. *Katalog redkikh i zamechatel'nykh okhotnich'ikh knig 1748–1917 gg. iz sobraniia M. V. Bulgakova.* Moscow: PTP Era, 2000.

——. "Russkie pisateli-okhotniki: Nikolai Alekseevich Nekrasov (1821–1877)." *Okhota i okhotnich'e khoziaistvo,* no. 8 (2008): 38–41.

Buslaev, F. I. *Moi dosugi.* Vol. 2. Moscow: Sinodal'naia tipografiia, 1886.

Campion, John. "Toward an Ecotropic Poetry." http://worldatuningfork.com/wp-content/uploads/2013/ 05/Toward-An-Ecotropic-Poetrywidermargins.pdf.

Carden, Patricia. "Finding the Way to Bezhin Meadow: Turgenev's Intimations of Mortality." *Slavic Review* 36, no. 3 (September 1977): 455–64.

Cartmill, Matt. "Hunting and Humanity in Western Thought (in the Company of Animals)." *Social Research* 62, no. 3 (Fall 1995): 773–87.

Carus, Paul. "Goethe's Nature Philosophy." *Open Court* 21 (1907): 227–37.

Chekhov, A. P. *Polnoe sobranie sochinenii i pisem v tridtsati tomakh.* Moscow: Nauka, 1974–83.

Chernov, N. M. *Dvorianskie gnezda vokrug Turgeneva.* Tula: IPP Grif, 2003.

——. *Provintsial'nyi Turgenev.* Moscow: ZAO Tsentrpoligraf, 2003.

——. *Spassko-Lutovinovskaia khronika (1813–1883).* Tula: IPO Lev Tolstoi, 1999.

Chertkov, V. G. "Zlaia zabava (Mysli ob okhote)." St. Petersburg: Tipografiia A. S. Suvorina, 1890.

Clayton, J. Douglas. *"Hunting in Russia" and "The Story of Dmitry."* Ottawa: Slavic Research Group at the University of Ottawa, 2008.

——. "Night and Wind: Images and Allusions as the Source of the Poetic in Turgenev's *Rudin.*" *Canadian Slavonic Papers* 26, no. 1 (1984): 10–14.

Cocker, Mark, and Richard Mabey. *Birds Britannica.* London: Random House, 2005.

Combes, Stacey A. "Neuroscience: Dragonflies Predict and Plan Their Hunts." *Nature* 517 (15 January 2015): 279–80.

Conrad, Joseph L. "Turgenev's Landscapes: An Overview." *Russian Language Journal* 41, no. 140 (Fall 1987): 119–34.

Costlow, Jane T. *Heart-Pine Russia: Walking and Writing the Nineteenth-Century Forest.* Ithaca, NY: Cornell University Press, 2013.

——. *World within Worlds: The Novels of Ivan Turgenev.* Princeton, NJ: Princeton University Press, 1990.

Costlow, Jane T., and Amy Nelson, eds. *Other Animals: Beyond the Human in Russian Culture and History.* Pittsburgh: University of Pittsburgh Press, 2010.

Czech, Kenneth P., ed. *Hunting Trips in the Land of the Czars.* Long Beach, CA: Safari, 2008.

Dal', V. I. *O pover'iakh, sueveriiakh i predrassudkakh russkogo naroda.* 2nd ed. St. Petersburg–Moscow: M. O. Vol'f, 1880.

——. *Poslovitsy russkogo naroda: Sbornik.* Moscow: Gosudarstvennoe izdatel'stvo khudozhestvennoi literatury, 1957.

——. *Tolkovyi slovar' zhivogo velikorusskogo iazyka v chetyrekh tomakh.* 3rd ed. St. Petersburg–Moscow: M. O. Vol'f, 1903–9.

Darwin, Charles. *On the Origin of Species by Means of Natural Selection.* 3rd ed. London: John Murray, 1861.

D'iakonov, V. I. "Sravneniia Turgeneva." *Turgenev i ego vremia* (Moscow-Petrograd, Gosudarstvennoe izdatel'stvo) 1 (1923): 77–141.

Dmitrieva, E. E., and O. N. Kuptsova. *Zhizn' usadebnogo mifa: Utrachennyi i obretennyi rai.* Moscow: OGI, 2003.

Dmitrieva, N. L. "Roza u Pushkina i Turgeneva." *Russkaia literatura* 3 (2000): 101–5.

Dobroliubov, N. A. *Sobranie sochinenii v trekh tomakh.* Moscow: Gosudarstvennoe izdatel'stvo khudozhestvennoi literatury, 1950–52.

Dostoevskii, F. M. *Polnoe sobranie sochinenii v tridtsati tomakh.* Leningrad: Izdatel'stvo Nauka, Leningradskoe otdelenie, 1972–90.

Dremov, I. "Po turgenevskim mestam." *Okhota i okhotnich'e khoziaistvo,* no. 9 (1958): 48–51.

Druzhinin, A. V. *Povesti, Dnevnik.* Moscow: Nauka, 1986.

Durkin, Andrew R. "The Generic Context of Rural Prose: Turgenev and the Pastoral Tradition." Edited by Robert A. Maguire and Alan Timberlake, 43–50. In *American Contributions to the Eleventh International Congress of Slavists: Literature, Linguistics, Poetics.* Bloomington, IN: Slavica, 1993.

——. "A Guide to the Guides: Writing about Birds in Russia in the Nineteenth Century." *Russian Studies in Literature* 39, no. 3 (Summer 2003): 4–24.

——. *Sergei Aksakov and Russian Pastoral.* New Brunswick, NJ: Rutgers University Press, 1983.

Egorov, O. A. *Ocherk istorii russkoi psovoi okhoty (XV–XVIII vv.).* St. Petersburg: Izdatel'stvo Dmitrii Bulanin, 2008.

——. "Zapiski okhotnika Orenburgskoi gubernii S. T. Aksakova i okhotnich'ia literatura do nikh." *Okhotnich'i prostory* 4 (1995): 241–54.

Eiges, I. R. "Myshlenie v obrazakh: Belinskii, Goncharov, Turgenev." Edited by N. K. Piksanov, 130–40. *Venok Belinskomu.* Moscow: Novaia Moskva, 1924.

Eikhenbaum, Boris. "The Sportsman's Sketches: An Introductory Essay." *Canadian-American Slavic Studies* 17, no. 1 (Spring 1983): 7–12.

Ellis, Richard M., Rupak Moitra, and Nigel North. "Turgenev's 'Living Relic': An Early Description of Scleroderma?" *Journal of the Royal Society of Medicine* 98, no. 8 (2005): 372–74.

Ely, Christopher. *This Meager Nature: Landscape and National Identity in Imperial Russia.* DeKalb: Northern Illinois University Press, 2002.

Erlewine, Robert. *Judaism and the West.* Bloomington: Indiana University Press, 2016.

Evgen'eva, A. P., ed. *Slovar' russkogo iazyka v chetyrekh tomakh*, Akademiia Nauk SSSR, Institut russkogo iazyka. 2nd rev. ed. Moscow: Izdatel'stvo Russkii iazyk, 1981–84.

Ewing, H. E. "The Speed of Insects in Flight." *Science* 87, no. 2262 (6 May 1938): 414–15.

Explication des ouvrages de peinture, sculpture, architecture, gravure, et lithographie des artistes vivants exposés au Palais des Champs-Élysées le 2 mai 1881. Paris: Charles de Morgues frères, 1881.

Fateev, S. P. "Priroda i chelovek v proze S. Aksakova i I. Turgeneva." *Voprosy russkoi literatury* (L'vov: Izdatel'stvo L'vovskogo universiteta) 1, no. 49 (1987): 95–100.

Fedosiuk, Iu. A. *Chto neponiatno u klassikov, ili Entsiklopediia russkogo byta XIX veka.* 2nd ed. Moscow: Izdatel'stvo Nauka, 1998.

Fet, A. A. "Karmannaia knizhka dlia nachinaiushchikh okhotit'sia s ruzh'em i legavoi sobakoi L'va Vakselia." *Sovremennik* 6 (June 1856): 55–64.

——. *Moi vospominaniia: 1848–1889.* Vol. 1. Moscow: Tipografiia A. I. Mamontova, 1890.

——. *Stikhotvoreniia i poemy.* Biblioteka poeta, bol'shaia seriia, 3rd ed. Leningrad: Sovetskii pisatel', Leningradskoe otdelenie, 1986.

Figes, Orlando. *The Europeans: Three Lives and the Making of a Cosmopolitan Culture.* New York: Henry Holt, 2019.

Filiushkina, O. V. "K voprosu o proiskhozhdenii *Zapisok okhotnika.*" *Spasskii vestnik,* no. 9 (2002): 133–50.

Finch, Chauncey, E. "Turgenev as a Student of the Classics." *Classical Journal* 49, no. 3 (December 1953): 117–22.

Flaubert, Gustave. *The Complete Works of Gustave Flaubert.* Vol. 8. London: M. Walter Dunne, 1904.

Flint, V. E., R. L. Boehme, Y. V. Kostin, and A. A. Kuznetsov, eds. *A Field Guide to Birds of Russia.* Translated by Natalia Bourso-Leland. Princeton, NJ: Princeton University Press, 1984.

Freeborn, Richard. "The Hunter's Eye in *Zapiski okhotnika.*" *New Zealand Slavonic Journal,* no. 2 (1976): 1–9.

Frost, Edgar L. "Hidden Traits: The Subtle Imagery of 'Zhivye moshchi.'" *Slavic and East European Journal* 36, no. 1 (Spring 1992): 36–56.

Fullenwider, Henry F. "The Goethean Fragment 'Die Natur' in English Translation." *Comparative Literature Studies* 23, no. 2 (Summer 1986): 170–77.

Generalova, N. P. *I. S. Turgenev: Rossiia i Evropa.* St. Petersburg: Izdatel'stvo Russkogo Khristianskogo gumanitarnogo instituta, 2003.

Generalova, N. P., A. Ia. Zvigil'skii, and V. A. Koshelev. "I. S. Turgenev (Semeistvo Aksakovykh i slavianofily)." *Russkaia literatura,* no. 4 (1995): 146–56.

Gershenzon, M. O. *Mechta i mysl' I. S. Turgeneva.* Moscow: Knigoizdatel'stvo v Moskve, 1919.

Gertsen [Herzen], A. I. *A Herzen Reader*. Edited and translated by Kathleen Parthé. Evanston, IL: Northwestern University Press, 2012.

——. *My Past and Thoughts*. Translated by Constance Garnett. Revised by Humphrey Higgens. 4 vols. New York: Knopf, 1968.

——. *Selected Philosophical Works*. Translated by L. Navrozov. Moscow: Foreign Languages Publishing House, 1956.

——. *Sobranie sochinenii v 30 tomakh*. Moscow: Izdatel'stvo Akademii Nauk SSSR, 1954–65.

——. *Who Is to Blame?* Translated by Michael R. Katz. Ithaca, NY: Cornell University Press, 1984.

Glotfelty, Cheryll, and Harold Fromm, eds. *The Ecocriticism Reader: Landmarks in Literary Ecology*. Athens: University of Georgia Press, 1996.

Goethe, Johann Wolfgang von. *The Collected Works*. Vol. 1. Edited by Christopher Middleton. Princeton, NJ: Princeton University Press, 1983.

——. *The Maxims and Reflections of Goethe*. Translated and edited by Bailey Saunders. New York: Macmillan, 1906.

Gogol', N. V. *Polnoe sobranie sochinenii*. Vol. 6. Leningrad: Izdatel'stvo Nauka, 1951.

Gomides, Camilo. "Putting a New Definition of Ecocriticism to the Test: The Case of 'The Burning Season,' a Film (Mal)Adaptation." *Interdisciplinary Studies in Literature and Environment (ISLE)* 13, no. 1 (Winter 2006): 13–23.

Goncharov, I. A. *Sobranie sochinenii v vos'mi tomakh*. Moscow: Khudozhestvennaia literatura, 1977–80.

Goncourt, Edmond de, and Jules de Goncourt. *Pages from the Goncourt Journals*. Translated and edited by Robert Baldick. New York: NYRB Classics, 2007.

Gregory, Patrick T., and Leigh Anne Isaac. "Food Habits of the Grass Snake in Southeastern England: Is *Natrix natrix* a Generalist Predator?" *Journal of Herpetology* 38, no. 1 (March 2004): 88–95.

Gromov, V. A. "Na okhote v Spasskom." *Okhotnich'i prostory* 25 (1967): 218–24.

——. "Pisateli-okhotniki i *Karmannaia knizhka* L. N. Vakselia." *Okhotnich'i prostory* 17 (1962): 260–67.

——. "Rasskaz mtsenskogo starozhila (Novye materialy ob I. S. Turgeneve)." *Okhota i okhotnich'e khoziaistvo* 8 (1960): 50–51.

——. "Ruzh'e i lira Turgeneva." *Okhotnich'i prostory* 20 (1964): 190–200.

——. "Zabytye vospominaniia o Turgeneve-okhotnike: Publikatsiia, predislovie i primechaniia V. Gromova. Na okhote s Turgenevym." *Okhotnich'i prostory* 24 (1966): 190–204.

Guski, A., and A. Seljak. "Portraits d'un chasseur: Tourguéniev et Nikolaï D. Dmitriev-Orenbourgsky. Essai sur un tableau disparu." *Cahiers Ivan Tourguéniev, Pauline Viardot, Maria Malibran*, no. 25 (2001): 193–201.

Gut'iar, N. M. *Ivan Sergeevich Turgenev: Biografiia*. Iur'ev: Tipografiia K. Mattisena, 1907.

Helfant, Ian. "S. T. Aksakov: The Ambivalent Proto-ecological Consciousness of a Nineteenth-Century Russian Hunter." *Interdisciplinary Studies in Literature and Environment (ISLE)* 13, no. 2 (Summer 2006): 57–71.

——. *That Savage Gaze: Wolves in the Nineteenth-Century Russian Imagination*. The Unknown Nineteenth Century. Boston: Academic Studies Press, 2018.

Herzen, A. I. See Gertsen, A. I.

Heschel, Abraham. *Die Prophetie*. Kraków: Nakładem Polskiej Akademji Umiejętności, 1936.

Hodge, Thomas P. "The 'Hunter in Terror of Hunters': A Cynegetic Reading of Turgenev's *Fathers and Children*." *Slavic and East European Journal* 51, no. 3 (Fall 2007): 453–73.

———. "Ivan Turgenev on the Nature of Hunting." *Words, Music, History: A Festschrift for Caryl Emerson. Stanford Slavic Studies* 29 (2005): 291–311.

Hoisington, Thomas H. "The Enigmatic Hunter in Turgenev's *Zapiski ochotnika*." *Russian Literature* 42 (1997): 47–64.

Homer. *The Odyssey of Homer*. Translated by Richmond Lattimore. New York: Harper Collins, 1975.

Hugo, Victor. *Les chansons des rues et des bois*. Paris: Librairie Hachette, 1884.

———. *Les châtiments*. Paris: J. Hetzel, 1890.

———. *Selected Poems of Victor Hugo: A Bilingual Edition*. Edited and translated by E. H. Blackmore and A. M. Blackmore. Chicago: University of Chicago Press, 2001.

Hull, Denison Bingham. *Hounds and Hunting in Ancient Greece*. Chicago: University of Chicago Press, 1964.

Hutchins, Michael, Dennis A. Thoney, and Melissa C. McDade, eds. *Grzimek's Animal Life Encyclopedia*. 2nd ed. Vol. 11: *Birds IV*. Detroit: Gale, 2004.

Iampol'skii, I. G. "Stikhotvorenie Turgeneva 'Pered okhotoi' i 'Psovaia okhota' N. A. Nekrasova." *Turgenevskii sbornik*. Vol. 5, 209. Leningrad: Izdatel'stvo Nauka, Leningradskoe otdelenie, 1969.

Ingham, Norman W. "Turgenev in the Garden." In *Mnemozina: Studia litteraria Russica in honorem Vsevolod Setchkarev*, 208–29. Munich: Fink, 1974.

Ionas, G. "Iulian Shmidt o tvorchestve Turgeneva." *Turgenevskii sbornik*. Vol. 5, 280–85. Leningrad: Izdatel'stvo Nauka, Leningradskoe otdelenie, 1969.

Isherwood, Christopher, and W. H. Auden. *The Dog beneath the Skin, or Where Is Francis?* London: Faber and Faber, 1935.

Iur'ev and Vladimirskii, eds. *Pravila svetskoi zhizni i etiketa: Khoroshii ton*. St. Petersburg: Tipografiia i Litografiia V. A. Tikhanova, 1889.

Izmailov, N. V., and L. N. Nazarova, eds. *Turgenevskii sbornik: Materialy k "Polnomu sobraniiu sochinenii i pisem" I. S. Turgeneva*. Vols. 2–3. Moscow-Leningrad: Nauka, 1966–67.

Jackson, Robert Louis. *Close Encounters: Essays on Russian Literature*. Boston: Academic Studies Press, 2013.

———. *Dialogues with Dostoevsky: The Overwhelming Questions*. Stanford, CA: Stanford University Press, 1993.

———. "The Turgenev Question." *Sewanee Review* 93, no. 2 (1985): 300–309.

———. "Turgenev's 'The Inn': A Philosophical Novella." *Russian Literature* 16, no. 4 (1984): 411–19.

James, Henry. *Partial Portraits*. London: Macmillan, 1894.

Jones, Christa C., and Claudia Schwabe, eds. *New Approaches to Teaching Folk and Fairy Tales*. Boulder, CO: University Press of Colorado for Utah State University Press, 2016.

Junkins, Donald. "'Oh, Give the Bird a Chance': Nature and Vilification in Hemingway's *The Torrents of Spring*." *North Dakota Quarterly* 63, no. 3 (Summer 1996): 65–80.

Kagan-Kans, Eva. "Fate and Fantasy: A Study of Turgenev's Fantastic Stories." *Slavic Review* 28, no. 4 (December 1969): 543–60.

——. *Hamlet and Don Quixote: Turgenev's Ambivalent Vision.* The Hague: Mouton, 1975.

——. "Turgenev, the Metaphysics of an Artist, 1818–1883." *Cahiers du Monde russe et soviétique* 13, no. 3 (July–September 1972): 382–405.

Kaledin, A. P., N. V. Kobozev, V. V. Pankratov, G. N. Semenova, and V. I. Chekharin, eds. "Kto est' kto v okhotnich'em obshchestvennom dvizhenii v Rossii." In *Russkaia okhota i kul'tura (1766–2000).* Vol. 2. Moscow: Tipografiia IPO profsoiuzov Profizdat, 2001.

Kamernitskii, A. V. *Okhota s sobakami na Rusi (X–XX vv.).* Seriia Mir okhoty. Moscow: Veche, 2005.

Kelly, Aileen M. *The Discovery of Chance: The Life and Thought of Alexander Herzen.* Cambridge, MA: Harvard University Press, 2016.

——. *Toward Another Shore: Russian Thinkers between Necessity and Chance.* New Haven, CT: Yale University Press, 1998.

Khomiakov, A. S. "Sport, okhota." *Polnoe sobranie sochinenii.* Vol. 1, 434–44. Moscow: Tipografiia P. Bakhmeteva, 1861.

Kinkead, Duncan T. "An Iconographic Note on Raphael's *Galatea.*" *Journal of the Warburg and Courtauld Institutes* 33 (1970): 313–15.

Kireevskii, N. V. *40 let postoiannoi okhoty: Iz vospominanii starogo okhotnika.* Moscow: Tipografiia V. I. Ryshkova, 1860.

Kiselev, A. L. *Prishvin i russkaia literatura.* Kuibyshev: Gosudarstvennyi pedagogicheskii institute imeni V. V. Kuibyshev, 1983.

Kistler, Mark O. "The Sources of the Goethe-Tobler Fragment 'Die Natur.'" *Monatshefte* 46, no. 7 (December 1954): 383–89.

Kleman, M. K. "Programmy 'Zapisok okhotnika.'" *Uchenye zapiski Leningradskogo gosudarstvennogo universiteta* 76, seriia filologicheskikh nauk 11 (1941): 88–126.

Kolbasin, D. I. "Na okhote s Turgenevym." *Iuzhnyi sbornik v pol'zu postradavshikh ot neurozhaia,* 139–47. Odessa: Shul'tse, 1892.

Kramer, Jeffrey, and Curt Meine. "Reconciling the Land Ethic and the Hunting of Wildlife." Center for Humans and Nature. https://www.humansandnature.org/does-hunting-make-us-human-reconciling-the-land-ethic-and-the-killing-of-wildlife. Online.

Krasnokutskii, V. S. "O nekotorykh simvolicheskikh motivakh v tvorchestve I. S. Turgeneva." In *Voprosy istorizma i realizma v russkoi literature XIX–nachala XX veka,* 135–50. Leningrad: Izdatel'stvo Leningradskogo universiteta, 1985.

Kudel'ko, N. A. "'Okhota pitala i literaturu': I. S. Turgenev i ego literaturnye posledovateli ob osobennostiakh natsional'noi okhoty." *Spasskii vestnik* 10 (2004): 112–18.

Kukol'nik, N. V. "Starina: Zimniaia i letniaia potekha na zveri." *Zhurnal konnozavodstva i okhoty* 1, no. 3 (March 1842): 29–38.

Kurliandskaia, G. B. *Esteticheskii mir I. S. Turgeneva.* Orel: Izdatel'stvo gosudarstvennoi teleradioveshchatel'noi kompanii, 1994.

——. "O filosofii prirody v proizvedeniiakh Turgeneva." *Voprosy russkoi literatury* (L'vov: Izdatel'stvo L'vovskogo universiteta) 2, no. 17 (1971): 44–53.

Kuz'mina, L. I. "Turgenev i khudozhnik N. D. Dmitriev-Orenburgskii." In *Turgenevskii sbornik: Materialy k Polnomu sobraniiu sochinenii i pisem I. S. Turgeneva*

3, edited by N. V. Izmailov and L. N. Nazarova, 264–71. Leningrad: Izdatel'stvo Nauka, Leningradskoe otdelenie, 1967.

LeBlanc, Ronald D. "'Tolstoy's Way of No Flesh: Abstinence, Vegetarianism, and Christian Physiology." In *Food in Russian History and Culture*, edited by Musya Glants and Joyce Toomre, 81–102. Bloomington: Indiana University Press, 1997.

Ledkovsky, Marina. *The Other Turgenev*. Würzburg: Jal Verlag, 1973.

Leopardi, Giacomo. *Operette Morali: Essays and Dialogues*. Translated by Giovanni Cecchetti. Berkeley: University of California Press, 1982.

Letopis' zhizni i tvorchestva I. S. Turgeneva . . .

—— *(1818–1858)*. Edited by N. S. Nikitina. St. Petersburg: Nauka, 1995.

—— *(1867–1870)*. Edited by N. N. Mostovskaia. St. Petersburg: Nauka, 1997.

—— *(1871–1875)*. Edited by N. N. Mostovskaia. St. Petersburg: Nauka, 1998.

—— *(1876–1883)*. Edited by N. N. Mostovskaia. St. Petersburg: Nauka, 2003.

Levinson, Paul. *Soft Edge: A Natural History and Future of the Information Revolution*. London: Routledge, 1998.

Long, A. A., and D. N. Sedley, eds. *The Hellenistic Philosophers*. Vol. 1. Cambridge: Cambridge University Press, 1987.

Longrigg, Roger. *The English Squire and His Sport*. New York: St. Martin's, 1977.

Lowe, David A., ed. *Critical Essays on Ivan Turgenev*. Boston: G. K. Hall, 1989.

Lubensky, Sophia. *Russian-English Dictionary of Idioms*. New York: Random House, 1995.

Lundblad, Michael. "From Animal to Animality Studies." *PMLA* 124, no. 2 (March 2009): 496–502.

MacKenzie, John M. *The Empire of Nature: Hunting, Conservation, and British Imperialism*. Manchester: Manchester University Press, 1988.

Maksimovič-Ambodik, N. M. *Emvlemy i simvoly (1788): The First Russian Emblem Book*. Facsimile edition, with an introduction and translation by Anthony Hippisley. Leiden: Brill, 1989.

Malle, Adolphe Dureau de la. "Mémoire sur l'alternance ou sur ce problème: La succession alternative dans la reproduction des espèces végétales vivant en société, est-elle une loi générale de la nature?" *Annales des sciences naturelles* 5 (1825): 353–81.

Manutchehr-Danai, Mohsen, ed. *Dictionary of Gems and Gemology*. Berlin: Springer, 2009.

Marchenko, N. P., and K. V. Zelenoi. *Litsa i sud'by: Portret XVIII–nachala XIX veka v sobranii Natsional'nogo khudozhestvennogo muzeia Respubliki Belarus'*. Minsk: Izdatel'stvo Chetyre chetverti, 2002.

Markov, B. I. *Moskva okhotnich'ia*. Moscow: Tsentropoligraf, 1997.

Marvin, Garry, and Susan McHugh, eds. *Routledge Handbook of Human-Animal Studies*. New York: Routledge, 2014.

Mashinskii, S. I. *S. T. Aksakov: Zhizn' i tvorchestvo*. 2nd ed. Moscow: Khudozhestvennaia literatura, 1973.

May, Rachel. "On the Idea of 'Russian Nature.'" *Russian Studies in Literature* 39, no. 2 (Spring 2003): 4–23.

McGuane, Thomas. *The Longest Silence: A Life in Fishing*. New York: Vintage Books, 2001.

McReynolds, Louise. *Russia at Play: Leisure Activities at the End of the Tsarist Era.* Ithaca, NY: Cornell University Press, 2003.

Menzorova, A. N. "O roli peizazha i muzyki v romane I. S. Turgeneva *Dvorianskoe gnezdo.*" *Trudy Chetvertoi nauchnoi konferentsii Novosibirskogo pedagogicheskogo instituta.* Vol. 1, 275–96. Novosibirsk, 1957.

Moe, Aaron M. "Toward Zoopoetics: Rethinking Whitman's 'Original Energy.'" *Walt Whitman Quarterly Review* 31 (2013): 1–17.

———. *Zoopoetics: Animals and the Making of Poetry.* Lanham, MD: Lexington Books, 2014.

Mondry, Henrietta. *Political Animals: Representing Dogs in Modern Russian Culture.* Studies in Slavic Literature and Poetics. Leiden: Brill Rodopi, 2015.

Morgan, Diane. *From Satan's Crown to the Holy Grail: Emeralds in Myth, Magic, and History.* London: Praeger, 2007.

Mostovskaia, N. N., and N. S. Nikitina, eds. *I. S. Turgenev: Voprosy biografii i tvorchestva.* Leningrad: Nauka, 1990.

Munsche, P. B. *Gentlemen and Poachers: The English Game Laws 1671–1831.* Cambridge: Cambridge University Press, 1981.

Nabokov, Vladimir. *Lectures on Russian Literature.* Edited by Fredson Bowers. New York: Harcourt, Brace, Jovanovich, 1981.

Nekrasov, N. A. *Polnoe sobranie sochinenii i pisem v piatnadtsati tomakh.* Leningrad: Nauka, Leningradskoe otdelenie, 1981–2000.

Newlin, Thomas. "At the Bottom of the River: Forms of Ecological Consciousness in Mid-Nineteenth-Century Russian Literature." Edited by Rachel May. *Russian Studies in Literature* 39, no. 2 (Spring 2003): 71–90.

———. "The Thermodynamics of Desire in Turgenev's *Notes of a Hunter.*" *Russian Review* 72 (July 2013): 365–89.

Nierle, Michael. *Die Naturschilderung und ihre Funktion in Versdichtung und Prosa von I. S. Turgenev.* Studien zur Geschichte der russischen Literatur des 19. Jahrhunderts (Frankfurter Abhandlungen zur Slavistik 11). Bad Homburg vor der Höhe: Verlag Gehlen, 1969.

Nikol'skii, N. "Iz zapisei o Turgeneve-okhotnike." *Okhotnich'i prostory* 6 (1956): 357–58.

Nikol'skii, V. A. *Priroda i chelovek v russkoi literature XIX veka (50–60-e gody).* Kalinin: Kalininskaia oblastnaia tipografiia, 1973.

Nonnos. *Dionysiaca.* Translated by W. H. D. Rouse. Introduction and Notes by H. J. Rose. Vol. 1. Loeb Classical Library. Cambridge, MA: Harvard University Press, 1940.

Nussbaum, Martha C. *The Therapy of Desire: Theory and Practice in Hellenistic Ethics.* Martin Classical Lectures, New Series. Vol. 2. Princeton, NJ: Princeton University Press, 1994.

O'Bell, Leslie. "The Pastoral in Turgenev's 'Singers': Classical Themes and Romantic Variations." *Russian Review*, no. 2 (April 2004): 277–95.

Odesskaia, M. M. "Russkii okhotnichii rasskaz XIX veka." In *Russkii okhotnichii rasskaz*, edited by M. M. Odesskaia, 5–14. Moscow: Sovetskaia Rossiia, 1991.

———. "Ruzh'e i lira: Okhotnichii rasskaz v russkoi literature XIX veka." *Voprosy literatury* 3 (May–June 1998): 239–52.

———. "*Zapiski okhotnika* I. S. Turgeneva: Problema zhanra." *Litteraria Humanitas* 7, 195–204. Alexandr Sergejevič Puškin v evropských kulturních souvislostech. Brno: Masarykova univerzita, 2000.

Ogareva, N. V. "Turgenev v poslednie gody zhizni: Iz vospominanii i pisem A. P. Bogoliubova, 1873–1883." *Literaturnoe nasledstvo* 76 (1967): 441–82.

Ortega y Gasset, José. *Meditations on Hunting.* Translated by Howard B. Westcott. New York: Charles Scribner's Sons, 1972.

Osnovskii, N. A. "Petrov den': Iz vospominanii okhotnika." *Sovremennik* 48 (1854): 177–208.

———. *Zamechaniia Moskovskogo okhotnika na ruzheinuiu okhotu s legavoiu sobakoiu.* 2nd ed. Moscow: Tipografiia Vedomostei Moskovskoi Gorodskoi Politsii, 1856.

Ostrovskii, A. G., ed. *Turgenev v zapisiakh sovremennikov. Vospominaniia. Dnevniki.* Moscow: Agraf, 1999.

Oxford English Dictionary. 3rd ed. Oxford: Oxford University Press, 2000.

Pahomov, George. "Nature and the Use of Paradox in Turgenev." *Zapiski Russkoi akademicheskoi gruppy v S.Sh.A.* 16 (1983): 47–56.

Pakhomov, N. P. "Istoriia odnoi druzhby (I. S. Turgenev i sem'ia Aksakovykh)." *Okhotnich'i prostory* 28 (1970): 192–203.

———. "I. S. Turgenev na okhote za granitsei." *Okhota i okhotnich'e khoziaistvo* 7 (1969): 40–41.

Paul, Alec. "Russian Landscape in Literature: Lermontov and Turgenev." In *Geography and Literature: A Meeting of the Disciplines,* edited by William E. Mallory and Paul Simpson-Housley, 115–31. Syracuse, NY: Syracuse University Press, 1987.

Pavliuk, R. S., and A. Iu. Kharitonov. *Nomenklatura strekoz (Insecta, Odonata) SSSR: Poleznye i vrednye nasekomye Sibiri.* Novosibirsk: Nauka, 1982.

Pearson, Irene. "Raphael as Seen by Russian Writers from Zhukovsky to Turgenev." *Slavonic and East European Review* 59, no. 3 (July 1981): 346–69.

Pechenina, Iu. A. "Priroda glazami rasskazchika." *Russkaia rech'* 5 (September–October 1987): 92–96.

Peterson, Dale E. "The Completion of *A Sportsman's Sketches*: Turgenev's Parting Word." In *The Poetics of Ivan Turgenev,* edited by David Lowe, 53–62. Washington, DC: Kennan Institute, 1989.

———. *Up from Bondage: The Literatures of Russian and African American Soul.* Durham, NC: Duke University Press, 2000.

Petri, William A., Jr. "Epidemic Typhus." *Merck Manual Professional Version.* https://www.merckmanuals.com/professional/infectious-diseases/rickettsiae-and-related-organisms/epidemic-typhus.

Petrov, S. M. *I. S. Turgenev: Zhizn' i tvorchestvo.* 2nd rev. ed. Moscow: Prosveshchenie, 1968.

Petrov, S. M., and V. G. Fridland, eds. *I. S. Turgenev v vospominaniiakh sovremennikov.* 2 vols. Moscow: Khudozhestvennaia literatura, 1983.

Petrovskii, N. A. *Slovar' russkikh lichnykh imen.* 6th ed. Moscow: Russkie slovari, 2005.

Pigarev, K. V. *Russkaia literatura i izobrazitel'noe iskusstvo: Ocherki o russkom natsional'nom peizazhe serediny XIX v.* Moscow: Izdatel'stvo Nauka, 1972.

Poliziano, Angelo. *The Stanze of Angelo Poliziano.* Translated by David L. Quint. University Park: Penn State University Press, 1979.

Porkorny. "Indogermanisches Etymologisches Wörterbuch." *Indo-European Etymological Dictionary*. Department of Comparative Indo-European Linguistics at Leiden University. http://www.indo-european.nl/cgi-bin/query.cgi?basename=\data\ie\pokorny&root=leiden.

Pritchett, V. S. *The Gentle Barbarian: The Work and Life of Turgenev*. New York: Ecco, 1977.

Pushkin, A. S. *Polnoe sobranie sochinenii v desiati tomakh*. Leningrad: Nauka, 1977–79.

——. *Pushkin on Literature*. Rev. ed. Edited and translated by Tatiana Wolff. Stanford, CA: Stanford University Press, 1986.

Pustovoit, P. G. *Roman I. S. Turgeneva* Ottsy i deti: *Literaturnyi kommentarii*. Izdatel'stvo Prosveshchenie, 1964.

Reardon, John. "Hemingway's Esthetic and Ethical Sportsmen." *University Review* 34 (October 1967): 13–23.

Reutt, Napoleon M. *Psovaia okhota*. 2 vols. St. Petersburg: Tipografiia Karla Kraiia, 1846.

Richards, Robert J. *The Tragic Sense of Life: Ernst Haeckel and the Struggle over Evolutionary Thought*. Chicago: University of Chicago Press, 2009.

Ripp, Victor. *Turgenev's Russia: From "Notes of a Hunter" to "Fathers and Sons."* Ithaca, NY: Cornell University Press, 1980.

Romanov, S. I. *Slovar' ruzheinoi okhoty*. Moscow–St. Petersburg: Izdanie Nikolaia Ivanovicha Mamontova, 1877.

Rosenholm, Arja, and Sari Autio-Sarasmo, eds. *Understanding Russian Nature: Representations, Values and Concepts*. Aleksanteri-papers 4. Saarijärvi: Gummerus Printing, 2005.

Rosenzweig, Franz. *Philosophical and Theological Writings*. Translated and edited by Paul W. Franks and Michael L. Morgan. Indianapolis: Hackett, 2000.

Rowland, Belinda, and Rebecca Frey. *Gale Encyclopedia of Alternative Medicine*. Edited by Jacqueline Longe. 2nd ed. 4 vols. Detroit: Gale, 2005. Online.

Rynda, I. F. *Cherty iz zhizni Ivana Sergeevicha Turgeneva*. St. Petersburg: Tipografiia A. S. Suvorina, 1903.

Sabaneev, L. P. *Okhotnich'i zveri*. Moscow: Terra, 1992.

——. *Sobaki okhotnich'i: Borzye i gonchie*. Moscow: Terra, 1992.

——. *Sobaki okhotnich'i: Legavye*. Moscow: Terra, 1992.

Sadovnikov, D. N. "Vstrechi s I. S. Turgenevym: 'Piatnitsy' u poeta Ia. P. Polonskogo v 1880 godu." *Russkoe proshloe* 3 (1923): 99–119.

Salonen, Hugo Tauno. *Die Landschaft bei I. S. Turgenev*. Helsinki: Kirjapaino-Osakeyhtiö Sana, 1915.

Schapiro, Leonard. *Turgenev: His Life and Times*. Cambridge, MA: Harvard University Press, 1982.

Sergeenko, P. A. *Kak zhivet i rabotaet gr. L. N. Tolstoi*. Moscow: Tipo-litografiia tovarishchestva I. N. Kushnerev, 1898.

Setschkareff, Wsewolod. *Schellings Einfluß in der russischen Literatur der 20er und 30er Jahre des XIX. Jahrhunderts*. Leipzig: Veröffentlichungen des Slavischen Instituts an der Friedrich-Wilhelms-Universität Berlin, 1939.

Shangina, I. I. *Russkii traditsionnyi byt: Entsiklopedicheskii slovar'*. St. Petersburg: Izdatel'stvo Azbuka Klassika, 2003.

Shapochka, V. V. *Okhotnich'i tropy Turgeneva*. Orel: Veshnie vody, 1998.

Shatalov, S. E., ed. *I. S. Turgenev v sovremennom mire*. Moscow: Nauka, 1987.

Shchukin, Vasilii. *Rossiiskii genii prosveshcheniia: Issledovaniia v oblasti mifopoetiki i istorii idei*. Moscow: Rosspen, 2007.

Shuvalov, S. "Priroda v tvorchestve Turgeneva." In *Tvorchestvo Turgeneva*, edited by I. N. Rozanov and Iu. M. Sokolov, 115–39. Moscow: Zadruga, 1920.

Šilbajoris, Rimvydas. "Images and Structures in Turgenev's *A Sportsman's Notebook*." *Slavic and East European Journal* 28, no. 2 (Summer 1984): 180–91.

Sinkankas, John. *Emerald and Other Beryls*. Phoenix: GeoScience, 1981.

Skokova, L. I. "Chelovek i priroda v *Zapiskakh okhotnika* Turgeneva." *Voprosy literatury* 6 (November–December 2003): 339–47.

——. Dialog Turgeneva s Russo o prirode i tsivilizatsii." *Spasskii vestnik* 10 (2004): 28–57.

Sloan, Phillip R. " 'The Sense of Sublimity': Darwin on Nature and Divinity." *Osiris* 16, Science in Theistic Contexts: Cognitive Dimensions (2001): 251–69.

Smirnov, Nikolai. "Pisateli-okhotniki (L. N. Tolstoi i I. S. Turgenev)." *Okhota i okhotnich'e khoziaistvo* 9 (1958): 41–45.

Solov'ev, S. M. *Sochineniia v vosemnadtsati knigakh*. Moscow: Golos, 1993.

Spinoza, Baruch. *Ethics*. Translated by Samuel Shirley. Indianapolis: Hackett, 1992.

Stamberg, L. "Obrazy i kompozitsiia *Zapisok okhotnika* I. S. Turgeneva." *Uchenye zapiski Tartuskogo universiteta* 47 (1957): 119–30.

Stewart, Frank. "Poetry and Wildness: Some Notes on the Hunt." *Ohio Review* 45 (1990): 345–67.

Stoppard, Tom. *Voyage (The Coast of Utopia, Part 1)*. New York: Grove, 2002.

Striker, Gisela. "Ataraxia: Happiness as Tranquillity." *Monist* 73, no. 1. Hellenistic Ethics (January 1990): 97–110.

Stuckrad, Kocku von. "Reenchanting Nature: Modern Western Shamanism and Nineteenth-Century Thought." *Journal of the American Academy of Religion* 70, no. 4 (December 2002): 771–99.

Tempest, Richard. *Russian Dreams: Pushkin, Chaadaev, Turgenev, Dostoevsky, Mandelshtam, Florensky*. London: Omega Books, 1987.

Tennyson, Alfred Lord. *The Works of Alfred Lord Tennyson*. Vol. 4. London: Macmillan, 1888.

Thiergen, Peter. " 'Priroda do otvratitel'noi stepeni ravnodushna': Alexandre Herzen et le scepticisme de son époque face à la nature." *Revue des études slaves* 78, nos. 2–3 (2007): 259–78.

Thoreau, Henry David. *A Week on the Concord and Merrimack Rivers*. Boston: James Munroe, 1849.

Time, Galina A. *Nemetskaia literaturno-filosofskaia mysl' XVIII–XIX vekov v kontekste tvorchestva I. S. Turgeneva (geneticheskie i tipologicheskie aspekty)*. Vorträge und Abhandlungen zur Slavistik, Bd. 31. Munich: Verlag Otto Sagner, 1997.

Tolstoi, L. N. *Polnoe sobranie sochinenii*. 90 vols. Moscow-Leningrad: Gosudarstvennoe izdatel'stvo khudozhestvennoi literatury, 1928–64.

Tolstoi, N. N. "Okhota na Kavkaze: Rasskazy N. N. T." *Sovremennik* 1 (January 1857): 170–232.

Tsakni, E. "Neizvestnyi portret Tolstogo." *Literaturnoe nasledstvo* 37–38 (1939): 698–99.

Turgenev, I. S. *Correspondance Ivan Tourguéniev–Louis Viardot: Sous le sceau de la fraternité*. Edited by Alexandre Zviguilsky. Paris: Hermann Éditeurs, 2010.

——. *The Essential Turgenev*. Edited by Elizabeth Cheresh Allen. Evanston, IL: Northwestern University Press, 1994.

——. *Fathers and Children*. 2nd ed. Translated and edited by Michael R. Katz. Norton Critical Edition. New York: W. W. Norton, 2009.

——. "A Fire at Sea." Translated by Oscar Wilde. *Macmillan's Magazine* 54 (May–October 1886): 39–44.

——. *Lettres inédites à Pauline Viardot et à sa famille*. Edited by Henri Granjard and Alexandre Zviguilsky. Lausanne: Éditions L'Age d'Homme, 1972.

——. *Literary Reminiscences and Autobiographical Fragments*. Translated by David Magarshack. Chicago: Ivan R. Dee, 2001.

——. *Pervoe sobranie pisem I. S. Turgeneva: 1840–1883 gg*. St. Petersburg: Tipografiia M. M. Stasiulevicha, 1884.

——. *Polnoe sobranie sochinenii i pisem v dvadtsati vos'mi tomakh*. 28 vols. Moscow–Leningrad: Nauka, 1960–68.

——. *Polnoe sobranie sochinenii i pisem v tridtsati tomakh*. 2nd ed. 30 vols. Moscow: Izdatel'stvo Nauka, 1978–. *Sochineniia*, vols. 1–12, 1978–86. *Pis'ma*, 17 vols. to date, 1982–. [Identified in citations as *Pssp*, followed by *S* for volumes of Works (*Sochineniia*) or *P* for volumes of Letters (*Pis'ma*).]

——. *A Sportsman's Notebook*. Translated by Charles and Natasha Hepburn. New York: Ecco, 2020.

Turgenev, I. S., and L. N. Tolstoi. *Rasskazy dlia detei I. S. Turgeneva i gr. L. N. Tolstogo*. Moscow: Izdanie P. A. Bers i L. D. Obolenskogo, 1883.

Unbegaun, B. O. *Russian Surnames*. Oxford: Oxford University Press, 1972.

Vaksel', L. N. *Karmannaia knizhka dlia nachinaiushchikh okhotit'sia s ruzh'em i legavoi sobakoiu*. St. Petersburg: Tipografiia Eduarda Pratsa, 1856.

——. *Karmannaia knizhka dlia nachinaiushchikh okhotit'sia s ruzh'em i legavoi sobakoiu*. 2nd rev. ed. St. Petersburg: Tipografiia Eduarda Pratsa, 1858.

——. *Karmannaia knizhka dlia nachinaiushchikh okhotit'sia s ruzh'em i legavoi sobakoiu*. 3rd ed. St. Petersburg: Tipografiia Eduarda Pratsa, 1870.

——. *Rukovodstvo dlia nachinaiushchikh okhotit'sia s ruzh'em i legavoi sobakoiu*. 4th rev. ed. St. Petersburg: Tipografiia Gogendel'den, 1876.

——. *Rukovodstvo dlia nachinaiushchikh okhotit'sia s ruzh'em i legavoi sobakoiu*. 5th rev. ed. St. Petersburg: A. S. Suvorin, 1898.

Valentino, Russell S. "A Wolf in Arkadia: Generic Fields, Generic Counterstatement and the Resources of Pastoral in *Fathers and Sons*." *Russian Review* 55, no. 3 (July 1996): 475–93.

Vasmer, Max [Maks Fasmer]. *Etimologicheskii slovar' russkogo iazyka v chetyrekh tomakh*. Translated by O. N. Trubachev. 3rd ed. St. Petersburg: Terra, 1996.

Vengerov, S. A. "Turgenev (Ivan Sergeevich)." *Entsiklopedicheskii slovar' Brokgauz-Efron*. Vol. 34, 96–106. St. Petersburg: Tipografiia aktsionernogo obshchestva Brokgauz-Efron, 1902.

Viardot, Louis. *Souvenirs de chasse*. 7th ed. Paris: Librairie de L. Hachette, 1859.

Voitolovskaia, E. L. "I. S. Turgenev o S. T. Aksakove." *Leningradskii gosudarstvennyi pedagogicheskii institut imeni A. I. Gertsena: Uchenye zapiski* 170 (1958): 109–35.

Vorontsov-Vel'iaminov, N. N. "Zapiski ruzheinogo okhotnika Orenburgskoi gubernii S. A-va." *Moskvitianin* 8, no. 2 (5 April 1852): 106–20.

Vysotskaia, V. V. "Dva tipa prostranstva v proizvedeniiakh Turgeneva: 'Gnezdo' i 'bezgnezdov'e.'" *Spasskii vestnik* 13 (2006): 121–30.

Waddington, Patrick. *A Catalogue of Portraits of Ivan Sergeyevich Turgenev (1818–83).* Wellington: Whirinaki, 1999.

——. *Turgenev and England.* New York: New York University Press, 1981.

——. "Turgenev's Notebooks for *Dym.*" *New Zealand Slavonic Journal* (1989–90): 41–66.

Wells, George A. "Goethe and Evolution." *Journal of the History of Ideas* 28, no. 4 (October–December 1967): 537–50.

Windle, Kevin. "'Hunters' Notes': Ornithology and Cultural Attitudes in Russian Literature of the Nineteenth and Twentieth Centuries." *Russian Studies in Literature* 39, no. 3 (Summer 2003): 25–47.

Wood, Harold B. "The History of Bird Banding." *Auk* 62 (1945): 257.

Woodward, James B. "The Triumph of Nature: A Re-examination of Turgenev's *Nakanune.*" *Russian Literature* 25, no. 2 (1989): 259–96.

——. "Typical Images in the Later Tales of Turgenev." *Slavic and East European Journal* 17, no. 1 (1973): 18–32.

Wynne-Tyson, Jon. *The Extended Circle: A Dictionary of Humane Thought.* London: Macdonald, 1990.

Zaitsev, Boris. *Zhizn' Turgeneva.* Paris: YMCA-Press, 1949.

Žekulin, Nicholas G. "*De gustibus disputandum est*: Turgenev's (Dis)agreements with His Hero Bazarov." In *Tusculum slavicum. Festschrift für Peter Thiergen,* edited by Elisabeth von Erdmann, Aschot Isaakjan, Roland Marti, and Daniel Schümann, 289–309. Basler Studien zur Kulturgeschichte Osteuropas, Bd. 14. Zürich: Pano Verlag, 2005.

——. "Early Translations of Turgenev's *Zapiski okhotnika* into German, French and English." *New Zealand Slavonic Journal.* Festschrift in Honour of Patrick Waddington (1994): 229–58.

——. "Ivan Turgenev." In *Russian Novelists in the Age of Tolstoy and Dostoevsky,* edited by J. Alexander Ogden and Judith E. Kalb. Dictionary of Literary Biography, vol. 238. Detroit: Gale, 2001.

——. "Turgenev as Translator." *Canadian Slavonic Papers* 50, nos. 1–2 (March–June 2008): 155–76.

Zemlianaia, Ol'ga. "I. S. Turgenev ob osobennostiakh natsional'noi okhoty." *Zvezda* 10 (1998): 150–55.

INDEX

Page numbers in *italics* refer to figures. T stands for I. S. Turgenev.